PRAISE FOR JOE FRIEL

"Twenty-five years of active multisport coaching has proven that Joe Friel has an unprecedented understanding of endurance sports. As a multiple triathlon world champion, I would consider Joe as one of the leading figures in triathlon coaching today. Joe's professional approach and practical understanding of sports physiology have helped many endurance athletes of all abilities reach their full athletic potential."

—Simon Lessing, five-time triathlon world champion

"Joe Friel has spent most of his life in devotion to the understanding and teaching of sport. Joe has managed to focus on the key components to athletic success while weeding out the noise."

—Justin Daerr, professional triathlete

"Whether you're a beginning triathlete or a seasoned pro, Joe Friel is the leading authority on triathlon training."

—Ryan Bolton, 2000 USA Olympic Team member

"Joe Friel's wealth of knowledge in triathlon is astounding, and he has a wonderful way of sharing that knowledge with all athletes from beginners to elite professionals."

—Siri Lindley, triathlon world champion

"Joe Friel is among the deans of triathlon coaching, and the newest edition of *The Triathlete's Training Bible* will be of great benefit to all triathletes interested in performance improvement."

—George M. Dallam, PhD, former USA Triathlon National Teams
Coach and coauthor of *Championship Triathlon Training*

"Joe Friel's training books have made the once 'crazy' sport of triathlon accessible to the public while also guiding seasoned athletes to their full potential."

—Barb Lindquist, 2004 USA Olympic Team member

YOUR BEST TRIATHLON

YOUR BEST TRIATHLON
Advanced Training for Serious Triathletes

JOE FRIEL

Boulder, Colorado

1830 55th Street
Boulder, Colorado 80301-2700 USA
(303) 440-0601 · Fax (303) 444-6788 · E-mail velopress@competitorgroup.com

Distributed in the United States and Canada by Ingram Publisher Services.

Library of Congress Cataloging-in-Publication Data
Friel, Joe.
Your best triathlon: advanced training for serious triathletes / Joe Friel.
    p. cm.
Includes bibliographical references.
ISBN 978-1-934030-62-2 (pbk.: alk. paper)
1. Triathlon—Training—Handbooks, manuals, etc. I. Title.
GV1060.73.F748 2011
796.429'57—dc22

                                                    2010040956

For information on purchasing VeloPress books,
please call (800) 811-4210 ext. 2169
or visit www.velopress.com.

This book is printed on 100 percent recovered/recycled fiber, 30 percent postconsumer waste, elemental chlorine free, using soy-based inks.

Cover design by Erin Johnson
Cover photo by John Segesta
Interior design by Anita Koury
Composition by Jane Raese
Illustrations and icons by Charlie Layton
Interior and back cover photos by Delly Carr

10   11   12 / 10   9   8   7   6   5   4   3   2   1

Contents

Preface

I HOPE YOU'VE READ *THE TRIATHLETE'S TRAINING BIBLE*. If you have, you may be wondering why I'd write another book about triathlon training. After all, it's been the best-selling book on the subject of triathlon training since 1997, when it first hit the bookshelves. I've revised it twice since then. More than 300,000 copies have been sold worldwide, and it's been translated into German, Chinese, and other languages. The book has been used by the national triathlon federations of many countries to train their coaches. Amateur and elite triathletes around the world tell me they learned how to train from my book. It has been very gratifying to make such a contribution to so many lives and to the sport.

So if that book has been so successful, why not just revise it again? Why is a whole new book on the subject needed? Well, there are lots of reasons. I'll explain.

As I've traveled around the world talking with triathletes at seminars, camps, and races, or communicated with them via e-mail, I've found that their comments often begin the same way: Something in the book was hard to understand. Some athletes have never implemented my principles into their training because they just weren't sure how to do it. After I answered their questions, there was an "aha" moment. They now understood. In this book I explain some of these misunderstood or perhaps complicated concepts from *The Triathlete's Training Bible* in a new way, using the same explanations that help people understand them when I am talking with them in person.

Here you will also find race-specific training plans for each period, with each of the workouts described in detail. That wasn't done in *The Triathlete's Training Bible*. The focus here is less on pedagogy and more on application. I'll tell you exactly what to do and how to do it.

In *Your Best Triathlon*, rather than just explaining how to train as a disinterested author, I'll write it from the perspective of your coach. The triathletes I've coached over the years have always come to understand the methods I use better than anyone else—with the exception of the coaches I've trained. I'll talk to you here just as I do with the athletes I coach during my weekly telephone conversations with them. This is when we get into the details of how to do a certain workout and why we're doing it this particular way. You will learn a lot about triathlon training and will be able to apply it right away.

In Part I, I'll describe some of the important principles from the first book from a new perspective while also introducing you to some new methods. Then in Parts II, III, and IV the serious training begins. Using a periodization format based on the seasonal timing and distance of your next important race, I'll walk you through the step-by-step process that goes into the preparation for an important triathlon.

Even if you didn't have any trouble getting it the first time around, a new perspective may reinforce the original ideas, resulting in greater mastery. Repetition is the key to full understanding and accurate implementation. Exposure to similar information, especially from a different point of view, may give you a greater depth of comprehension. After all, it may have been many years since you first read *The Triathlete's Training Bible*.

If you are a student of training who has read *The Triathlete's Training Bible* very closely, you may find some differences in what you read here. That's because the world of training is not static. It is constantly evolving. New technology often results in different ways of viewing old methods, and I continue to be a student of training who is always looking for better ways. This often results in change and even contradictions from what I have previously written.

I like it when triathletes ask me to sign their well-worn, dog-eared, thoroughly highlighted and tabbed books, whether it is *The Triathlete's Training Bible*, *The Cyclist's Training Bible*, or one of the other books I've written over the years that they are holding in their hands. It's apparent that these athletes have been deeply involved in the process of learning and not just reading to finish a book. You'll get a lot more from this book—and ultimately race better—if you do that also. The more tattered this book becomes, the more you will learn. Mark it up!

What else can you do to make this book—and me—your coach? You could read a chapter at the same time as your training partner and discuss what you are learning whenever you get together for a workout. But realize that talk and good intentions are not enough. It takes action to become a better athlete. Apply what you are learning. Try out some of the methods the very first chance you get. Start following the training plans at the ends of Chapters 4 through 12 based on where you are in the season right now.

What should you do if you come across something you don't understand, or something you are reluctant to try because you are unsure what to do? Go to my blog (joefrielsblog.com) and do a search for the topic. There's a good chance you will find what you are looking for, as there are years of information stored there on a wide variety of subjects. If that doesn't help, then send an email to support@ trainingbible.com. Briefly describe your quandary, and one of our TrainingBible coaches will get back to you with an answer. If your question is simple and does not require a lot of time to research or address, there is no charge for this service. I do need to warn you that if your question is complex, we may suggest a consultation with one of our coaches, and there's a fee for that. Keep your question brief and to the point to avoid that cost.

I do a few weekend seminars, one-day clinics, and multiday camps around the world on training for triathlon. These are listed on our Web site (TrainingBible.com). Consider attending one to learn about triathlon firsthand and to get your questions answered.

The ultimate way to become a better triathlete is to hire a coach. If you have high goals and are pressed for time, this is the best way to not only race better, but also grow as an athlete. There are thousands of great coaches around the world. You can find one through your national triathlon federation or at TrainingPeaks (training-peaks.com), a Web site devoted to the enhancement of training and performance of endurance athletes.

One final point: This book is not meant to be read cover to cover. Treat it as a reference guide. After Part I, start reading with the chapter that corresponds to where you are in your season. Chapter 3 will help you to figure out where to begin based on how many weeks remain until your most important race of the season. Consult the training plan at the end of the first chapter you read, modifying it as needed to fit your lifestyle. As you are about to finish a 3- or 4-week training block, read the next chapter to begin preparing for the following block. If you are now at the start of your training for a new season, continue straight on through and go to Chapter 4, which describes how to train as your season begins. Then follow the training plans at the end of each chapter as you progress through the season.

The training plans at the ends of Chapters 4 through 12 are just like the ones I write for the athletes I coach. At the start of the season, the Prep and early Base blocks, the workouts are quite simple. As the season progresses the workouts become increasingly complex. By Base 3 (Chapter 7), you may well be scratching your head as you look at the training plan tables. Don't worry: Each training session listed in the plan is explained in great detail earlier in the chapter.

So let's get on with it. For the next several hundred pages I'll be your coach. We will work as a team as you get ready for the best triathlon you've ever had.

—*Joe Friel*
Boulder, Colorado

Acknowledgments

FIRST OF ALL I WANT TO THANK THE HUNDREDS OF ATHLETES I have coached during the last 30 years who have allowed me to tinker with their training and their lifestyles while I grew as a coach. Without their willingness to try new ways of training, this book and my coaching career would never have happened. Thank you!

There are many who contributed to this book's growth from an idea in my head to what you now hold in your hands. Thanks go to the following people:

- Hunter Allen for answering my many questions on training with power and using WKO+™ software
- Tudor Bompa, PhD, for his seminal work, *The Theory and Methodology of Training*, which provided guidelines over many years as my coaching philosophy developed
- Loren Cordain, PhD, of Colorado State University for answering the nutrition questions posed by my athletes and me
- My son and business colleague, Dirk Friel, for sharing his thoughts on the many uses of WKO+™
- Sports psychologists Cheryl Hart of the University of Louisville and Christina Maddox, also my client, for their insightful thoughts on mental training
- Renee Jardine of VeloPress for once again taking a gamble on a book idea of mine, getting its format and me organized, and doing a great job of keeping the project on course
- Connie Oehring and Katherine Streckfus, also of VeloPress, for their much-needed and very professional editing
- Nate Koch at Endurance Rehabilitation in Scottsdale, Arizona, for assistance with my understanding of core strength and injuries
- Jeff Kitchen of Endurance Rehabilitation for meticulously testing the athletes I coach and providing me with accurate and detailed results to ponder
- Wolfgang Oswald, an outstanding physical therapist at Endurance Rehabilitation, for introducing me to new concepts in injury treatment while taking care of my aging body
- Physical therapist Mark Saunders of Physio4Life in the United Kingdom for comments on and graphic illustrations of good and poor core strength

Finally, I want to thank my supportive and loving wife, Joyce, who managed my speaking engagements while I worked on this project. She continues to put up with my 4:00 a.m. tinkering at the computer while I study and write about things that fascinate me.

Part I

YOUR BEST TRIATHLON

The first three chapters lay the foundation for your best triathlon by developing an understanding of what it takes to race to your potential. I will tell you the same things I talk about with the athletes I coach. I will also explain the qualities I look for in athletes who have high goals. This will provide focus for your training, which is described in Parts II through V.

In Chapter 1 you will set a seasonal goal that will put you on the path to training as you've never trained before. I'll also tell you what to look for in a race to maximize your potential for success. Then we'll try to predict how you will do in that race.

The purpose of Chapter 2 is to develop a deeper understanding of what it takes to be the best triathlete possible. We will delve into what fitness really is, what's holding you back, the many nuances of power, and the characteristics of good triathletes.

We'll review the main concepts of seasonal planning in Chapter 3. Even if you read about this in *The Triathlete's Training Bible*, it's important to refresh your memory before you begin to lay out your Annual Training Plan. You'll soon be on your way to swimming, biking, and running with more confidence and putting your skills together for your best possible performance on race day.

Let's get started!

Your Race

YOUR BEST TRIATHLON. It's a daunting task. If you are like most of the triathletes I coach, you've been racing for a few years and have had some success. Now you've decided it's time to see how good you can be if you get focused. I'm certain that by working together with a common goal, we can pull it off. It won't be easy, but that is what makes the challenge so much fun. Just thinking about becoming the best triathlete possible is motivating. Imagine what it will feel like to cross the finish line having achieved your goal. Getting from where you are now to that point several weeks from now will place many demands on you. I'll be there with you each step of the way as you follow the race preparation training detailed in Chapters 4 through 11.

The starting point for this journey is deciding what "best triathlon" means for you. This decision involves goal-setting. Next you'll need to choose a race. Just as I do with the triathletes whom I personally coach, I will help you with both tasks. This chapter is designed to help you set a precise goal, choose the race that's right for you, and consider what it will take to be successful on race day.

GOAL SETTING

I know you've heard it before, but I'm going to say it again: You must have well-defined and measurable goals if you want to excel at anything in life, and that includes your best triathlon. Vague and open-ended goals are cop-outs, a way of avoiding a decision that needs to be made. The higher your goal is relative to what you have achieved in the past, the more important it is that you be precise about that goal and have a plan for achieving it. An undefined goal without a plan is just a wish.

Creating and planning for a well-defined, ambitious goal can be a bit scary. These tasks demand action. They require hard and long training sessions wedged in between other activities in your life and accompanied by hard work, fatigue, soreness, and the possibility of failure. But, most of all, higher goals within the sport of triathlon are intimidating because they require you to balance everything in your life—family, career, friends, household responsibilities, community involvement, other interests, and training. If your goal is ambitious, you can expect it to have a significant impact on your life.

I once went to a talk given by a successful ultradistance runner. He described a relentless training regimen during which he spent every spare minute running on trails. He ran before work, during his lunch break, after work well into the night, and for entire weekends. He had won the Western States 100-Mile Ultramarathon that year and was obviously pleased with this accomplishment. During the question-and-answer session after the race, someone asked how all of that training had affected the rest of his life. He answered that he'd lost his job, his wife had divorced him, and he had no friends. "But," he said, as he held up the belt buckle that is awarded to the winner, "it was all worth it!" I'm not sure I agree with that, but to each his own. He had accomplished his goal, albeit at a high price.

I doubt that reaching your goal will be quite so costly, but there will be a cost. I wouldn't recommend giving up family, friends, and career for it. The higher your goal, however, the greater the sacrifice. And it will likely be a sacrifice for others, too. Those around you, especially your family, will have to change their lives somewhat to accommodate your passion. They will endure late meals and huge blocks of time when you aren't available. They'll take over your household chores, deal with your occasional overtraining grumpiness, bend their activities to fit your training schedule, and much more. Before you start down this path to triathlon excellence, it's best to discuss it with the people who will be affected. If they don't enthusiastically support your pursuit of this goal, your chances of success are slim, and you should reconsider.

Don't take this important step lightly. Excellence isn't easy. If it were, everyone would be excellent.

From this point forward, I'm going to assume, just as I do with all of the athletes I coach, that you have the full support and blessing of your family and friends for your ambitious goal. So let's get on with understanding your goal.

Refining Your Goal

If you hired me to be your coach, I would need to know more about you. This is a long process where I ask lots of specific questions. You would start by telling me your goals, which I would help you define. This part requires some introspection on your part, and in order to create a similar process, your responses need to be honest and thoughtful. In the end, you'll have a more specific, achievable goal to strive for.

Why this goal? Is it really something you want, or is it something someone else wants you to do—or perhaps something you think someone else wants you to do? (I see this issue occasionally, for example, with women athletes who want to achieve the same goals that their husbands have set for themselves.)

How can you be more specific? What do you mean by "faster"? Faster at which race? How much faster? What does "place higher in your age group" mean? Five places higher? Top 10? On the podium?

Are you being realistic? A common goal of the athletes I coach is to qualify for a major event such as a national championship, a world championship, or Ironman Hawaii. Have you qualified before? What kind of race performance did it take to qualify? Have you researched the time commitment you will need to make in order to qualify? Perhaps you want to win a special race. What is the course like? What is the typical weather? How have you done in the past in this race? Who is your competition, and how good are they?

Accommodating Your Goal

Now we can consider what is standing between you and success. Immediately you might think of improving your muscular endurance on the bike or swimming with more power. We'll tackle your "limiters" later in this chapter. First let's talk about the changes you'll need to make. More than likely you will have to shift your priorities and rearrange your life to achieve your goal. How will you do that? This is the hard part. Dreaming about goals is fun and exciting, but figuring out how to achieve them is difficult.

If I could just tell you what to do with your training without concern for the rest of your life, it would be easy. Based on what I'd discovered about you and your goal, I could create a training plan for you to follow over several weeks that could practically guarantee triathlon success. In fact, that's what I've done in this book, leaving the hard part—how to make it happen—up to you. Just train both long and intensely and you'll achieve very high performance goals. But will the multitude of changes in your day-to-day life be worth it? Only you can answer that question.

Everyone wants to be successful; few have the will to make it happen. Once you have a clear, precise goal, write it on a slip of paper and place it where you will see it every day.

RACE SELECTION

Your goal may have already determined what race will be your focus. If so, you are pretty much set to start training. Perhaps it's your goal to qualify for Ironman® Hawaii, a national championship, or some other event with multiple qualifiers. Or perhaps your goal is to produce a fast time for a given distance, and the particular race doesn't matter much. Regardless, you will need to choose a race to make your goal viable.

This focus race is called the "A-priority" race, which means it's the most important. You may even have one or two more A-priority races planned for this season. Three is the maximum. But in this book we will focus on one of them—the most important one. The A race. For this one you will build to a high level of fitness and then taper your training so that you come into great form on race day. If everything goes right, you will have race fitness like you have never experienced before. The buildup to this race-readiness is a long and complex process that I will take you through, step by step, in Chapters 4 through 11.

There will also likely be B- and C-priority races on your schedule. In Chapter 3 we will develop an annual training plan that includes all of these races. The B-priority races are not quite as important to you as the A races; they are stepping-stones along the path. You want to do well in them, so we'll schedule a few days of rest prior to each B race. But we won't peak your fitness for them. And as soon as they are over, you will return to training for the A race. The C races are not very important. Essentially, they are hard workouts. There is no rest before these, and your results are of little consequence. You will still give them your best effort because you do these as tune-ups for more important races, as learning experiences if you are new to triathlon, or perhaps even as social events if friends are doing them. The more experienced you are and the longer your A (or A-priority) race is, the fewer C-priority races you should do.

Timing

The first consideration is how much time you have to train and where you currently are in the season. If you've recently finished the previous season, it's early winter, and you've been rather laid back with your training, then we need at least 24 weeks to get ready. If it's late winter or early spring and you have just completed your Base period so that you have good aerobic fitness, then you'll need 11 to 12 weeks to get ready. If it's summer and you've already started racing, allow a minimum of 6 to 7

IRONMAN: RUN A MARATHON FIRST?

An athlete once wrote to me to ask for advice about whether to do an early-season marathon as a short-term goal to stay motivated. He was planning on doing the Ironman later in the season and wondered whether doing a marathon in March would help him build toward the Ironman. His question is a common one among competitive athletes, and it takes on new importance when you are training for your best triathlon. The problem is that a significant recovery is needed after a marathon. If you approach the marathon with a specific goal beyond the goals of yoru A-priority race, you could jeopardize your greater goals.

There is no compelling reason to do a marathon when training for an Ironman. But there are many reasons why you shouldn't. The athlete mentioned one—the necessary recovery afterward, which may last a month if you set a new personal best. During this time you'd be losing running fitness. There's also an increased risk of injury and a loss of focus on swimming and cycling. Trying to set a personal best in a marathon makes it an A-priority race. Too many of your resources (time and energy) will be shifted to running as a result. And, besides, the pace you run in an Ironman is nowhere near the pace you run in a marathon personal-record attempt.

You'd be much better served by training for a half-marathon in the months leading up to an A-priority Ironman. One of the many upsides of this, one that I really like, is that you train faster than when training for a marathon. The key to training is not how much training you do, but how much quality there is in your training. This generally equates to the intensity of your training. Faster training means faster running. I sometimes have sub-10-hour Ironman triathletes run fast in the late Base period, because in the Build period the running becomes much slower and is done at the goal Ironman pace in order to become more racelike. This is a pace that you could do all day if you hadn't just finished a 4 km swim and 112 mile ride.

If your A-priority race will be an Iron-distance race, there is nothing wrong with wanting to run a marathon—especially if you've never done one before. But you need to plan that so it doesn't interrupt your Ironman training, since that is your greater goal. When it comes time to run, keep your effort and ego in check so your best triathlon is still within reach.

weeks. These estimates are minimums. Generally, the more time you have until the race the better, so long as it's not more than about 30 weeks. If the A race is more than seven months off, then it's a good idea to schedule another A race about 12 weeks before. We'll peak for the first A race and then return to training for the second. The details of scheduling and planning are discussed in Chapter 3.

Location

There are some real advantages to choosing a race that's close to home. Long-distance travel is often disruptive to final race preparation because of jet lag, exposure to illness on airplanes, fatigue, strange food, mental stress, and more. Typically, the closer to home the race is—in your home town or a short drive away—the better your race performance. In the days and hours before the race, you can sleep in your own bed and eat your own food while keeping extra stress in your life low. This ideal location is seldom an option, however.

Terrain

The terrain profile of the A race should also be considered relative to where you train. If you pick a race that is very hilly but you live someplace flat, you're at a distinct disadvantage. Although you can simulate hills in training (a tactic I'll explain in later chapters), it's never the same as running or riding up a steep or long hill. Hills often determine the outcome of races. A few years ago when I was coaching a pro triathlete who was especially good on hills, I compared how course profiles related to the outcomes of races. What I found was that the hillier the course, the closer the bike performance was to overall race placement. The flatter the course, the more closely the run split time was related to race outcome. In other words, if it is a hilly course, the advantage goes to strong cyclists over strong runners. But a flat course puts the strong runner at an advantage. Of course, there are always athletes who are exceptions, and you may be one of them. Select a course based both on the terrain where you train and on your strength as a cyclist or runner.

Altitude

Altitude can significantly impact race performance. If you live near sea level or up to about 2,000 feet, it's generally not a good idea to pick an A race in Colorado or another high-altitude location such as Albuquerque, New Mexico; Flagstaff, Arizona; or Laramie, Wyoming. This warning is especially true if your goal is a fast time. You will be 2 to 20 percent slower, depending on how high the race is, than you are on your low-altitude training course. Of course, everyone will be at least a little slower than they would be at sea level. If your goal is a high placement, realize that those who live at high altitude have a definite advantage if their fitness is the same as yours coming into the race.

If you correctly time your arrival at a high-altitude destination, there are a few ways to curb your losses. One effective strategy is to arrive at the race site less than 24 hours before the start, because the body begins to experience the negative effects of high altitude in the second day of exposure. These effects include changes in heart rate, hydration status, body acidity and alkalinity, carbohydrate utilization, blood iron levels, and immune system function. Some people experience nausea and shortness of breath with initial exposure. It takes about 4 weeks at high altitude for your body to fully recalibrate. Within just 2 weeks, your body should undergo significant adaptation. So if you can go to the high-altitude race venue at least 2 weeks early, you have a second option. But during this 2-week block your training is likely to suffer, and fitness may be lost. A third option is to rent or buy an altitude tent for your home and sleep in it every night for at least 4 weeks prior to the race. In the first week to 10 days, steadily take the simulated altitude up to about 7,000 feet (2,100 meters). Get a minimum of 8 hours per day in the tent. Realize that you may not sleep as well as normal. Some athletes also experience claustrophobia. The benefits from high-altitude exposure last about 3 weeks, but there is a lot of individual variation.

High-altitude races—those higher than about 5,000 feet (1,500 meters)—are seldom a good choice for the low-altitude athlete seeking a peak performance. If you have a choice, avoid these for your A race.

Climate

Another race condition that requires adaptation is heat. Cities such as Phoenix, Houston, New Orleans, Atlanta, and Miami can be extremely hot in the summer. If you are from a northern city where it's relatively cool, such conditions will present even greater difficulties for you than changes in altitude. As with altitude, it takes about 2 weeks to adapt to heat, and during those 2 weeks your training, especially running, will suffer. Other than stiff competition, heat is the biggest challenge you will face in racing. I once coached a pro who wanted to qualify for the U.S. Olympic triathlon team at a race in Dallas in May. At start time the temperature was 93° Fahrenheit (34° Celsius) with high humidity. Everyone struggled in the muggy heat that day. He qualified because he'd spent 2 weeks in the Dallas area prior to the race, training in the heat of the day. He was better adapted than most. Don't plan on a fast time if you are racing someplace hot.

You may not have a choice in many of these race-venue considerations. Kona is always hot and humid in early October, so if you are to race well at the Ironman World Championship, or in any other hot climate, you need to do all you can to get ready for the heat. You could go to the race site 2 weeks before race day and do most of your runs and all of your rides in the late morning and early afternoon. If you have to stay home, another option is to ride an indoor trainer in a sauna or on the deck of an indoor-pool facility for an hour or longer every day for 2 weeks. (Be sure to clean your bike after a humid, sweaty ride.) If there is a treadmill available for use in the sauna or at the pool (although this is unlikely), include some running as well.

Air quality is another concern at some race venues. The extreme air pollution in some cities will definitely have an impact on your performance. In the Americas, Mexico City stands out as such a location. Many big cities in India, Africa, and Asia also fall into this category. Adaptation is not an option. In fact, if there are no other concerns (such as altitude and heat, which are both issues in the case of Mexico City), avoid going to such a race location until the latest possible time.

Competition

Who among your competitors is likely to be at the race? You may want to compare several race options with this question in mind. If your goal is winning, earning a podium position, achieving a top-10 finish, or qualifying for another race based on age-group placement, then you should know who your competition is likely to be. You can find out by asking the best athletes, talking with the person in your age group who always knows what the others are doing (every category has such a person), checking the blogs of known competitors, finding results from previous years to see who frequently races in a given event and what their times were, and schmoozing at races.

Picking and Knowing a Race

All or some of these variables may already have been decided for you. Your A race may be a national or world championship. Do what you can to play to your strengths, but don't panic about the elements that are beyond your control. Once you make a decision, we can begin equipping you for the challenges you anticipate.

Once you've decided on a race, you need to learn all you can about it. There may be subtle course nuances such as off-camber corners, craggy running trails, a shallow swim, prevailing winds, ocean currents, rough pavement, or a poorly organized packet pickup. The better you know the race, the better you can prepare for it. While training, you want to visualize the course whenever possible. So how can you find out the details? Do you have previous experience with this race? Do you know anyone else who has done it? Check the race Web site for details. A video of the course may be available online or through a vendor. Do an Internet search. Use Google Earth to check out course details. Don't leave your knowledge of the course to chance—you don't want any surprises when you arrive at the race venue.

PREDICTING A GREAT RACE

I believe it is possible to predict with a high degree of confidence how you'll do in your most important race once the training is done. Of course, from where you sit now, it's difficult to say how it will all play out. I believe there are four factors that determine success, assuming you have the potential to achieve a realistic but challenging goal.

1. FINAL 12 WEEKS OF TRAINING

Research suggests that the final 84 days are the most important in your preparation for an endurance event. In periodization talk, these weeks comprise the Build and Peak periods. This emphasis doesn't lessen the importance of the Base period that precedes the last 84 days. In order to train well in Build, you must have a solid fitness base.

During the Build period, you must avoid gaps in training for any reason, including the most common ones: unusual commitments (your spouse and boss will love this one), injury, burnout, illness, and overtraining. Any of these complications will put your chances of success well below 50-50. It's not simply great workouts during these 84 days that do the trick; it's consistent training. You can't miss workouts. Ever. The trick is moderation and the wise expenditure of energy. You *must* be smart enough to avoid illness and injury and keep from digging a deep hole of fatigue.

2. RACELIKE WORKOUTS IN THE BUILD PERIOD

During the Build period, your workouts must increasingly take on the demands of the race for which you are training. That concept seems simple enough, but I often learn of athletes violating this principle. They train for an Ironman by doing short, fast intervals, or they train for an Olympic-distance race by going increasingly longer distances at a slow pace.

A key to success is doing workouts that mimic the race in some way. The more racelike these workouts, the better your chances of success on race day. This is why, if you are doing an Ironman, I will have you do "Big Day" workouts twice in the last 84 days (as explained in Chapter 8). On the Big Day you will do 8 hours of

HITTING 84 DAYS

Some time ago I coached a triathlete who became sick 87 days before his Hawaii Ironman qualifying race. The illness lasted for about 10 days, and then there was a period of about a week during which he transitioned back into normal training. Altogether, about 17 days of focused training were lost right at the start of the Build period. By the time he was back to normal, there were 70 days remaining before the race. We were unable to make up that lost time, and he failed to qualify. We aimed for a second qualifier 10 weeks later, allowing 1 week for him to partially recover from the first Ironman race and gradually beginning to work our way back to normal training during the second week. Now there were 56 days left. However, 14 of those days would be reserved for tapering and peaking, so we actually had only 42 days to build fitness. We were unsuccessful a second time, although he certainly had what it took to qualify and had done so before. Basically, an entire season was lost because of a 10-day illness at the start of the critical 84 days.

Ironman-paced training and eat the way you plan to eat on race day. There are 90 minutes for recovery between each of the disciplines. If these two workouts go well, you have a high chance of success.

3. THE IDEAL COURSE AND CONDITIONS

Some events, such as championships, are tied to given courses. You must train to do as well as you can on a particular course by improving your limiters and taking advantage of your strengths whenever possible. But if you have the option of choosing a course, be sure to pick one that matches your abilities. Important considerations, as described earlier, include course length, hills, turns, terrain, water conditions, altitude, and weather—especially rain, snow, heat, humidity, and wind.

Your other concern is competition. You have no control over who shows up in your race category, but with some research and previous experience, you can probably make an educated guess. Knowing who the other athletes are and how well they generally race may help you make a decision about which race to select.

If the course and conditions don't match up well with your strengths, then your chances of success are diminished. If you have options, select a race that you feel confident about.

4. DESIRE

How badly do you want it? A peak race performance will take you to your limits. In other words, it will hurt. Are you willing to suffer to achieve your goal? Hard races have a way of showing what we are made of. When that time inevitably comes late in the race, do you have what it takes to hang on, or do you often crack? This kind of talk sounds like macho posturing, and maybe it is. But wanting it is a big part of what competition is about. It takes great motivation to continue when your body is screaming at you to stop. Some people seem to be very good at pushing through suffering, which may be as much a physical ability as a mental one. Others may simply be better designed to tolerate pain. Then again, it may be something that their lives have prepared them to handle. Do you suffer well? If so, your chances of success are high.

/ / /

AS YOU START DOWN THE PATH to your A-priority goal race, keep these four keys to success in mind. Most of the variables that affect these four factors are in your control. If you can successfully plan for and execute all four, I'd be willing to place a bet on you in Las Vegas.

Now that you've set your goal and selected a race, let's take a closer look at what it will take for you to succeed.

Your Fitness

NOW THAT WE'VE DEFINED AND EXAMINED your goal in detail, it's time to look at what you will need to accomplish that goal. If you've set a high goal, as I expect you have, you will need to attain a high level of fitness in order to succeed.

Exercise physiologists generally agree that there are only three things you can improve to become physiologically fit for endurance sports performance: aerobic capacity, lactate threshold, and economy. Ultimately, these are the reasons you train. So what are these things, and how do you improve them?

AEROBIC CAPACITY

Also referred to as "VO$_2$max," this term refers to your ability to use oxygen to produce energy. The more oxygen your body can process, the more energy you can produce and the greater your output (power or pace). It's common to find that the fastest athletes in a race have the highest aerobic capacities of the entrants. Slower race results typically correlate with lower aerobic capacity. But don't think that knowing your VO$_2$max will tell you how fast you will go or how well you will do compared with others in your race category. The two other physiological factors— lactate threshold and economy—also play a major role in race outcomes. One of these by itself does not constitute all of what it takes to race fast.

Aerobic capacity is literally at the heart of success in endurance sport. Improvements in aerobic capacity largely have to do with how much blood (which contains oxygen) the heart pumps to the working muscles with every beat. This "stroke volume" has a lot to do with how much aerobic capacity you have. A purpose of training is to improve your stroke volume. There are basically two ways to achieve such improvement. The first is to focus on the volume of your training. The heart responds to lots of time spent at higher-than-resting intensity (above about 50 percent of VO_2max) by becoming more efficient and effective, which ultimately means pumping more blood per beat.

High-intensity intervals will also improve your aerobic capacity, especially when you do them at the power or pace associated with your VO_2max. At this intensity, your heart rate approaches maximum capacity, so these efforts are very hard. This method will produce a higher stroke volume sooner than if you rely only on volume. Most experienced athletes employ both strategies.

There are other physiological contributors to aerobic capacity, such as aerobic enzymes found in the muscles, blood-vessel diameter and ability to dilate, and blood volume and the related hematocrit (ratio of red blood cells to total volume of blood). Many athletes seem to believe their lungs are the deciding factor when it comes to aerobic capacity, but training produces insignificant changes in lung volume.

Body weight also affects aerobic capacity. The formula for determining VO_2max is expressed in terms of milliliters of oxygen consumed per kilogram of body weight per minute. Consequently, if you lose body weight—especially fat, as opposed to sport-specific muscle—your VO_2max will increase and the effort at any given power or pace will be easier. Most of us have experienced this change at both ends of the weight spectrum. When we gain weight, it's harder to run or ride a bike uphill because our VO_2max decreases.

Aerobic capacity is primarily dependent on who your parents were. Research (Bouchard 1986) has shown that identical twins have nearly identical aerobic capacities. Although genetics probably sets the boundaries for the upper limit of your VO_2max, proper training can take you near the upper limit. However, bear in mind that two other physiological factors also contribute to endurance performance.

LACTATE THRESHOLD

Although aerobic capacity gets a lot of ink in triathlon magazines, the competitive triathlete should focus the bulk of his or her hard training on lactate threshold. If you've been training and racing seriously for three or more years, your aerobic capacity isn't likely to change much. But you may be able to significantly improve your lactate threshold.

What is lactate threshold? We need to start with a little biochemistry to understand this measure of intensity.

As your body uses carbohydrate to create energy, it creates a by-product called "lactic acid" inside the working muscle cells. As the intensity of a workout increases, this liquid begins to seep out of the muscle cell into the surrounding space and bloodstream. In so doing, it changes its composition by giving off hydrogen ions. It's now called "lactate." Despite its bad reputation, lactate is actually a beneficial substance for the body during exercise because it is used to create more energy so that exercise may continue. It's the hydrogen that is the real bogeyman because it is what causes the burning sensation in your muscles and the heavy breathing at high effort levels. Measuring lactate levels in the blood is a convenient way of estimating how much acid is in the body. The more intense the workout, the greater the amount of lactate released into the blood—and the more hydrogen ions interfering with muscle contractions. (By the way, neither lactate nor hydrogen causes the muscle soreness you may experience the day after a hard workout.)

Lactate threshold is sometimes referred to as "anaerobic threshold." Although sports scientists may argue about the differences between these two terms, for athletes there is little reason for concern. It's essentially the high intensity at which you begin to "redline." On a perceived exertion scale of 1 (low) to 10 (high), you redline at about 7 or 8. Whatever your heart rate, power, or pace is at this moment is your lactate threshold intensity. The higher this threshold is as a percentage of your aerobic capacity, the faster you will race, especially in steady-state events such as triathlons. Fit athletes commonly find that their lactate thresholds fall in the range of 80 to 85 percent of their aerobic capacities.

Most well-conditioned athletes can sustain lactate threshold for about an hour. Hunter Allen and Dr. Andrew Coggan, authors of *Training and Racing with a Power Meter*, have created a term to describe this intensity—"functional threshold." This level is the average bike power (functional threshold power) or running pace (functional threshold pace) you can maintain for one hour. Simple.

If you are using heart rate to determine your training zones, your lactate threshold heart rate (LTHR) is your average heart rate for a one-hour race effort. Because LTHR is unique to each sport, your heart rate zones will also be unique to each sport.

The body has two ways of improving your lactate threshold as a result of training. It can come to better tolerate the acid, and it can also become more effective at removing the acid. As with all aspects of fitness, the way to train your body to tolerate and remove hydrogen ions is by training at your lactate threshold. This, then, is the best marker of training intensity. That's why I base heart rate zones on lactate threshold rather than on maximum heart rate.

ECONOMY

The last of the big three physiological fitness determiners is economy. Sports scientists understand less about this one than the other two, but it may be the most important. It has to do with how efficiently you use oxygen while exercising. Measuring oxygen used is just another way of measuring energy during exercise, because, in the human body, how much oxygen you use also tells you how much energy you're expending. Your economy is much like the economy rating for a car—how many miles per gallon of gas. However, in the case of exercise, it's how many milliliters of oxygen per mile.

The longer the race is, the less important aerobic capacity becomes and the more important economy is. This is because at the longer distances, you exercise at a lower percentage of your aerobic capacity. So having a big VO_2max won't be of great benefit. But in a long race, poor economy will add up to a lot of wasted energy—and a slow performance.

You can do lots of miles and mix in high-intensity intervals to boost your aerobic capacity, but economy is a bit different. You have control over some things, but there are many you can do nothing about. For example, we know that for swimming, being tall with long arms and legs and big feet improves economy. If you have a long femur relative to your total leg length, you will have greater cycling economy. For running, being short and small leads to better economy. An endurance athlete's economy is improved by having a greater percentage of slow-twitch muscle fibers. There are other physiological improvements we would make if we had control over them, such as increasing our number of mitochondria (the little powerhouses in the muscle cell that produce energy). These are all things over which we have little or no control.

So how can you improve your racing efficiency and use fewer milliliters of oxygen per mile? Improve your swimming, biking, and running techniques. You must realize that if you decide to go this route and make changes to your current technique in one or more of the sports, there will be a period during which you will become less efficient. This will show up as a higher-than-normal heart rate at any given speed or power. It may take weeks if not months to make the new technique feel natural. At that point you should be able to swim, bike, or run faster at the same heart rates as before.

Other solutions that are beneficial for cycling and running involve reducing excess body weight and using lighter equipment. There are also sport-specific improvements that may be made. The most notable is aerobars, along with other aerodynamic equipment such as special wheels, helmet, and bike frame. As a swimmer, you can improve economy by improving the flexibility of your shoulders and feet, especially the ability to point your toes. Interestingly, research (Gleim and McHugh 1997) shows that having less flexibility in the ankle joint makes for more economical running because it appears to improve the release of energy stored in your calf muscle with each foot strike.

Training components that improve economy are intensity and frequency. Swimming, biking, and running at a high speed or power have been shown to make athletes more economical at all speed and power outputs, including the lower range. But this formula doesn't work both ways: Going very slowly doesn't pay off with greater economy at the high end of speed and power.

Frequency is one of the best ways to improve your technique and, ultimately, your efficiency. This holds true even if each session is very brief. For example, if you have only two hours a week to devote to becoming a more efficient swimmer, swim four times a week for 30 minutes each time. More frequent, short sessions will improve your efficiency faster than a few longer workouts.

Plyometric exercises have also been shown to improve economy in both runners and cyclists. These exercises involve explosive jumping, bounding, and hopping drills. For the run, brief, powerful hill repeats are much like plyometrics. You will find such repeats included in the suggested workouts in Chapter 6.

There is still a great deal of debate about whether or not traditional strength training with weights improves economy. I believe it does, as I have seen many of the athletes I've coached over the years improve their performances remarkably after a winter of lifting weights—provided they did exercises that closely mimicked the movements of the sport. Doing curls is unlikely to make you a better runner, but doing step-ups may help.

To summarize the three physiological fitness determiners: Remember that aerobic capacity is largely the result of your genetics, as optimized by steady training over many years. The longer your race is, the less significant your aerobic capacity is, even though it doesn't hurt to have a high VO_2max. Lactate threshold is highly trainable, and you should see a steady improvement in your speed or power when you reach this threshold. Economy may be the best determiner of performance of the three. But, as mentioned earlier, we don't know a lot about it, and much of what is known to be important is out of your control. The things over which you do have some measure of control often take a long time to accomplish (e.g., changing your technique), are difficult to achieve (e.g., lower body weight), or are expensive (e.g., a lighter bike).

LIMITERS

I wrote extensively about limiters in *The Triathlete's Training Bible*. This concept is so critical to your race success and to understanding the workouts in Chapters 4 through 12 that it deserves further explanation.

Like all triathletes, you have physiological strengths and weaknesses. Hopefully you have more strengths than weaknesses if you have a few years' experience in the sport. By now you probably know what your weaknesses are. Because these may prevent you from having your best triathlon, they merit special attention in your training. Not all weaknesses stand between you and success. The only ones we need to address in your training are the ones that overlap with the demands of your A-priority race. These *race-specific weaknesses* are called "limiters." For example, if your weakness is climbing long hills, but your A-priority race is flat, then that weakness is not a limiter. But if the course is hilly, then this weakness is a limiter and must be addressed. In this case, your training must focus on climbing. Realize also that limiters may vary by sport; that is, a race-specific weakness in one sport does not mean you have the same weakness in the other two sports.

To help focus this discussion, I describe training, regardless of the sport, as being based on six "abilities." This is an approach I learned from Tudor Bompa, PhD, a former Romanian sports scientist who is currently a professor at York University in Toronto and is often referred to as the "Father of Periodization." Figure 2.1 illustrates these six abilities.

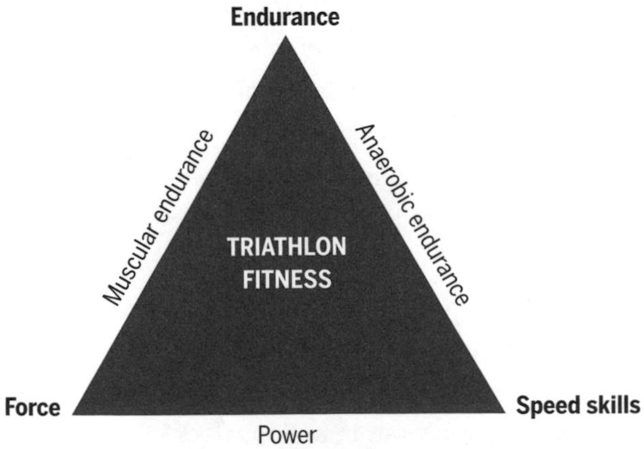

Notice the three corners of the triangle in Figure 2.1. These are the "basic abilities," the ones upon which the "advanced abilities" on the sides are based. Basic abilities must be reestablished every year, especially in the Base period. The advanced abilities are the primary focus of the Build period. (Periodization is discussed in Chapter 3.) We will look at the basic abilities first.

FIGURE 2.1 The six racing abilities

THE BASIC ABILITIES

Although the basic abilities are the focus of your Base period, they are also critical to your training in the Build period. Until these abilities are well developed, the advanced abilities, which determine race performance, will be weak. Keep in mind that fitness for a particular sport is unique to that sport—you cannot improve your fitness for swimming by doing workouts on your bike. In sports science a training principle called "specificity" suggests that one's aerobic capacity, lactate threshold, and economy are unique to a given sport and that there is very little crossover. Carefully consider how the abilities apply to the three sports individually, not collectively.

The three basic abilities are described here with the abbreviations and icons that are used in the training plans in Chapters 4 through 12.

Aerobic Endurance (AE)

Without a doubt, this is the most important of all the abilities for triathlon. But I've found it is one that triathletes pay little attention to. They would much rather do the hard workouts involving the advanced abilities because aerobic endurance training seems relatively easy. As a result, many athletes never come close to achieving their highest potential fitness. What a shame.

Triathlon is an endurance sport and depends heavily on the aerobic system to deliver oxygen and fuel to the working muscles, where aerobic enzymes create the energy needed for swimming, biking, and running long distances. For this system to work effectively, the heart, lungs, blood, and muscle chemistry need fine-tuning. This is accomplished by training at low effort, heart rate, pace, and power. If you train too intensely, then these components of the aerobic system start to shut down, allowing the anaerobic systems to take over. Triathlon is not an anaerobic sport. It is fully aerobic whether you are training for an Ironman- or a sprint-distance race.

To develop aerobic endurance, do long, steady workouts in each sport at a relatively low intensity. Zone 2 heart rate, pace, or power is the intensity that best builds aerobic endurance. Go higher than zone 2 and you start to develop anaerobic endurance systems. Go lower than this and you are not working hard enough to challenge the aerobic systems.

The outcome we're seeking in this type of training is for you to become faster at low efforts. By the end of the Base period, you should swim, bike, and run faster in zone 2 than you did at the beginning of the period. A great example is Mark Allen, an icon of the sport who won Ironman Hawaii six times between 1989 and 1995. His wins came after he discovered the benefits of aerobic endurance training at low heart rates. He used a heart rate of 155 as the upper limit of his running intensity—

that's his zone 2. When he first started, he was running an 8:15-per-mile pace (5:09/km) at this heart rate. Within a year he was running 5:20 per mile (3:20/km) at the same heart rate. He had become 35 percent faster without working any harder.

If aerobic endurance is a limiter for you, it will show up when doing long workouts. You will gradually slow down late in the session, or your heart rate will rise steadily. Aerobic endurance is explained in greater detail with workout examples in Chapter 6.

Speed Skills (SS)

Speed skills are often neglected in cycling and running, though I expect you are working to improve in this area in swimming—at least I hope you are. Training for speed has to do with your technique in each sport. It's a component of economy, as described earlier. It involves lots of drills. Drills used to develop speed skills in each sport are described in the Base period part of this book (Chapters 5–7).

The word "speed" as used here means not how fast you are, but how fast your arms or legs move when you swim, bike, and run. This is your cadence (cadence is discussed in greater detail in the "Muscular Power" section later in this chapter). Typically, when athletes are learning a new skill, they start by making the movement slowly, at a low cadence. But as they become more skilled, their arm or leg movement becomes faster until they are able to make the movement at the cadence demanded by the sport.

For example, one of the most basic skills in running is putting the foot down flat on the ground, or nearly so, with each step. When I teach this technique, I start by describing the proper foot strike and asking the athlete to stand up and try it while stationary. I simply have the athlete lift a foot and put it down slowly while I watch and make corrections until it is being done properly. Then we add a slow skipping drill in which the athlete uses the new foot-strike skill while moving forward. Next the athlete runs at a low cadence until he or she can put the foot down that way consistently. Once this is achieved, the athlete runs at increasingly higher cadences while putting the foot on the ground correctly. While it might sound easy in theory, this learning process can take weeks, if not months. To improve speed skills, you need to remain focused.

It takes a long time to develop speed skills because you are retraining the nervous system to perform in a different way. You are changing things you have been doing for a long time, perhaps years. New nervous-system pathways must be built while old ones are allowed to fade away.

Just as with aerobic endurance, as your speed skills improve, you will swim, bike, and run faster without working any harder. But at first the result will be just the opposite. You'll find that you are indeed working harder with the new technique and perhaps even going slower. You'll feel awkward, and your heart rate will likely be higher than it was with your old technique. This reaction will challenge you, but if you stay with the improved technique, you will eventually reap the benefits. It takes patience and confidence to be a good athlete. Success doesn't happen overnight.

It's sometimes difficult to know whether speed skills are a limiter for you. The best way to find out is to have a coach or knowledgeable athlete watch you swim, bike, and run to see if your movements are efficient and effective.

Force (Fo)

Racing fast requires you to apply muscular strength to the water when swimming, to the pedals when riding, and to the ground when running. This is called force. If you are weak—that is, lacking force—you will never swim, bike, or run fast, especially when you must deal with environmental conditions such as rough water, wind, and hills. Triathletes with good force thrive in such situations.

Workouts to improve force involve doing repetitions at a very high intensity against resistance. This could involve lifting heavy weights with exercises that mimic the movements of the sport, swimming with drag devices or paddles, or biking and running uphill or into a strong wind. Force workouts are explained in greater detail in Chapters 4, 5, and 6.

If force is a limiter for you, it will be apparent when you swim in rough water or bike or run uphill or into a strong wind. The weak athlete will slow down considerably and begin to "fight" the resisting condition. Technique will fall apart. If force is a limiter, you will also have slower swim, bike, or run splits in races relative to others in your age group when these conditions are present.

THE ADVANCED ABILITIES

For the advanced and competitive triathlete, the advanced abilities are the keys to success in racing at all distances. These are the three sides of the triangle in Figure 2.1. Of the three, the ones that are the most important for triathlon are muscular endurance and anaerobic endurance. But as the race duration becomes longer, anaerobic endurance has less impact on performance. The power ability is of little value to triathletes, with the possible exception of those who do draft-legal races, a type of racing almost exclusive to pros in World Cup events.

Muscular Endurance (ME)

Muscular endurance is the most important of the advanced abilities for triathlons of all durations. It has to do with the capacity to maintain a fairly high force for a relatively long time. It results from the interplay of the basic abilities of aerobic endurance and force. As these abilities improve in the Base period, so does muscular endurance. In Chapter 6, which describes the Base 2 period, you will see the first ME workouts. These are merely introductory to begin the transition from AE and Fo to ME. By the Build 1 period (Chapter 8), much of your training will be ME intervals or steady-state efforts, done primarily in zones 3 and 4. There is a close relationship between how much ME training you do, how well these workouts go, and your race performance.

Muscular endurance will be a limiter for you if your aerobic endurance or force is not well developed. The other obvious indicator is a poor race performance based on low fitness.

Anaerobic Endurance (An)

In order to have good anaerobic endurance, you must have good aerobic endurance and speed skills from your Base period training. Therefore, anaerobic endurance training does not start until Build 1 for those who do these workouts. This type of training is done at very high intensities, such as heart rate zone 5b, which is about 10 beats per minute above lactate threshold. These workouts are best left for the fastest athletes, who are frequently close to or above their thresholds when competing in sprint- and Olympic-distance races. Such training can yield nice rewards, such as improved aerobic capacity and economy, but it comes with a high risk. The chances are great for injury; a weakened immune system, resulting in illness; and overtraining. The greatest benefit is likely to be in swimming, again primarily for competitive triathletes, because this leg usually starts very fast with an anaerobic effort lasting for a few minutes before the pace calms down.

Never take anaerobic endurance workouts lightly. You must be ready for them both physically and mentally. It sometimes helps to have a training partner for these sessions, but make sure your partner's ability level is similar to yours and that he or she understands what the session is about. It is *not* about seeing who can "win" the workout.

Anaerobic endurance is likely to be a limiter for you if you race in sprint- and Olympic-distance races and your aerobic endurance or speed skills are weak. You will also have difficulty keeping up with the more fit athletes in races at the start of the swim and during surges on the bike or run.

Power (Po)

Power workouts are all about sprinting. If you watch bike races, especially the flat stages in the first few days of the Tour de France, you will see the best examples of power in endurance sports. At the end of a flat stage, it often comes down to a sprint in the final 200 meters. That is seldom the case in triathlon. As a triathlete, the power ability is unlikely to be a limiter for you, so time spent working to develop it is largely wasted. There are no power workouts in this book because the focus is on nondrafting triathlon training.

MUSCULAR POWER

Despite having just told you that the power ability is of little value in nondrafting triathlons, we're going to explore power from a different perspective. What follows is *not* about sprinting at the end of the race. It's about racing faster.

To race fast with good muscular and anaerobic endurance, what you need is muscular power and the aerobic engine to sustain it. We'll get to the aerobic engine and how to develop it in later chapters. For now let's develop a greater understanding of power in swimming, biking, and running.

Again, be aware that I am not referring to the power (Po) ability for sprinters described in the preceding section. The term "power" here refers to your capacity to maintain muscular output.

What is muscular power? There are many ways to describe it, but let's look at it from a physics perspective. In physics, power is the product of force and velocity. As a formula, it is expressed as:

$$\text{Power} = \text{Force} \times \text{Velocity}$$

In physics shorthand, this formula is $P = FV$. So whenever F or V increases while the other remains the same, P also increases. If F or V decreases and the other remains constant, then P also decreases. It's just simple math.

The best endurance athletes don't have maximal force or maximal velocity. Power athletes—the sprinters in swimming, cycling, and running—do have maximal force and velocity. They have large muscles to create lots of force and very high cadences, which is what "velocity" refers to. On the other hand, elite endurance athletes have *optimal* force and velocity. Just as with Goldilocks, neither of these elements is too high or too low for the endurance athlete. They are just right.

Does this explanation help you to understand power? Perhaps not. So let's break down the two components—force and velocity—into terms that make sense to endurance athletes.

Force has to do with the activity of muscles. When they contract, as the thigh muscles do when you push down on a bicycle pedal, force is applied—in this case, to propel the bike forward. When force is applied to the water when swimming, or to the ground when running, it also moves you forward. As the muscle's strength increases, so does force. But there is a limit to how much force is needed in endurance sports. At some point the muscle can become stronger—and larger—than is necessary to move the body. Beyond this point the extra muscle mass becomes an excessive load that must also be moved over the course, thus wasting energy. That's why elite endurance athletes are generally lightly muscled. And of course the primary movers in endurance sports are the slow-twitch muscles, which remain small relative to fast-twitch muscles even when trained for greater force production.

Force improvements allow you to use a higher gear on your bike and therefore cover more ground with each revolution of the cranks. Greater force also helps you to run and swim with a longer stride and stroke. As these changes take place, if your cadence (velocity) doesn't change, then you will swim, bike, and run faster. It's that simple.

Now let's look at velocity in the formula. This refers not to your speed or pace over the course but rather to how quickly your legs move when cycling and running and how quickly your arms move when swimming—your cadence. Cadence is usually measured in terms of revolutions—how many cycles the arms or legs make—per minute (rpm). As with force, the endurance athlete is seeking optimal cadence, not maximal cadence—which is for sprinters. And optimal cadence seems to vary by sport. The best endurance athletes in cycling and running tend to have cadences of about 85 to 95 rpm when counting one leg only. Elite endurance swimmers seem to have cadences in the range of 40 to 55 rpm when counting both arms, which is the common way to count strokes in swimming.

Cadence on the bike and run is easy to figure: Just count every time your right foot completes a revolution or strikes the ground for one minute. It's a little trickier in swimming. Table 2.1 offers an optimal two-arm count per 25 yards or meters based on your time for 100 yards or meters.

So how can you improve force and velocity? Force—and therefore power—can be increased by overloading the muscles. Methods for doing this include lifting weights using exercises that mimic the movements of the sport. The most effective methods, however, involve using gravity, or drag, to overload the muscles while doing the sport. Cyclists and runners may do maximal sprints up a short, steep hill for about six revolutions. For swimming, wear a T-shirt while doing six-revolution sprints. There should be long recoveries after each sprint for all sports. You can't make a tired muscle stronger, so full recovery is needed. Two to four of these sprints done two or three times a week should produce measurable improvements in force within 8 weeks. Be aware that force sprints like the ones described here put a lot of stress on joints, tendons, and muscles. The risk of injury is high, especially if your technique is poor or you have a history of frequent injuries. (These workouts are described in greater detail in Chapter 6.)

| TABLE 2.1 Optimal Stroke Count ||
100 m TIME (min:sec)	STROKE COUNT (40–55 rpm)
1:10	12–16
1:20	13–18
1:30	15–20
1:40	17–23
1:50	18–25
2:00	20–28

Most age-group athletes have low bike and run cadences and high swim cadences. Moving into the optimal ranges for each sport will also boost power (if force doesn't decline). This change results from persistent and ongoing devotion to an optimal cadence. The starting point is to become aware of your cadence and change it slowly over the course of several weeks. If you are consistent in your training, you should see changes within two months, although you may not be quite at the optimal range yet. For cadence, you are making changes in the nervous system, which can be slow to respond, especially if you have been training with a nonoptimal cadence for many years. (Workouts for cadence improvement are included in Chapters 5 through 8.)

As you begin to change velocity, you are likely to see a step back in performance. At any given swim or run pace or bike power, your heart rate and effort are likely to be higher than they were previously. That's normal and must be endured for some period if you are ever to become more powerful. You must be patient to become powerful.

Power and Weight

When riding a bike uphill or running, you are working to overcome gravity. For the bike, I'm sure that's obvious. Riding up a hill means that gravity is trying to pull you back down. That's what makes climbing on a bike so challenging. Running probably doesn't seem as difficult because when running there is only a little bit of vertical movement occurring with each stride. Although the vertical displacement is not great, it's happening about 170 times per minute. That's a lot of times. If the vertical displacement with each stride is only one inch (although many age-group runners bounce up and down much more than an inch with each step), that means you are lifting your body's center of gravity 170 inches—14 feet (425 cm)—every minute. If you run for an hour, you've produced 283 yards (257 m) of vertical displacement. That's an 85-story skyscraper you've climbed. Huge!

Now imagine that you are riding your bike up a steep hill or running along a flat road, as usual, only this time you're wearing a backpack filled with 10 pounds (4.5 kg) of rocks. It's obviously far more difficult when wearing the backpack. Why? Because as the weight of an object (you, your equipment, and the backpack with rocks) increases, the pull of gravity also increases. That's why you have a bathroom scale—to measure the pull of gravity on your body. We refer to that as your weight. Increases in weight will require you to use more energy while riding uphill or running. Notice that there is no change in your power when you put on the weighted backpack; only a change in weight.

Now imagine the opposite. You've got a new bike that weighs 10 pounds less than your old clunker. It's easier to ride up the hill, isn't it? Or imagine that you've lost excess body fat, and your bathroom scale says you are now 10 pounds lighter. What will happen to your running? You'll run faster at the same energy rate. Again, no change in power; only a change in weight.

Every extra pound (450 g) added to your body and equipment "costs" you about 1.5 watts of power on a steep hill climb on your bike and about 2 seconds per mile when running. A few extra pounds one way or the other directly affects how fast your race times are.

There's no doubt that the weight of your body and equipment has a lot to do with how well you perform in triathlon. If we can reduce your weight without changing your power, you will go faster. Conversely, if we can increase your muscular power with your weight remaining the same, you will also go faster. The best combination is to increase power and reduce weight. Much faster!

Here's a simple guide for determining what your body weight means to performance. Divide your weight in pounds (or kilograms) by your height in inches (or centimeters). The typical high-performance male triathlete is in the range of 2.1 to 2.3 pounds per inch (0.38–0.41 kg/cm), and the typical high-performance female triathlete is 1.9 to 2.1 pounds per inch (0.34–0.38 kg/cm). This doesn't mean that you can't excel if you are above these common ranges. It simply means that you must also have a higher-than-normal power output per pound (or kilogram) to overcome the greater weight.

Reducing your excess body weight and the weight of your bike and running shoes will potentially pay off with faster race times. But there's risk associated with weight reduction. If you lose muscle—especially the muscles that are used for swimming, biking, or running—you are likely to be slower. Replacing heavy components on your bike with the lightest (and most expensive) equipment available raises the risk of that component failing during a race. For example, lightweight tires are one of the most effective weight-reducing changes you can make because they lower the rotating weight. The downside is that they are more likely to have a puncture. A super-lightweight saddle is more likely to break when you hit a pothole. Featherweight handlebars have been known to snap when a powerful rider is climbing out of the saddle. Running in racing flats may increase your risk of injury. Lowering your racing weight provides both reward and risk.

Of course, for riding a bike on a flat road or an indoor trainer (regardless of whether the front wheel is raised or not) and for swimming, weight is not critical. The tug of gravity on your body and equipment is not as great. In fact, a big triathlete riding a bike on a flat course is generally faster than a small triathlete because being big usually means having more power. That's why if your weight is above the pounds-per-inch ranges suggested here, it's best to select flat racecourses when possible.

Power and Drag

As explained earlier, a higher weight is not a big issue when riding a flat racecourse or swimming, because the pull of gravity is insignificant in both cases. However, there is an outside force that will slow you down in both cases, and that is drag. Drag has to do with aerodynamics on the bike and hydrodynamics for swimming.

As body parts or equipment interfere with the smooth flow of air or water as you move forward, you're forced to use more power to overcome the drag. The faster you go, the greater the impeding drag of air and water and the harder you have to work. Here again, it pays to be big. If you're thinking that a large body creates more drag, you're right. But the increase is relatively minor compared to the drag of a smaller triathlete. The frontal area of a 200-pound triathlete in the aero position on a bike is only slightly greater than that of a 150-pound rider. But the power of the bigger rider is generally much greater. So overcoming the small difference in drag by applying more power is not a big deal. The same goes for swimming. If both athletes have an excellent aero position on the bike and a compact swim stroke, the larger triathlete has an advantage due to much greater power.

Regardless of your size, the starting place for better aerodynamics is having a bike that fits properly and is designed for triathlon. If these two factors are right, then the next has to do with how you are positioned on the bike relative to the wind. This generally means achieving a setup that offers a small frontal area with a flat back, low head, and narrow shoulder position. The aerodynamic characteristics of the wheels are of secondary importance. And finally, the number of things that stick out into the wind from the bike and from your body have a small but cumulative effect on aerodynamics. This may be your helmet, clothing, cables, handlebars, wide tires, and so on.

I have the athletes I coach get a bike fit every winter, even if it's the same bike they raced on the previous season. Things change. You may have become stronger or more flexible, the distance of your most important race may be different or the course hillier, you may have had a niggling injury or lost weight late in the season, or perhaps something else has changed. There are many other possibilities. The bike fit should be done by a professional fitter who understands triathlon. Setting up a triathlon bike is not the same as setting up a road cyclist for a time trial. Those cyclists don't have to run at the end of their ride. Do not do your own bike fit or have a friend do it, no matter how experienced you or the friend is. This is critical. You don't want to invest a lot of sweat, time, and money in preparing for your best triathlon ever only to perform poorly because your bike was not set up right.

For swimming, how much frontal area you present to the oncoming water is critical. Something that really stands out to me when I watch excellent swimmers is how little water they disturb. It's as if they are swimming through a long, narrow tube. They keep their heads, arms, and legs inside the tube. Enabling this is a long posture in the water, like the position of a speedboat. These swimmers have a long arm extension that results in a hip roll (not the other way around) and keeps their feet inside the shoulder-width tube. The poor swimmer not only lacks fitness but has arms, legs, feet, and head sticking out in all directions, increasing drag and the need for power to overcome it. They require a much larger tube. This poor positioning compounds their lack of swim fitness. When it comes to swim training, economy is critical—much more so than for cycling or running. I will emphasize proper mechanics over fitness repeatedly in the training chapters that follow. You must improve your stroke. I've never coached a triathlete yet, including any pro, who didn't have room for improvement in his or her swim technique.

Just as with a bike fit, have a professional swim instructor help you with your swimming mechanics. Again, this is best done by a teacher who understands triathlon. Find one who uses an underwater camera to see exactly what you are doing. The slower you swim, the more important it is to have such instruction done frequently. If swimming is your primary limiter, then shoot for once a week. The best time of the year to work on swim instruction is the Base period. But if you started reading this book during the Build period and swimming is a limiter for you, then seek out an instructor now and begin to work on becoming more hydrodynamic. Don't wait.

Power and Pacing

Distributing power evenly throughout a race is perhaps the hardest skill for triathletes, regardless of ability, to master. Keeping your pace right on the bike is especially challenging. Much of this has to do with your emotions. As you exit the water, clear the first transition (T1), and start the ride, there is a lot of excitement around you. You feel great, so you start the bike portion extremely fast—much faster than a pace you can sustain for the entire distance. Because of this mistake, you eventually are forced to slow down and finish with a slower bike split than you are capable of. It's the most common mistake triathletes make.

The even distribution of power in a race is called "pacing." I find that proper pacing is one of the most difficult things to teach in coaching. For proper pacing, an athlete has to learn to take it a bit easier at the beginning of a run, ride, or swim in order to have a faster ride overall and a fast finish. But most athletes are not patient enough to take it easy at the start, or they have trouble shaking the feeling that starting out extra-fast will lead to a better time. The problem is that when you go out overly fast, you create a lot of acid buildup that then stays with you for the rest of the bike ride and causes you to slow at a greater rate than would have been the case had you been more conservative early on.

I have the athletes I coach divide the bike course into four segments and have a strategy for each. These segments may be of equal length. Another way of doing it, which may be even better, is to set these segments by terrain changes. One segment may be hilly, another has a prevailing headwind, or perhaps one requires lots of cornering. With this approach, the sections are unlikely to be of equal length. Regardless of how the bike course is divided, here is how I suggest you mentally manage each segment.

SEGMENT 1

In the first segment, simply try to hold back. This is the hardest thing you will do in the entire bike portion. If you have a power meter, it's much easier to do. You establish a power goal for the first quarter and then watch your handlebar computer to make sure you are on pace. I do not recommend using a heart rate monitor for this purpose because your heart rate is affected by your excitement about the race. If you don't have a power meter, you can rely on perceived exertion—how hard it feels. It should feel very, very easy—far easier than what your mind is telling you to do. This may result in only a 3 percent reduction of power, but it will feel much greater. If you start breathing hard, then you went out much too fast. Another way of knowing you got the pacing right is that other athletes will pass you. They're going too fast and will eventually drop back. If you're passing others, then you're going too fast.

SEGMENT 2

In the second segment, if you don't have a power meter, watch your heart rate and speed closely. Realize that if it's a windy day or you're on a hilly course, then speed has little meaning. A power meter, again, makes this task simple. Just ride at your goal for average power in segment 2. If you are using a heart rate monitor, which may now start to give you dependable information, stay in your goal zone for the bike leg. Do not let your heart rate rise above the goal heart rate. If you are using perceived exertion, the effort is only slightly harder than for the first segment. Stay in tune with your technique and breathing while being careful not to get caught up in "racing" everyone around you. Save the racing for the run. Concentrate on your own race—not that of others.

SEGMENT 3

The third segment is typically the toughest. If you started out too fast, you will now slow down. The purpose of the first half of the race is to prepare you for this section. If you controlled your effort and were patient in segment 1, you will now be able to maintain average power, heart rate, or speed, although the effort will feel much harder than earlier. In other words, perceived exertion is now rising rapidly even though your body is not working any harder than before. During this segment you may well say to yourself, "I'm not doing very well. Going too slow. Someone's going to pass me." That's normal. Expect it. Everyone will think that during this segment. Maintain focus and effort. Pay attention to your race, not that of others.

You may find it useful to play "pedaling games." Count pedal strokes as "1-2-3, 1-2-3," etc. On "1" apply more force, and let up on "2-3." This means each leg will get a five-stroke "rest." Or try a five-beat count. "Sing" a song in your head that has the right tempo for your pedaling. Do whatever you need mentally to get through this section of the race. It is by far the most challenging portion even if you paced properly earlier. If you didn't, then this part is incredibly depressing and you are likely to surrender here.

SEGMENT 4

In the fourth segment, you know there are only a few miles left. The end is mentally in sight. It's like a horse smelling the barn—you know you can finish strongly. Maintain your power or heart rate. Perceived exertion will rise slightly again. Focus on someone up the road. Concentrate on that target. Keep the effort steady and begin to prepare for the second transition (T2). Mentally rehearse T2, including where your bike is racked, how you will put on your running shoes and other equipment, where you exit the transition area, and how you will start the run. Go through the steps in your head a couple of times. In the last few hundred yards of the bike leg, bring your attention back to the present moment. Be aware of those around you. This point in the race is when a crash is likely to happen.

This pacing won't happen on race day if you don't do it in training. That's where proper pacing is learned. When doing interval workouts, such as the ones suggested in later chapters, do them with negative splits, using the same strategy you will employ for the segments in the race. That means you hold back a bit on the first interval and then try to make each successive one a bit harder than the first. You can do the same when riding steady-state efforts in training. Don't wait until race day to practice this. I guarantee that it won't happen if you've never done it in workouts. Make it a habit.

Another element of successful pacing that must be practiced is riding the hills so as to optimize performance. On all hills, including small rollers you hardly even notice, ride slightly harder than your goal power or perceived exertion on the uphill side and slightly easier on the downhill side. This will help you gain time while giving your legs a small break. This technique also needs to be rehearsed on small hills when doing intervals and steady-state rides.

Patience and confidence are the keys to successful pacing. If you are impatient or lack confidence in your ability, the tendency is to start much too fast on the bike and then limp home in the fourth segment. I'm afraid this is what nearly all triathletes do—but it doesn't have to be that way. You'll never realize your potential as a triathlete until you develop and follow a pacing strategy. This requires both mental control and physical practice.

THE RIGHT STUFF

Excellence in sport is not just about physical power. It also has a lot to do with mental and emotional power. The following describes what I have found in working with hundreds of athletes over the past 30 years.

Excellence is not for everyone. It's far too difficult for the great majority of those who participate in sport. In fact, those who seek excellence are often ridiculed because they are different from their peers. Thus, it isn't easy to seek excellence. Humans are social animals; we don't like being outcasts. It's much easier to go along with the crowd than to stand out.

But there are athletes who pull it off, and with great aplomb. Have you ever noticed how young pro athletes often try to give the impression that nothing about their training or dedication to the sport is unusual? They've learned to give the appearance of being just like everyone else, even though their performance in competition tells us otherwise. Going out of their way to be laid-back is how they cope with the dilemma and prevent others from branding them as strange. That's a good strategy that I recommend to anyone who truly seeks excellence: Try not to give the air of someone who is seeking excellence. Appear ordinary in every way you can.

This discussion basically comes down to how I select the athletes whom I agree to work with. How do I know if a particular person could be successful? The following is a list of what I think are the best mental predictors of excellence in sport, in their order of importance. I rate these right up there with, and even above in some cases, the success predictors discussed at the end of Chapter 1. The mentally powerful athlete will figure out a way to make success happen. Do you have these qualities?

HIGH MOTIVATION

This quality is more important than all the others combined. If the athlete isn't highly motivated, excellence is highly unlikely. In fact, the other predictors are of little value without motivation. This goes well beyond giving lip service to goals. The truly motivated athlete is on a mission and has a hard time keeping him- or herself in check. This person often needs a coach to pull on the reins to prevent overtraining, injury, illness, and burnout. If the coach has to use a whip, then it's a losing cause no matter how talented the athlete is.

Neither the coach nor anyone else will ever give the athlete motivation; it must come from within. When I'm interviewing athletes, I ask lots of questions to find out how truly motivated they are. For example, I ask how often they train with other athletes versus alone. The low-motivation athlete will frequently need companionship. If you are motivated, then all of the following predictors of excellence will eventually fall into place. You will make them happen.

DISCIPLINE

This quality is very simple. The disciplined athlete will make daily sacrifices and make do with hardships in order to excel. This person doesn't miss workouts under any conditions short of a disaster. Weather is an insignificant factor for the disciplined athlete because he or she knows that the small stuff is important. He or she doesn't get sloppy with diet, recovery, equipment, or anything else that has to do with goals.

Discipline is not easy. Others can accept motivation, but they have a hard time dealing with people who are disciplined. You've got to make light of or even hide your discipline in the company of friends if you want to be accepted by your peers.

CONFIDENCE

Some people seem to live life with an unwavering belief in themselves and their actions. These folks are rare. I've met very few athletes who didn't have some concerns about how well suited they were for the task at hand. There's a sliding scale of confidence, and most of us are somewhere in the middle. To move closer to the high-confidence end, all we typically need is some success. Success breeds confidence.

Look for success every day in everything you do. Never dwell on failures. Seek out and relive successes all day, every day.

FOCUS

This quality could also be called "purpose": The athlete knows where he or she wants to go in the sport. There is no confusion about direction. Daily training is a purposeful activity that will lead to excellence. Each hard workout (and accompanying recovery) is a small building block that eventually results in excellence. But you have to take it one step at a time, which brings us to the last predictor.

PATIENCE

According to Malcolm Gladwell in his book *The Outliers*, it takes about 10,000 hours for a person to become a master of anything. Before reading his book, I had never tried to quantify mastery in terms of hours, but experience told me that performing at the highest level in sport takes something on the order of 10 years of serious training, regardless of when you started in life. So I think Gladwell is probably right. There are certainly exceptions, or at least it appears that way on the surface. But when an athlete comes along who seems to go to the top right away, we often find on closer examination that he or she had been developing outside the recognized success pathways.

Patience has another level that goes beyond this long-term approach to success. This is a more immediate, daily component associated with the ability to pace appropriately early on in workouts and races. Athletes who seem unable to learn this skill are less likely to be successful than those who master it.

I've never met anyone who didn't have the capacity to develop each of these mental abilities. No one achieves high levels of accomplishment in any activity, including triathlon, without being highly motivated, disciplined, focused, and patient.

Your Training

AS YOUR COACH, I'm making many training decisions for you, just as I do for the athletes who are my clients. Of course, you're going to have to make some decisions on your own. This chapter is designed to help you understand how to make big-picture training decisions so that on race day you are in good form and ready for a peak performance.

Once I know an athlete's race goals and a great deal about him or her, the next step is to lay out a plan for accomplishing the goals. This plan is based on "periodization" and includes everything from a seasonal overview to individual workouts. I think you will find my Annual Training Plan very helpful as you plan for your best triathlon ever. You can either use the Annual Training Plan form from the appendix in this book or download an electronic version under the "Forms" heading at TrainingBible.com/resources.aspx. TrainingPeaks.com provides all of the other tools necessary to design your season. Chapters 7 through 9 of *The Triathlete's Training Bible* cover the planning process in great detail.

PERIODIZATION

Periodization is a widely accepted training approach. It is used by nearly every successful athlete in the world, regardless of sport. All of the athletes I have ever coached believed that they should use it in planning for their peak race performance, too. Not a single one has ever wanted to do it a different way. But many have admitted that they find the subject confusing. Actually, nothing about periodization is inherently complicated. It's rather simple.

Periodization is just a way of planning how best to use your resources—time and energy—to achieve your race goals. As with almost any aspect of your life, planning improves your chance of success. This book does almost all of the planning for you. At the end of each of the periodization chapters (4 through 12) is a training plan. Each of these training plans follows the guidelines of periodization. So you really don't need to become an authority on the theory. But I believe that an informed athlete trains better than one who is uninformed, so I want to explain periodization to you just as I do for those whom I personally coach.

Keep It Simple

The periods of training refer to time—Prep, Base, Build, Peak, Race, and Transition. I use these titles not because I want to but because I have to. If every triathlete did his or her A-priority race on the same day every year, then I could refer to training time frames using specific months of the year. If, for example, everyone, including you, was racing the last weekend in May, I could talk about how you would all plan your training in November, December, January, and so on. It would be quite simple and easy to understand. But everyone's A races are not on the same day— or even in the same month—so the names of the months simply won't do. Hence the period names.

Table 3.1 explains what the periods mean in terms of the primary purpose of training during each and how long each lasts. Once you understand that these terms are nothing more than labels for periods of time and that each has a general training purpose, the next challenge is to understand the application of periodization to training. It may already be apparent from the "Primary Purpose" column in Table 3.1.

TABLE 3.1	The Purpose and Length of Training Periods	
PERIOD	PRIMARY PURPOSE	TYPICAL LENGTH
Prep	Prepare to train	2–4 weeks
Base	Develop basic abilities, emphasizing duration	12 weeks
Build	Develop advanced abilities, emphasizing intensity	8–9 weeks
Peak	Taper and do "minirace" workouts	2 weeks
Race	Rest and prepare to race	1 week
Transition	Recover physically and mentally	1–8 weeks

Over the past several decades, sports scientists have proposed many ways to explain periodization. One explanation is that it is a method for gradually increasing physical stress over the course of many weeks. Others describe it as a methodical system for gradual physical adaptation that avoids exhaustion. Still others explain that it has to do with the alternation and progression of high and low workloads. It has also been referred to as a cyclical system for the practical application of the principles of training. These definitions could go on and on, becoming increasingly vague and complex, but it doesn't have to be that way. I believe the explanation of periodization-based training can be boiled down to one simple sentence: Using periodization means that the closer in time you get to the race, the more like the race your workouts must become.

If this is all you know about periodization and you adhere to it, you'll do fine. Because when all is said and done, the most important question is: Are you prepared to race? If you can answer that question affirmatively—which you can if your workouts have been like the race—then you will have a great performance. If you're not sure of your race-readiness, then you haven't made your workouts enough like the race. It's that simple.

Racelike Training

So what does it mean to make your workouts like the race? It has to do with three things: how frequently you do racelike workouts, how intense your racelike workouts are, and how long your racelike workouts are. Let's take a closer look at each of these concepts.

RACELIKE WORKOUT FREQUENCY

In keeping with my simple definition, early in the training year—during the Prep and first few weeks of the Base period—your training is quite different from your A race. For example, the training plan provided in the next several chapters calls for you to do some weight lifting during these periods. At no time in a triathlon do you stop to lift weights; strength training is not racelike at all. So, given my definition, what do you think should happen to weight lifting as the season progresses into the late Base, Build, Peak, and Race periods? Weight lifting should become an infrequent workout with a low priority.

Becoming more frequent during this same period are workouts that are like your race. Thus, by the time you get to the late Build and Peak periods, many of your workouts will be like miniraces. Now, obviously, you can't do a minirace every day. You would very quickly become overtrained if you tried to do so. You have to have easy days and basic-ability maintenance days between the racelike workouts. If your A race is sprint-distance, you can do a racelike workout about once a week in the last few weeks before the race. In fact, you can do a lot of sprint-distance races during this time. But if you are training for an Ironman, there's no way you can do an Iron-distance race every week. You can, however, do portions of the race, such as long bike rides and long runs, on a weekly basis. As a coach, I have Ironman tri-athletes do abbreviated Ironman races twice in the Build period with several weeks separating them (you'll find these "Big Days" in the Chapter 8 and 9 plans). That's frequent enough to prepare for the specific demands of that particular type of race, but not so frequent as to cause breakdown.

So the frequency of racelike workouts depends on the race you are training for. You will see this become quite obvious in Chapters 8 and 9 as you follow the Build period plans I've written for you.

RACELIKE WORKOUT INTENSITY

For the experienced and competitive triathlete, the key to success is intensity. This does not mean swimming, biking, and running as fast as you can; it means training at intensities that are appropriate for your A-race goals. For example, if your A-race goal running pace is 7 minutes per mile, then the closer you get to the race, the more time you must spend running at a 7-minute-mile pace—especially after a bike ride. By race day, running at that pace should feel like second nature. But in the Base period, you won't do much 7-minute-mile-paced running. You'll do runs that are much slower and some that are even faster. They are not specific to your goal pace, but they have a purpose that will become clear when you get to Chapters 5, 6, and 7.

RACELIKE WORKOUT DURATION

Notice that in the preceding paragraph, I did *not* say the key to success for the ex-perienced and competitive triathlete is how long his or her workouts are. Endur-ance athletes tend to believe the length of their workouts is what their training is all about. That's the case if you are new to the sport, because novices have to build the endurance to finish the race. But once you have a good level of endurance, which you should achieve after about three years of serious training, duration is no lon-ger the key to your success.

This is not to say that workout length is unimportant for the advanced athlete. It's just less important than intensity. Early in the season, especially in the Base pe-riod, your workouts will be quite long. Your longest workouts will be in the last few weeks of Base, which I call Base 3. In the following Build period, there will actually be a slight shortening of your longest sessions as the intensity becomes more race-like. That will prepare you for the race much better than if you simply did more and more miles slowly, as most self-coached athletes do.

That's really all there is to periodization. Make the workouts increasingly like your race by appropriately increasing the frequency of your racelike workouts, making the intensity of these workouts more like the race, and training at durations that are also appropriately racelike. All of this will lead to a best race ever.

PLANNING YOUR SEASON

Having talked with and answered questions for hundreds of athletes over the past 30 years, I can guess with some certainty that you're not keen on planning. You would prefer to simply jump ahead to the training plan at the end of a chapter and start following it. You may get lucky and pick the right chapter. But if you don't, then you will just make your season worse. At some point you will be forced to figure out what you did wrong, and then you'll try to correct your mistake within weeks or even days of your A race. Much of your training will have been wasted and your race performance compromised. Dedicating an hour or so now to planning your season will greatly increase your chances of success.

If it's now winter and your training is just starting up again following a break, then this is the perfect time to begin planning. Even if you're already well into your racing season as you're reading this book, it's a good idea to plan the remainder of the season. After this chapter, you'll need to jump to the chapter in this book corresponding to where you are in the season, and in order to determine which chapter that is, you'll need to know how to identify the periods. You will use the Annual Training Plan form to list the types of workouts you've been doing (aerobic endurance, force, speed skills, muscular endurance, anaerobic endurance, and power) and when you did them. You may not have thought of your workouts earlier in the year as falling into these categories, but with the help of Chapter 2 you should be able to label the types retrospectively.

If you are now in midseason, be sure to also indicate on the Annual Training Plan when you took your last rest break. Later in this chapter we'll review why such breaks are critical to building fitness and are an integral part of your planning.

What follows is a summary of the planning process, as discussed in Chapters 7, 8, and 9 of *The Triathlete's Training Bible*. Included are some insights into common mistakes I've found athletes make when using those chapters to plan their season. (For a comprehensive, step-by-step description of how to design the periodization plan for your season, see Chapter 7 of *The Triathlete's Training Bible*.)

Your Training Blocks

The most common way to manage time and energy using periodization is to train in subperiods, which are commonly called "blocks." In scientific periodization lingo, they are referred to as "mesocycles." The Base and Build periods described in Table 3.1 are divided into blocks that are typically 3 to 4 weeks long. I call them Base 1, Base 2, Base 3, Build 1, and Build 2. The first 2 or 3 weeks of each block are devoted to developing greater fitness, and the last week is for recovering and testing progress.

The final week of each Base and Build block includes a few days of rest and recovery because fatigue accumulates throughout a training block. Older athletes will find that they need these rest weeks more frequently than younger athletes, so the older triathlete trains in 3-week blocks. The younger athlete trains in 4-week blocks.

Athletes always ask me, "How old is old?" In this case, "old" is defined not by how many candles are on your birthday cake but by how quickly you recover after long or highly intense workouts and how your body copes with accumulating fatigue. Getting older seems to slow down the recovery process. Nobody knows why. If you often find that 48 hours after a hard workout you are still quite tired and find it difficult to do another hard workout, or if you start feeling overly tired after 2 weeks of training, then you are an "older" athlete and need to train in 3-week blocks. I've seen this occur in athletes in their 40s. But I've also seen athletes in their 50s who recover quickly and can train in 4-week blocks. There is no number that tells us definitively; age categorization is different for everyone. If you are unsure, the only advice I can give you is to use 3-week periods if you are over 50. By then, slow recovery is fairly common. You may even find that in the Base period you cope quite well and can use 4-week blocks, but in Build you need more frequent rest—if so, go with 3-week blocks then. Pay close attention to how your body responds to the hard workouts, and make training-block alterations as needed.

Table 3.2 shows the organization of training blocks according to your recovery-based age. Only the Base and Build blocks are affected by this adjusting. The durations of the other blocks remain as listed in Table 3.1. Note that for older athletes, Table 3.2 calls for repeating Base 3 and Build 2. Thus, they would go through the blocks in this order: Base 1, Base 2, Base 3, Base 3, Build 1, Build 2, and Build 2. This means that the Base period is 12 weeks long, the same as for younger athletes. The older athletes' Build period is 9 weeks long, and for younger athletes it is 8 weeks.

TABLE 3.2	Training-Block Durations Based on Age	
BLOCK	**YOUNGER ATHLETES**	**OLDER ATHLETES**
Base 1	4 weeks	3 weeks
Base 2	4 weeks	3 weeks
Base 3	4 weeks	3 weeks (repeat Base 3)
Build 1	4 weeks	3 weeks
Build 2	4 weeks	3 weeks (repeat Build 2)

Your Training Weeks

In periodization talk, training weeks are "microcycles." They don't have to be a week long, but I will refer to them as "weeks" anyway. Some athletes make them longer or shorter. That can be difficult to do, especially if you have a lifestyle built around a five-days-a-week job or school and have weekends off. Trying to do a long bike ride on a weekday can be difficult if you have to be at work by 8 a.m. Although I'd really prefer to separate long runs and bike rides by 72 hours or more, weekends usually work best for these workouts for most triathletes. The training plans in this book are designed with such a lifestyle in mind. Although it would be quite a scheduling challenge, the plans found here can be altered if for some reason a seven-day cycle doesn't work for you. The two groups of athletes who often change the duration of their microcycles are pros and retired people, who have much more latitude with their lifestyles and can train using any pattern they find beneficial. If in doubt, stick with seven-day weeks.

During the 2 or 3 fitness-development weeks in the Base and Build training blocks, the training is challenging. It is common to make each of these weeks slightly harder as the block progresses. This increased training load may come from making the workout durations longer (in the Base period), from increasing workout frequency (also in Base), and from increasing intensity (in the Build period). For the latter, you might do more intervals in week 2 than you did in week 1, or the recovery time between intervals might be shortened. Increasing intensity does not necessarily mean going faster.

Let's return to the rest-and-test weeks mentioned earlier. Actually, I don't devote an entire week to resting and testing, but when I wrote *The Triathlete's Training Bible*, I allowed for a slightly longer rest and recovery break in these weeks. In the past several years, I've discovered that an advanced triathlete can reduce the number of days devoted to rest. The more fit you are, the faster you bounce back, and we have learned much about how to speed recovery. A shortened rest break is suitable for older triathletes who are fit as well as for younger ones, but the older athletes need recovery breaks more often.

You will find in the training plans at the ends of Chapters 5 through 9 that the rest-and-test weeks (the final week of each block) devote Mondays, Tuesdays, and Wednesdays to light training. Advanced athletes typically recover better by doing short, low-intensity training rather than by doing nothing at all. During these three days you must do what is necessary to speed recovery. This includes nutritional adaptation and other methods of expediting recuperation (as described in the following chapters). By Thursday, if you did a good job of recovering over the preceding three days, you should be ready for a short swim test to measure progress. I put the swim test rather than a bike or run test on this day simply because any fatigue remaining on Thursday will likely be in your legs. If you aren't ready for a short swim test by Thursday, then you will need to push it to a later day in the week.

Fridays in the rest-and-test weeks call for a short bike test and nothing more. The run test is scheduled for Saturdays because running is the most stressful of the three sports. By Saturday you should be feeling pretty good, and since you should be rested, the run test is followed by a run workout. Sundays in rest-and-test weeks are much the same as the preceding Sundays in the block, with a scheduled bike workout.

Your Workouts

The heart of training is the workout. This is when you create the potential for fitness. Notice the word "potential." Fitness is not created in workouts—it occurs in the recovery period following a long or intense training session, when the body changes by adapting to the stress you previously placed on it. The major change that happens during a workout is that fatigue is created.

Fatigue is a good thing. If there is no fatigue, then the body doesn't need to adapt. Therefore, fatigue is your sign that you accomplished something. Unfortunately, some athletes become addicted to fatigue and want to always be in a fatigued state. Athletes who seem to enjoy fatigue are prime candidates for the overtraining syndrome. As I mentioned earlier, fatigue must be shed when the accumulation becomes too great. That's why there are easy days and rest weeks. I have already discussed rest weeks, and I'll come back to easy days a little later in this chapter.

Workouts must have a purpose, and you should always be aware of what that purpose is as you begin a session. You must then stay focused on that purpose. It is usually to improve or maintain an ability, as discussed in Chapter 2. These are the hard workouts that leave you fatigued. Of course, the other common purpose is to recover—workouts with this purpose are the easy ones. Athletes often become confused and forget what the purpose of each workout is, especially when they are around other athletes. This confusion may happen, for example, if a group of riders comes along while you are in the middle of a bike workout. You jump in with them, and all of a sudden you're "racing." Your purposeful workout is replaced by a random workout that has no relationship to either your sport or your limiters. It's wasted time at best. But it also means you didn't do anything that day to get ready for your A race. Going anaerobic with a bunch of roadies will not make you a better triathlete; it will make you a worse triathlete. Know the purpose of your workout, and keep your focus.

There are only two things you can do to make a workout hard: You can make it longer, or you can make it more intense. Of course, you can also make it longer *and* more intense. In the Base period the workouts emphasize duration—the make-it-longer method. Intensity also increases a bit during the Base period, but not as much as duration. In the Build period intensity increases while duration stays the same as in Base or is reduced slightly.

As mentioned before, "intensity" in this case does not mean trying to go faster and faster with every subsequent workout. Workout intensity is directly tied to your race goals. In the race, what do you want your pace, heart rate, power, or perceived exertion to be for each sport? The answer to that question determines the intensity of your hard workouts in the Build period. All you should do then is focus on getting more and more time at that level of intensity to build race-specific fitness. I have to say this again because it seems that most athletes do not fully understand how important it is: For the advanced athlete, how long your workouts are and how many miles, kilometers, or hours you train in a week is not the ultimate determinant of how race-fit you are—intensity is. Trying to continually increase duration or olume in the Build period will not adequately prepare you for a fast race. To race fast, you must train fast, not slow and long. Once your workout duration and weekly volume are established in the Base period, you have accomplished all you can in this regard. At that point, turn your attention to the intensity of training, and keep it there.

Consistency and Moderation

The biggest mistake most self-coached athletes make is to not train consistently. It's not that they don't want to train consistently; it's just that they frequently violate an even more basic tenet of smart training that is at the heart of consistency— moderation. When you moderately increase training stress (workout duration and intensity) in conservatively measured amounts, you wind up training consistently week after week. But if you pile on huge doses of stress with overly long or hard workouts, or you skip a rest week, you greatly increase your risk of injury, burnout, illness, and overtraining. Any one of these problems will interrupt your consistency. When there is a break in training for a few days, fitness is lost and you have to step back in training and begin over again. Many athletes experience this once or twice each season and as a result never realize their full potential.

TROUBLESHOOTING TRAINING INTERRUPTIONS

The training plans in the following chapters are built around these basic tenets of consistency and moderation. If you closely follow one of these plans, you should develop excellent fitness and come into form at the right time for your A race. I fully expect, however, that something will happen to interfere with your training even if you do everything right. This type of problem could happen a couple of times as you follow the plan, so it's quite likely that you will have to vary your training to accommodate an interruption. Here's a quick guide to modifying your training plan when workouts are missed. Make a mental note to return to this section the first time it happens.

Three or fewer days missed. Return to training as if nothing happened. Don't try to make up the missed workouts, because cramming more workouts into a few days creates the potential for a breakdown and another loss of time. It's simply not a big deal to miss a couple of workouts if it happens rarely.

Four to seven days missed. This may be the hardest scenario to deal with. If the lost time was due to illness, as is quite often the case, you probably won't really be ready to return to normal training right away even if the symptoms are gone. Your body's chemistry has probably changed, which will affect your capacity for exercise. This change will show up as a high heart rate and a higher level of perceived exertion at common paces and power outputs. In this case, you will need to treat it as more than seven days missed even though you are starting back into training again.

If the missed training was not due to illness and you are ready to get started right away, you will need to make some adjustments to the plan. The first change is to consider the lost training time a rest week. This is necessary even though it will throw off the scheduling of training for your A race. Your training blocks will no longer be synchronized to bring you to a peak of form on the day of the race. There are a couple of ways to resolve this dilemma. The first option, if you are in the Base or Build period, is to reduce the length of the current block by a week. If you still aren't synchronized, do the same for the following block. The second option is to reduce the Peak period from 2 weeks to 1. Neither of these options is perfect because both will result in less fitness being developed. But that's the reality of missing a week of training. You can't have it both ways—you can't miss several workouts and still have the same fitness as if no training was missed.

Once you are ready to train again, you will need to step back and make up two or three key workouts—one in each sport. Decide which were the most important ones missed, given your limiters, and reschedule them. Rescheduling may well mean pushing other workouts further ahead in the plan. Eventually something will have to give; you'll either have to miss one of the culminating workouts or decide you are progressing well enough to skip or modify one of the sessions remaining in the plan. There are simply too many variables for me to be able to tell you exactly how to handle your situation. Give it a lot of thought.

One or two weeks missed. If this gap was due to illness and you were in the Build period, start back into training with a Base 3 training block. If you were in the Base period, go back to Base 1 or even Prep training. Stay with that until you feel normal when working out. You will know because your heart rate and perceived exertion will match your pace and power as they did before you got sick. If in doubt, give it another day or two.

When your training vigor returns, repeat the last week of hard training you did before the interruption. If that week goes well, then begin moving forward with your training from that point. If it doesn't go well, repeat that week again. At some point you will need to leave out 1 to 3 weeks, or even more, of planned training. That could mean omitting Build 2 and/or the first week of the Peak period.

More than two weeks missed. If you were in the Build period when this training pause happened, then return to Base 3 and start again from there. If you already were in the Base period, then back up one block from where you left off. As in the previous scenarios, you will have to leave out some significant portion of your plan. The priority for omissions is the first week of Peak, Build 2, and Build 1, in that order.

If any of your training time was lost in the last week of Build 2 or the Peak period, continue with your training as if nothing happened. But as with all of these scenarios, if the lost time was due to illness, be conservative with intensity as you start back; opt to train primarily in zones 1 and 2 until you are back to normal.

EASY MEANS EASY

The starting point for consistency and moderation in training is the recovery workout. Sometimes the hardest part of training is going easy. As I was writing this book,

I had the opportunity to go for a bike ride with two of my coaching clients who were visiting. They and I had recovery rides scheduled, as we all had hard workouts planned for the following day and had had hard workouts the day before. I could tell they were having a hard time "going for a walk" on a bike, which was what we had agreed to do. At one point I had to chase one of them down to get the effort low again. When we were done, the other told me he had never had such a low heart rate on a bike ride.

Since they were both starting their Build periods, their training had to be either hard or easy—never in between. "Hard," of course, is related to the event for which you are training. It doesn't mean maximum effort all the time. "Easy" means zone 1. If you make the easy days easy, the hard days can be hard. As a result, race fitness will improve. If, on the other hand, easy becomes moderate, then hard also becomes moderate because you will be too tired to push the effort higher. And so there is little fitness progress. Recovery days *must* be easy. The harder the hard workouts, the easier the easy ones.

/ / /

WITH THESE PRINCIPLES IN MIND, it's time to start swimming, biking, and running.

Part II

PREP, BASE 1, BASE 2, AND BASE 3

It's time to start swimming, biking, and running.

As when building a house, we have a lot of foundation work to do. The Prep and Base periods are a time when you are developing this foundation, so this stage can't be skipped or rushed. A poor foundation for fitness will show up later in your training, just as it would in house construction. For the athlete, injuries and slow pacing are the equivalent of cracked walls and sagging floors.

For these next several weeks, you will be training to train. What this means is that you'll do workouts that are not quite specific to triathlon racing. Not until the Build period will the training sessions take on the characteristics of the race you're training for. In the next few weeks the workouts will be more general than they will be later on. Gradually shifting your training from general to specific over several weeks will bring you to a peak of fitness at just the right time.

I've seen it happen time and time again in the hundreds of athletes I've coached over the past 30 years. I'm certain it will work the same way for you if you are patient and stick to the plan.

In many ways the Base period is the most important time of the entire season. If training goes well now, you will be able to do very high-quality workouts in the Build period. If it doesn't go so well, you won't be able to train to your potential later on, and you'll be more likely to break down because of overtraining, illness, and injury.

Now on to the training.

Prep

4

THE LENGTH OF THE PREP BLOCK depends on how many weeks there are until your A-priority race. If you precisely follow the periodization model described in the previous chapter, you need 23 or 24 weeks to train for your race, depending on whether you are a younger athlete or an older one (see Chapter 3). All weeks above and beyond your 23 or 24 weeks make up your Prep block. Ideally, your Prep period will be 2 to 6 weeks. If you have less than 23 or 24 weeks until the race, then you'll need to do some head scratching to figure out what to omit. You may even have to leave out the Prep block, though anytime you omit a training block some fitness potential goes unrealized. It may be a tough decision, but making those decisions is part of the challenge of being a self-coached athlete.

In the Prep block the training will be easy. It only takes about 12 weeks to fully build race-specific fitness once you've established the basic abilities described in Chapter 2. Race-specific fitness is what allows you to go fast for a long time, but the intervals and other hard workouts focusing on advanced abilities need not start until about three months before your A-priority race. Getting into the heavy breathing too soon with too much volume means that you must try to maintain that level week after painful week or lose all of your hard-earned fitness. That's difficult—if not impossible—to do for an entire race season. About the only way to accomplish it is to take a long break from training in the spring and then start over again. I'm sure you aren't willing to do that.

The solution, of course, is to spend time in the winter thoroughly developing basic-ability fitness with long aerobic endurance workouts, skills development, and muscular force training. The Prep block begins this process and is the first step down the path to your best triathlon.

Objectives for Prep

1. **Gradually return to normal training.** I hope that after your last race of the previous season you took some time away from structured training. Just as you need easy training days and weekly rest periods, you need annual recovery breaks. Focused training day after day, week after week, month after month is a sure way to become stale as an athlete. So if you've been taking some time off and perhaps messing around with a wide variety of fun exercise activities for the past few weeks, as you should have, I'm sure you are chomping at the bit to get going again. That's what you will do in the Prep block. But the training won't be demanding. You will ease back into a routine so that when it's time to begin the Base 1 block you are back to normal training.

2. **Begin developing aerobic endurance and speed skills.** In Prep you will begin working on the basic abilities described in Chapter 2—aerobic endurance, speed skills, and force. The first two will come along as you focus on them while swimming, biking, and running. But you'll also do some cross-training to further build aerobic endurance. You're encouraged to do activities other than the three primary sports during this block.

3. **Develop general muscular force with weight training.** In the Prep block you will start a gym-based weight lifting regimen to build greater muscular strength. This starts with a total-body program and morphs into a transitional phase to get you ready for the Max Strength phase in Base 1. I'll get you started on this in Chapter 5.

4. **Reduce risk of injury.** I hate injuries. I'm sure you do, too. There's nothing worse than having trained for months with your fitness progressing nicely and then getting an injury that forces you to greatly reduce your training—or even to stop working out entirely—for days or weeks. All of your hard-earned fitness can be lost. You will take steps in the Prep block to prevent injuries for the rest of the season, thus improving your chances of getting consistent training and achieving race-day fitness.

Coaching Tips for Prep

Preparing for your triathlon goes well beyond physical training. As I'm sure your race experience has taught you, what you do when not training is often just as important as your workouts. Keep this in mind as you read the following. These are the key topics I discuss with the athletes I coach as we enter the Prep training block.

MINDSET

Training is not just physical. Your mind plays an important role as you build fitness and improve as a triathlete. To fully benefit from the workouts in this training block you must understand your purpose and stick to it.

As you start back into training with the Prep block, you will experience a feeling of excitement accompanied by a desire to quickly improve your fitness. I've seen this attitude in nearly every athlete I've ever coached. They all want to hurry the process. Training with other triathletes often increases this sense of urgency. It may seem that everyone is more fit than you. I hear that a lot this time of year. As a coach, I think it's great that you are not in race shape now while your training partners are.

Why? There are still several months until your first important race of the season. Getting in great shape now and trying to maintain it for the next 20 or so weeks simply isn't going to work. Your fitness is either getting better or getting worse. It's never constant. Once you reach a peak of fitness there is no place to go but down. Early-season fitness means a poor performance later on. Avoid the urge to train as if you had a race coming up soon. Allow your body to gradually ramp up. Stop trying to "win" workouts. Praise your training partners for how fit they are and let them dominate now when it doesn't matter.

Use this time to ease back into training. You're simply preparing the body and the mind for what comes next in the Base period. You don't want to have great fitness now—that would be a mistake on a grand scale. Simply take the first step down a long path that will lead to your best triathlon ever. The process can't be rushed, so have patience.

INJURY PREVENTION

You're going to spend the next several weeks training to race better than you ever have before. Unfortunately, there are lots of little injury demons lurking out there just waiting to pounce on you and ruin your plans. They would love to give you a sore knee, hip, Achilles, shoulder, back, or something else. And it wouldn't be hard for them to do it. Wouldn't it be great if you could get rid of the demons now? You can and should. There are three things you can do to greatly reduce your potential for injury this season.

The first thing you can do is see a medical specialist for a head-to-toes assessment of your physical make-up. I have each of the athlete's I coach do this every year in the Prep block. It greatly reduces the likelihood of an injury later on when the training load increases and your body is under a lot of stress.

It may cost you a couple hundred dollars for a thorough exam, depending on your medical insurance coverage, but it's money well spent if you have a good practitioner. Choose a physician or specialist who has a background in sports medicine and understands what triathletes do in training and racing. A health care professional who tends to work only with aging people who are sedentary or with people who have work-related injuries would not be appropriate. If you don't know who to go to, ask around and find out who works with a lot of athletes. Your general practitioner may be able to recommend a specialist if you tell him or her what you are looking for.

What you want the specialist to do is identify weak muscles, inadequate core strength, leg-length discrepancies, joints that have too much or too little range of motion, rigid or hypermobile arches, and anything else that could cause injury. After the exam the practitioner should provide you with strength and stretching exercises to improve your muscular and joint balance. He or she should also give you special instructions about how to prevent injury. This may include tips on workouts or movements to avoid (such as running hard downhill), the type of running shoe that might be best for you, any orthotic devices needed for your shoes, whether to put a shim in your bike cleats, and what to tell your bike fitter about your needs.

Once you have done this you are well on your way to an injury-free season. But there are still things you can do to improve performance while also reducing the risk of injury.

BIKE FIT

I go to lots of races as a spectator, and I'm always amazed at how poorly many triathletes have their bikes set up. They invest hours and hours of training time, carefully watch every kilocalorie of food they eat, buy the most expensive equipment available, pay a wad of money to enter the race—and then ride a bike that doesn't fit right and significantly reduces their performance. What a waste.

But when I ask triathletes how well their bikes fit, they always tell me they made the fit themselves and it's just right. You simply cannot set your own bike. You need to have someone do this who knows what he or she is doing. Eyeballing it won't do anymore. Take your bike to a professional fitter. Ask around at bike shops to find a good one who understands triathlon. It's not the same as setting a time trial bike for a road cyclist. They don't have to run after crossing the finish line.

As I mentioned in Chapter 2, I have all of the athletes I coach do a bike fit every winter, in the Prep block, even if it's the same bike they rode last year and they have no problems on it. Things change from season to season. Get a bike fit every year even if you don't think you need one.

The fitter will want to know a few things about you, such as what you found out in your physical exam; whether you have any problems when riding, such as a sore knee or hands that "go to sleep"; and the type of A-priority race you're doing this season. This last point is critical to fitting a triathlon bike.

To race well on a tri bike you need balance between power and aerodynamics. There will always be a trade-off involved here. If you opt for more power, you will need the front end to be positioned higher, which increases drag and compromises aerodynamics. If you want to go for the most aero-possible position, you'll give up some power. The proper balance is somewhat dependent on the course you are racing. The hillier or more technical the course, the more you need power. The opposite is also true: The flatter and less technical the course, the more you should lean toward aerodynamics. The set-up for an Ironman-distance race must place greater emphasis on comfort, whereas aerodynamics matter more for short-course racers. These are the sorts of things a good fitter has going on in his or her mind while talking with you and looking at your bike set-up.

SKILLS ASSESSMENT

When it comes to swimming and running, the equivalent of a poor bike fit is poor biomechanics. Inefficient and ineffective swim and run techniques not only slow you down but also increase your risk of injury. In the Prep block I meet with each of the athletes I coach to assess these skills and determine what we need to work on to reduce the risk of injury and increase speed. It's very difficult to evaluate your own technique. Have a coach do this and offer suggestions. This is best done with video. Avoid coaches who overwhelm you with changes you need to make. You should only work on one or two changes at a time, and the ones you choose to work on must be the most critical for your current level of performance. Once they are mastered, then you can move on to the next most important change.

It's best to set up some sort of ongoing technique review with this coach, since movement skills don't change overnight. In the Prep and Base periods, meet with him or her frequently as you are refining your movement patterns. If you start working on them now, by the Build period you should have them pretty well dialed in.

NUTRITION

The younger an athlete is, the less effect a poor diet seems to have on health and performance. The older an athlete is, the more critical diet is to health and performance. At least that is what I have observed in coaching athletes of all ages for more than 30 years. It's strictly my opinion, as there is no research on this topic, and though I really don't know the reasons why, it appears to be the case.

Perhaps it's because young athletes generally train with a higher workload than older athletes and burn more calories. Burning more calories means they can eat more food—they may get enough of the micronutrients they need for optimal health and performance from the "good" part of their diet, and if they eat junk food, they simply burn it off in the extra work they do. That's the Walmart model: A small percentage of a large volume may be the key for the younger athlete.

It also may be strictly a health issue. It could be that the systemic defenses of the young athletes are so effective that it doesn't take much for them to maintain a sound body. By this theory, older athletes may need to take in more vitamins and minerals than younger ones because their immune systems are weaker.

So if you're an older athlete, could you eat more junk food and just use supplements to get what your body may need? I don't think so. There is some evidence that vitamin and mineral supplements are ineffective and may even be harmful. For example, vitamin E, when eaten in foods that contain it, has been shown to be an effective antioxidant. But as a supplement it has shown no benefit, according to clinical studies (e.g., McGinley, Shafat, and Donnelly 2009). Beta carotene, when eaten in a carrot, is good for your health, but when the beta carotene is removed from the carrot and taken as a supplement, it actually has negative consequences for health in the form of greater risk for cancer (Bjelakovic et al. 2007). If you're taking pills to boost health and perform better, you may be accomplishing nothing or even doing harm. You're much better off getting the micronutrients you need from real food rather than supplements.

I only recommend two supplements to those I coach. The first is omega-3, usually taken in a fish oil capsule. The Western diet is poor when it comes to omega-3 and it has potential benefits not only for performance, but also for health. The other is vitamin D, which I recommend in the winter for any athlete who lives someplace located above about 40 degrees north latitude. Our bodies make their own vitamin D when exposed to sunlight. Just 15 to 30 minutes outdoors on a sunny day, with your face and arms exposed, should be sufficient for your body to make enough vitamin D, according to most experts. But in cold weather, athletes either train indoors or cover up when outside. Once summer rolls around again there is little reason to continue taking the vitamin. If you cover every inch of your body with a heavy sunscreen all summer, then you may need vitamin D, too. Taking these supplements is not necessarily the best option. I'd much rather my clients get these nutrients from eating fish and from ensuring adequate exposure to the sun. I cannot guarantee the supplements will produce the desired results, as we're still waiting for that research to be done.

There is no research showing that a "healthy" diet is beneficial for performance, but there are a few things the research generally agrees on when it comes to diet and health. The most obvious is that vegetables and fruits are beneficial. I have absolutely no doubt that the health of an older athlete who has a poor diet will improve if he or she simply eats more of these two food groups, and I've seen it happen. But I wouldn't expect to see a significant difference in a younger athlete who made the same change. The older athlete may see a positive shift in performance from eating more veggies and fruits. The benefits may be direct or indirect—for example, the athlete may have fewer breakdowns due to illness, and therefore more consistent training. As discussed in Chapter 3, consistent training is far more effective for performance than inconsistent training.

I tell the athletes I coach that 80 percent of what they eat should be regular meals containing vegetables, fruits, and lean meats, especially fish, game, and free-ranging animals. The other 20 percent should be in the form of foods eaten immediately before, during, and right after a workout to promote performance and recovery. I also tell them they don't have to be perfect. It's okay to cheat a little. Just make sure that it really is only "a little."

Prep Workouts

The workouts listed in the training plans at the end of the chapter are designated by abbreviations for some of the abilities discussed in Chapter 2. In the Prep block you will train in only two of them: aerobic endurance (AE) and speed skills (SS).

Force (Fo) workouts are also included in the Prep plans, but they are listed as strength training sessions done in a gym (AA or MT). The strength workouts are detailed in Appendix C.

AEROBIC ENDURANCE AND SPEED SKILLS WORKOUTS

In the Prep period almost all of your swim, bike, and run workouts will focus on aerobic endurance and speed skills (AE + SS). The other abilities—force, muscular endurance, and anaerobic endurance—will be developed in the training periods that follow.

An aerobic endurance workout is done in zone 2. If you know your heart rate zones for the bike and run you can use them here. But in the Prep block, intensity does not need to be that precise. It's all right to simply swim, bike, and run at what feels like an "easy" effort. By that I mean you will not experience labored breath-

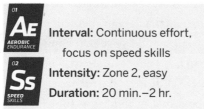

AE AEROBIC ENDURANCE
Interval: Continuous effort, focus on speed skills

Ss SPEED SKILLS
Intensity: Zone 2, easy
Duration: 20 min.–2 hr.

ing and you will sense that you could maintain the effort for a very long time—as in several hours. Focusing on speed skills while swimming, biking, and running aerobically in the Prep block merely means that you are aware of and self-correcting your technique as you exercise. In Base 1, speed skills training, and all of your training, becomes more structured. In Prep, since you are just getting back into training after a break, workouts are much less regimented.

CROSS-TRAINING WORKOUTS

The plans at the end of this and the following chapters include two categories of workouts—primary and optional. The ones in italic are optional. The primary workouts are in bold red type. An optional workout may be done in place of a primary workout on a given day or may be done in addition to a primary workout. In Prep, the optional sessions are of only one type—cross-training ("x-train"). You may do one of these instead of the scheduled bike or run when one is listed.

Cross-training should always be an option in the winter months when the weather isn't good enough for you to train outside. If a bike ride is scheduled on a day when the weather is poor, you can ride indoors on a trainer or do a workout in another sport. Being forced indoors by snow, rain, high winds, and short daylight hours can get tiresome, especially after a few days in a row. Cross-training instead is a good option at those times. In the winter I'd rather have you somewhat under-trained but enthusiastic than the other way around.

At this point in the season we are focusing your training on the cardiovascular and respiratory systems. This means your heart, blood vessels, blood, and lungs. These "central" systems don't know the difference between swimming, biking, running, and other types of aerobic exercise. It's all the same as far as they are concerned. That's why it's all right to do some training with activities that aren't specific to triathlon. All the cross-training will prepare you for the later work, and that is what the Prep period is for. Over the next few weeks, your training will continue to become more specific to triathlon, so resist the temptation to train as if you had a race next week.

Winter sport activities are perfect cross-training alternatives at this time of year. Below we'll look at some of the common choices for cross-training workouts for the Prep period. Feel free to do any others you enjoy, even if they aren't listed, so long as they are aerobic. You may also combine one or more of these activities to produce a longer session with a lot of variety. Feel free to substitute any of the following when "x-train" is listed on your schedule as an option. Just be sure to keep the effort easy so that the central systems are developed.

Hike. This is a favorite, especially for those who live near the mountains. You can hike with someone who is not an athlete, such as a friend or your spouse, and no particular skills are needed. Just pick a trail and start walking briskly. Move along at a good pace, especially on the uphills. To challenge yourself a bit, wear a loaded backpack. Twenty to thirty pounds will do it.

Cross-country ski. This is another popular winter workout in snowy areas. Cross-country skiing is great for developing cardiovascular and respiratory fitness. It also works the upper body, and you can do long workouts without a high risk of injury.

Snowshoe. Snowshoeing skills can be picked up quickly and you can do it any time there is enough snow covering the ground. Using ski poles will also work the upper body.

Gym machines. Your gym may have equipment you can use to get a good aerobic endurance workout without swimming, biking, or running. Common types are stair climbers, cross-country skiing simulators, rowing machines, elliptical trainers, and the like. Be sure to get someone to teach you proper rowing technique before you spend much time on a rowing machine. Using incorrect form can put you at risk for back strain.

Mountain bike. Riding off-road not only is great for the cardiovascular and respiratory systems but also develops better pedaling skills and is great fun. The workouts are best left unstructured. Simply ride on a variety of terrains. Small hills covered with loose gravel are especially good for improving pedaling, as this forces you to keep even tension on the chain rather than mashing the pedals.

Force Workouts

I encourage you to lift weights in the winter and even year round because it develops total-body muscular fitness. If you don't have weights or machines available, be creative. Leg exercises can be done with a loaded backpack. Rubber stretch cords, available in sporting goods stores and online, are also a good option for increasing resistance.

Note that in the Prep block your training plan calls for Anatomical Adaptation (AA) and Maximal Transition (MT) weight workouts. You'll find basic instruction for these workouts in Appendix C; for more detail on the periodization of your gym-based force training, see *The Triathlete's Training Bible* (Chapter 13). In the first part of Prep there are three weight workouts per week. In the rest-and-test week there are only two. By the last week of Prep you should be doing the MT workouts.

Prep Testing

In your rest-and-test week at the end of the Prep block, the daily and weekly volume will not be significantly different from that of previous weeks. The stress of training is quite low already in this period, so it's not necessary to reduce the training load further. Although it's called a "rest-and-test week," you should not be experiencing significant fatigue at this time. Your training proceeds much as it did in the previous weeks, only with some testing included.

The tests will establish your heart rate training zones for the bike and run. Testing for swim pace, run pace, and bike power will be done at the end of the Base 1 block. We're testing the bike and run heart rate zones at this point because you will be using your heart rate monitor for these sports in Base 1, which begins next week. We will not be using heart rate for swim workouts at any time during training. I've nevertheless included a simple pace test for swimming, however, just as an optional baseline measurement.

When it comes to heart rate zones, what we want to determine is your lactate threshold heart rate (LTHR). It is also sometimes referred to as the anaerobic threshold heart rate. There are other names for it that aren't as common, but we'll just call it your LTHR. This is the heart rate at which labored breathing begins. On a difficulty scale of 1 to 10, with 10 being very, very hard, LTHR occurs at about 7. Some athletes describe it as the intensity at which they begin to redline. An LTHR effort cannot be sustained for a long time. It's uncomfortable, to say the least. The test description below will give you a better idea of just how uncomfortable.

Your LTHR will be different for every sport, and that is why we need to do separate tests for biking and running. The reason is that LTHR is a function of how much muscle is required to overcome resistance, especially gravity. The LTHR for running is almost always higher than it is for biking. That's because there is some vertical oscillation with running—you bounce up and down slightly. With every step you have to overcome gravity, which requires a great deal of muscle and effort. In biking, particularly on a flat road, there is no vertical oscillation and the effort needed to overcome the pull of gravity remains constant. Far fewer muscles are called upon to propel the bike forward than are called upon to propel your body forward in running. The heart doesn't have to work as hard in biking; therefore your LTHR will probably be lower on the bike than when you are running, usually by 5 to 10 beats per minute.

Many coaches recommend finding your max heart rate instead of LTHR. I prefer the LTHR method for two reasons: first, because I believe it's far more important to know the point at which you redline than to know how high you can push your heart rate, and second, because LTHR is much easier to find. Most athletes can't push themselves hard enough to find their true maximum heart rate. A max-heart-rate level of effort is very painful. Usually, what an athlete thinks is a max-heart-rate effort is actually "peak" heart rate—the highest the athlete found that day, but not the highest possible. LTHR is roughly 20 to 30 beats per minute lower than your max. That alone makes finding LTHR easier.

The more important point here is that we want the results to accurately reflect your intensity and effort. Having the same max heart rate as your training partner doesn't mean you have the same lactate threshold heart rates or that you should both train at the same heart rate zones. LTHR is not always the same percentage of max heart rate. This concept is easier to explain with an example.

Let's say two triathletes who are training partners share a common max heart rate of 172 on the bike. But triathlete A has an LTHR that is 90 percent of max (155), and triathlete B has an LTHR that is 82 percent of max (141). If they are scheduled to do a workout at 85 percent of max heart rate (146), the effort triathlete A experiences will be far easier than the one B experiences. Triathlete A is aerobic, whereas B is anaerobic. B is suffering while A is cruising along. They aren't achieving the same results at all. B is developing his anaerobic systems, and A is building aerobic fitness. Such a physiological system discrepancy will show up in every workout at every level of intensity from low to high. That's why we will only try to determine your LTHR. We don't care what your max heart rate is. It's an interesting number, but of little consequence to your training.

THE RUN AND BIKE FIELD TESTS

There are various ways to find your LTHR. One way is to do graded exercise tests and short time trials, and I describe these in *The Triathlete's Training Bible*. You can use these in your bike and run testing at the end of the Prep block. But there's an easier way to do it that takes only 30 minutes. Just warm up for 20 to 30 minutes and then run or ride as hard as you can for 30 minutes. This is best done on a flat course with no stops and little or no traffic. For running, a track works well, and for cycling a little-used country road will do. You'll see how to schedule the tests later in the Training Plans at the end of this chapter.

The best location for the bike test would be a cycling velodrome, but you're not likely to have one in your area. In addition, riding a bike on a velodrome takes some getting used to, so you don't want your first time there to be a test. You can do the bike test on an indoor trainer, if necessary, or the run test on a treadmill, but doing the tests indoors can be mentally challenging and give you lower heart rate readings. If you live at a northern latitude, you may have no other options, but make sure you have at least one fan to keep you cool during the tests.

The road is a better option for most triathletes. Just be aware of the danger associated with riding or running hard on the open roads. Keep your head up and pay close attention to traffic and intersections. Finding LTHR is not so important that you need to put yourself at risk of an accident. Be careful.

Because we are taking the average heart rate of the last 20 minutes of the test effort, I am frequently asked if you should go hard for the first 10 minutes. The answer is most definitely yes. Go hard for the entire 30 minutes. But be aware that most people doing this test go too hard the first few minutes and then gradually slow down. If you took the average for the entire half hour, the data from that burst would give you a skewed and inaccurate result. You'll be doing these tests periodically to recheck your LTHR, and the more you do them, the more accurate your results will be, because you will learn to pace yourself better at the start.

You can do these tests during actual races—either a "stand-alone" bike time trial or a running race—but suitable races can be very difficult to find at this time of year. If you do a race for test purposes, it needs to be about 60 minutes in duration rather

The 30-minute test should be done *as if it were a race* for the *entire* 30 minutes, whether you are running or on your bike.

Warm-up	20–30 min.
Main set	30 min. hard, race effort
Cooldown	As needed, easy

At 10 minutes into the test, click the lap button on your heart rate monitor. Hit the lap button again at the end of the 30-minute effort. After your cooldown, see what your average heart rate was for the last 20 minutes. This number is an approximation of your LTHR.

than 30. The reason is that you go harder when in a real race—in a 60-minute race you would likely go about as hard for the whole hour as you would go for only 30 minutes in a workout. In workouts we give in to the fatigue that sets in after a half hour or so, whereas in a race we keep pushing harder as we approach the finish.

Whichever way you do it, avoid starting too fast. Proper pacing is critical not only for testing but also for racing in triathlon, and now is as good a time as any to start working on pacing skills. Hold back just a little at the start of each test. I tell the athletes I coach to go out about 3 percent easier than they would if they were really pushing themselves. If you hold back a bit in the first few minutes, you won't fade as much, if at all, in the second half, and you will get better test results. The more accurate the results, the better your training will be, and the better you'll race later on.

Another option for determining your LTHR is to have a professional handle the testing for you at a clinic, university lab, or health club. You may even have a bike shop or running store in your area that offers such testing. I've found there is a lot of variability in such testing when it comes to defining what LTHR is, however. The technician's opinions, methodologies, protocols, testing equipment, and software may give you numbers that are very different from what you would find in a field test. If you go this route, tell the technician that you are trying to find the heart rate you could maintain for about an hour in a race. This is sometimes referred to as a "functional threshold heart rate." The real advantage of professional testing is that all the variables that can have a significant effect on the results are carefully controlled.

Once you have found your LTHR in biking, go to Table B.2 in Appendix B to set your zones. Simply find your LTHR and read across the columns to the right to find your zones.

After determining your run LTHR, go to Table B.3 in Appendix B to find your training zones.

SWIM FIELD TEST

The swim field test is optional because we are not concerned with your heart rate in the pool; we don't really need to know your pace zones yet. That information will be necessary as you enter Base 2, so pace testing in the pool will occur at the end of Base 1. But there's nothing wrong with establishing a fitness baseline for swimming now with a simple pace test.

Although the swim pace test is simple, it is by no means easy. After warming up, you will swim 1,000 yards or meters as hard as you can. You'll want to pace yourself by holding back just a bit at the start.

If you decide not to test your swimming this week, simply do another AE + SS workout in its place.

Warm-up	10–15 min.
Main set	Swim 1,000 m at hard, racelike effort
Cooldown	

Divide your total time for the 1,000 by 10 to find your pace per 100 yards or meters. This is referred to as your "T-time" and is a good indicator of your fitness for endurance swimming. Over the course of the season it should gradually get faster.

Your Prep Training Plan

I suspect this is what you've been waiting for: weekly training plans. Each of the following plans is laid out first by the distance of the A-priority race for which you are training. Then for each distance there are two suggested weekly plans. The first is for the initial part of Prep. This block is a bit different from the other blocks in that the number of weeks is not precisely specified; instead it depends on the number of weeks until your first A-priority race. You may do a Prep block for only two weeks, or it could be six or more. Regardless, for the first week or weeks of Prep follow the "training week" plan. In the last week of Prep, follow the rest-and-test-week plan.

Note that I've referred to these weekly plans as "suggested." It is not possible to design a generic training plan that works for everyone. There are simply too many variables. These could be lifestyle-related, such as your work or school schedule, or even have to do with the days on which your masters swim group meets. So you may need to move the workouts around to better fit your routine.

The first rule for doing this is to evenly space the workouts by sport as well as you can. For example, notice that in the first plan below, swim workouts are scheduled for Tuesdays, Thursdays, and Saturdays. That's a fairly even spacing, and it leaves only a single two-day gap, with no swimming on Sunday and Monday. Otherwise, there is only a single off-day between your swims. It would be poor spacing to swim on Tuesday, Wednesday, and Thursday, as that would leave a four-day gap without swimming (Friday through Monday). It's the same for the bike and the run. Try to avoid big gaps with days of no training for any of the three sports. During periods when you don't work out in a sport, there is a loss of fitness. You need to minimize that loss.

Here's how to read the abbreviations. Say on a given day the suggested plan calls for a bike ride designated as "AE 1:00–1:30." That means to do an aerobic endurance ride with a duration of 1 to 1.5 hours. When two or more ability abbreviations are connected by a "+" sign, it means a workout includes all of those abilities. For example, a run of "AE + SS" means to warm up (assumed for every workout), then train at an aerobic effort with a focus on speed skills, and cool down (also assumed for each workout).

For most workouts in your training plan there are time ranges for the durations of the sessions, such as "0:45–1:00." This means your workout may be 45 minutes to 1 hour long. How long you choose to make it depends on what your level of fitness is, how well you have recovered from the previous workout, and how much time you have available, given your job and other demands on your time.

As I mentioned earlier, the plans throughout this book include primary workouts (in red type) and optional workouts (in italic type). You may choose to replace a primary workout with an optional workout that better fits your goals, or you may do the optional workout in addition to the primary workout.

SPRINT-DISTANCE TRAINING **PREP**

T R A I N I N G   W E E K S

SPORT	SWIM	BIKE	RUN	STRENGTH	DAILY VOLUME
MON				AA or MT 1:00	1:00
TUES	AE + SS 0:20–0:40		AE + SS 0:30–0:45		0:50–1:25
WED		AE + SS 0:45–1:00 or *cross-train*		AA or MT 1:00	1:45–2:00
THURS	AE + SS 0:20–0:40		AE + SS 0:30–0:45		0:50–1:25
FRI		AE + SS 0:30–0:45 or *cross-train*			0:30–0:45
SAT	AE + SS 0:30–0:45		AE + SS 0:45–1:00 or *cross-train*	AA or MT 1:00	2:15–2:45
SUN		AE + SS 1:00–1:30 or *cross-train*			1:00–1:30
VOLUME BY SPORT	1:10–2:05	2:15–3:15	1:45–2:30	3:00	8:10–10:50
WORKOUTS	3	3	3	3	12

R E S T   &   T E S T   W E E K

SPORT	SWIM	BIKE	RUN	STRENGTH	DAILY VOLUME
MON				MT 1:00	1:00
TUES	AE + SS 0:20–0:40		AE + SS 0:30–0:45		0:50–1:25
WED		AE + SS 0:45–1:00 or *cross-train*			0:45–1:00
THURS	Te or AE + SS 0:20–0:40		AE + SS 0:30–0:45		0:50–1:25
FRI		Te + AE + SS 0:45		MT 1:00	1:45
SAT	AE + SS 0:30–0:45		Te + AE + SS 0:45–1:00		1:15–1:45
SUN		AE + SS 1:00–1:30 or *cross-train*			1:00–1:30
VOLUME BY SPORT	1:10–2:05	2:30–3:15	1:45–2:30	2:00	7:25–9:50
WORKOUTS	3	3	3	2	11

Notes: Rec = Recovery. Optional workouts may be done in place of or in addition to a primary workout. Detail on the workouts can be found in the chapter. Strength workouts appear in Appendix C.

OLYMPIC-DISTANCE TRAINING PREP

TRAINING WEEKS

SPORT	SWIM	BIKE	RUN	STRENGTH	DAILY VOLUME
MON				AA or MT 1:00	1:00
TUES	AE + SS 0:40–1:00		AE + SS 0:45–1:00		1:25–2:00
WED		AE + SS 0:45–1:00 or cross-train		AA or MT 1:00	1:45–2:00
THURS	AE + SS 0:40–1:00		AE + SS 0:45–1:00		1:25–2:00
FRI		AE + SS 0:45–1:15 or cross-train		AA or MT 1:00	1:45–2:15
SAT	AE + SS 0:40–1:00		AE + SS 1:00–1:15 or cross-train		1:40–2:15
SUN		AE + SS 1:15–1:45 or cross-train			1:15–1:45
VOLUME BY SPORT	2:00–3:00	2:45–4:00	2:30–3:15	3:00	10:15–13:15
WORKOUTS	3	3	3	3	12

REST & TEST WEEK

SPORT	SWIM	BIKE	RUN	STRENGTH	DAILY VOLUME
MON				MT 1:00	1:00
TUES	AE + SS 0:40–1:00		AE + SS 0:45–1:00		1:25–2:00
WED		AE + SS 0:45–1:00 or cross-train			0:45–1:00
THURS	Te or AE + SS 0:40–1:00		AE + SS 0:45–1:00		1:25–2:00
FRI		Te + AE + SS 1:00		MT 1:00	2:00
SAT	AE + SS 0:40–1:00		Te + AE + SS 1:00–1:15		1:40–2:15
SUN		AE + SS 1:15–1:45 or cross-train			1:15–1:45
VOLUME BY SPORT	2:00–3:00	3:00–3:45	2:30–3:15	2:00	9:30–12:00
WORKOUTS	3	3	3	2	11

Notes: Rec = Recovery. Optional workouts may be done in place of or in addition to a primary workout. Detail on the workouts can be found in the chapter. Strength workouts appear in Appendix C.

TRAINING PLAN — PREP

LF IRONMAN

HALF-IRONMAN-DISTANCE TRAINING **PREP**

T R A I N I N G W E E K S

SPORT	SWIM	BIKE	RUN	STRENGTH	DAILY VOLUME
MON				AA or MT 1:00	1:00
TUES	AE + SS 0:45–1:00		AE + SS 0:45–1:00		1:30–2:00
WED		AE + SS 0:45–1:15 or *cross-train*		AA or MT 1:00	1:45–2:15
THURS	AE + SS 0:45–1:00		AE + SS 0:45–1:00		1:30–2:00
FRI		AE + SS 0:45–1:15 or *cross-train*		AA or MT 1:00	1:45–2:15
SAT	AE + SS 0:45–1:00		AE + SS 1:00–1:30 or *cross-train*		1:45–2:30
SUN		AE + SS 1:30–2:00 or *cross-train*			1:30–2:00
VOLUME BY SPORT	2:15–3:00	3:00–4:30	2:30–3:30	3:00	10:45–14:00
WORKOUTS	3	3	3	3	12

R E S T & T E S T W E E K

SPORT	SWIM	BIKE	RUN	STRENGTH	DAILY VOLUME
MON				MT 1:00	1:00
TUES	AE + SS 0:45–1:00		AE + SS 0:45–1:00		1:30–2:00
WED		AE + SS 0:45–1:15 or *cross-train*			0:45–1:15
THURS	Te or AE + SS 0:45–1:00		AE + SS 0:45–1:00		1:30–2:00
FRI		Te + AE + SS 1:00		MT 1:00	2:00
SAT	AE + SS 0:45–1:00		Te + AE + SS 1:00–1:30		1:45–2:30
SUN		Te or AE + SS 1:30–2:00 or *cross-train*			1:30–2:00
VOLUME BY SPORT	2:15–3:00	3:15–4:15	2:30–3:30	2:00	10:00–12:45
WORKOUTS	3	3	3	2	12

Notes: Rec = Recovery. Optional workouts may be done in place of or in addition to a primary workout. Detail on the workouts can be found in the chapter. Strength workouts appear in Appendix C.

IRONMAN-DISTANCE TRAINING **PREP**

T R A I N I N G   W E E K S

SPORT	SWIM	BIKE	RUN	STRENGTH	DAILY VOLUME
MON				AA or MT 1:00	1:00
TUES	AE + SS 0:45–1:00		AE + SS 0:45–1:00		1:30–2:00
WED		AE + SS 0:45–1:15 or *cross-train*		AA or MT 1:00	1:45–2:15
THURS	AE + SS 0:45–1:00		AE + SS 0:45–1:00		1:30–2:00
FRI		AE + SS 0:45–1:15 or *cross-train*		AA or MT 1:00	1:45–2:15
SAT	AE + SS 0:45–1:00		AE + SS 1:00–1:30 or cross-train		1:45–2:30
SUN		AE + SS 1:30–2:00 or *cross-train*			1:30–2:00
VOLUME BY SPORT	2:15–3:00	3:00–4:30	2:30–3:30	3:00	10:45–14:00
WORKOUTS	3	3	3	3	12

R E S T   &   T E S T   W E E K

SPORT	SWIM	BIKE	RUN	STRENGTH	DAILY VOLUME
MON				MT 1:00	1:00
TUES	AE + SS 0:45–1:00		AE + SS 0:45–1:00		1:30–2:00
WED		AE + SS 0:45–1:15 or *cross-train*			0:45–1:15
THURS	Te or AE + SS 0:45–1:00		AE + SS 0:45–1:00		1:30–2:00
FRI		Te + AE + SS 1:00		MT 1:00	2:00
SAT	AE + SS 0:45–1:00		Te + AE + SS 1:00–1:30		1:45–2:30
SUN		AE + SS 1:30–2:00 or *cross-train*			1:30–2:00
VOLUME BY SPORT	2:15–3:00	3:15–4:15	2:30–3:30	2:00	10:00–12:45
WORKOUTS	3	3	3	2	11

Notes: Rec = Recovery. Optional workouts may be done in place of or in addition to a primary workout. Detail on the workouts can be found in the chapter. Strength workouts appear in Appendix C.

Base 1

YOUR TRAINING BECOMES more structured in the Base 1 block. Whereas Prep was a time of play rather than focused training, Base 1 starts you down the path that will eventually culminate with your race. From the beginning of Base 1, there are 23 or 24 weeks until your A-priority race; by the end of Base 1 there will only be 19 or 20 weeks left.

The target race is so far off it may not seem important or compelling to you now. Some athletes continue to play around with their workouts, avoiding the structure of consistent training. Others take the opposite route, deciding that one can't start training too hard too soon. They do lung-searing intervals in mid-winter when they still have six months until the big race. These athletes will often achieve a high level of race fitness, albeit without much base fitness, and then spend the next several months trying to maintain it. If you get into race shape now, there is nowhere to go but down. Remind yourself of this when you find it hard to resist doing high-intensity workouts. Hold back on the urge to "hammer" with training partners, and instead, remain true to your first major goal for this new season—to have the highest level of fitness ever on the day of your A-priority race when it counts.

Objectives for Base 1

1. **Begin to develop an aerobic endurance base.** Triathlon is first and foremost an endurance sport. If your aerobic endurance is poor, you will never achieve truly high fitness for swimming, biking, and running. Over the next few weeks you will keep the intensity of your triathlon-specific workouts low. This will stimulate your body to make several physiological changes: It will begin building a more dense capillary network to better deliver fuel and oxygen to your muscles; it will increase the amount of blood your heart can pump with every beat; and it will increase the aerobic enzymes in your muscles so you become more effective at burning fat for fuel. There will be many other changes taking place as well. If you make your workout intensity too high, the workout will become anaerobic instead of aerobic and you will miss out on these positive changes. Be sure to follow the instructions in this chapter regarding the intensity of workouts. It will take most, if not all, of the Base period to develop a good aerobic endurance base.

2. **Refine speed skills.** The Base 1 training plans found at the end of this chapter include many speed skills (SS) workouts. Before doing truly long or intense workouts, it is critical that you become highly skilled at making the movements of the sport efficiently so as to not waste energy. When the hard training begins you must be smooth and graceful. One way to gauge your efficiency is to notice how quietly you move when training. Efficient swimmers don't slap the water with their hands or kick like a motorboat. They swim quietly. Skilled cyclists keep the chain turning quietly over their gears with round circles. They don't thrust the pedals down, pedaling in squares. The best runners run as if on eggshells. There is no foot slapping sound. Always swim, bike, and run as if you were trying to sneak up on someone. Be quiet and efficient.

3. **Increase force with strength training.** Like it or not, the hardest training you will do in Base 1 will happen in the gym. In this period, swimming, cycling, and running will be done at low exertion levels, while strength training will be intense. In the Prep block you should have prepared for this by having gone through several Anatomical Adaptation (AA) and Max Transition (MT) sessions. These should have gradually become harder as the loads increased and the repetitions decreased. Now you should be ready for the heaviest loads (with the fewest reps) of the entire year. You can gain a lot of force

from strength training that will improve your swim, bike, and run power. But whenever there is a lot to be gained from a workout, there is also a lot to be lost. In other words, both the rewards and the risks of strength training are great. Be careful and conservative when lifting heavy loads. Injuring your back, a knee, or anything else could end your season before it really gets going. Our purpose here is to be much stronger by the end of Base 1. Proceed with caution while being conservative with load progression.

Coaching Tips for Base 1

Preparing a best-ever race performance involves a lot more than just swimming, biking, and running. Here are some other things I believe are important at this time.

MINDSET

I've found that many of the best triathletes lack confidence. Some have become quite good at hiding their weakness in this area by acting cocky, talking loudly, cracking jokes, and using other masking behaviors. I suppose that to some extent everyone lacks confidence when standing on the start line for a tough, season-defining race. I have had athletes I coach, including pros, admit to me that they were worried they couldn't pull it off that day. This kind of honesty is rare, though; most athletes are unwilling to talk about their weaknesses in the area of mental attitudes, which is too bad. The time to address this issue is not on race morning, but now. You can train yourself to have a good mental attitude just as you can train your body to go faster.

Many years ago I coached a female pro cyclist who had lots of potential but could never seem to rise to the top at the big races. She was a powerhouse on the bike. But her shy demeanor—she would hide to warm-up before races—was pretty obvious. When I talked with her on the phone she told me of all the things she was "no good at." It quickly became obvious that it wasn't physical ability that was holding her back, but mental attitude. I talked with her about doing three simple things to build confidence. I learned these from talking with confident athletes and sports psychologists. I highly recommend them for all athletes. Here they are.

Relive Successes

The last 10 minutes before falling asleep at night, give or take a minute or two, is the most peaceful time of your waking hours. You are no longer bombarded with telephones, email, advertising, and other demands on your attention. Your mind is entirely your own for these few minutes. Use this time to your mental advantage by reliving one success from your training or racing that day.

It doesn't have to be something big. It may just be that you climbed one hill particularly well, or finished a hard and intimidating workout. Go back and replay that memory "tape" as if it were a video recording. Use your senses to enhance the memory. What did it feel like? How did it look? Was the wind blowing? Were you hot or cold? I'm sure you get the idea. Fall asleep reliving that day's success. Over time you will build up a vault of successes—some big and some small. The big ones will come in handy on race day when doubt begins to creep into your mind. At those moments, relive the biggest successes. I call these your "anchors."

Act as If . . .

Have you ever noticed the posture of confident people? They always stand tall and proud. In fact, I believe that it's impossible to feel confident while looking at your feet with a drooping head and slouched back. When you feel threatened or weak, act as if you are confident by standing erect and looking people in the eye. You'll be amazed at what that does for your actual sense of confidence. Your posture will soon lead to greater confidence. Fake it until you make it.

Quiet Self 1

In his excellent book *The Inner Game of Tennis* (Gallwey 1974), now a classic of sports literature, author Timothy Gallwey says that we have two "selves"—Self 1 and Self 2. Self 2, as he describes it, is the you that is the "doer" who is meek and hardworking. Self 1 has a parental voice and thrives on finding fault with Self 2, and Self 2 accepts the critique at face value. When Self 1 senses a weakness, this self tells Self 2 that failure is certain. And, of course, Self 2, being the victim, agrees, but promises to "try hard." As long as Self 1 is allowed to have control, low confidence is assured. Don't allow that to happen. When you hear that little voice in your head saying, "You can't do it," embolden Self 2 to become angry and say, "It can be done and I'm going to do it!" This is a great time to go back and grab one of those big successes from your success vault while standing tall and proud.

So what happened to the pro cyclist I coached, the shy one who would hide during the warm-ups? She practiced the methods described here and even took acting lessons. Then she went on to win the U.S. National Pro Championship that summer, finishing fifth in the race, scoring the highest finish by an American pro that year. It was an exceptional season, and confidence was no longer an issue for her.

You can become more confident, also. The time to start working on your attitude is now. Don't wait until the race season starts. It will take several weeks to improve your mindset in this area, and you will still experience lapses from time to time. Hang in there.

NUTRITION

Since your volume is slowly rising in Base 1 while the intensity of swimming, biking, and running is low, it's important to be careful with your diet. This is a time to make sure your body weight is stable or even beginning to come down a bit after your season-ending Transition block and the very low-key Prep block. The key is limiting your starch intake. These are carbohydrates that get into the bloodstream very quickly as a sugar and are likely to wind up as unwanted body fat. Starches are great for recovery after long or highly intense workouts. But when it comes to Base 1, they have limited value. Starches include such foods as bread, bagels, cereal, corn, rice, potatoes, and pasta. Typically, the whiter these foods are the more sugar they put into your blood and the fewer vitamins and minerals they have to offer.

You may find it difficult to limit starches in your diet as they are very satisfying to eat. Your brain primarily uses sugar for fuel, and because starchy foods put a lot of sugar into your blood quickly, the brain is happy when you eat them. That's why we crave starches and find them so hard to resist. Rather than tempting yourself daily, it's best to keep the ones you are most strongly attracted to out of your pantry. Don't buy them and you are less likely to eat them. The problem, of course, is that the rest of your family may not agree. This is one of the many challenges you face as an athlete. I can't tell you what to do, as every family is different. Do your best to come to an agreement.

You will also find that it's difficult to avoid starchy foods when eating out. Nearly every item on a restaurant's menu includes at least one starch, usually potato. Most restaurants will let you substitute a nonstarchy vegetable for a starch. Now is the time to get in the habit of choosing healthier foods from menus and to gain control over what you eat in general.

Does this mean you shouldn't eat carbohydrates during Base 1? No, not at all. We tend to think "carb" just refers to starchy foods. Although starchy foods are one type of carbohydrate—and the most powerful when it comes to getting sugar into your bloodstream (a good thing when you need to recover quickly)—they are not the only kind of carb. Others include fruits and vegetables. This is where you want to get most of your carbs at this time of year. Not only are fruits and veggies less likely to flood your body with body-fat-producing sugar, they are also much richer in vitamins, minerals, and fiber than starches. And these are all nutrients that will improve your health and vitality as an athlete.

COMMON CONCERNS OF BASE 1

Some of the greatest challenges of the entire year happen in Base 1. Instead of the long, warm days of summer beckoning you out for a workout, it may be cold and rainy. It gets dark early, and the busy holiday season puts demands on your time—not to mention the challenges it presents for your diet. Here's what I tell the athletes I coach about how to deal with these Base 1 blues.

Weather and Short Days

I've coached athletes on nearly every continent. No matter where they live there are times of the year when weather forces them indoors. For those in the northern latitudes, the winter Base period occurs during a time of cold weather, snow, ice, and short daylight hours. Running and swimming aren't generally affected all that much, but riding a bike definitely is.

When it comes to bike training, expect some lost training time due to nasty weather conditions. The starting point for dealing with this reality is to deemphasize cycling in the Base 1 block. Concentrate on swimming, running, and strength work in the gym during these training weeks. Your bike workouts will be less frequent and shorter than in later periods. You may even occasionally substitute cross-country skiing or snowshoeing for bike workouts. Although these sports will maintain your cardiovascular system, they won't develop the muscular fitness specific to riding a bike. The only way to get that is to ride a bike. So whenever the weather allows, get in the longer, aerobic endurance bike sessions recommended for Base 1. With some luck, you'll have clear weather on the weekends or other days off from work or school to get outside on the bike.

Your other rides will more than likely be done indoors on a trainer. The training plan for the Base period, spelled out in detail later in this chapter, assumes that the weather is acceptable every time a bike workout is scheduled. That's obviously not going to always be the case. When the plan calls for a bike session of more than an hour and you are forced to ride indoors, cut the workout in half, but ride no less than one hour. You should still do the "meat" of the session, whether its objective is aerobic endurance, speed skills, force, or muscular endurance. You may not be able to do everything to the extent called for in the plan. That's all right. Just do what you can given the time limitations.

The reason I reduce the length of indoor bike workouts in Base 1 and Base 2 and allow for the substitution of cross-country skiing and snowshoeing is that riding day after day for long durations indoors is mentally taxing. I'd much rather have you be enthusiastic but slightly undertrained than the other way around. By the time you reach Base 3, however, you must get the entire workout in regardless of the weather. At this point training becomes too critical to give up big chunks of cycling time in response to the whims of Mother Nature. This is especially the case if you are training for an Ironman-distance race. Music, movies, television shows, and video recordings of previous Ironman races may be necessary to help you get through what is otherwise a very boring workout.

If the weatherman predicts good weather for days when a long bike ride isn't on the agenda, you can rearrange the week's workouts to get in the entire bike session when the getting is good. That may mean moving a gym, swim, or run workout to another day, or postponing a bike session focusing on abilities such as speed skills, force, and muscular endurance, which can more easily be done on an indoor trainer, so that you can do the aerobic endurance training when the weather permits.

Weight Loss

During the Transition block at the end of your last race season, you probably gained some weight. That is to be expected. And if it's only a few pounds, that's probably a good thing. Trying to stay at your optimal race weight year round is not good for your health or your psyche. Staying focused on maintaining race weight 12 months of the year, regardless of your training load, requires a monk-like lifestyle of continual sacrifice and near suffering.

So I hope you've gained some weight over the past few weeks, but the Base period is the time to start trimming down any excess beyond your best training weight. Training weight is a bit heavier than race weight. Your training weight by the end of the Base period may be roughly 3 to 5 percent more than your race weight—the weight you will have on the day of your first A-priority race. If you achieve this by the end of the Base period, the higher workload of the Build period should be enough to gradually bring your training weight down to your racing weight by race day.

The extra calories you are burning as you move into the Base period may be enough to help you accomplish this initial weight loss. If not, you'll need to become more aware of your eating habits and modify them accordingly. Keeping a food log is a proven way of doing this, and you can find such a log at TrainingPeaks.com.

The hard part of this weight-loss problem is that the Base period often includes the holiday season.

Holidays

In the Northern Hemisphere, athletes are often well into their first Base period of the triathlon season when the holiday season begins. And you know what that means: Tempting foods, especially pastries and other sweets, are at your fingertips daily. Training is often interrupted by parties, travel, and family activities, and all of these things make it difficult to maintain a healthy diet. You are not alone. Every athlete I've ever coached, including pros, has had to deal with the same problem. You will lose some fitness and may even gain some weight. That's a given. Your challenge is to keep both the fitness losses and the weight gains to a minimum. It isn't easy, but it is possible. You have to build up a strong will and learn some new skills.

The key to dealing with the parties is planning. If you know when you have to be at various places, you can plan your training around the activities. This may mean rearranging your day to fit in a workout. You might do a long aerobic-endurance workout the day before a holiday activity, for example, which could leave an easy and short recovery workout for the day of the event itself.

Travel can be very disruptive to training. If traveling to grandma's, you may be without a bike, pool, and gym for several days. But again, with some planning, you need not lose fitness. Perhaps it's a good time to take your running up a notch, for example. Or there might be a YMCA or gym in grandma's area that allows use of the facility for a weekly fee. If you focus on running during your travel days, then when you return home you can maintain the running gains with shorter and less frequent workouts while devoting more time to the missed swim and bike training.

You simply must be flexible during the holidays. Realize that you will slide backward a bit, but don't stress out over it. Have a plan for dealing with it, and get back to focused training as soon as possible.

Base 1 Workouts

Base period workouts account for a significant proportion of the fitness an athlete has on race day. I'd guess as much as 80 percent of race-day fitness comes from the Base period. I've seen pros and age groupers alike achieve remarkable results in lab and field tests and in early-season races after developing nothing more than their basic abilities—aerobic endurance, speed skills, and force. And yet many athletes consider base training a waste of time. It just seems too easy.

But if you consistently follow the plan laid out in Chapters 5–7, I can practically guarantee that you will have your best fitness ever before even starting the

Build period. I've seen it happen many, many times. Perhaps you've never trained like this before in the Base period. If that's the case, you're about to learn how beneficial Base training can be.

AEROBIC ENDURANCE WORKOUTS

In Base 1 we will not be concerned with monitoring intensity as precisely as we will in the following months. For now, here's the general rule of thumb: Make all of your swim, bike, and run workouts easy. In terms of heart rate, power, and pace, that means you should not go above zone 2. Actually, I'd prefer that for now you train using a rating of perceived exertion (RPE) of no greater than 4 on a 1-to-10 scale, with 1 being super easy and 10 meaning as hard as you can possibly push yourself. RPE 3 to 4 means easy to moderate. If you have a riding partner, you should be able to talk to him or her easily as you ride. This level is perfect for now whenever your training plan calls for an AE workout. There is at least one of these every week in each sport.

SPEED SKILLS WORKOUTS

Speed skills training is perhaps the most neglected ability for triathletes. Now is the time to do something about that. Improving your sport-specific skills is just another way of improving your fitness. Although most athletes don't think of their technique in a sport as being related to fitness, being more skilled means wasting less energy. And that means you can go faster or farther for the same energy cost as before your skills improved. Let's examine what you should be doing to improve your speed skills for each sport.

Swim Speed Skills

When it comes to skills, swimming is more like tennis and golf than biking and running. Tiny changes in swim technique can result in huge improvements in performance. For most triathletes swim speed skills are the most important area to work on out of all the training abilities. Until you develop all of the subtle nuances of breathing, body rotation, hand entry, catch and pull, the flutter kick, and other swimming skills, there is little reason to work on any other aspect of fitness in swimming. If your skills are weak, devoting significant amounts of training time to other abilities will only further ingrain your poor technique. Learn to swim skillfully before you focus on fitness in swimming.

Even if your swim skills are solid, you need to maintain them. Base 1 is the time to check that you are swimming with good technique. It's easy to get sloppy with

THE COMBINED WORKOUT

A combined workout is one that includes two or more abilities to be trained. The SS + AE session includes a speed skill set and an aerobic endurance set. You may use a little creativity here to combine the abilities in a way that best suits your needs. To do such a workout, after warming up, start with a speed skill set, then do an aerobic endurance set. The mix, or how much of each you do, depends on your needs. If your speed skills are your primary limiter, then include a long speed skill portion followed by a shorter aerobic endurance set. Or reverse the emphasis if aerobic endurance is weaker.

form at other times of the year when you're working on going faster. Little changes can sneak up on you over time, resulting in diminished performance. Correcting these bad habits now will result in faster swim times at your first A-priority race.

Refining your swim speed skills is a five-step process that will take several weeks to complete.

Step 1: Assess your swim skills. Get a swim instructor to shoot an underwater video of you swimming. Watch the video together and note where changes are needed. I think you'll find that seeing is believing: You could simply have the coach watch you swim from the pool deck, but it wouldn't be as effective as seeing what's going on under the water and watching your movements at slow speeds. If the coach sees something incorrect or inefficient in your stroke, you might disagree unless you see it for yourself. Sometimes we think we're doing it one way when we're really doing it another. The video confirms what you are doing without question.

Step 2: Prioritize the skill changes you need to make. First address the skills that will improve your posture in the water. A common error is poor head position—looking more forward rather than down. A related error is swimming with the hips low in the water. Your next priority is the skills to develop the catch-and-pull phase of the stroke. Finally, work on your kick technique.

Step 3: Begin working on one skill at a time. Refine the top-priority skills first. With each skill, start by learning to make the movement correctly at a very slow speed. If, for example, you're working on improving your catch, learn to do it first on dry land with the assistance of a coach. Then try the same motion standing in the water, bent over at the hip. Again, do it very slowly. Next, swim slowly, concentrating on the catch. You can further isolate your catch with swim aids such as a snorkel and pull buoy.

Gradually wean yourself from the aids as the skill progresses. As the skill becomes ingrained, begin to make the movement at faster cadences until you are able to make the catch correctly when swimming with a racelike cadence. Then do the same for the next skill on your list.

Steps 4 and 5: Work on second- and third-priority skills in the same way. Throughout this process of improving your swim skills, continually assess your progress. Have someone take more underwater video footage each time and have a coach help with the analysis.

Fatigue is the enemy of skill development. When you are learning or refining skills, you'll find that short and frequent workouts with short sets are best. I typically have triathletes swim for 20 to 40 minutes, several days each week, in Base 1. These workouts often are simple 25 meter or 25 yard repetitions focusing on the skill we're developing. After each 25, stand at the wall and think about anything you want—the weather, a work project, or whatever. Then it's time to bring the focus back to the key movement again as you begin the next 25. The athletes I coach do this simple swim workout more than any other in the Base period.

In the training plans at the end of this chapter you will find a weekly swim session called "SS + AE." This is a "combined" workout, your first of what will eventually become many such combinations during the remainder of the season (see sidebar, "The Combined Workout").

Interval: 25 m
Intensity: RPE 3–4, easy to moderate
Duration: 20–40 min.

Bike Speed Skills

What could be complicated about pedaling a bicycle? Your foot is clipped into a pedal, which is fastened to a fixed-length crank arm that rotates around a single point on the bike. How could that possibly take any skill at all? I'll have to admit that the skill needed for pedaling a bicycle is not nearly as complicated as that needed for swimming. On a 1-to-10 scale, with 10 representing a sport based in skill to an extremely high degree, such as golf, swimming might be an 8, and pedaling a bike might be a 4. So there is still some skill involved. It's just not as challenging to master as swim skills are.

Before starting to work on pedaling speed skills, you need to make sure your bike is correctly fit to your body. For more information on this step, see the "Bike Fit" section in Chapter 4.

To work on pedaling speed skills, you'll be doing drills two or three times each week in Base 1. The purpose of the drills is to improve the distribution of force to the pedal throughout the entire 360-degree range of the stroke.

Triathletes who are efficient at pedaling a bike are especially good at the top, bottom, and recovery sides of the pedal stroke. These are the ranges that are difficult to get right. At the top they transition efficiently from pedaling up and back to pedaling forward and down. At the bottom of the stroke they do just the opposite without wasting energy. Riders who are not very good at pedaling make these transitions too late. This wastes a tiny amount of energy in every stroke. In an Olympic-distance triathlon you may do 5,000 to 6,000 pedal strokes. That is potentially a lot of wasted energy.

Efficient cyclists slightly reduce the weight resting on the pedal on the recovery side, or backside, of the stroke. Inefficient riders let the foot and leg on the recovery side rest on the pedal, causing the other leg, the one driving the pedal down, to work harder to lift the dead weight of the recovery leg. Again, this wastes a lot of energy.

Note that I haven't said anything about the front side of the pedal stroke. This side is easy to get right. Pushing the pedal down does not require much in the way of skill. The problem is that inefficient riders focus only on the down stroke. They "mash" the pedals, typically with a lot of excess, side-to-side, upper-body movement. This also wastes a tremendous amount of energy.

Interval: 3–5 min.
Intensity: RPE 3–4, easy to moderate
Duration: 30–75 min.

A few common pedaling drills will improve your cycling if you commit to doing them every week. They may be mixed together in a single technique workout or added to other workouts.

Isolated leg training (ILT) drill. This is the quintessential pedaling drill, the one you should do a lot in Base 1. On an indoor trainer, unclip one foot and rest it on a chair next to the bike so you can pedal with only one leg. With the bike in a low gear, turn the crank at a comfortably high cadence. You'll notice that it's difficult to get through the top of the stroke, the 12-o'clock position. Focus on smoothing out this top transition. At first you may only last a few seconds before the hip flexors fatigue. When that happens, switch to the other leg. When the second leg fatigues, clip both feet in and pedal for a few minutes, applying what you have learned from the single-leg pedaling. Repeat the drill several times throughout the workout.

A variation on this drill involves using PowerCranks™. These are cranks like the ones you have on your bike now, except they aren't connected in the bottom bracket, so each leg pedals independently of the other. If you get these it's best to mount them on a spare bike so you don't have to change crank arms when you want to do different workouts.

Toe touch drill. In this "mind" drill you focus on your feet. Every time your foot approaches the top of the stroke, imagine that you can push your foot forward in your shoe, touching your toes to the front end of the shoe. Of course, you won't be able to do this, but trying will cause you to transition more smoothly through the 12-o'clock position. Pedal in an easy gear, going slowly as you learn how to make this movement. As you master the drill you'll be able to turn the pedals faster.

Top-only drill. This is another foot-focused drill. Pedal the bike by keeping the top of your foot in constant and firm contact with the inside top of the shoe. Try not to push down on the pedal at all. The actual pedaling is done just with the up-stroke. Don't apply excessive upward force. Make the pedaling movement gentle and smooth.

9-to-3 drill. As you pedal the bike, imagine that you can drive the pedal forward from the 9-o'clock position on the backside to 3-o'clock on the front side of the stroke without going through 12 o'clock. Keep the gearing low so that you can pedal easily.

Spin-up drill. During a ride, shift to a low (easy) gear and gradually increase your cadence higher and higher until it is so fast that you begin to bounce on the saddle. Then return to a normal cadence. Each "spin-up" should last 30 seconds or so. Bouncing indicates that you have reached and slightly exceeded your optimal high cadence. Your foot is still pushing down at the bottom of the stroke (the 6-o'clock position). Because the crank arm can't get any longer, your butt comes off of the saddle as you push down on the pedals. This drill is best done with a cadence meter on your handlebar computer so you know what the top-end cadence is. The goal is to raise your highest, optimal cadence by learning to smoothly transition back and up at the bottom of the stroke.

High-cadence drill. Throughout a workout insert high-cadence intervals of several minutes each. During each of these intervals increase your cadence to a level that is just slightly uncomfortable and then maintain it for the length of the interval. Use a low (easy) gear. Recover between the intervals for several minutes while pedaling at your normal cadence. Over the course of several weeks, extend the duration of each interval and the combined interval time for the workout.

Speed-skill drills can be worked into your ride as conditions allow and repeated as much as you like. Use your time on an indoor trainer to get in more focused technique work.

Fixed-gear drill. This drill requires a fixed-gear bike. Your local bike shop can help you set up such a bike. It will have only one chainring, one cog, and no derailleurs or freewheel. When the wheels go around, the pedals also go around, and you can't coast. When riding a fixed-gear bike you must learn to relax and let the bike do the work. The first few times you ride it, go someplace flat with no traffic and no stop signs. A large parking lot early in the morning would be perfect. Keep the workouts short at first. Be forewarned that this is a dangerous workout until you master riding the "fixie."

Mountain biking. This isn't a drill, but riding a mountain bike off-road on hilly courses is good for improving pedaling skills. When you ride a mountain bike up a steep hill on a loosely packed surface such as dirt or gravel, you must learn to keep even tension on the chain. If you mash the pedals, the back wheel will slip and you won't make any progress. Saying you are learning to keep even tension on the chain is just another way of saying you are learning to pedal smoothly and efficiently.

Run Speed Skills

Continuing with my 1-to-10-point scale to rank sports based on how important skill is to performance in them, if swimming is an 8 and pedaling a bike is a 4, then running is a 6. In other words, there's a very good chance we can improve your running times by simply refining your running skills. Speed skill is so important to running that I have the athletes I coach do drills and other skill-enhancing workouts every week throughout the year, much as with swimming. The skills that need mastering are simple and few, but important enough to matter.

Biomechanically, there are only two things you can do to run faster. You can run with a faster cadence or you can run with a longer stride. The fastest endurance runners in the world, the Kenyans, do both of these. Force training will help you to develop a longer stride. That is taken care of with strength training in Base 1 and run-specific force training in Base 2. So the place for you to start now in improving your running efficiency is with cadence. Let's examine how you can do that.

The next time you go to a race or watch one on television, check the cadence of a few elite runners. To do this, count every time a runner's right foot strikes the road for 20 seconds and then multiply by three. What you'll find is that the Kenyans are running at a cadence of 94 to 98 even late in a long race such as a marathon. The others generally have a cadence of 90 to 94. The only way these lower-cadence runners can keep up with the Kenyans is to lengthen their strides, but that's inefficient because it produces excessive vertical oscillation. They start to bounce up and down a bit too much—and since the finish line is in a horizontal plane, energy expended vertically is mostly wasted. See Figures 5.1 and 5.2 for illustrations of good and poor running form.

How can you apply this lesson? Count your cadence the next time you are out for a run. If you're like most age-group triathletes it will be in the range of 76 to 86. And the slower an age grouper runs, the lower his or her cadence typically becomes. Elite runners tend to keep their cadence about the same even when running slowly. They've trained their nervous systems to fire at a set rate that isn't appreciably altered by pace. Pace is how fast the body is moving; cadence is how often the feet strike the pavement. Besides reducing vertical oscillation, running with a higher cadence means the foot spends less time in contact with the ground. That results in running faster. Until your foot comes off the ground you aren't going anywhere.

So let's work the other direction now—from foot contact time back up the chain to cadence—to see how we can improve your running times. To minimize foot contact time, you need to reduce the angle at which your foot comes in contact with the road surface. If you land on the heel with your toes pointing skyward at about a 30-degree angle, which is common for slower runners, it will take a long time for the forefoot to be lowered to the pavement and then to rock forward and finally

FIGURE 5.1 Efficient running form: midfoot strike with foot slightly ahead of center of gravity

FIGURE 5.2 Inefficient running form: long recovery pendulum, heel strike well in advance of center of gravity, excessive vertical oscillation

come off the ground at the toes. This will take only a few more milliseconds than putting your foot down flat on the pavement and then toeing off, but those extra milliseconds for each foot strike add up by the finish line, especially if you have a slow cadence.

It's all right to have a very slight heel-first contact with the road—a lot of good distance runners do. But it should be so slight that someone you're running toward would not be able to see the bottoms of your shoes. You can check this for yourself by having a friend or spouse shoot a video of you running at the camera. Do you see black soles? If so, you have an exaggerated heel strike. Minimizing it will speed you up.

How can you minimize the heel strike? The answer has to do with your knee. The only way to land on your heel is to lock, or nearly lock, your knee out straight. This is what you would do if you were running fast and trying to stop abruptly. You would straighten your knee and land on your heel. Running this way is like running with the brakes on. No wonder it slows you down.

The fastest way to experience flat-footed running is to run with your shoes off. Most running shoes, with their thick, rubber heels, seem to be saying to us, "land here." As soon as you take them off you're back to the way our ancient ancestors ran on the grassy plains of Africa. We're also running the way the Kenyan kids learn to run—without shoes.

Strides drill. I have the triathletes I coach do a drill called "strides" almost every week in the Base period. If they can do this drill without shoes, all the better. Often they can't, because snow and cold weather in a winter Base period make this impractical. But whenever possible I encourage them to do the drill shoeless, even if it's on a treadmill. Another option is to do the drill in lightweight racing shoes or in "water walkers"—light, slipper-like shoes that fit snugly around the foot and are designed for the beach. Strides are best done in a park or other grassy area that has a very slight downhill grade (about 1 percent for 150 yards or so).

STRIDES

Warm-up	10–15 min.

Take off your shoes (or put on water walkers or thin-soled racing flats).

SS set	6–8 × 20 sec., run down the slope.
	Walking recoveries on uphill

The 20-second strides interval should be a fairly fast run, but not as fast as you could go. In other words, hold back just a little bit. Focus on a flat-footed landing with the knee slightly bent. Count every time your right foot strikes the ground. Your goal is 30 to 32. That's a cadence of 90 to 96. Don't try to go above 96.

Note a landmark where you completed the 20-second stride. If you start at the same spot for each 20-second stride, as the workout progresses and you warm up even more you will finish farther down the course, which means that your stride is getting longer (since your cadence remains steady). You're now running more like a Kenyan.

The hard part—at least for most type-A triathletes—is that you must turn and walk back to the start point each time. Fatigue is the enemy of skill development, and by walking back up the hill you will make sure you are as fresh as possible for the stride efforts.

Skipping drill. As your fitness improves you can insert drills into the walking portions. Start by doing skips—the same kind of skipping you did as a kid. Do 50 total skips on the recovery. This will further ingrain the new landing technique while building foot and lower leg strength. Later in the Base period, you can do these skips for height. How high can you skip? Skipping for height builds power in your legs, which in turn automatically increases stride length.

Cadence drill. When you are out for your normal Base training runs, check your cadence occasionally and try to raise it by 1 or 2 rpm for a few minutes. This will feel awkward at first, as if you are running with baby steps, and your heart rate will probably rise even though you aren't going any faster. It will take a while for your nervous system to adapt to a higher cadence. During this time you may think you are going the wrong direction with training. That's common, but eventually you will run faster as your body adapts.

FORCE WORKOUTS

Triathletes who are deficient in force will never swim, bike, or run fast because they lack power. You need power for speed in all three sports, and you need it to climb hills in biking and running and to plow through rough water in swimming. Having sufficient force, the ability to overcome resistance, is a critical aspect of power. Let's examine power from a physics perspective and then tie it into our world of triathlon.

Power is defined as force multiplied by velocity, and it is a critical part of your training in Base 1. The power formula (Power = Force × Velocity) relates to all three sports, but it's probably easiest to understand with cycling.

Velocity is easy. That's your cadence when riding a bike. So if you turn the cranks at 100 rpm, you are creating more power than if you turn them at 80 rpm, assuming you are in the same gear. But the higher your cadence, the more likely you are to get sloppy with your pedaling technique. That's why you'll be doing so much work on your speed skills on the bike in Base 1 (and in the other sports, too). Your speed skills must be balanced by greater force if you want to become an effective rider (or swimmer or runner).

Force is the amount of muscular effort you generate in pushing the pedal down. Let's say you're pedaling at 90 rpm in a high gear, such as 53×14. It takes a lot of hard effort (force) to push the pedal down, but the bike travels a relatively long distance on every revolution of the pedals. Had you chosen a lower gear, such as 39×18, the bike would not go as far on one turn of the cranks, but it would be easier to push the pedals down. So a higher gear requires you to apply more force to the pedals, but you go a greater distance with each stroke. That's good.

To have power on the bike, you must be able to turn a high gear at a high cadence. That's all the equation means for cycling: In a sense, Power = Force $\times$ Velocity (or $P = F \times V$) is just a shorthand way of saying the same thing. In swimming and running, it is the same principle, only here we are talking about stroke or stride length instead of gear size. The bottom line is that you can go faster by increasing force or velocity—or both. Either of these changes will make you more powerful and therefore faster. In this section we will discuss how you can improve force in order to become a more powerful athlete. The key to force is greater strength in the muscles that you use to swim, bike, and run.

There are two training routes to improving the ability of your muscles to produce force. The first is strength training in the gym. The other is the sport-specific development of force while swimming, biking, and running. I like to have athletes start with a short strength-training phase in the Base 1 block and then transition to sport-specific training for force in the Base 2 and Base 3 blocks, while maintaining the gains made in the weight room. Although strength training with weights is not the same thing as swimming, biking, and running, it gets your muscles ready for the sport-specific phase, which is where the greatest gains are eventually made.

Major Movers Strength Training

Many triathletes don't like strength training, or what is usually called "weight lifting." That's understandable. It's not like being outside in the fresh air riding or running. And it can be a bit intimidating to be working out by all of those bulky weight lifters moving massive loads. When we skinny triathletes go to a serious gym and lift comparatively small loads, we stand out like sore thumbs. But bear in mind that there's a reason for putting yourself through this: A few weeks in the gym lifting weights should improve the strength of the muscles responsible for moving you forward and may ultimately make you faster. It won't happen overnight, but by engaging in strength training in Base 1, you will be starting the process.

The research on resistance training for endurance athletes does not offer clear answers as to the benefits. Some studies have found no benefits whatsoever for endurance athletes who engage in strength training, while others have shown significant improvements in economy for swimmers, cyclists, and runners. The positive studies suggest that resistance training makes the slow-twitch muscles, your primary endurance muscles, stronger, allowing them to do more of the work of swimming, biking, and running, and thus reducing the amount of work done by the fast-twitch muscles. Fast-twitch muscles use mostly carbohydrate for energy, whereas slow-twitch muscles rely on fat. Anytime you can shift the workload from fast-twitch to slow-twitch muscles, you will waste less of your limited stores of carbohydrate and thus improve economy. The bottom line is that this allows you to go faster for a longer period of time.

I've had the athletes I coach lifting weights since the 1980s, usually with good results. But not everyone benefits from training this way. I've coached a number of athletes, usually younger males, who already had excellent strength. I've also trained a number of body builders and power lifters making the move to endurance sport who certainly did not need more strength building in the weight room. They needed more time swimming, biking, and running to build endurance. The athletes who tend to get the most benefit from resistance training are women, older men, and those— men or women—who are "ectomorphs," which means they have light bones and slight muscles.

The exercises I recommend are listed and illustrated in Appendix C, and they will most likely be familiar to you if you have experience with strength training. For now, let's review the practical applications of resistance training as they relate to periodization.

In the Prep block, you started resistance training with the Anatomical Adaptation (AA) phase by using light weights and high repetitions as you learned to do the strength exercises with proper technique. This stage is critical to success with this type of training. It's a good idea to have a personal trainer at your gym help you master the movements of each exercise in order to get the most out of your force training. The potential reward from lifting weights is great, but there is also considerable risk. You can easily injure your back or a knee with poor technique or by attempting to lift too much too soon.

Like any other sport, lifting weights involves skills that must be learned. Be cautious and conservative with loads, especially when you are tired. Warm up well before your workouts, and start each exercise with loads you know you can safely manage. Be especially cautious with any exercise involving standing while moving heavy loads, such as squats—the riskiest of all of the triathlon exercises. If you have a history of knee or back problems, or if you are older and have not lifted weights before, I recommend that you avoid such high-risk exercises. Give it careful consideration, but if in doubt, don't do squats and other high-risk exercises.

Although squats are also a high-reward exercise, I'd rather have inexperienced or risk-prone athletes do leg presses or step-ups, which aren't quite as risky. If you decide it's best to avoid squats this year, perhaps you can try them next year, once you've established a solid strength base. Strength training should be viewed as a long-range activity that produces results gradually over time. It's not something you can do for a month and reap benefits from immediately. That way of thinking leads to injury.

After a few AA resistance-training sessions in the early Prep block, you advanced to the Maximum Transition (MT) phase, with increasing loads and 10 to 15 reps in a set. Now you are ready for the heart of the gym-based program.

If you have experience with resistance training, in the Base 1 block you should be in the Maximum Strength (MS) phase. This phase is risky, but the upside has great potential. As described in Appendix C, you now should be doing a limited number of exercises with an emphasis on few reps (3 to 6) and high loads. I can't emphasize enough how risky this is. Be very conservative and cautious. If you are new to resistance training or are prone to back or knee injuries, repeat the MT phase in Base 1 and avoid the MS phase.

You may only need about eight MS sessions, depending on how quickly you improve. Once you achieve the MS load goals for a given exercise, do not increase the loads further. Do more reps instead as you continue to increase loads in the other exercises.

By the end of Base 1 you should be done with the MS (or MT) phase. You are ready to move into Strength Maintenance (SM) for the remainder of the Base and Build periods while continuing to develop your force with sport-specific training. In Base 2 you will begin sport-specific force training.

Core Strength Training

We read a lot about core strength training these days, but I've found most people don't know what it really means. Most people think it means strengthening the abdominal muscles. That's true, but it's not the whole story. Core training goes well beyond that. Core strength could be called "torso" strength, because it has to do with all the muscles, both large and small, from your armpits to your groin. These core muscles stabilize the spine, support the shoulders and hips, drive the arms and legs, and transfer force between the arms and legs.

When a triathlete has poor core strength, it may show up in several different ways, most obviously in running. Poor core strength is evident in a dropping hip on the side of the recovery leg with the support-leg knee collapsing inward regardless of what the foot may be doing. Especially in running, injury is common when core strength is inadequate.

In swimming and cycling poor core strength is less obvious, even though it's still just as much of a problem. In swimming it may result in "fishtailing"—the legs and hips wiggling from to side as the hand and arm "catch" is made. Sometimes fishtailing is due to faulty stroke mechanics, however, so it should not automatically be attributed to a lack of core strength. In cycling, a weakness in the core muscles can show up as a side-to-side rocking of the shoulders and spine when the pedal is pushed down, even when the saddle is the right height and the rider is not excessively mashing the pedals. But there is little doubt, even if it's not obvious, that poor core strength results in a loss of power in the water and on the bike.

How do you know if your core strength is adequate? One way is to have a physical therapist do an assessment. Find one who works with endurance athletes and tell him or her that you would like a head-to-toe exam to pinpoint weaknesses and imbalances that could reduce performance or lead to injury. Ask for recommendations about how to correct any problems found. These fixes may be strengthening exercises, flexibility exercises, or postural improvement.

The therapist should make sure you are doing the exercises correctly and send you home with specific instructions about what you can do on your own. The instructions will most likely include pictures of the moves with a step-by-step guide. The exam generally takes about an hour, and it will be expensive if your insurance doesn't cover it. But it provides a great start on core strengthening, and I have each of the athletes I coach do this every winter.

Although it's somewhat less effective than having a physical therapist evaluate you, another way to check your core strength is to have someone take a video of you running. When you review it, you'll be looking for the dropping recovery-side hip mentioned above. You're likely to miss the details, as for the untrained eye there appears to be little difference in techniques even when the movement faults are very noticeable to someone who knows what to look for. Use a treadmill and shoot the video from the back. Tuck your shirt in so you can watch the waistband of your running shorts on the video, and see if it dips when the recovery leg swings through. Also check the knee of the supporting leg to see if it is buckling in slightly. You will probably have to view the video in slow motion several times to see any of these unwanted movements.

If you view the video and determine that you need to improve core strength, you might want to see a physical therapist after all. But if you want to continue to go the self-help route, I'd recommend getting a copy of the book *Core Performance Endurance* by Mark Verstegen. This is one of the best books I've found on core strength training for endurance athletes.

During each of your gym workouts in Base 1, include core strengthening exercises and continue the most effective of these as you move into the Strength Maintenance phase in the following blocks. I also recommend that you do some core strengthening throughout the week whenever the opportunity is available. This could involve doing one core exercise before or after a workout or while relaxing in the evening before bed. A little of such work done frequently is more effective than a lot of it done infrequently.

RECOVERY WORKOUTS

While the Prep block was a rather low-key time of easy workouts as you returned to training, by Base 1 your training should now feel a bit more challenging. You may find that you can manage the primary workouts of the Base 1 plan easily enough that you want to do some of the optional sessions as well. For now, these "extra" workouts should be for recovery. Fit and experienced athletes tend to recover faster when they do light exercise as opposed to taking a day off from training. A recovery workout (noted as *Rec* in the plans at the end of the chapter) has a short duration and is low in intensity—zone 1 only. Making the duration long or bumping the intensity above zone 1 will only increase your training stress for the week and may well reduce the quality of your next primary workout.

So these recovery sessions are only used to speed recovery. But you'll get another benefit from doing them. As the frequency of swimming, biking, or running increases, economy improves. As described in Chapter 3, economy has to do with how much fuel the body uses to produce energy. An economical swimmer, cyclist, or runner—like a car with good fuel economy—wastes little precious energy, and in the case of a triathlete this means using more fat for fuel, thus sparing carbohydrate.

If you are new to the sport or find that you don't recover very quickly, as is often the case with older triathletes, these recovery sessions are best avoided. You will bounce back faster by simply resting up from the main workouts.

Base 1 Testing

At the end of your Prep block you should have done some field testing to confirm your heart rate training zones for biking and/or running. These tests are described in Chapter 4. If for some reason you didn't do the field tests at the end of the Prep block, then do them as soon as possible in Base 1. Heart rate changes little during the season unless you take an extended break from training, as may have been the case after your last A-priority race at the end of last season. We'll still have you do some testing at the end of Base 1, however, to check your progress.

The testing will not yet involve technology such as a power meter or pacing device (although you will need heart rate monitors for the run and bike tests). If you already have the more advanced tools, you can collect and analyze data for functional threshold power (FTPw) and functional threshold pace (FTPa). However, you need not be too concerned with power and pace now as they will change rapidly in the next few weeks as your fitness improves. In fact, this is what serious training is all about—getting faster while heart rate stays constant. If you do not have these devices, consider purchasing them at this point. In Base 2 you will use run-pace and power zones for many of your workouts.

The following tests should be done in the last week of Base 1. Reduce your training load for at least two days beforehand, as fatigue will give you inaccurate information.

Swim Field Test

In the last week of Base 1, after at least two days of easy training to allow for recovery, swim a 1,000 meter or 1,000 yard time trial as described in Chapter 4. The purpose now is to gauge your progress after the weeks of being focused on technique in this block. The average 100 meter or 100 yard time will also serve as a guide for how fast to swim in your workouts in Base 2.

This pace is commonly called your "T-time"—your pace for 100 meters or yards. It is similar to your lactate threshold heart rate or your functional threshold power or pace. The swim intensity for the workouts described in Base 2 and all following blocks is based on your T-time. So if a workout calls for you to swim a given distance at T-time, the pace for each 100 meters or yards, or any portion thereof, should be what you found in your most

Interval: 1,000 m
Intensity: Race pace
Duration: Time trial

recent test. If it says to swim at, say, "T-time + 10 seconds," you would add 10 seconds to your T-time for each 100.

Bike Field Test

Bike field testing for Base 1 is done with a 30-minute time trial. Other graded-exercise tests are suggested in *The Triathlete's Training Bible*; these may also serve your purpose now, but I have come to rely much more on the 30-minute test. It is a simple test, and the results have been quite reliable for the athletes I coach.

A challenge you may face with testing on the road now is wind, cold weather, and rain or snow. So you may be forced to test indoors. I've found that athletes usually get lower numbers when they are indoors for the 30-minute time trial. This is probably due to the greater heat buildup and the lack of adequate cooling indoors, and perhaps also to the greater mental stress of riding hard on a trainer. If you must test indoors, then I'd suggest doing the graded exercise test found in *The Triathlete's Training Bible* (Chapter 5).

For the 30-minute time trial, find a road with no stop streets and with light traffic. It may be either flat or very slightly uphill. Avoid testing on a course with significantly rolling hills or steep downhill sections, and remember this course so you can use it again in the following blocks. If you did the test in the Prep block, use the same course now so that you can compare results. Do the test after two to four days of reduced training so that you are rested. Testing while fatigued will not provide useful information.

Warm-up	20–30 min., increasing intensity and cadence
	Ride easy to recover
Test set	30-min. time trial, hard as you can

At 10 minutes, press the lap button on your heart rate monitor so you can capture three pieces of data: your average heart rate for the first 10 minutes, your average heart rate for the last 20 minutes, and your average heart rate for the entire 30 minutes. Note that this does *not* mean you are going easy the first 10 minutes. The entire 30 minutes is done at maximal effort.

The data we are most interested in is your average heart rate for the last 20 minutes. This is a good predictor of your lactate threshold heart rate and is used to establish your training zones. If you have a power meter, your average power for the entire 30 minutes (not just the last 20 minutes) is a good indicator of your functional threshold power (FTPw).

Run Field Test

Run field testing is much the same as bike testing. There are two bits of data we are looking for: your lactate threshold heart rate and your functional threshold pace (FTPa). The run test is very similar to the bike test described above. Run solo so you can get a true idea of your potential.

Warm-up	20–30 min.
Test set	30 min., hard as you can

Hit the lap button on your heart rate monitor 10 minutes after starting the test and again at the end of the test.

If this procedure were followed in a race, your heart rate would be too high for what we are looking for. To find LTHR from a race the event would need to take about an hour. The reason for this is that you go much harder in a race than in a solo workout.

Your average heart rate for the last 20 minutes is a good approximation of your LTHR. Your pace for the entire 30 minutes is what we will use for your FTPa. In testing during the other blocks, we will probably find that your LTHR stays nearly stable while your FTPa gets faster. That's what we hope happens.

If you do not have a pacing device and you are certain of your running LTHR, I recommend doing a different test at this point. I call it an "aerobic time trial." It's a very simple test done on a running track or a flat, measured road. A track is preferable, as running in circles generally neutralizes mild wind. It's also safer and there are fewer things to interrupt your focus.

AEROBIC TIME TRIAL

Warm-up	10–20 min., slowly elevating heart rate to 10 beats per minute below LTHR
Test set	Steady run, keeping heart rate at 9–11 bpm below LTHR

When your heart rate reaches the correct level, begin a steady run at that heart rate plus or minus 1 beat per minute (9 to 11 beats per minute below LTHR). The distance is based on the A-priority race for which you are training:

Race Distance	Test Interval
Sprint	1 mile
Olympic	2 miles
Half-Ironman	3 miles
Ironman	4 miles

Watch your heart rate monitor closely to make sure you stay in a tight range of 9 to 11 beats per minute below LTHR. This is the hard part. Don't try to "win" the test by going above the range. If this heart rate range forces you to slow down, that's fine. In fact, you should probably expect that to happen at this time in the season. With this field test we are establishing a pace baseline for your running fitness. In a few weeks you will revisit this test to see how much progress you have made.

LAB OR CLINIC TEST

Another option is to substitute a lab or clinic test for a bike or run field test. Lab tests for swimming are rare. The test for biking or running is commonly referred to as a VO_2max test, or a gas-analysis test, and is available at many health clinics, university physiology labs, health clubs, triathlon stores, bike shops, and running stores. This isn't a necessity, but it can prove valuable. I have everyone I coach do one of these at about this point in the season every year. I will often have them repeat it at the end of a second Base period later in the season. I'd highly recommend you do it, if only for one sport. If you have to choose, I'd usually recommend the bike testing. But if your running is a limiter and biking is a strength, then you may want to consider doing a run test instead.

Although there is some expense involved, what you find out about your physiology may indicate the sort of training you need to emphasize in the coming weeks. A knowledgeable test technician should help you to analyze and interpret the data. Not only will you find out what your VO_2max is (don't be too concerned about this, as your fitness is not very high right now), you'll also learn how your body uses fat and carbohydrate during exercise at various intensities, which is invaluable, especially for Ironman-distance athletes. You'll also be able to confirm your lactate threshold heart rate and your bike and/or run functional thresholds, on which your training zones are based.

Assuming the test and the technician proved helpful, consider going back to the same facility again later in the season as you wrap up your second Base 3 block prior to your next A race (see Chapter 13 for more on this). By this time your fitness should have improved greatly, especially VO_2max. The comparison of data with the previous test results should give you great insight into how your training has gone over the course of the early part of your season and may even point you in a new direction for the remainder of the year.

Your Base 1 Training Plan

There are two suggested weekly plans below for each race distance. Be sure to select the pair that reflects the distance of the A-priority race for which you are training. The first plan in each set for a given distance is for the first two or three weeks of the Base 1 block. If you recover slowly, as is common for some older athletes and those new to triathlon, then follow the training-week plan in this table for only two weeks; for the third week, follow the rest-and-test-week plan. If you recover relatively quickly, meaning you do not experience heavy or nearly debilitating fatigue early in the third consecutive week of hard training, then do three weeks of the training-week plan and one week of the rest-and-test-week plan. The only way to know how quickly you recover is through experience. If you are unsure, then try following the three-on, one-off plan. You can then make changes going forward as you learn more about your capabilities.

As in the Prep block plans, there are both primary and optional workouts in the Base 1 plans. The primary workouts are indicated in bold red type. These are the workouts I strongly suggest you do every week. The optional workouts are in italic. Do some or all of these workouts if you are a high-volume trainer or if you need to focus on a discipline that is a limiter. Putting in extra time and attention every week will help you to improve more rapidly in that sport.

Earlier in this chapter, workouts are described for each of these swim, bike, and run abilities and for strength training. Refer to those sections to see what the details of your workout should be on any particular day below.

The durations of the workouts are listed as either minutes ("0:20") or hours and minutes ("1:30"). There is a suggested duration range for each workout. You may be able to start at the high end of the range in the first week of Base 2. That is highly likely for the shorter-distance races. But for half-Ironman and Ironman athletes, it's best to start at the low end of the range and increase the duration weekly so that you finish the block doing the upper ends of the suggested durations.

Note that there is an optional short SS run following the bike ride on Sundays. The purpose here is to concentrate on running with good form when you are tired. Simply start the run and immediately concentrate on the weakest aspect of your running skills. This may be cadence, posture, the footstrike, or any number of other common technique errors. This is a very brief run. Focus on only one skill, the one that is your greatest limiter. Keep the rate of perceived exertion at 3 to 4—easy to moderate.

SPRINT-DISTANCE TRAINING **BASE 1**

T R A I N I N G   W E E K S

SPORT	SWIM	BIKE	RUN	STRENGTH	DAILY VOLUME
MON	*Rec* 0:15–0:30			MS or MT 1:00	1:00–1:30
TUES	SS 0:20–0:40	*Rec* 0:45–1:00	SS 0:30–0:45		0:50–2:25
WED		SS 0:45–1:00	SS 0:30–0:45	MS or MT 1:00	0:45–2:45
THURS	SS 0:20–0:40		SS 0:30–0:45		0:50–1:25
FRI	*Rec* 0:15–0:30	SS 0:30–0:45		MS or MT 1:00	1:30–2:15
SAT	SS + AE 0:30–0:45	*Rec* 0:30–0:45	AE 0:45–1:00		1:15–2:30
SUN		AE 1:00–1:30	SS 0:15–0:30		1:00–2:00
VOLUME BY SPORT	1:10–3:05	2:15–5:00	1:45–3:45	2:00–3:00	7:10–14:50
WORKOUTS	3–5	3–5	3–5	2–3	11–18

R E S T   &   T E S T   W E E K

SPORT	SWIM	BIKE	RUN	STRENGTH	DAILY VOLUME
MON				MS or MT 1:00	1:00
TUES	SS 0:15–0:30		SS 0:20–0:30		0:35–1:00
WED		SS 0:30–0:45			0:30–0:45
THURS	Te 0:30–0:45		SS 0:20–0:30		0:50–1:15
FRI		Te or SS 0:45			0:45
SAT	SS 0:15–0:30		Te 0:45–1:00		1:00–1:30
SUN		AE 1:00–1:30	SS 0:15–0:30		1:00–2:00
VOLUME BY SPORT	1:00–1:45	2:15–3:00	1:25–2:30	1:00	5:40–8:15
WORKOUTS	3	3	3–4	1	10–11

Notes: Rec = Recovery. Optional workouts are in italic. The optional SS runs on Sunday are intended to follow the bike ride. Detail on the workouts can be found in the chapter. Strength workouts appear in Appendix C.

OLYMPIC-DISTANCE TRAINING **BASE 1**

T R A I N I N G   W E E K S

SPORT	SWIM	BIKE	RUN	STRENGTH	DAILY VOLUME
MON	*Rec* 0:15–0:30			**MS** or **MT** 1:00	1:00–1:30
TUES	SS 0:40–1:00	*Rec* 0:45–1:00	SS 0:45–1:00		1:25–3:00
WED		SS 0:45–1:00	*SS* 0:30–0:45	*MS* or *MT* 1:00	0:45–2:45
THURS	SS 0:40–1:00		SS 0:45–1:00		1:25–2:00
FRI	*Rec* 0:15–0:30	SS 0:45–1:15		**MS** or **MT** 1:00	1:45–2:45
SAT	SS + AE 0:40–1:00	*Rec* 0:45–1:00	AE 1:00–1:30		1:40–3:30
SUN		AE 1:15–1:45	*SS* 0:15–0:30		1:15–2:15
VOLUME BY SPORT	2:00–4:00	2:45–6:00	2:30–4:45	2:00–3:00	9:15–17:45
WORKOUTS	**3–5**	**3–5**	**3–5**	**2–3**	**11–18**

R E S T   &   T E S T   W E E K

SPORT	SWIM	BIKE	RUN	STRENGTH	DAILY VOLUME
MON				**MS** or **MT** 1:00	1:00
TUES	SS 0:30–0:45		SS 0:30–0:45		1:00–1:30
WED		SS 0:45–1:00			0:45–1:00
THURS	Te 0:30–0:45		SS 0:30–0:45		1:00–1:30
FRI		Te or SS 1:00			1:00
SAT	SS 0:30–0:45		Te 1:00–1:30		1:30–2:15
SUN		AE 1:15–1:45	*SS* 0:15–0:30		1:15–2:15
VOLUME BY SPORT	1:30–2:15	3:00–3:45	2:00–3:30	1:00	7:30–10:30
WORKOUTS	**3**	**3**	**3–4**	**1**	**10–11**

Notes: Rec = Recovery. Optional workouts are in italic. The optional SS runs on Sunday are intended to follow the bike ride. Detail on the workouts can be found in the chapter. Strength workouts appear in Appendix C.

HALF-IRONMAN-DISTANCE TRAINING **BASE 1**

T R A I N I N G   W E E K S

SPORT	SWIM	BIKE	RUN	STRENGTH	DAILY VOLUME
MON	Rec 0:20–0:30			MS or MT 1:00	1:00–1:30
TUES	SS 0:45–1:00	Rec 0:45–1:00	SS 0:45–1:00		1:30–3:00
WED		SS 0:45–1:15	SS 0:30–0:45	MS or MT 1:00	0:45–3:00
THURS	SS 0:45–1:00		SS 0:45–1:00		1:30–2:00
FRI	Rec 0:20–0:30	SS 0:45–1:15		MS or MT 1:00	1:45–2:45
SAT	SS + AE 0:45–1:00	Rec 0:45–1:00	AE 1:15–1:45		2:00–3:45
SUN		AE 2:00–3:00	SS 0:15–0:30		2:00–3:30
VOLUME BY SPORT	2:15–4:00	3:30–7:30	2:45–5:00	2:00–3:00	10:30–19:30
WORKOUTS	3–5	3–5	3–5	2–3	11–18

R E S T   &   T E S T   W E E K

SPORT	SWIM	BIKE	RUN	STRENGTH	DAILY VOLUME
MON				MS or MT 1:00	1:00
TUES	SS 0:30–0:45		SS 0:30–0:45		1:00–1:30
WED		SS 0:45–1:00			0:45–1:00
THURS	Te 0:30–0:45		SS 0:30–0:45		1:00–1:30
FRI		Te or SS 1:00			1:00
SAT	SS 0:30–0:45		Te 1:15–1:45		1:45–2:30
SUN		AE 2:00–3:00	SS 0:15		2:00–3:15
VOLUME BY SPORT	1:30–2:15	3:45–5:00	2:15–3:30	1:00	8:30–11:45
WORKOUTS	3	3	3–4	1	10–11

Notes: Rec = Recovery. Optional workouts are in italic. The optional SS runs on Sunday are intended to follow the bike ride. Detail on the workouts can be found in the chapter. Strength workouts appear in Appendix C.

IRONMAN-DISTANCE TRAINING **BASE 1**

T R A I N I N G   W E E K S

SPORT	SWIM	BIKE	RUN	STRENGTH	DAILY VOLUME
MON	*Rec* 0:20–0:30			**MS** or **MT** 1:00	1:00–1:30
TUES	**SS** 0:45–1:00	*Rec* 0:45–1:00	**SS** 0:45–1:00		1:30–3:00
WED		**SS** 0:45–1:15	*SS* 0:30–0:45	*MS* or *MT* 1:00	0:45–3:00
THURS	**SS** 0:45–1:00		**SS** 0:45–1:00		1:30–2:00
FRI	*Rec* 0:20–0:30	**SS** 0:45–1:15		**MS** or **MT** 1:00	1:45–2:45
SAT	**SS + AE** 0:45–1:00	*Rec* 0:45–1:00	**AE** 1:30–2:00		2:15–4:00
SUN		**AE** 2:00–3:00	*SS* 0:15–0:30		2:00–3:30
VOLUME BY SPORT	2:15–4:00	3:30–7:30	3:00–5:15	2:00–3:00	10:45–19:45
WORKOUTS	**3–5**	**3–5**	**3–5**	**2–3**	**11–18**

R E S T   &   T E S T   W E E K

SPORT	SWIM	BIKE	RUN	STRENGTH	DAILY VOLUME
MON				**SM** 0:45	0:45
TUES	**SS** 0:30–0:45		**SS** 0:30–0:45		1:00–1:30
WED		**SS** 0:45–1:00			0:45–1:00
THURS	**Te** 0:30–0:45		**SS** 0:30–0:45		1:00–1:30
FRI		**Te** 1:00			1:00
SAT	**SS** 0:30–0:45		**Te + AE** 1:15–1:30		1:45–2:15
SUN		**AE** 2:00–3:00	*SS* 0:15		2:00–3:15
VOLUME BY SPORT	1:30–2:15	3:45–5:00	2:15–3:15	0:45	8:15–11:15
WORKOUTS	**3**	**3**	**3–4**	**1**	**10–11**

Notes: Rec = Recovery. Optional workouts are in italic. The optional SS runs on Sunday are intended to follow the bike ride. Detail on the workouts can be found in the chapter. Strength workouts appear in Appendix C.

Base 2

SERIOUS TRAINING BEGINS IN BASE 2. In Prep and Base 1, you were training to train, doing general-fitness workouts with a lot of cross-training. This was important for laying the groundwork for what was to follow. You should now be ready to take it up a notch. With about 19 weeks until your A-priority race, you need to start training more specifically. General training, such as lifting weights and other cross-training, now fades into the background as swim, bike, and run sessions become longer and more intense.

Training in Base 2 and Base 3 has been compared with building the foundation for a new house. Construct a solid foundation, and the house will be sound and free of cracked walls and sagging corners. Rush through it, cut corners, and generally do a poor job of constructing the foundation, and it will be obvious in the finished house. The poorly built house will be likely to collapse when it is stressed by harsh conditions. Good home builders know just how important the base of the house is.

However you like to think about it, the bottom line is that Base 2 is when the fitness for your best triathlon begins to take shape. Everything you do after this block is dependent on what you accomplish in the next few weeks. Though racing season has not yet begun, this is not still the "off-season." That term implies that little of significance is happening, and that is not the case now. This is a time that is critical to your success later on. You need to have clearly defined objectives for Base 2 and a plan for accomplishing them. The higher your goals are for your racing this season, the more important this period of training is.

Objectives for Base 2

1. **Emphasize aerobic endurance.** In Base 2 you will improve your aerobic endurance. You'll know this is happening because long workouts will be less demanding by the end of Base 2. If you have a power meter or run-pacing device, you'll actually be able to precisely measure this improvement through a technique called "decoupling" that I will explain later in this chapter.

2. **Continue refining speed skills.** In Base 2 you will maintain and improve upon the swim, bike, and run speed skills that you started working on in earnest in Base 1. After several weeks of focusing on technique you should be noticeably more skilled. You may already be at a peak of skill in one or more of the sports. For those in which you are still a bit rough around the edges, speed skill training receives continued emphasis. For your strong sports, you go into a maintenance mode.

3. **Develop specific force.** In Base 2 you will convert the force developed in the weight room into swim-, bike-, and run-specific force. By the end of Base 2, this will be evident when you ride or run up hills. It won't show up for swimming until you do your first lake or ocean swim in rough water.

4. **Begin building muscular endurance.** In Base 2 you will begin building muscular endurance. This is the key to success in your A-priority race. We'll only just start the construction of this key ability in Base 2. It will improve more in Base 3, and in the Build blocks it will be the focus of your training.

The biggest mistake that many triathletes make in the Base period is to skip ahead of the basic-ability workouts described in this chapter in order to get to the truly hard sessions of the Build period, such as high-intensity intervals, hill repeats, and "racing" with training partners. Athletes commonly omit the Base period because the workouts seem too easy, and they feel that they aren't working hard enough. If you bypass the Base 2 training objectives, your fitness will not be as great later on as it would have been if you had taken several weeks to lay down a solid foundation. Hang in there with me for these few weeks. What you do now is critical to your success later on.

Coaching Tips for Base 2

You will face many challenges in Base 2 that are unique to this time in the season. Here are the most common ones, the ones I am most likely to discuss with the athletes I coach. In this block you can continue to work on the mindset skills introduced earlier as you attend to the new ones mentioned below. We'll also look at the special nutritional and weight-management concerns of this block and how to deal with the continuing cold weather.

MINDSET

Many, perhaps most, athletes don't fully grasp how important the Base period is. The workouts don't seem all that hard. There are long workouts in zone 2, very short repetitions for work on skills, a bit of muscular-endurance work that may not seem all that hard, and some weight lifting. If you are like most of the triathletes I coach, what you want to do is intervals and racelike group workouts, thinking that's where the real fun is, and you're tempted to skip the Base period entirely.

I frequently hear about triathletes doing just this. They skip the Base workouts and go straight to the Build period. Sometimes they do what they call "reverse periodization," which means going hard in the winter and doing the long stuff in the summer. They train with lung-searing intervals and racelike group workouts when their first A race is still five or more months away.

This is like building the house first and saving the foundation for later. In the final analysis, it doesn't work all that well. I call these folks "Christmas Stars." They're in great shape by late December and can "beat" all of their training partners in workouts. But by June they are burned out and getting slower as their motivation wanes. (I should point out here that there's an exception to this rule: Higher intensity in the Base period, followed by more duration in the Build period, is not uncommon for some Ironman-distance triathletes, and it can be a legitimate training approach. It follows the principle of making the workouts become increasingly like the race as race day approaches.)

Now if your goal for this season is simply to have fun, then being a Christmas Star is all right. Of course, "fun" can be defined in many ways. Since you're reading this book, I assume that for you fun means performing better in your most important races. I could be wrong. You may not care about the outcomes of your most important races. If what you really want is to sweat a lot and feel tired every day, then you don't need periodization. Just do whatever you feel like doing.

This is a conversation I've had on only rare occasions with the athletes I've trained. Athletes who hire coaches willingly relinquish control over an important part of their lives to their coaches. That takes a lot of trust. Many self-coached athletes don't trust others to guide them and need this little talk more often. They sometimes don't even seem to trust themselves. They have little direction, and may train randomly, doing what a training partner suggests one week and what they read in the most recent triathlon magazine the next.

When you're tempted to abandon the plan, resist that temptation. Think long-term rather than seeking the short-term gratification of a racelike workout in mid-winter, the time when you need to be developing base fitness. Following the plan will mean you race better when it truly counts. Trust me on that—I've seen it happen many times.

NUTRITION

One of the common objectives of the Base period is to improve aerobic endurance. Your body will realize many physiological benefits as your aerobic endurance improves, such as an increase in muscle capillaries, greater heart-pumping capacity, and more plentiful muscle enzymes for converting fat to energy. Related to this last benefit is your body's greater preference for using fat for fuel while sparing glycogen as your aerobic endurance improves. This means a greater reliance on a fuel source each of us has plenty of—fat. Regardless of how skinny you are, you have enough body fat stored to fuel several back-to-back Ironman triathlons. The problem is accessing it.

If you were to stop training for a few weeks, your body would begin to lose its preference for fat. It would gradually shift toward a preference for using carbohydrate instead, which is stored in the body as glycogen and glucose. When you started exercising again after this time off, most of the energy used in your workouts would come from glycogen and glucose, and your body would not be very good at accessing its fat for fuel. That would be a problem. It would mean that during workouts, just to finish, you would have to continually feed your body sugar from sports drinks, bars, gels, and other sources. There's a limit as to how much sugar your gut can process during exercise, so you would face a double-headed problem: Besides having to keep feeding yourself sugar, you would not be able to take in enough sugar to fuel your engine, so your pace would slow down despite what would feel like a high effort. This is the early stage of "bonking."

In the Base period, assuming it comes on the heels of having had a break from high-workload training, it will take many weeks of long aerobic-endurance workouts to train your body to once again preferentially use fat for fuel. In a winter Base period, the holiday season, with all of its pastries and sweets, may have compounded this shift. You want—actually, you need—to speed up the fueling changes your body goes through as you begin to increase the duration of your workouts. What you eat now plays a role in this change.

The body prefers to use whatever it is given the most of when it comes to fuel. If you eat a diet high in carbohydrate, which at some times in the year is necessary (more on that in later chapters), it will prefer to use sugar for fuel. If you feed it more fat while reducing carbohydrate, it will learn to use fat for fuel. That's a good thing because it augments your aerobic endurance training.

The idea that eating fat is bad for your health grew out of the 1950s and refuses to go away. Like many "old wives' tales," there's an element of truth to it. Some types of fat are definitely bad for your health and should be avoided. The worst is hydrogenated fat, often referred to as "trans fat." This is a fat that nutrition science gave us about 60 years ago to avoid what was perceived as a problem—too much saturated fat in our diets in the form of butter and as an ingredient in many processed foods. The scientific solution was eventually discovered to be worse than the original problem. Avoid trans fats. On food labels, it will appear in the list of ingredients as a partially hydrogenated oil. You'll find them in some breads and most snack foods.

The "good" fats are found in such foods as walnuts, macadamia nuts, avocadoes, fish, shellfish, flaxseed oil, olive oil, canola oil, and the meats of range-fed animals and wild game. In the Base period, slightly increase your consumption of these foods while slightly decreasing your intake of sugar and starchy foods. In this latter category are foods such as bread, bagels, cereal, corn, rice, and potatoes. These are best eaten immediately following long workouts to speed recovery. Don't make the mistake I come across with some athletes, who become so focused on avoiding starch and sugar that they shy away from them following exhaustive workouts. That's a mistake: Do not entirely avoid carbohydrates or even starches. We want to slightly shift your diet toward fat and away from carbohydrate during the Base period.

It's all right to "cheat" on your diet—in fact, you should. Having a small dessert after a meal will not have negative consequences for performance and may do wonders for your peace of mind. My favorite is gourmet, double-chocolate cookies. On days that I work out, I'll have one or two of them for dessert after dinner. Having an occasional baked potato or infrequent pasta side dish is also fine. What we're trying to avoid in the Base period is a diet dependent on moderate- to high-glycemic carbohydrate foods. And be sure to emphasize healthy fats. This dietary shift will contribute to your aerobic endurance fitness.

COMMON CONCERNS OF BASE 2

The following are some of the common challenges faced by triathletes during a winter Base 2 block. Some of these may not pertain to your unique circumstances. For example, while body-weight management is a concern for many athletes, there are some for whom it is a nonissue. They seem to eat whenever and whatever they want with no weight gain. For some the problem is just the opposite—they find it difficult to maintain weight, especially when training at high volume. For others, particularly those who live in warm and dry places, weather is seldom a factor when it's time to work out in the winter. In fact, you may have training challenges in the Base period that are unusual for other athletes. This is when having a coach or trusted and knowledgeable training partner is beneficial.

Weight Management

I hope that if you needed to lose some body fat at the start of the season, you accomplished that in Base 1. But if it was a considerable amount of weight to lose, then that project may well continue into Base 2 and perhaps even beyond.

Weight management essentially comes down to skills. If there are sweet foods you know are tempting, then don't keep them in your pantry. When the time is right to eat such foods (for example, after a long workout), then allow yourself a small portion. This may mean going to the store to buy it in a small quantity. If excess remains after you've satisfied your craving, put it in an inaccessible place, such as the top shelf in the back. The less of such foods you have in your kitchen and the more difficult it is to reach them, the less likely you are to give into temptation.

Cold and Wet Weather

Sometimes getting outdoors for a workout in the winter simply comes down to having the right equipment. Depending on the weather where you live, you may need several sets of base-layer clothing; warm jackets that you can both bike and run in; arm, leg, and shoe covers for cycling; tights for running; hats; helmet liners and covers; light and heavy gloves; neck and ankle gaiters; and a rain jacket. If people want to know what to buy you for a holiday gift, these are the types of things you can suggest. You can never have too many of them.

Of course, much of your training is still going to be indoors, so you will also need a bike trainer, a treadmill, and an indoor pool. Having a workout room in your house with all of these, along with strength equipment, is a great luxury. But whatever you can have readily available at home will make indoor training more accessible and more likely to be done. The alternatives are to belong to a health club or to have access to a city recreation center that has all of this available.

If you have the budget for it, you might also consider buying a cyclocross bike or a mountain bike. They can give you more opportunities to ride outdoors when a triathlon or road bike simply can't handle the road conditions. Fenders, knobby tires, a headlight, and a taillight for your bike can also be helpful this time of year.

Training Partners

Having others to work out with is a great motivator, but training partners can be either a help or a hindrance in your quest to have your best triathlon. On the positive side, a good training partner will push and motivate you when you need it. He or she will also be willing to go easy when your plan calls for it. Such a person is hard to find, though, so you might consider having more than one training partner. You could easily have different people to work out with for each of the three disciplines. And within each of these pairings, you might have some who are good to train with on harder training days and others who are good at going easy when your plan calls for it.

These may also be training groups. One of the best ways to improve your swimming, for example, is to train with a masters group. Similarly, a cycling group out of a local bike shop or club can also be beneficial. But look for a cycling group that doesn't "hammer," and also one that obeys traffic laws. In the winter, a spinning class at a local health club can break the monotony of yet another ride on the indoor trainer watching television. Look for an instructor who understands triathlon—especially winter Base training—and isn't trying to simply entertain the class by making the workouts ridiculously hard.

Be aware that a training partner may also hold back your progress. There are at least two types of triathletes to avoid as training partners. One is the athlete who wants to make every workout a race. This athlete will always want to touch the wall first in a swim, have his or her wheel in front of yours, and stay half a stride ahead. Your workouts will be too intense training with such people. The key to good training for racing is to get the intensity nailed down precisely—not to go as hard as you can.

The other type to avoid is the triathlete who thinks your goal is unrealistic, who has a negative outlook on life, who badmouths others behind their backs, and who is good at pointing out everybody's faults, including yours. Avoid all such people like the plague. They will prove to be an obstacle you must overcome in training to achieve your race goal. There is far more to be lost by training with such athletes than to be gained.

Base 2 Workouts

In the Base 2 block, you take a step up in serious training as you prepare for your A-priority triathlon. Total weekly training time remains about the same as in Base 1, but there are changes in how that time is distributed. The biggest training change you will see is a shift from an emphasis on strength training to an emphasis on the three triathlon disciplines, especially cycling. If you are a strong cyclist but weak in one or both of the other sports, it would be a good idea to include some of the optional swim or run workouts found in the training plan tables at the end of this chapter.

There are four physical abilities we will need to improve during Base 2 and Base 3. A description of each of these follows. The ones we'll emphasize the most are aerobic endurance, speed skills, and force. These must be well-developed before you start into the Build period. In Base 2 you will also begin to work on muscular endurance. This ability is dependent on the prior development of aerobic endurance and force. If you got a good start on these in Base 1, then we can expect muscular endurance to progress well.

Getting muscular endurance to an A-priority race level takes some time, as this ability is slow to develop. Training for it starts now and continues into the Build period, when it becomes the major training focus regardless of your race distance. High-level triathlon performance is dependent on excellent muscular endurance. But the primary focus, for now, is aerobic endurance.

AEROBIC ENDURANCE WORKOUTS

This is the most important ability to be developed in your Base period. Building the aerobic system—the capacity to use oxygen and fuel to create energy for swimming, biking, and running—is crucial to your success as a triathlete. After all, triathlon is an aerobic sport whether your A-priority race is sprint- or Ironman-distance.

The aerobic endurance workout is a long-duration workout done at or slightly above your aerobic threshold (AeT). This is zone 2 intensity for heart rate, power, and pace. In Base 2, you will use heart rate for aerobic-endurance cycling and running workouts. Basing the intensity of these workouts on heart rate makes sense because heart rate remains relatively stable throughout the year, whereas power and pace will change rapidly as you start back into serious training. It also makes sense because building the cardiovascular system is a primary purpose of aerobic endurance training. In swimming, where using a heart rate monitor is problematic, you will use pace, which you should have established with a T-time test at the end of the Prep block.

Aerobic endurance workouts are key training sessions in Base 2. I would like to see you complete every one of them for each sport. But for the first time in the season you may now start feeling the effects of accumulating fatigue before you come to your next rest-and-test week. If this happens, then lower the intensity of the aerobic endurance session to zone 1 and make it a recovery workout. If, during a swim, bike, or run, your fatigue is even greater than you had thought originally, stop the workout and call it a day. That goes for any workout, but it's especially true for aerobic endurance. There is nothing to be gained by dragging yourself through any session. You will only increase the risk of illness, injury, burnout, and overtraining.

Following are descriptions of the key workouts you will do in Base 2 for aerobic endurance. They are built into your general training plan at the end of this chapter.

Swim Aerobic Endurance

This may be a steady, continuous swim or broken into intervals. Each interval should be 500 to 1,000 meters or yards, with 20- to 40-second recoveries between intervals. You can determine how many intervals by race distance using the table that follows. If your swim times tend to be on the slow end of your age-group results, or if you prefer to think in terms of time instead of distance for your swim workouts, that's fine.

The pace to swim these AeT intervals is based on your time for the 1,000-meter or 1,000-yard time trial that you did in the last week of Base 1. Using Table 6.1, find your

TABLE 6.1 Swim Zone 2 Pace	
TIME 1,000 m/yd	PACE/100
9:35–9:45	1:09–1:12
9:46–9:55	1:11–1:14
9:56–10:06	1:12–1:15
10:07–10:17	1:13–1:16
10:18–10:28	1:14–1:17
10:29–10:40	1:15–1:19
10:41–10:53	1:17–1:21
10:54–11:06	1:19–1:22
11:07–11:18	1:20–1:23
11:19–11:32	1:21–1:25
11:33–11:47	1:23–1:27
11:48–12:03	1:24–1:28
12:04–12:17	1:26–1:31
12:18–12:30	1:28–1:32
12:31–12:52	1:30–1:34
12:53–13:02	1:32–1:37
13:03–13:28	1:34–1:39
13:29–13:47	1:36–1:40
13:48–14:08	1:39–1:44
14:09–14:30	1:40–1:45
14:31–14:51	1:44–1:49
14:52–15:13	1:46–1:51
15:14–15:42	1:49–1:55
15:43–16:08	1:52–1:57
16:09–16:38	1:55–2:01
16:39–17:06	1:57–2:03
17:07–17:38	2:02–2:08
17:39–18:12	2:05–2:12
18:13–18:48	2:10–2:17
18:49–19:26	2:13–2:20
19:27–20:06	2:18–2:25
20:07–20:50	2:22–2:30
20:51–21:37	2:28–2:36
21:38–22:27	2:33–2:41
22:28–23:22	2:38–2:47
23:23–24:31	2:45–2:54
24:32–25:21	2:52–3:01

Note: Paces are based on a 1,000 meter or 1,000 yard time trial.

Determine the total time for your AE set based on race distance and either swim continuously or break it into intervals. At least once each week, swim a long set at your zone 2 swim pace.

Goal Event	AeT Distance	AeT Duration
Sprint	1,500–1,800 m	20–25 min.
Olympic	1,800–2,200 m	28–32 min.
Half-Ironman	2,400–2,600 m	35–40 min.
Ironman	2,800–3,200 m	42–48 min.

For example, if your race is an Olympic-distance triathlon, the workout might look something like this:

Warm-up	10–15 min.
AeT set	4 × 500 m at pace zone 2
	30-sec. recoveries
Cooldown	10 min.

1,000 time in the column on the left. The corresponding "Zone 2" column is your 100 pace for the AeT intervals.

When you start this workout, the pace will seem slow. You will be tempted to go faster, but don't do it! Stick with the workout plan. As the workout proceeds, the sets will become increasingly harder even though the pace has not changed. This is when you will begin to reap the aerobic endurance rewards of AeT training. If you find it difficult to maintain your pace as the workout proceeds, then your aerobic fitness is incomplete and you need to continue doing this workout at least once a week.

It's time to stop any given workout if your breathing becomes labored during the session. Another sign that it's time to stop the workout is if your rating of perceived exertion on a 1-to-10 scale exceeds 6 (moderate). If, using these guidelines, you are forced to stop this workout the first time you do it, and you seem to be otherwise well-recovered and healthy, then you should retest with a 1,000 meter or 1,000 yard time trial, or take a look at the data in your log for the day you originally did the time trial to see if you got the math right.

When you can easily hold the targeted pace for the entire set, your aerobic endurance is well established. At that point you can reduce the frequency of this workout to once every other week to maintain the ability. But do at least four of these swim sessions in Base 2 even if you find they are easy early on.

Bike Aerobic Endurance

The aerobic endurance bike ride, like the aerobic endurance swim, is like Chinese water torture. What seems easily managed at the start of the ride eventually becomes challenging as the workout progresses. You have to have the patience to stay with the proper intensity early in the session to reap the benefits later on. You'll be tempted to go faster. Don't do it. (This is one of the numerous reasons why I so often say that patience is a necessary trait for anyone who wants to be a good endurance athlete.) Ride for a long time at AeT and you'll soon learn what aerobic endurance is all about.

Ride steadily for an extended time at your zone 2 heart rate.

Race Distance	AeT Duration
Sprint	1 hr.
Olympic	2 hr.
Half-Ironman	3 hr.
Ironman	4 hr.

Stop the workout when your RPE exceeds 6 on a 1-to-10 scale or if the speed at which you are riding becomes ridiculously slow even though your heart rate remains the same. If you have a power meter, stop the workout when your power drops 10 percent from what it was in the first 30 minutes.

As you do this workout once a week over the course of several weeks, you should find it easier to go farther while your speed and power remain relatively constant for the entire ride. Later in this chapter, in the section on your training plan, you will see how this workout progresses throughout Base 2.

Your zone 2 heart rate is based on testing done at the end of the Prep block. Using that test result, find your lactate threshold heart rate (LTHR) in Table 6.2. The "Zone 2" column is the heart rate range in which you should do aerobic endurance rides.

TABLE 6.2 | **Bike Zone 2 Heart Rate**

LTHR	HEART RATE	LTHR	HEART RATE
137	109–122	167	136–149
138	110–123	168	137–150
139	110–124	169	138–151
140	111–125	170	139–151
141	112–125	171	140–152
142	113–126	172	141–153
143	113–127	173	142–154
144	114–128	174	143–155
145	115–129	175	144–156
146	116–130	176	145–157
147	117–131	177	146–158
148	118–132	178	147–159
149	119–133	179	148–160
150	120–134	180	149–160
151	121–134	181	150–161
152	122–135	182	151–162
153	123–136	183	152–163
154	124–137	184	153–164
155	125–138	185	154–165
156	126–138	186	155–166
157	127–140	187	156–167
158	128–141	188	157–168
159	129–142	189	158–169
160	130–143	190	159–170
161	130–143	191	160–170
162	131–144	192	161–171
163	132–145	193	162–172
164	133–146	194	163–173
165	134–147	195	164–174
166	135–148		

Note: Zones are based on lactate threshold heart rate (LTHR).

The first time you do this workout in Base 2, start with a duration that's about half of the duration mentioned above for your A-priority race. Make the workout a bit longer each week at a rate determined by how quickly you seem to be adapting to it. When you find it's becoming easy to complete the A-priority-race duration for this workout as described above, with speed and power holding steady, begin doing these rides in the upper half of zone 2. When that becomes easy, it's time to do this workout only every other week. But be sure to do at least six of these rides before advancing—four in Base 2 and at least two in Base 3.

This workout is best done alone. Doing such a ride with a group or partner presents problems. The greatest is that not everyone's zone 2 heart rate produces the same speed.

The best way to do this ride is to have a power meter onboard in addition to your heart rate monitor. Although you will use a heart rate monitor to set the effort, what happens to power is the real story. The relationship between power and heart rate has a lot to teach you about your cycling fitness (see the sidebar, "Measuring Aerobic Fitness for Cycling").

This workout is beneficial even if you don't have a power meter. You just can't accurately measure your progress without a power meter or know for certain when you've achieved good aerobic fitness. About all you can do without the meter is pay close attention to how you feel. If you are in good aerobic condition, you should be able to finish the ride strongly, though you may feel tired. If you're totally whipped

MEASURING AEROBIC FITNESS FOR CYCLING

For triathletes, aerobic fitness is the most important ability of the six I've discussed throughout this book. We've only actually been able to measure and analyze it with a field test for a few years. The following describes how I do that for cycling.

Figures 6.1 and 6.2 present examples of two riders doing a steady, multi-hour, zone 2 ride. All you see here are the aerobic endurance portions of the workouts. The warm-ups and cooldowns are not shown. However, the warm-up, is especially important in this workout because you will use it to elevate your heart rate to zone 2. Although the rider in Figure 6.2 has a relatively high heart rate, he is still riding in zone 2. He just happens to have a higher LTHR than the rider in Figure 6.1.

In both examples, the riders are doing an excellent job of maintaining a steady heart rate, as evidenced by the "heart rate" line staying almost flat on both charts. But notice what happens to the "power" line. In Figure 6.1, power closely parallels heart rate. That's good: The rider is staying strong throughout the ride. There is no fading of power (or slowing down, even though that's not a precise way to measure output on a bike). I call this separation of heart rate and power "decoupling." This rider has good aerobic endurance.

For the rider in Figure 6.2, however, the decoupling is excessive, as evidenced by the fade in power as heart rate remains steady. In the

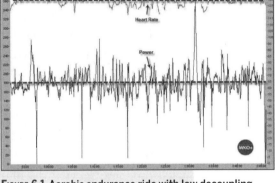

FIGURE 6.1 Aerobic endurance ride with low decoupling

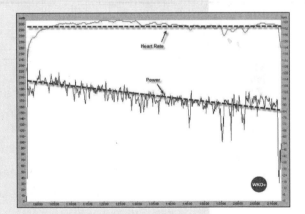

FIGURE 6.2 Aerobic endurance ride with excessive decoupling

data it looks like railroad tracks separating. The rider is losing power output and slowing significantly as the ride progresses.

From these two examples, I can tell you unequivocally that rider 1 has much better aerobic endurance than rider 2. If all they had were heart rate monitors, we wouldn't know this kind of information. Heart rate is only effective when we can compare it with something else. By itself, it tells us nothing about aerobic fitness.

later in the ride and struggling just to limp home, though your heart rate remains in zone 2, your aerobic fitness probably needs a lot more work. If this is the situation for you, continue doing this workout weekly until you can finish strongly.

Run Aerobic Endurance

There is little difference between the aerobic endurance bike workout and the aerobic endurance run. The purpose of both is to elevate your heart rate to zone 2 and then maintain it for an extended period.

This workout is best done on a flat or slightly rolling course. Avoid hilly courses, as the downhill sections will cause the heart rate to drop. Attempting to keep the heart rate elevated as you descend a steep hill means running quite fast, which means lots of impact force, increasing your risk of injury. If you have no choice but to do this run on a hilly course, then allow your heart rate to fall on the downhills. That's better than ending up with an injury. You can also do this workout on a treadmill, though that isn't perfect, either, because it can be so boring. Moreover, on a treadmill the terrain never changes, so the load on the muscles never changes, which also increases your risk of injury.

You won't be holding zone 2 for this duration the first time you do this workout. You will start with a much shorter duration, perhaps 20 to 40 minutes, and build gradually to the race-based workout duration listed above. Again, realize that the

Warm-up	10–20 min., run slowly, raising HR steadily into zone 2
AE set	Build set to be 45 min. to 2.5 hours, based on goal race
Cooldown	10 min.

Once you reach zone 2, pay close attention to your heart rate monitor to ensure that you stay there throughout the session. Use the table below to determine the duration of your AE effort.

Race Distance	*AE Duration*
Sprint	45 min.
Olympic	1.5 hr.
Half-Ironman	2 hr.
Ironman	2.5 hr.

total workout will be longer than the aerobic endurance portion because of the warm-up and cooldown. The cooldown can be very short, however. Combined, these will account for perhaps 30 minutes at most.

As in the bike workouts, your zone 2 heart rate for running is based on the 30-minute time trial test you did at the end of the Base 1 block. With this test you should have discovered your lactate threshold heart rate (LTHR) for running. Find your LTHR in the lefthand column of Table 6.3. The corresponding range in the "Zone 2" column is the heart rate to be used for your aerobic endurance run.

Keep in mind that having good bike aerobic endurance doesn't mean that you have good running aerobic endurance, too. It may take you longer to develop one than the other. Refer to the sidebar, "Measuring Aerobic Fitness for Running," to find out how your running endurance is coming along.

If you don't have a pacing device such as a runner's GPS or accelerometer, assess your progress based on how you feel during the aerobic endurance portion of the run, especially the latter part. Using the 1-to-10 scale, your perceived exertion for this run should not exceed 6. If it does, allow your heart rate to drop down into zone 1 and call it a day. Over the course of a few weeks you should gradually be able to extend the duration of this workout until you can achieve your objective time.

TABLE 6.3 Run Zone 2 Heart Rate

LTHR	HEART RATE	LTHR	HEART RATE
140	120–126	171	146–156
141	120–127	172	146–156
142	121–129	173	147–157
143	122–130	174	148–157
144	123–131	175	149–158
145	124–132	176	150–159
146	125–133	177	151–160
147	125–134	178	152–161
148	126–135	179	153–162
149	127–135	180	154–163
150	128–136	181	155–164
151	129–137	182	155–165
152	130–138	183	156–166
153	131–139	184	157–167
154	132–140	185	158–168
155	132–141	186	159–169
156	133–142	187	160–170
157	134–143	188	160–170
158	135–143	189	161–171
159	136–144	190	162–172
160	137–145	191	163–173
161	137–146	192	164–174
162	138–147	193	165–175
163	139–148	194	166–176
164	140–149	195	166–177
165	141–150	196	167–178
166	142–151	197	168–178
167	142–152	198	169–179
168	143–153	199	170–180
169	144–154	200	171–181
170	145–155		

Note: Zones are based on lactate threshold heart rate (LTHR).

MEASURING AEROBIC FITNESS FOR RUNNING

It's possible to use a speed-distance device such as a GPS or accelerometer, in addition to your heart rate monitor, to measure your aerobic fitness. If you use one of these devices, though, it is all the more important that you are on a mostly flat course. As of this writing, these units don't normalize speed based on uphills and downhills. Eventually such devices will probably be able to tell you what your pace would be if you were on flat terrain regardless of the hills you are actually running. I expect the next generation of this technology to include such a feature.

If you're using a speed-distance device, when the workout is over you can download the data and compare heart rate with speed. (I recommend WKO+ software, available at Trainingpeaks.com.) As with the bike, we'd like the graphic display of these two variables to remain parallel (coupled) throughout the run. If they decouple significantly—more than 5 percent—then your aerobic endurance is not well established. Realize that they may stay coupled for the early portion of the run but then decouple in the latter part. Where they begin to separate is the limit of your current aerobic endurance.

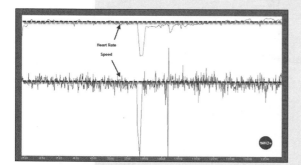

FIGURE 6.3 Aerobic endurance run with low decoupling

Figure 6.3 shows a runner with good aerobic endurance—at least for the duration of this workout. Figure 6.4 illustrates decoupling in an aerobic endurance run. Notice that the decoupling increases less than halfway into the workout. Should the athlete in Figure 6.3 run longer, he may also experience decoupling.

Decoupling may result from inadequate aerobic fitness or from heat, dehydration, wind, or changes in the run surface (such as sand versus asphalt). I've found athletes can generally adapt to heat. If, in the first hot days of summer, you decouple earlier in the workout, it simply means that you have not yet adapted to the weather change. You can either avoid the

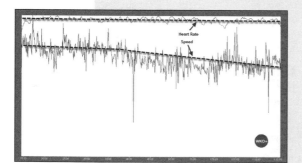

FIGURE 6.4 Aerobic endurance run with excessive decoupling

heat by running earlier in the day, or adapt to the heat. If your race will be in warm conditions, then adapting is the better strategy. As you adapt, the decoupling will diminish.

Although perceived exertion sounds nice, in reality it can be difficult to gauge your effort accurately—and running with a training partner almost always causes the standard to shift higher. In other words, when you're running with a buddy, what would have been a 7 or 8 when running alone is called a 6. For this reason it is generally best to do this workout by yourself. Running with someone who is faster or slower than you will cause you to go higher or lower than zone 2. Neither of these will make you more fit when it comes to this ability. You need to stay in the proper zone. As the Base 2 block progresses, you should be able to move the targeted intensity to the upper half of zone 2.

Once your aerobic endurance is fully developed, it's time to do this workout less often than when you were establishing your aerobic fitness level. You can reduce the frequency by half. So if you were doing an aerobic endurance run once a week, you can now do it once every other week. The best time to reduce the frequency of aerobic endurance work in one sport is not necessarily the best time to reduce it in another. Each sport should be considered separately. But do be certain that your aerobic endurance is sound before moving into the Build period. If you make a mistake here, make it on the side of doing too many workouts for this ability. Do at least six AeT workouts per sport in the Base 2 and 3 training blocks.

When you reduce the frequency of aerobic endurance training in a sport, you open up a workout slot for another type of ability. This slot may now be used for additional speed skills, force workouts, or muscular endurance training, depending on where your limiter is. Let's discuss those options now.

SPEED SKILLS WORKOUTS

Speed skills training continues in Base 2 with workouts similar to those you did in Base 1 but with minor adjustments. The drills in Base 1 that were complete workouts in themselves are now built into workouts for other abilities. In swimming, for example, some of the drills that have proven to be effective for you should be continued into Base 2 as a part of the warm-up for every swim session. For your strong sports, speed skill training takes on a secondary importance. So if cycling is your strength, you can still do some work on your pedaling skills; it just won't be done as often as in Base 1. Do just enough drill work to maintain your skills in your strong sport.

Here's how speed skill training differs from what you did in Base 1.

Swim Speed Skills

In Base 1 swimming, an entire workout could consist of technique drills; now the drills are incorporated into the warm-ups and cooldowns of workouts that focus on the other abilities—aerobic endurance, force, and muscular endurance. If swimming is your sport limiter, however, then you need to devote a significant portion of each workout to technique refinement, focusing especially on the drills that seem to help you the most. If you've been working with a swim instructor and making good progress, then continue the relationship, if possible. By the end of the Base period we want your swim speed skills to be well-honed.

Swimming with a masters group can also prove beneficial. I always suggest to the athletes I coach that they find a masters group with a swim coach on deck at each workout who is good at helping swimmers work on technique. It's also a good idea to tell the coach that you'd appreciate any help he or she may provide in the way of technique instruction. Some coaches are a bit hesitant to offer stroke advice, so let the coach know that you want to improve your stroke and need all the help you can get.

Base 2 is a good time to get some underwater videos made of your swim stroke. Some masters swim teams do this regularly. If yours doesn't, ask if the coach has an underwater camera and would mind shooting some footage of your stroke and then looking at it with you. There is often a fee for this, but it is perhaps the most effective thing you can do to get faster if your swim speed skills are a limiter. Videos don't lie. If you think you've been doing it the right way but see in the film that you aren't, you are more likely to make a concerted effort to change. The underwater camera is a great tool for all swimmers, regardless of ability. I'd suggest using it at least once every four weeks in the Base blocks.

Bike Speed Skills

Speed skill training on the bike continues into Base 2, only it now becomes part of the workouts for the other abilities, just as in swimming. When you are warming up or cooling down, do drills such as spin-up, toe touch, high cadence, 9-to-3, and top only (all described in Chapter 5). For indoor trainer rides, warm up with the isolated-leg-training drill. And on days when you need a break from the aero bike, ride a mountain bike or fixed-gear bike for a change of pace. Actively apply what you have learned about pedaling technique when doing your bike workouts. You must concentrate on technique frequently to keep the old bad habits from returning.

Run Speed Skills

I have the triathletes I coach do some form of the basic strides drill year round (see Chapter 5 for a description of the drill). It seems you can never devote too much time to improving your run technique. I once coached a pro triathlete who was an

All-American runner in college and considered one of the fastest runners in triathlon. I still had him work on technique year round.

If you do not have a history of calf, Achilles, or plantar fascia injuries, then you may substitute "uphill strides" for the strides workout you've been doing. Uphill strides are described in the next section.

FORCE WORKOUTS

By the end of Base 1, if you came into the block with lots of experience in strength training, you should have completed six to eight sessions of Max Strength (MS) weight lifting. If this season was your first of weight lifting, then you would have done the same number of sessions of Max Transition (MT) training. In either case, you should be aware that you are considerably stronger as you start Base 2. One of your objectives for this block is to convert that newly developed gym strength into swim-, bike-, and run-specific strength.

Swim Force

If your swim speed skills are still improving rapidly when you start Base 2 training, it's best not to start muscular force training yet. Wait until it is apparent that your gains in swim skills are beginning to plateau. If you are new to swimming or have never worked on technique before, it may take more than the four weeks of Base 1 to see significant improvement and an acceptable level of skill. If this is your situation, then don't do force workouts at this time. Replace those workouts in the suggested schedules later in this chapter with speed skills sessions like those you did in Base 1. But if your swim technique improvements seem to have stabilized, which is what I would expect for a seasoned triathlete, then it's time to begin force training in the pool.

Force workouts for swimming are simple. All you do is warm up and then swim very high-effort 25 meter or 25 yard intervals. You must go all out on each of these 25s to build force, but don't go so fast that your technique breaks down. After each 25, stand at the wall twice as long as the time you spent doing the 25. For example, if you swim a 25 in 20 seconds, stand at the wall to fully recover for 40 seconds. That's a very long recovery in swimming. But it's necessary because we are trying to build your muscular strength. It takes a maximum effort to fully stress the muscle, so long recoveries are necessary. If you shorten these significantly or do even an easy swim after each 25, you won't achieve the results we are after here. This is not an aerobic endurance workout—allow your swim muscles to rest.

After a thorough warm-up, repeat this Force set up to three times:

3 × 25 m, hard efforts

For the recoveries, stand at the wall after each 25, spending twice as long at the wall as it took to complete the effort. After three 25s with corresponding rest periods, swim an easy 50 meters or yards, then stand at the wall until you are fully recovered before beginning the next set.

Start with one set and add another every third workout in Base 2 until you are doing three sets. These may be one portion of a longer workout that includes other sets, such as speed skills for maintenance of technique, aerobic endurance, or muscular endurance. If this workout is paired with the training of other abilities, make the force portion the first set after the warm-up. The reason is that you can't make a tired muscle stronger. To reap the benefits of this workout, you must be fresh when starting it and follow the recovery guidelines.

To make this workout even more challenging, wear a T-shirt while doing the high-effort 25s. That will increase drag, causing your swim muscles to work much harder than normal. Remove the shirt during the recovery swims. Be careful not to get sloppy doing this workout. We don't want to build force at the expense of speed skills. No amount of force is worth poor technique and bad skill habits. Swim the 25s hard, but not so hard as to become sloppy with your form.

Advanced swimmers may need to increase the drag even more to get a benefit. A sweatshirt may be used in place of the T-shirt in that case. Another alternative is to use paddles, either with or without the shirt.

Be certain you are ready for these add-ons when you do them. Force training has an element of risk not found in aerobic endurance or speed skills workouts. The risk is that you will injure a shoulder due to the high effort. This is most likely to happen if your technique is poor. So, again, don't do these workouts until you have developed good swim form.

If you're doing these reps correctly, you should experience pressure against the palm of your hand throughout the pull phase of the stroke. If you're having trouble with this, bend your wrist when your arm reaches a full extension so that the fingers point toward the bottom of the pool, then start your straight-back pull. Do not

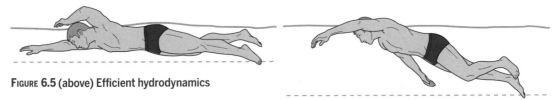

FIGURE 6.5 (above) Efficient hydrodynamics

FIGURE 6.6 (right) Inefficient hydrodynamics

push down on the water with your fingers pointing straight ahead. Keep the fingers pointing down. As before, don't let your technique break down in order to increase hand pressure. These reps should be very short, usually 25 yards or meters and no longer than 50, because you must stay very focused. Concentrate on maintaining good form (see Figures 6.5 and 6.6).

Bike Force

Force workouts on the bike are best done with a power meter, as the data will tell you precisely how hard you are working and allow you to gauge your progress. But you can do these workouts without measuring power by relying on your perceived exertion. A heart rate monitor is of no use here because the intervals are so short.

The key to this workout is how much force you apply to the pedals. Start with a gear such as 53 × 17 for the first set of three intervals. The selected gear should be

After a thorough warm-up, repeat this Force set 3 times:

3 × 6 revolutions, hard as you can
2-min. soft-pedal recovery between intervals
5-min. soft pedal between sets

Before starting the interval, stop pedaling and allow the bike to slow down. It should almost come to a complete stop. Then start the interval by driving the pedals down with great effort. Stay seated throughout the interval. If you are using a power meter, aim for at least twice your functional threshold power (FTPw) on each interval. The cadence will be very slow at first but increasing as the interval progresses. Count each time your right foot completes one revolution, stopping on the sixth.

only slightly challenging. For the second interval, set the shifter to a higher gear, such as 53 × 16, and for the third set select a very challenging gear such as 53 × 14. The gears you use and how challenging they are will be determined largely by the course you are using.

These intervals may be done on flat terrain; on a short, low-gradient hill (4 or 5 percent); or on an indoor trainer (with the rear-wheel resistance high to prevent slipping). Force intervals may be paired with another ability, such as speed skills or aerobic endurance, in Base 2. If you combine them with a second ability, do the force intervals early in the session after warming up.

You will probably feel like the 5 minutes between sets is too much recovery. Remember, with this workout you are working on developing greater muscular force—not endurance. Fatigue is counterproductive for building force. If you are fresh for every hard effort, you will get more benefit from this workout than if you skimp on the recoveries and become progressively more fatigued. If you are tired, the force you apply will not be as great and you won't get the same results. It's even okay to take too much rest between the force intervals.

As I mentioned earlier, force workouts are risky. The downside of this workout on the bike is that it risks injury to the knees. If you are prone to knee problems, then don't do this workout. No amount of fitness is worth an injury. Even if you have no history of knee problems, it's best to be cautious. Start with one set and then add a set every time you do the workout. Do this workout once or twice a week.

Run Force

Developing greater running force will automatically make your stride longer. Combine that with the higher cadence you have been working on in speed skills training, and your running is sure to improve. But it won't happen overnight. Your aerobic system must also improve to allow you to maintain the combined higher cadence and longer stride. And the nervous and muscular systems must also adapt to the changes. All of this will take some time as the body slowly adapts. By the start of the Build period in a few weeks, if you've been diligent about both speed skills and force training, you will be running faster at the same effort as when you started the Base training. You must be patient and persistent to realize the improvement.

Uphill-strides workouts for force are done on either a short, very steep hill or on something like the stairs you find in a football stadium or basketball arena. If in the past you have had Achilles, calf, or plantar fascia injuries, then you are better

After a thorough warm-up, repeat this Force set 3 times on stairs or hills:

3 × 6 stride-building efforts
Walking recovery between intervals
5 min. easy jogging between sets

The first set should be at an intensity that is less than what you would call "challenging." Each successive set is done at a slightly higher level to build force. Run as hard as you can on the third set—but not so hard that your technique breaks down.

Begin each interval from a standing (not running) position. Count six right-foot strikes and stop on the sixth. If you are running stairs, you may need to take two or even three steps with each stride depending on the width and rise of the stairs. Turn around and walk back down the hill or stairs. Do not run down. Jog easily for five minutes after each set.

off using the stairs. Do not do this workout if you are currently experiencing discomfort in any of these areas. The ankle flexion is significant when running up a steep hill and puts a tremendous load on those soft tissues. I prefer stairs for this workout, but they are harder to find than hills.

This is a very risky workout. Be cautious with its progression. Once a week is best for most athletes, but do this no more than twice a week with at least 96 hours between the workouts. Start with one set and add another each week for the first three weeks of Base 2. If you have "glass legs," you would be wise not to do it at all. In that case just continue doing downhill strides for speed skill. Not all of the athletes I coach do the uphill-strides workout, as many are injury-prone. I'm very conservative when it comes to risky running workouts. You must avoid injury.

MUSCULAR ENDURANCE WORKOUTS

For the advanced triathlete, muscular endurance is the key to high performance. In the Build period it will be the primary focus of your training regardless of the distance of your A-priority race. Muscular endurance is slow to develop, so we will start working on it in Base 2 with tempo workouts, and in Base 3 the intensity will be bumped up to the lactate-threshold level. In Base 3 this stress will gradually

TABLE 6.4 Swim Zone 3 Pace	
TIME 1,000 m/yd	PACE/100 m
9:35–9:45	1:04–1:08
9:46–9:55	1:06–1:10
9:56–10:06	1:07–1:11
10:07–10:17	1:08–1:12
10:18–10:28	1:09–1:13
10:29–10:40	1:10–1:14
10:41–10:53	1:12–1:16
10:54–11:06	1:13–1:18
11:07–11:18	1:14–1:19
11:19–11:32	1:15–1:20
11:33–11:47	1:17–1:22
11:48–12:03	1:18–1:23
12:04–12:17	1:20–1:25
12:18–12:30	1:22–1:27
12:31–12:52	1:24–1:29
12:53–13:02	1:26–1:31
13:03–13:28	1:28–1:33
13:29–13:47	1:29–1:35
13:48–14:08	1:32–1:38
14:09–14:30	1:33–1:39
14:31–14:51	1:36–1:43
14:52–15:13	1:39–1:45
15:14–15:42	1:42–1:48
15:43–16:08	1:44–1:51
16:09–16:38	1:47–1:54
16:39–17:06	1:49–1:56
17:07–17:38	1:53–2:01
17:39–18:12	1:57–2:04
18:13–18:48	2:01–2:09
18:49–19:26	2:04–2:12
19:27–20:06	2:08–2:17
20:07–20:50	2:12–2:21
20:51–21:37	2:18–2:27
21:38–22:27	2:22–2:32
22:28–23:22	2:27–2:37
23:23–24:31	2:34–2:44
24:32–25:21	2:40–2:51

Note: Paces are based on a 1,000 meter or 1,000 yard time trial.

increase to prepare you for the challenging workouts to come in the buildup to your race.

Muscular endurance is the ability to maintain a moderately high output for a moderately long period of time. Muscular endurance workouts are either long, steady-state efforts or long intervals with short recoveries. The intensity is zone 3 to zone 5a for heart rate, pace, or power. In Base 2 you will only be doing zone 3 efforts, which I call "tempo."

Swim Muscular Endurance

In Base 2, do long sets of swim muscular endurance efforts at a zone 3 pace. Your training objective is to get in 20 to 40 minutes of such training in a single workout at least once a week.

  Interval: 1,000 m repeats
Intensity: Zone 3 pace
Duration: 20–40 min. in zone 3

Getting the pace right is critical for the muscular endurance workout if you are to get the benefits we're after. Table 6.4 is based on your 1,000 meter or 1,000 yard time trial from Base 1. It will help you determine your zone 3 pace per 100. Divide these zone times by 4 to establish your 25 pace, or divide by 2 if you are swimming in a long-course (50 meter or 50 yard) pool.

It's fine to do this workout twice in a week, or to combine it with aerobic endurance, speed skills, or force training to form a single workout session. In workouts combining skills, speed skills and force work should come early in the session, before the muscular endurance set, and aerobic endurance training should follow muscular endurance.

A typical combined-ability swim session in Base 2 might look like this, beginning with a warm-up and ending with a cooldown:

Speed skills set
Force set
Muscular endurance set
Aerobic endurance set

Bike Muscular Endurance

As with swimming, muscular endurance training for cycling begins in Base 2 with zone 3 tempo workouts. Start developing this ability by doing long work intervals with very brief recoveries that are about 10 percent of the preceding work-interval length. So after a 10-minute interval there is a 1-minute recovery. This is just long enough to get a mental break from the focused workout. Each interval is done in the aero position (keep your head up and eyes on the road ahead).

In Base 2, get in 20 to 60 minutes of such training in a single session.

Start near the lower end of the interval range and add a few more minutes each week in Base 2. Don't rush to the upper end. Be patient, allowing your body to adapt gradually. One of these workouts each week is adequate, but some advanced triathletes training at a high weekly volume (more than about 18 hours a week) may be able to do two such sessions per week. This may be especially beneficial if muscular endurance on the bike is your limiter.

Use Table 6.5 to determine your zone 3 heart rate based on your lactate thresh-

TABLE 6.5 Bike Zone 3 Heart Rate

LTHR	HEART RATE	LTHR	HEART RATE
137	123–128	167	136–149
138	124–129	168	137–150
139	125–130	169	138–151
140	126–130	170	139–151
141	126–131	171	140–152
142	127–132	172	141–153
143	128–133	173	142–154
144	129–134	174	143–155
145	130–135	175	144–156
146	131–136	176	145–157
147	132–137	177	146–158
148	133–138	178	147–159
149	134–139	179	148–160
150	135–140	180	149–160
151	135–141	181	150–161
152	136–142	182	151–162
153	137–142	183	152–163
154	138–143	184	153–164
155	139–144	185	154–165
156	139–145	186	155–166
157	141–146	187	156–167
158	142–147	188	157–168
159	143–148	189	158–169
160	144–148	190	159–170
161	144–150	191	160–170
162	145–151	192	161–171
163	146–152	193	162–172
164	147–153	194	163–173
165	148–154	195	164–174
166	149–154	200	182–191

Note: Zones are based on lactate threshold heart rate (LTHR).

Interval: 10–20 min.

Intensity: Zone 3 heart rate or power

Duration: 20–60 min. in zone 3

old heart rate. If you have a power meter you may use it instead of heart rate for zone 3 workouts. Your functional threshold power (FTPw) as determined by testing at the end of the Prep or Base 1 blocks establishes your power zones. To set your zone 3 power for Base 2 tempo training, multiply your FTPw by 0.76 for the low end and 0.90 for the high end.

Power zone 3 = 76 to 90% of FTPw

PACE-BASED RUNNING ZONES

Running pace zones are based on your functional threshold pace (FTPa). Pace-based zones are often more reliable than heart rate–based training zones since heart rate is affected by so many variables, such as diet, weather, excitement, and more. Basing your training on pace is usually more reliable. The problem is that the technology behind speed-distance devices such as GPS units and accelerometers leaves much to be desired. You may well find that you get inaccurate data from time to time. Nevertheless, I would highly recommend training with pace as your intensity guide when running on relatively flat courses.

If you don't know your FTPa, then go back to Chapter 2 and read about how to find yours. To find both ends of the range for your tempo running pace, multiply your FTPa by 1.06 and 1.13.

Pace zone 3 = 1.06 to 1.13% of FTPa

It is easiest to do this if you convert the FTPa time to minutes and hundredths of a minute. For example, a 1 mile FTPa of 7 minutes and 30 seconds would be 7.50 minutes. In this example, to determine the upper (slower) end of zone 3, multiply 7.50 by 1.13, producing a pace of 8.48 (8 minutes, 29 seconds). (To calculate the number of seconds, multiply 0.48 by 60 (48 percent of 60 seconds). To find the faster end, multiply your 1 mile FTPa by 1.06. The result is 7.95 (7 minutes, 57 seconds). In this example, the runner would do tempo workouts in the range of 7:57 to 8:29 per mile. (If you use kilometers, the percentages remain the same.)

Run Muscular Endurance

The muscular endurance workouts and training pattern for running are similar to those for cycling. If you have a history of running injuries, I'd suggest doing tempo training in the form of intervals instead of a long, steady run. Taking brief recovery jogs every few minutes gives you an opportunity to assess your feet and legs to see if there is anything unusual going on related to past injuries or portending new ones. I've found that runners are generally unwilling to stop a steady run even if they feel something that isn't quite right in a leg or foot tendon, the most likely areas of injury. Don't hesitate to stop if you notice something; you can sacrifice one workout to prevent an injury. If you are not prone to injury, then you can run the tempo workouts as long, uninterrupted efforts.

Whether you are doing your tempo runs as intervals or as a steady-state effort, find a course that is relatively flat and has a soft but firm surface. Avoid concrete and asphalt. Some cities have running paths that are excellent for such training. Or you may do them on hiking trails—just be sure there are no roots or jagged rocks to contend with. Another option is a track, as most tracks provide an excellent surface for running. The only potential problems are the boredom and the continual left turns for such a long workout. To counter the turning problem, change directions every

TABLE 6.6   Run Zone 3 Heart Rate

LTHR	HEART RATE	LTHR	HEART RATE
140	127–133	171	157–163
141	128–134	172	157–164
142	130–135	173	158–165
143	131–136	174	158–166
144	132–137	175	159–167
145	133–138	176	160–168
146	134–139	177	161–169
147	135–140	178	162–170
148	136–141	179	163–171
149	136–142	180	164–172
150	137–143	181	165–173
151	138–144	182	166–174
152	139–145	183	167–175
153	140–146	184	168–176
154	141–147	185	169–177
155	142–148	186	170–178
156	143–149	187	171–179
157	144–150	188	171–179
158	144–151	189	172–180
159	145–152	190	173–181
160	146–153	191	174–182
161	147–154	192	175–183
162	148–155	193	176–184
163	149–155	194	177–185
164	150–156	195	178–186
165	151–157	196	179–187
166	152–158	197	179–188
167	153–159	198	180–189
168	154–160	199	181–190
169	155–161	200	182–191
170	156–162		

Note: Zones are based on lactate threshold heart rate (LTHR).

Interval: 6–12 min., with 1-min. or
2-min. jogging recoveries

Intensity: Zone 3

Duration: 20–40 min.

*Start these runs as intervals and
work up to a steady-state effort.*

few minutes. When running the "wrong" way (clockwise), always go to the outside lanes of the track so as not to interfere with other runners.

If you are using heart rate for the tempo workouts described here, see Table 6.6 for your training zone.

COMBINED WORKOUTS

In Chapter 5, I explained that combined-ability workouts would become more common in the remainder of the season. Many such sessions are suggested in the training plans at the end of this chapter. There is some latitude for creativity, especially when it comes to how much of each ability to include in a given workout. Here are the combined workouts that are scheduled for the Base 2 block.

Swim Combined Skills Workouts

The speed skills and aerobic endurance (SS + AE) workout you will find in the Base 2 training plans at the end of this chapter was explained in Chapter 4 (see p. 58). Just as in Base 1, this session starts with a warm-up and is followed by speed skills drills focusing on your weakest swim skill. Following the drills, swim an AE set as described earlier in this chapter. You can also include drills for your skills limiter at the beginning of your cooldown.

In the training schedules at the end of the chapter, you will also find a rather complex swim workout for speed skills, force, and muscular endurance (SS + Fo + ME). The Fo and ME sets within this workout are described earlier in this chapter, and you can work some SS drills into your warm-up. You have some latitude in how much time or distance you devote to each of these training abilities. If your swim force is the greater limiter of the three, then devote more of the workout to that. Be sure to do the abilities within the session in the order listed: You'll start with speed skills, then do the force drills, and end with muscular endurance.

Bike Combined Skills Workouts

Your Base 2 training schedule suggests two combined workouts: one for speed skills and muscular endurance (SS + ME) and one for speed skills and force (SS + Fo).

In both workouts, you should include one or more speed-skill drills, as described in the "Bike Speed Skills" section of Chapter 5, in your warm-up. Then begin the muscular endurance or force portion, following the instructions provided earlier in this chapter.

Run Combined Skills Workouts

In the Base 2 training schedule there are two run combined workouts listed. The first is for speed skills and muscular endurance (SS + ME). This is simple. Just do a speed skills set following your warm-up and then a muscular endurance run. Both types of workouts are described above.

The other combined run workout is a test with aerobic endurance work (Test + AE), which occurs during the rest-and-test week. As you did in Base 1, complete the test described below after your warm-up, allow yourself a few minutes to recover, and then run steadily with your heart rate in zone 2 for the remainder of the workout.

Combined Bike-Run Workouts

Often called "bricks," the combined bike-run workouts are critical to your success in triathlon. When you've just finished a bike ride, running feels very different from the way it feels when done alone, especially if the ride is long or hard. The purpose of such workouts is to learn to adapt to these strange sensations and to learn to run with good form and appropriate pacing even when you are tired.

In the schedules at the end of the chapter, you'll see a long AE bike workout and also a short AE run planned for Sundays. These are meant to be done as a combined session. So following the ride, put on your running shoes and start the short run. At this time in the season you don't need to be concerned about making a particularly quick transition. But also don't take a long break after the ride. You should start running within five minutes of stepping off the bike. As the run starts, go immediately to a pace that will raise your heart rate to zone 2. As you may have done in Base 1, focus on only one of your skill limiters during the run.

RECOVERY WORKOUTS

The recovery workouts (Rec) suggested in the training schedules at the end of this chapter are optional. If you are an experienced athlete who typically trains with high volume, then it's a good idea to do Rec workouts. If your volume is low, you can omit them if you like.

Base 2 Testing

In Base 2 testing we will continue to gauge your progress and confirm that we have your training zones right. As the workouts become more intense, it is increasingly important that you train at the right pace and power. (It also becomes more important to have devices that measure these). While pace and power should be showing slight improvements by the end of Base 2, heart rate is unlikely to change. We only need to confirm that your lactate threshold heart rate is correct for biking at this point, as you should have confirmed your running LTHR at the end of Base 1. As in previous training blocks, the testing in Base 2 should occur in the last week of the period following a few days of rest and recovery. The following are the tests to do at that time.

SWIM FIELD TEST

Repeat the swim T-time test you did at the end of Prep and Base 1. If training has gone well over the past few weeks, you should see some improvement in your time, but probably not by much. In fact, the improvement may be so slight that the conditions for testing that day negate your improved fitness. Warmer pool water, a poor night of sleep, or a hard day at work the day before are all examples of things that could slow you down just a bit. So don't be too upset if you see what appears to be a slight backward slide in performance.

Warm-up	10–15 min.
Test set	Swim 1,000 m, hard race effort
Cooldown	As needed, easy

To find your T-time, divide your total time for the 1,000 m by 10.

A result that is a few seconds slower is simply not a big deal at this time of year, and such a result is even likely if you are making a lot of changes to your stroke mechanics. But if you experience a significant loss of time, on the order of 10 percent or more, then it's time to reevaluate your swim training. This may be the time for you to join a masters swim group, find a coach, or take swimming lessons to refine your stroke.

BIKE FIELD TEST

Because bike training increases in Base 3, we will recheck your heart rate zones on the bike at this point. If you have a power meter, we will also establish your new power zones. In Base 3, power is the preferred intensity metric on the bike. A power meter is a great investment if you want faster race times. If you have one or decide to buy one now, invest the time to learn how to use it properly, too.

In the last week of Base 2, repeat the same bike test you did at the end of the Prep block, as described in Chapter 4. This should confirm your lactate threshold heart rate, which is what your heart rate zones are based on.

As before, if you have a power meter, your average power for the entire 30 minutes predicts your functional threshold power. By now you should see positive changes in power as your fitness improves. Although your input (effort as reflected by heart rate) doesn't change with rising fitness, your output (power for biking and pace for swimming and running) does change.

Do the time trial as if it were a race for the *entire* 30 minutes.

Warm-up	20–30 min.
Test set	30 min. hard, race effort
Cooldown	As needed, easy

At 10 minutes into the test, click the lap button on your heart rate monitor. Hit the lap button again at the end of the 30-minute effort. After your cooldown, see what your average heart rate was for the last 20 minutes. This number is an approximation of your LTHR.

RUN FIELD TEST

If you have a speed-distance device (accelerometer or GPS), repeat the 30-minute time trial that you did at the end of the Prep and Base 1 blocks, as described in Chapter 4. If you do not have the device, do this test only if you are unsure of your heart rate zones for running. They should have been established by the end of Base 1, if not earlier in the season.

As at the end of Base 1, if you do not have a pacing device and you are certain of your heart rate zones, repeat the aerobic time trial.

Warm-up	10–20 min., slowly elevate heart rate to 10 beats per minute below LTHR
Test set	Steady run, keeping heart rate at 9–11 bpm below LTHR

When your heart rate reaches this level, begin a steady run at that heart rate plus or minus 1 beat per minute (9 to 11 beats per minute below LTHR). The distance you run is based on the A-priority race for which you are training:

Race Distance	Test Interval
Sprint	1 mile
Olympic	2 miles
Half-Ironman	3 miles
Ironman	4 miles

Compare your new time with your time at the end of Base 1. The amount of change tells you how much you improved. The time should be slightly faster or about the same. If it is slightly slower, don't despair. There are so many variables that go into field testing—such as wind, rest, diet, and other factors—that small swings one way or the other should not be concerns. Over the long term, as in eight weeks or more, you should see measurable, positive changes related to your fitness.

Your Base 2 Training Plan

As you can see in the suggested Base 2 training schedules that follow, the workload is increasing. The biggest change is that the muscular endurance workouts are being added. It's not unusual for an athlete to recover quickly when the emphasis is on the basic abilities (aerobic endurance, speed skills, and force), while recovering more slowly when muscular endurance is included. So although you may have easily followed a three-weeks-on and one-week-off training pattern in Base 1, in Base 2 you may need to shift to two-on and one-off. This is especially true for older athletes and those who are new to the sport. The only way to find out is through experience. Try three-on and one-off and see how you do. If you are tired and the workouts are low quality in the third week, then go to two-on and one-off. You may want to continue this pattern in Base 3 and throughout the Build period.

There have now been two workout categories added to the mix since Base 1—muscular endurance (ME) and strength maintenance (SM). The other abilities remain the same as in Base 1. All of the workouts for each of those listed below are described earlier in this chapter.

SPRINT-DISTANCE TRAINING **BASE 2**

T R A I N I N G   W E E K S

SPORT	SWIM	BIKE	RUN	STRENGTH	DAILY VOLUME
MON	*Rec* 0:15–0:30			SM 0:45	0:45–1:15
TUES	**SS + ME** 0:30–0:45	*SS or Rec* 0:45–1:00	**Fo** 0:45–1:00		1:15–2:45
WED		**SS + ME** 1:00–1:15	*SS* 0:30–0:45		1:00–2:00
THURS	**SS + Fo** 0:30–0:45		**SS + ME** 0:45–1:00		1:15–1:45
FRI	*Rec* 0:15–0:30	**SS + Fo** 1:00–1:30		SM 0:45	1:45–2:45
SAT	**SS + AE** 0:45–1:00	*Rec* 0:30–0:45	**AE** 1:00–1:30		1:45–3:15
SUN		**AE** 1:30–2:00	*SS* 0:15–0:30		1:30–2:30
VOLUME BY SPORT	1:45–3:30	3:30–6:30	2:30–4:45	1:30	9:15–16:15
WORKOUTS	**3–5**	**3–5**	**3–5**	**2**	**11–17**

R E S T   &   T E S T   W E E K

SPORT	SWIM	BIKE	RUN	STRENGTH	DAILY VOLUME
MON				SM 0:45	0:45
TUES	**SS** 0:15–0:30		**SS** 0:30–0:45		0:45–1:15
WED		**SS** 0:45–1:00			0:45–1:00
THURS	**Te** 0:30–0:45		**SS** 0:30–0:45		1:00–1:30
FRI		**Te** 1:00			1:00
SAT	**SS** 0:15–0:30		**Te + AE** 0:45–1:15		1:00–1:45
SUN		**AE** 1:30–2:00	*SS* 0:15–0:30		1:30–2:30
VOLUME BY SPORT	1:00–1:45	3:15–4:00	1:45–3:15	0:45	6:45–9:45
WORKOUTS	**3**	**3**	**3–4**	**1**	**10–11**

Notes: Rec = Recovery. Optional workouts are in italic. The optional SS runs on Sunday are intended to follow the bike ride. Detail on the workouts can be found in the chapter. Strength workouts appear in Appendix C.

OLYMPIC-DISTANCE TRAINING **BASE 2**

T R A I N I N G   W E E K S

SPORT	SWIM	BIKE	RUN	STRENGTH	DAILY VOLUME
MON	*Rec* 0:15–0:30			SM 0:45	0:45–1:15
TUES	SS + ME 0:45–1:00	*SS or Rec* 0:45–1:00	Fo 0:45–1:00		1:30–3:00
WED		SS + ME 1:00–1:15	SS 0:30–0:45		1:00–2:00
THURS	SS + Fo 0:45–1:00		SS + ME 0:45–1:00		1:30–2:00
FRI	*Rec* 0:30–0:45	SS + Fo 1:00–1:30		*SM 0:45*	1:00–3:00
SAT	SS + AE 0:45–1:00	*Rec* 0:45–1:00	AE 1:15–1:45		2:00–3:45
SUN		AE 1:30–2:00	SS 0:15–0:30		1:30–2:30
VOLUME BY SPORT	2:15–4:15	3:30–6:45	2:45–5:00	0:45–1:30	9:15–17:30
WORKOUTS	3–5	3–5	3–5	1–2	10–17

R E S T   &   T E S T   W E E K

SPORT	SWIM	BIKE	RUN	STRENGTH	DAILY VOLUME
MON				SM 0:45	0:45
TUES	SS 0:30–0:45		SS 0:30–0:45		1:00–1:30
WED		SS 0:45–1:00			0:45–1:00
THURS	Te 0:30–0:45		SS 0:30–0:45		1:00–1:30
FRI		Te 1:00			1:00
SAT	SS 0:30–0:45		Te + AE 1:00–1:30		1:30–2:15
SUN		AE 1:30–2:00	SS 0:15		1:30–2:15
VOLUME BY SPORT	1:30–2:15	3:15–4:00	2:00–3:15	0:45	7:30–10:15
WORKOUTS	3	3	3–4	1	10–11

Notes: Rec = Recovery. Optional workouts are in italic. The optional SS runs on Sunday are intended to follow the bike ride. Detail on the workouts can be found in the chapter. Strength workouts appear in Appendix C.

TRAINING PLAN — BASE 2

TRAINING PLAN — BASE 2

HALF-IRONMAN-DISTANCE TRAINING **BASE 2**

T R A I N I N G   W E E K S

SPORT	SWIM	BIKE	RUN	STRENGTH	DAILY VOLUME
MON	*Rec* 0:20–0:30			SM 0:45	0:45–1:15
TUES	SS + AE 0:45–1:00	*SS* or *Rec* 0:45–1:00	Fo 0:45–1:00		1:30–3:00
WED		SS + ME 1:00–1:30	*SS* 0:30–0:45		1:00–2:15
THURS	SS + Fo + ME 0:45–1:00		SS + ME 0:45–1:00		1:30–2:00
FRI	*Rec* 0:20–0:30	SS + Fo 0:45–1:00		*SM* 0:45	0:45–2:15
SAT	SS + AE 0:45–1:00	*Rec* 0:45–1:00	AE 1:30–2:00		2:15–4:00
SUN		AE 2:30–3:30	AE 0:15		2:45–3:45
VOLUME BY SPORT	2:15–4:00	4:15–8:00	3:15–5:00	0:45–1:30	10:30–18:30
WORKOUTS	3–5	3–5	4–5	1–2	11–17

R E S T   &   T E S T   W E E K

SPORT	SWIM	BIKE	RUN	STRENGTH	DAILY VOLUME
MON				SM 0:45	0:45
TUES	SS 0:30–0:45		SS 0:30–0:45		1:00–1:30
WED		SS 0:45–1:00			0:45–1:00
THURS	Te 0:30–0:45		SS 0:30–0:45		1:00–1:30
FRI		Te 1:00			1:00
SAT	SS + ME 0:30–0:45		Te + AE 1:15–1:45		1:45–2:30
SUN		AE 2:30–3:30	AE 0:15		2:45–3:45
VOLUME BY SPORT	1:30–2:15	4:15–5:30	2:30–3:30	0:45	9:00–12:00
WORKOUTS	3	3	4	1	11

Notes: Rec = Recovery. Optional workouts are in italic. The AE runs on Sunday are intended to follow the bike ride. Detail on the workouts can be found in the chapter. Strength workouts appear in Appendix C.

IRONMAN-DISTANCE TRAINING **BASE 2**

T R A I N I N G   W E E K S

SPORT	SWIM	BIKE	RUN	STRENGTH	DAILY VOLUME
MON	*Rec* 0:20–0:30			**SM** 0:45	0:45–1:15
TUES	**SS + AE** 0:45–1:00	*SS or Rec* 0:45–1:00	**Fo** 0:45–1:00		1:30–3:00
WED		**SS + ME** 1:00–1:30	**SS** 0:30–0:45		1:00–2:15
THURS	**SS + Fo + ME** 0:45–1:00		**SS + ME** 0:45–1:00		1:30–2:00
FRI	*Rec* 0:20–0:30	**SS + Fo** 0:45–1:15		*SM* 0:45	0:45–2:30
SAT	**SS + AE** 1:00–1:15	*Rec* 0:45–1:00	**AE** 2:00–2:30		3:00–4:45
SUN		**AE** 3:00–5:00	**AE** 0:15		3:15–5:15
VOLUME BY SPORT	2:30–4:15	4:45–9:45	3:45–5:30	0:45–1:30	11:45–21:00
WORKOUTS	**3–5**	**3–5**	**4–5**	**1–2**	**11–17**

R E S T   &   T E S T   W E E K

SPORT	SWIM	BIKE	RUN	STRENGTH	DAILY VOLUME
MON				**SM** 0:45	0:45
TUES	**SS** 0:30–0:45		**SS** 0:30 0:45		1:00–1:30
WED		**SS** 0:45–1:00			0:45–1:00
THURS	**Te** 0:30–0:45		**SS** 0:30–0:45		1:00–1:30
FRI		**Te** 1:00			1:00
SAT	**SS + ME** 0:30–0:45		**Te + AE** 1:30–2:00		2:00–2:45
SUN		**AE** 3:00–5:00	**AE** 0:15		3:15–5:15
VOLUME BY SPORT	1:30–2:15	4:45–7:00	2:45–3:45	0:45	9:45–13:45
WORKOUTS	**3**	**3**	**4**	**1**	**11**

Notes: Rec = Recovery. Optional workouts are in italic. The AE runs on Sunday are intended to follow the bike ride. Detail on the workouts can be found in the chapter. Strength workouts appear in Appendix C.

Base 3

BASE 3 HAS BEEN DESCRIBED as being like a pyramid: The broader the base of the pyramid, the higher the peak you can build on it. The "width" of the base has to do with how much training you do—your volume. Now is the time for your training volume to reach its highest level, regardless of the distance of the race you are training for. You should have about 15 weeks remaining until your A-priority race. Your training will step up in volume, and intensity will continue to trend upward, becoming slightly harder than in Base 2.

If you are training in 3-week blocks with 2 weeks on followed by a rest-and-test week, you will do the Base 3 period twice, for a total of 6 weeks in Base 3. This is a typical way of training for older athletes, for novices, and often even for young, experienced athletes training at very high volume for Ironman-distance races. If you do not fall into any of these categories, do a 4-week Base 3. At the end of this block you should be ready to move into the Build period, which emphasizes race intensity.

Our purpose now is to ensure that you can manage the stress load of a higher volume of training. In a few weeks, when you enter the Build period, we'll start to shift the stress from volume to intensity. Making that transition gradually lowers the risk of injury.

Objectives for Base 3

1. **Maintain aerobic endurance.** By now, after 6 to 8 weeks of emphasizing it, your aerobic endurance should be at a high level. That means your decoupling of heart rate and power, or heart rate and pace, should consistently be less than 5 percent. If you don't have a power meter or pacing device, or WKO+ software to make these determinations, then you have been relying heavily on perceived exertion and comparing that with heart rate during workouts. If so, at your zone 2 heart rate you should be able to train for a long time in each sport and feel as if your effort and speed remain constant for your longest workouts. In Base 3 you will do some workouts to exclusively maintain aerobic endurance, and combined-ability workouts will become much more common.

2. **Maintain speed skills.** Just as with aerobic endurance, your speed skills should be very solid by this point in training. The newer you are to any of the three sports, the more change you should have noticed in this area. The most critical is swimming. Regardless of what the workout calls for in Base 3, you must never allow your swim technique to become loose and sloppy. The same goes for running and cycling. You've devoted a lot of time to mastering the techniques of the three triathlon disciplines. Don't lose it now by thinking the changes you have practiced so hard to attain are permanent. They aren't. It's very easy to fall back into old patterns if you're not paying attention. You must be diligent about maintaining the gains you've made and always trying to improve upon them.

3. **Develop force in hills.** Force training now graduates from short intervals to longer sessions in which force is combined with other abilities. This essentially means doing hilly aerobic endurance and muscular endurance workouts for the bike and run. Pool workouts emphasizing muscular endurance will also include a force set. Combining other abilities with force will begin to prepare you for the unique, intensity-focused stresses of the Build period.

4. **Create greater muscular endurance.** In Base 2 you started down the path of developing muscular endurance. This ability is the key to fast triathlon racing, so in Base 3 we will take it up another notch. When you reach the end of Base 3 I want your zone 3 and 4 workouts to feel like they are second nature to you, because you will need to be ready to do a lot more of this kind of training in Build 1 and Build 2.

Coaching Tips for Base 3

Every step along the path to a peak performance in your A-priority race is important. But I've found that the Base 3 period is when athletes usually make the greatest gains in their quest for success. It's also the first time in the season when problems may arise. The following are areas of concern I often address with the athletes I coach.

MINDSET

In Base 3 the training takes a decided step up. The volume is quite high and the intensity also continues to rise. And for that very reason, resting properly when you are supposed to be resting becomes even more important than before.

When you were in the Prep and Base 1 blocks, recovery was not a big deal. Now everything about your training hinges on it. If you don't recover well, the quality of your training will decline, as will your fitness and eventually your performance. Burnout, injury, illness, and overtraining are always lurking, waiting for you to make a mistake by doing too much. You must allow yourself to recover on easy days. There will also be days when you need to omit a workout or even take an entire day off from working out. Can you do that?

I hope you can, but I've coached athletes who could not. They went well beyond being highly motivated to achieve their goals; they were obsessed with training. They made decisions to keep going when they shouldn't have. Deep down, they knew they were wrong. They knew it was counterproductive for their optimal athletic performance, but they couldn't help themselves, and this ultimately produced only failure.

Do you believe that more is better? The USA Triathlon Federation used to have a motto that simply said, "Never enough." That was a terrible motto, and I'm glad they eventually got rid of it. There certainly are times when it is "enough." And you need to recognize those times. There's no question that training to the point of exhaustion, injury, or illness is not in your best interest as an athlete. Obsessive behavior must be recognized and avoided.

OBSESSIVE OR HIGHLY MOTIVATED?

Answer these questions:

- Do you drive yourself to complete workouts even when you are tired, injured, or sick?
- Do you find it very difficult to take a day off from training?
- When you do take time off, is there an overwhelming feeling of guilt?
- Have you been adding extra workouts or time to the training plans in the previous chapters?

If you answered yes to any of these questions, you may have moved beyond healthy motivation to become obsessive with exercise.

Obsessive behavior is not healthy. It will not help you become a better athlete; instead, it will prevent you from achieving your race goal. But what can you do about it? The first step is to fully acknowledge that you are training obsessively and to recognize that if this behavior continues you will not be successful with your goals. Next, stop yourself from doing one thing each week that you know is obsessive, such as adding time to a planned workout, or swimming, biking, or running on a day off. Enlist the help of your family. Ask them to point out when you are training obsessively and encourage you to stop. Train with partners who are not obsessive about their training. When you have an easy or short workout scheduled, do it with someone who is not as fit as you are and allow that athlete to set the pace. On rest days, do other things you enjoy besides training. This may be reading, getting a massage, watching a movie, getting caught up on work, or spending time with family or friends. If you are still having trouble after you try these things, do yourself a favor and see a counselor who specializes in treating obsessive behavior. They should be experienced in doing cognitive-behavioral therapy with their clients.

NUTRITION

Training in Base 3 is challenging. But your training plan over the past several weeks has gradually stepped up the workload so you should be ready for it. With recovery becoming increasingly important, your diet is becoming increasingly important. Along with taking enough time off from your training and getting enough sleep, diet is one of the factors that will determine your success. Your body needs to have the right nutrients to feed your recovery and your performance.

Eating isn't just about what you eat, though; it's also about when you eat it. By now, if you are working at near your limit, you are in a constant state of recovery. I tell the athletes I coach that there are actually five stages to their recovery throughout the day and that each of these stages is unique in terms of what foods are eaten. Here are the five stages.

Stage 1: Before the Workout

The only time this point in your day really presents a problem for your diet is if you are doing a long or intense workout first thing in the morning, especially if it's swimming or running. Before a hard bike ride, there are more options available, but even then, if the ride involves training at zone 4 and higher, you may need to be careful with what and how much you eat.

From a nutritional perspective, the perfect way to resolve the early-morning, preworkout conundrum is to get out of bed two hours before the workout and have breakfast. But if you have a 5:00 a.m. swim or run planned, that is unlikely to happen—you just won't be hungry for breakfast at 3 a.m., and it would disturb your sleep to get up and eat then. Instead, you'll want to sleep as late as you can, hop out of bed, grab your swim or run gear, and head out to the pool or road. Should you eat anything? If so, what should you eat?

Let's take the first question: Should you eat anything? If the workout is to be long or intense, you definitely should. During the night, while sleeping, your body used a large portion of its carbohydrate stores. You need some fuel in your tank now. If it is a short workout, you won't need much, especially if you had an adequate meal the night before. You could grab a quick snack, such as a piece of fruit.

If it's a long or intense workout, you need to take in enough calories to fuel your body without causing an uncomfortable lump to be in your stomach. Eating too much could even cause temporary hypoglycemia, which could make you feel lightheaded and dizzy within minutes of starting the workout, especially if it's a run. Instead of trying to eat a big meal, try using gel packets.

You can take in a couple of gel packets while sitting on the edge of the pool before jumping in, as you're still wiping the sleep out of your eyes. If you are running, squeeze them down as you're putting your shoes on and then chase them with a big gulp of water. The point is, take the gel packets less than 10 minutes before starting your workout. The gel won't sit in your stomach the way real food would. You'll be ready to train with a few hundred extra calories onboard. And you won't become lightheaded because it takes a bit longer than 10 minutes for your body to respond to the carbs you just took in. Once exercise begins, sugar is processed differently than when resting.

A couple hundred calories may not be enough if the workout is very hard or long. So keep a bottle of sports drink on the swim deck, or, for a run, wear a bottle holster or waist-belt container with sports drink. You could also carry more gels and have plain water available. This brings us to stage 2.

Stage 2: During the Workout

During exercise that lasts 90 minutes to two hours or more, you are likely to need some carbohydrate to maintain intensity. Expending your carbohydrate stores will cause you to gradually, even imperceptibly, slow down. The more aerobically fit you are, the longer you can go without additional sugar intake. In this context, aerobic fitness means that your body has a preference for burning fat for fuel.

The amount of carbohydrate you need to take in during exercise for these longer workouts depends not only on aerobic fitness but also on body size, the intensity of the workout, the duration of the workout, and your experience with refueling. The likely range is 100 to 400 calories per hour once you start refueling. A big athlete doing a long, high-intensity workout will need to take in more calories than a small athlete doing a lighter workout. You will need to experiment to see what works best for you.

The calories should come primarily from carbohydrate. Although there is some research showing that protein is beneficial during exercise, especially in very long sessions, there are also studies that have found no benefit. Some long-course athletes have reported feeling bloated when adding protein to their sports drink. This is likely because it slows the processing of the digestive system. While you're experimenting, see if adding protein during your longest workouts works for you. If not, stick with carbs.

For long-course triathletes I recommend considering fluids and fuel as being independent of each other. This is because they are two entirely separate needs. You should drink when thirsty, not when the clock hits a certain time. Forget the old saw that says, "When you're thirsty it's too late." That bit of misinformation has led many Ironman athletes to drink too much and become bloated. Fuel, however, should be consumed regularly, and so a schedule makes sense here.

Here's the problem: If you take in enough of a sports drink to meet your caloric needs, you are likely to take in too much water and cause bloating. But if you use a sports drink only when you are thirsty, you are likely to run short of fuel. The solution is to carry water on your bike and get water at run-course aid stations, while having fuel onboard in the form of gels, blocks, or whatever it is you like. If you prefer the sweet taste of a sports drink to plain water, it's fine to make a light mix. But consider it primarily as a fluid, not a fuel, and use it only when you are thirsty, drinking until your thirst is abated. Whatever you decide to do, rehearse it during your longest bike and run workouts. Don't wait until race day to see if it works.

For short-course racing, it's fine to use a fluid-fuel sports drink mix, since you won't need a lot of either. It isn't until about four hours that this problem of fluid and fuel becomes great enough to warrant a solution like the one described above.

Stage 3: Immediately After the Workout

The first 30 minutes or so after a long or intense workout is a crucial time when it comes to nutritional recovery. Your muscles are now very sensitive to carbohydrate and will gladly grab and store any that happens by in the bloodstream. If you do a good job of refueling in this postworkout window, it will pay off for your next workout.

Immediately after a workout, take in at least three calories of carbohydrate for every pound of body weight. It's best if the calories taken in at this stage are in liquid form, as liquids are processed faster in the gut than solids. There are many commercial products available that fill this need. And it may be beneficial to add a small amount of protein to this postworkout recovery drink.

This restocking of carbohydrate should only be done following long or highly intense workouts. After short and easy workouts this is just extra calories that may be turned into fat.

Stage 4: In the Hours After the Workout

This stage of nutritional recovery after highly stressful workouts continues for as long as the workout lasted. For example, after a hard two-hour session, focus your diet on carbohydrate, along with some protein, for two hours. Of course, the first 30 minutes of this two hours was stage 3 recovery, leaving 90 minutes for stage 4.

During stage 4 recovery, your food choices shift away from liquid sources of carbohydrate and toward solids. This is a great time to eat starchy foods, especially potatoes, yams, and sweet potatoes, which are also alkaline-enhancing. Now is also the time to eat grains such as bread, cereal, a bagel, pasta, corn, or rice. It's a good idea to include some fruits and fruit juices as well because they are rich in carbohydrate and also alkaline-enhancing. Alkaline foods may help to counteract the acidic trend your body experiences with hard training, thus speeding recovery.

Because you are likely to have a meal now, in stage 4 also eat some animal protein. This could be egg whites, turkey breast, fish, or shellfish. Get your protein at this time from real food, not from powders or other potions.

Don't force-feed your muscles in stage 4. Eat when you are hungry, and stop eating when your appetite is satisfied. Don't be concerned with counting grams of nutrients. Keep it simple. Just eat.

Stage 5: The Rest of the Day

In the previous four stages the emphasis was on the macronutrient carbohydrate along with a bit of protein. Your body's carbohydrate stores should now be well stocked. In stage 5, you must focus on micronutrients—vitamins and minerals.

AVOID PILLS

I'm afraid we've come to believe that vitamins should come in a pill. That's not a good way to view nutrition. Get your vitamins and minerals by eating real food, because we know it works. Humans have thrived on food for hundreds of thousands of years. It's only in the past 50 years that we've come to rely on pills as a source of micronutrients. In fact, there is now some research indicating there may be problems with this way of getting your vitamins and minerals.

Vegetables are the most micronutrient-dense foods. I've found that most of the athletes I coach don't eat enough from this food group. In stage 5, cut back on your intake of starchy foods (the ones mentioned above in stage 4) and replace them with veggies. Also include lean animal protein and fruit. You will have fewer colds, recover faster, and perform much better. I've seen it happen time after time with the athletes I've coached.

If you are doing two or three workouts in one day, stage 5 may be very brief. In fact, it may only happen once, near the end of the day, so it's all the more important on these days that you eat micronutrient-dense foods when you get the opportunity. Don't just fill up on sweets and starches.

COMMON CONCERNS OF BASE 3

Your training is now significantly harder than it was earlier in the season. One of the things that makes it harder is the hill training you'll now be doing. But what if you don't have any hills where you live? Or maybe it's just the opposite—you have too many hills and not enough flat terrain. What should you do? This is a common concern that will be addressed in this section. Training is also becoming more like your race. Now you will begin to work on one of the most important elements of racing a triathlon—pacing. Let's start by examining this most critical aspect of your race preparation.

Pacing

Perhaps the most challenging task before you is to learn how to pace a race properly. Nearly all triathletes start the bike leg of a race too fast and then fade as the race progresses. If you are racing for a high finishing place in your age group, starting the swim fast is usually the right thing to do. You need to get into position in order to draft with the swim leaders. The bike is a different story, however. I've seen athletes in an Ironman-distance race set a 40 km personal best time in the opening miles. That's not a good idea, because there are still 87 miles to go.

Starting too fast on the bike, regardless of the race distance, is easy to do. You are rested, you're motivated to perform well, and there is lots of excitement around you. If you hold back, lots of riders will pass you. So you put the pedal to the metal and the next thing you know you're redlined, with a zone 5b heart rate and heavy breathing. Your muscles are rapidly becoming acidic and your gut is shutting down. That's how a poor race performance starts. If you race this way, you will never realize your full potential as a triathlete.

Although it is almost a certainty that you will race better by holding back a bit at the start, it is a rare athlete who actually does it. The best races in long, steady-state endurance events are usually accomplished with what is called "negative-split" pacing. This means that on a flat course, the first half of the race is slightly slower than the second half. The first half of the race should take about 51 percent of the finish time, and the second half 49 percent. Nearly all world records in distance-running events and cycling time trials are set with something close to 51–49 pacing. If the course is not flat, or there is a headwind going out and a tailwind coming back, then the principle applies to how you expend energy—start conservatively and finish strongly.

Proper pacing is the most basic skill for success in endurance sports, and you must work on it frequently in training. But training doesn't have the same emotional baggage that racing has. Holding back at the beginning can be very difficult to do when scores of people are passing you. It takes discipline, patience, and self-confidence to restrain yourself. You must realize that those who pass you early in the race will come back to you later. Failure to get this basic skill right generally means you will not live up to your potential in triathlon.

The key to successful negative splitting in a race is to mentally prepare yourself to hold back initially on the bike. To race with negative-split pacing, you must train with negative-split pacing. Keep the 51–49 principle in mind for all of your workouts, especially those that are high in intensity, such as intervals. Each work interval should start slightly slower than it finishes, and the first interval should be the slowest of them all. Another effective time to rehearse 51–49 is when riding with other athletes. Pace yourself so that you finish stronger than when you started the workout.

When the athletes I coach master this skill, their race performances improve remarkably. Yours can, too. But it takes lots of practice.

No Hills

Base 3 includes a lot of force work. There is nothing that will exactly simulate the pull of gravity as you ride or run up a hill, but there are some things you can do to work the muscles to build greater force if you live in an area with only flat terrain, such as Kansas or Florida.

Let's start with the bike. Typically, places that are flat are also windy. Make the wind an ally. When a workout calls for force training in the hills, find a headwind instead. Sit up with your hands on the bars and select a higher gear than you would normally use as you ride into the wind doing the hard efforts.

More options are available for running in a flat location. One is to use a weight vest; another is to drag an automobile tire behind you. For the latter, tie a rope to a tire and fasten the other end to a belt around your waist. It's not high-tech, but it works. You can also do hilly workouts on a treadmill that has a gradient setting. Although these alternatives will build the force component of muscular endurance, which is a primary purpose of hill work, they are not the same as running up a real hill.

If these options do not work for you, then simply do the flat versions of the muscular endurance and aerobic endurance workouts.

Too Many Hills

Base 3 workouts do not always require hills; sometimes a flat route is what you need. If you live someplace like the mountains of Colorado, where there simply is nowhere to do flat workouts, you will need to make some adjustments when doing steady-effort workouts such as aerobic endurance rides and runs. There are two options. One is to ride an indoor trainer or run on a treadmill when the schedule calls for steady-effort heart rates, power, or pace. The second is to find the least hilly route possible and do circuits on it while holding back on the uphill portions. This, by the way, is a better problem to have than no hills at all.

Base 3 Workouts

In Base 3 the weekly training volume increases, with the greatest changes scheduled for the bike and run. This block often comes in the last few weeks of winter and early spring, so you may now be able to spend more time on the road, especially on the bike. That should make it somewhat easier to increase the volume. As with Base 2, if you are weak in one of the three disciplines—and who isn't?—consider dedicating some additional time to it. You may choose to ramp up your training with the optional workouts that address your limiting sport. If adding more volume isn't possible given your lifestyle or training capacity, consider moving some training time from your strongest sport to your weakest.

Besides increasing your training volume over that of Base 2, you should also slightly increase the total amount of higher-intensity training done in Base 3. By this I don't mean that you try to swim, bike, or run as fast as possible, but rather that you do more training that is appropriate for the distance of the A-priority race you're training for. The training intensity for a sprint-distance triathlete will be very different from the training for an Ironman triathlete. The muscular endurance workouts suggested here will satisfy this need.

The following are your Base 3 workouts. Refer back to this section when you come to the training plans at the end of this chapter.

AEROBIC ENDURANCE WORKOUTS

The aerobic endurance workouts remain the same as in Base 2 for each of the three sports. The biggest change now is how often these are done, because you also need to fit in other workout abilities, especially force and muscular endurance.

If you glance ahead to the training plans for your race distance at the end of this chapter, you will find that there are alternate aerobic endurance–only and aerobic endurance–force workouts (AE and AE + Fo) on the weekends for the bike and run. This means that on one weekend you should do an aerobic endurance workout just as you did in Base 2. The following weekend do a combined aerobic endurance and force workout in the same sport (the details of combined workouts are described later in this chapter). I alternate these for the athletes I coach so that on one weekend they do an AE run on Saturday and an AE + Fo bike ride on Sunday. The next weekend these are reversed, with an AE + Fo run on Saturday and an AE bike ride on Sunday.

Notice that in the rest-and-test week plan, the weekend calls for AE for both sports. This means that if you train in four-week blocks, there are only three weeks where you will alternate AE and AE + Fo workouts. In other words, for the three weeks, you will do two AE workouts and one AE + Fo workout in one sport, and one AE workout and two AE + Fo workouts in the other sport. So which combination should you choose? If your aerobic endurance is not quite as strong in one sport as the other, select the combination that gives you two AE sessions in three weeks for that sport. Let's consider an example to better understand.

Let's say that "Bill" trains in four-week blocks. His aerobic endurance is stronger on the bike than for the run. So on the first weekend of Base 3, he will opt to do an AE run on Saturday and an AE + Fo bike ride on Sunday. On the second weekend, he will reverse these and do an AE + Fo run on Saturday and an AE bike ride on Sunday. For the third week he repeats what he did on the first weekend. And since the rest-and-test week calls for AE workouts for both of these sports on the weekend, he will finish Base 3 having done three AE runs, one AE + Fo run, two AE rides, and two AE + Fo rides. He has emphasized aerobic endurance training for his weaker sport in Base 3. That's good, because this is his last chance to optimize it before starting the Build period.

If your aerobic endurance is the same for the bike and run, then do the AE + Fo workout on weekends 1 and 3 in the sport in which your limiter is force. If both aerobic endurance and force are equal for bike and run, then do the bike AE workout on weekends 1 and 3. This is your last chance to get it to a high level, and since the bike makes up about half of the race time, this plan is likely to have the greatest payback.

Anytime you have an AE or AE + Fo workout scheduled but you feel exceptionally tired, turn the workout into an active recovery session by dropping the intensity down into zone 1. Or feel free to omit the scheduled workout and take the time for passive recovery. Too much fatigue can lead to injury, burnout, illness, and overtraining.

SPEED SKILLS WORKOUTS

It's now been at least six weeks since you started working diligently on your swim, bike, and run skills. If one or more of these were exceptionally poor at the start of Base 1, you should be aware of great gains by now. If so, that alone will make you faster in that sport. In Base 3, we start cutting back on this emphasis so we can develop more fitness. But this doesn't mean that speed skills are any less important. You must never allow your technique to erode back to where it was just a few weeks ago. It is still critical to your continued success.

Swim Speed Skills

The big change with speed skills in Base 3 is that there are fewer such ability-focused workouts. In swimming your warm-ups emphasize speed skills just as they did in Base 2, however. Continue doing the drills from previous chapters that have proven beneficial. If you haven't started doing so, I'd strongly suggest that you swim with a masters group that has a coach on deck at least once a week. Getting feedback from an experienced coach is the best way to ensure correct technique. Underwater video is always an excellent learning tool, and it's made all the more valuable by having a knowledgeable coach critique it with you.

Bike Speed Skills

At least one session each week will be devoted to speed skills on the bike. Continue doing the drills from Chapter 5 that have proven most effective. A new option is to simply do the SS workout while staying focused on pedaling at a comfortably high cadence. I will often have a rider who needs to improve his or her pedaling skills, and who typically pedals at 80 rpm, simply ride for an hour or longer while averaging at least 90 rpm. I tell the athlete that I don't care what the power, heart rate, or speed of the workout is. I only want to see a high average cadence. This means the athlete must stay focused on technique for the entire session, and that is good not only for technique but also for focus.

Run Speed Skills

The weekly run workout for speed skills is the strides session described in Chapter 5. This involves a warm-up in which you gradually increase the effort, followed by six to eight 20-second sprints. Recover after each sprint by taking a walk back to the starting point. Although I said earlier that these could be done barefoot to make your feet and lower legs stronger, you may not have been able to do that in Base 1 or 2 because of snow or freezing temperatures. Now that it is warming up, it may be possible for you to run unshod. Barefoot striding is a fun workout to do early in the morning when there is light dew on the grass—it's a great way to start the day. Just as with swimming and biking, in running you need to make sure that the skills you have developed doing drills such as these do not disappear when you do workouts emphasizing other abilities.

FORCE WORKOUTS

In Base 3 there is a decided step backward in the emphasis on force. There are no longer any workouts dedicated to force only; instead, it is now always combined with another ability, such as muscular endurance or aerobic endurance. Below are the basics of force training for each sport. The details are covered more fully in the "Combined Workouts" section of this chapter.

Swim Force

In swimming, the force set of a workout is done early in the session, before endurance training. For the force sets suggested in the training plan at the end of this chapter, continue with the sets you were doing in Base 2. That means very short, high-intensity efforts for 25 meters or yards, done with paddles or a drag device, such as while wearing a T-shirt. Continue taking long recoveries after each hard repetition. As always, the most important element when training at a high intensity is to never let your technique break down. Form is critical! You can't make a tired muscle stronger. Fatigue only improves endurance. Nothing else.

Bike Force

Although swim training for force is pretty much unchanged in Base 3 from the previous block, there is a big shift in such workouts for the bike. Whereas in Base 2 you did short, high-intensity efforts, in Base 3 you will ride up hills on the bike while doing muscular endurance intervals or aerobic endurance rides. The hills may be shallow or steep, so long as there is variety. If you live in a hilly area the length of the hills will probably vary. But try to spend more time on the shorter climbs for now. By "shorter," I mean hills that take about 5 minutes or less to go up. Use a slightly bigger gear than usual when climbing so that your cadence is lowered.

Run Force

Force training for the run is much like that for the bike. You are now moving toward a maintenance mode for force, as it is combined with either muscular endurance or aerobic endurance sessions. These combined workouts are done on hills, with an emphasis on those that take about 5 minutes to crest. Running uphill requires you to push a little harder to overcome gravity, so the experience is much like shifting to a higher gear on a bike.

MUSCULAR ENDURANCE WORKOUTS

Muscular endurance is now becoming a much more important part of your training. In Base 3 you will step up the muscular-endurance intensity a bit, reaching lactate threshold or slightly below it. For the bike and run, muscular endurance workouts are done on hills now, as described above in the "Bike Force" and "Run Force" sections.

Swim Muscular Endurance

Base 3 intervals are shorter than Base 2 intervals. You will be doing 300s to 500s with very short recoveries (on the order of 20 to 30 seconds per recovery). These Base 3 intervals are done at a zone 4 or 5a pace (see Table 7.1).

Race Distance	ME Interval	Total ME Session
Sprint	300–400 m	1,000 m
Olympic	300–400 m	1,500 m
Half-Ironman, Ironman	400–500 m	2,000–3,000 m

Interval: 300–500 m;

20–30-sec. recoveries

Intensity: Zones 4 and 5a

Total Distance: 1,000–3,000 m

Bike Muscular Endurance

In Base 3 we step up the intensity of the bike muscular endurance work to zone 4 or 5a. These are lactate threshold intervals (or FTPw, if you are using a power meter). The work intervals are now about 5 minutes long with brief recoveries. Because these intervals are repeats on hills, your recovery will be the descent time. Keep these as short as possible. It generally takes about half as long to go down the hill as it took to climb it.

These intervals are done in the aero position. Get in 10 to 30 minutes of total work-interval time in a single workout once a week.

Duration: 10–30 min.

Interval: 5-min. hills;

recover on descents

Intensity: Zones 4 and 5a

  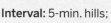

Use Table 7.2 to determine your zone 4 and zone 5a heart rates based on your lactate threshold heart rate. If you are using a power meter, you must know your functional threshold power to establish your zones. This should have been part of your Base 2 testing. You will set your zone 4 power for Base 3 muscular endurance intervals by finding 91 percent and 105 percent of your FTPw. These are the upper and lower ends of the range.

Zone 4 Power = 91 to 105% of FTPw

TABLE 7.1	Swim Zone 4–5a Pace
TIME 1,000 m/yd	**PACE/100 m**
9:35–9:45	0:58–1:03
9:46–9:55	0:59–1:01
9:56–10:06	1:00–1:06
10:07–10:17	1:01–1:07
10:18–10:28	1:02–1:08
10:29–10:40	1:03–1:09
10:41–10:53	1:05–1:11
10:54–11:06	1:06–1:12
11:07–11:18	1:07–1:13
11:19–11:32	1:08–1:14
11:33–11:47	1:10–1:16
11:48–12:03	1:11–1:17
12:04–12:17	1:13–1:19
12:18–12:30	1:14–1:21
12:31–12:52	1:16–1:23
12:53–13:02	1:18–1:25
13:03–13:28	1:20–1:27
13:29–13:47	1:21–1:28
13:48–14:08	1:23–1:31
14:09–14:30	1:24–1:32
14:31–14:51	1:27–1:35
14:52–15:13	1:29–1:38
15:14–15:42	1:32–1:41
15:43–16:08	1:34–1:43
16:09–16:38	1:37–1:46
16:39–17:06	1:39–1:48
17:07–17:38	1:43–1:52
17:39–18:12	1:46–1:56
18:13–18:48	1:50–2:00
18:49–19:26	1:53–2:03
19:27–20:06	1:56–2:07
20:07–20:50	2:00–2:11
20:51–21:37	2:05–2:17
21:38–22:27	2:09–2:21
22:28–23:22	2:14–2:26
23:23–24:31	2:20–2:33
24:32–25:21	2:25–2:39

Note: Paces are based on a 1,000 meter or 1,000 yard time trial.

PACING ME INTERVALS

I've found that most athletes start intervals much too hard. Learning to properly pace your A-priority race starts now, so become proficient in pacing during your interval training. If you can't control pace in a workout, you certainly can't do it in a race. Intervals are mini-races, so pace them properly.

On the bike, you may use either a heart rate monitor or a power meter to gauge the intensity of the muscular endurance intervals. As the intervals get shorter, using a power meter offers a slight advantage, as heart rate is slow to respond at the start of an interval. If you are using heart rate, during the first few minutes of an interval you will have to guess at the effort. Your heart rate will be trying to "catch up" with your pacing. The same holds true for RPE. The perceived exertion of the first interval will always seem easier than that of the following intervals. This is when you must hold back even though you know you could go much faster. If you go as hard as is possible on the first one, the others, especially the last one, will be incredibly hard. You may not even be capable of finishing it. To finish strongly, you must learn to hold back at the start of an interval set. This is the same mind-set you must establish for racing. To finish the race strongly, you must hold back in the early stages.

TABLE 7.2   Bike Zone 4–5a Heart Rate

LTHR	HEART RATE	LTHR	HEART RATE
137	129–140	167	156–170
138	130–141	168	157–171
139	131–142	169	158–172
140	131–143	170	159–173
141	132–144	171	161–174
142	133–145	172	161–175
143	134–145	173	162–176
144	135–147	174	163–177
145	136–148	175	164–178
146	137–149	176	165–179
147	138–150	177	166–180
148	139–151	178	167–181
149	140–152	179	167–182
150	141–153	180	168–183
151	142–154	181	169–184
152	143–155	182	171–185
153	143–156	183	172–186
154	144–157	184	173–187
155	145–158	185	173–188
156	146–159	186	174–189
157	147–160	187	175–190
158	148–161	188	176–191
159	149–162	189	177–192
160	149–163	190	178–193
161	151–164	191	179–194
162	152–165	192	179–195
163	153–166	193	180–196
164	154–167	194	181–197
165	155–168	195	182–198
166	155–169		

Note: Zones are based on lactate threshold heart rate (LTHR).

Run Muscular Endurance

Hill interval: 5-min. repeats;
recover on the descent
Track interval: 5-min. repeats;
90-sec. recoveries
Intensity: Zones 4 and 5a,
moderately hard
Duration: 10–20 min. total

In the running muscular endurance workouts you will do intervals that are about 5 minutes long. These may be done on a track, a relatively flat road, or a hill that takes about 5 minutes to run up. The recoveries, when on the track or a flat road, are about 90 seconds long. On a hill they are simply as long as it takes you to descend the hill. The combined muscular endurance and force workout, done on a hill, is described in the "Combined Workouts" section on p. 158.

The work intervals should add up to 10 to 20 minutes per session. One such session each week is perfect for most triathletes in Base 3. But if you are training at a high volume, such as 18 or more hours each week, you may want to do two of these sessions weekly, especially if run muscular endurance is a limiter for you.

For the intensity of these intervals, use either a rating of perceived exertion of about 7 to 8 on a 10-point scale, which feels moderately hard but sustainable for perhaps 30 minutes, or heart rate zones 4 and 5a (see Table 7.3).

TABLE 7.3 Run Zone 4–5a Heart Rate

LTHR	HEART RATE	LTHR	HEART RATE
140	134–143	171	164–174
141	135–144	172	165–175
142	136–145	173	166–176
143	137–146	174	167–177
144	138–147	175	168–178
145	139–148	176	169–179
146	140–149	177	170–180
147	141–150	178	171–181
148	142–151	179	172–182
149	143–152	180	173–183
150	144–153	181	174–184
151	145–154	182	175–185
152	146–155	183	176–186
153	147–156	184	177–187
154	148–157	185	178–188
155	149–158	186	179–189
156	150–159	187	180–190
157	151–160	188	180–191
158	152–161	189	181–192
159	153–162	190	182–193
160	154–163	191	183–194
161	155–164	192	184–195
162	156–165	193	185–196
163	156–166	194	186–197
164	157–167	195	187–198
165	158–168	196	188–199
166	159–169	197	189–200
167	160–170	198	190–201
168	161–171	199	191–202
169	162–172	200	192–203
170	163–173		

Note: Zones are based on lactate threshold heart rate (LTHR).

COMBINED WORKOUTS

Combined-ability workouts, as briefly described in the two previous chapters, make up a large portion of your weekly training in Base 3. This is because your training is increasingly taking on the demands of your A-priority race.

Racing does not involve just one ability. All of the abilities I've discussed play a role in the outcome. You must have good speed skills, good force, good muscular endurance, and good aerobic endurance to race well. The combined workouts will help you put it all together. In the Build blocks, there will be an even greater emphasis on mixing the abilities in each session. Following are the combined workouts you will find in the training plan tables at the end of this chapter.

Swim Combined Workouts

The SS + AE and SS + Fo + ME swim workouts are explained in Chapters 4 and 6 in the "Combined Workouts" section (see pp. 58 and 130). The only new combined workout introduced in Base 3 is SS + ME + AE. The three sets within this workout should be completed in the order listed: first, speed skills, then muscular endurance, then aerobic endurance.

For this three-part workout, after the warm-up, or as a part of it, include speed skills drills focusing on your greatest swim flaw (Chapter 5, pp. 80–81). By now you should have a good idea of what that flaw is and what is necessary to correct it. This should be accomplished by the end of Base 3. The amount of time you devote to speed skills in this session and others depends on how formidable this flaw is. Make a concerted effort now to fix it. In swimming, poor speed skills are much more detrimental than any other weakness.

Race Distance	ME Interval	Total ME Session
Sprint	300–400 m	1,000 m
Olympic	300–400 m	1,500 m
Half-Ironman, Ironman	400–500 m	2,000–3,000 m
Warm-up/SS set	Drills to work on SS limiter	
ME set	300–500 m, zone 4 or 5a, *swim 25 m recovery or rest 20–30 seconds*	
AE set	10–20 min. steady zone 2 pacing	
Cooldown/SS set	If needed, swim easy or do additional drills	

Each of the ME hard efforts is done at zone 4 or 5a for pace, as shown in Table 7.1. Recover at the wall for about 20 to 30 seconds after each effort, or swim an easy 25. Be very aware of stroke mechanics and also of pacing (see "Common Concerns of Base 3" above for more on pacing).

The AE set within this workout is 10 to 20 minutes of steady zone 2 pacing, as shown in Table 6.1. Be sure to stay focused on good swim mechanics throughout this set. Typically, by this time in the season, this set is easy enough that no cooldown is necessary. But you may want to finish with a drill focused on your speed skills limiter.

Bike Combined Workouts

In Base 3 there are two combined-ability bike workouts: ME + Fo and AE + Fo. Although the force component still involves hills, you will apply less force to the pedals than in previous combined workouts because the emphasis is now greater for muscular endurance and aerobic endurance. You're essentially in a maintenance mode presently when it comes to force. These two combined workouts are unique in that the abilities are merged rather than only combined. Here's how to do them.

For the ME + Fo workout, the perfect hill for your warm-up and muscular endurance sets would be about a mile long and have a steady grade of 4 or 5 percent, with no intersections and only light traffic. If you don't have such a hill handy, the grade could be as low as 2 percent or as much as 8 percent. (See "Common Concerns of Base 3" on p. 149 if there are no hills where you train.) Your hill may even take less or more than 5 minutes to climb, but it's best that it fall in the range of 3 to 8 minutes for this workout.

Interval: 5-min. rolling hills, riding in an aero position
Intensity: Zones 3 and 4; in a slightly higher gear without going anaerobic
Duration: Build to 30 min. with each subsequent ride

Once you are warmed up, do several intervals on this hill totaling 10 to 30 minutes of combined climbing time. For example, it could be four climbs of 5 minutes each for a total of 20 minutes. The first time you do this workout, start closer to the 10-minute end and add a few more minutes each week thereafter. Use a slightly higher gear than you normally use for climbing this hill, selecting one that has one or two fewer teeth engaged on

Warm-up	5-min. hill climb
ME + Fo sets	2–6 × 5-min. hill climb in zone 4 or 5a
	Ride in an aero position, using a slightly higher gear than normal
	Recover on the descent
Cooldown	Ride easy

Note: This is an optional workout. To adjust this to be a simple ME workout, do the 5-minute intervals on a flat route.

the rear-wheel gear cluster. Stay in the aero position as you climb. The intensity is heart rate zones 4 and 5a or power zone 4. Power is the preferred intensity metric for the session. Heart rate lags behind power at the start of each interval, forcing you to guess how hard to go for a couple of minutes. Your recovery after each climb is the descent time. Sit up, relax, and get back to the starting point at the bottom of the hill as quickly as you can.

You will notice that ME + Fo is an optional workout in Base 3. The other option is to work on muscular endurance only. The optional ME is done just as described above, only on a flat course. You may opt to do this and omit the high-gear force part of the workout if you have a high risk of injury due to knees that are often tender after hilly or long bike rides. It's better to be healthy than fit, and force training is particularly risky.

The other combined-ability bike workout in Base 3 is AE + Fo. It is done on alternate weekends, as described in the "Aerobic Endurance" section above. This session is somewhat unstructured. To do this workout you will ride a hilly course—preferably one with climbs of less than 5 minutes—working at a high intensity on the climbs, going easy on the descents to recover, and riding the flatter portions in zone 2. The higher intensity climbs are done in heart rate or power zones 3 and 4.

Avoid going anaerobic. Shift to a slightly harder gear for each climb, just as you did in the ME + Fo workout, so that you emphasize the force ability. This is a long ride, so it's likely to build a lot of fatigue before you're done. It's best to make this ride somewhat shorter than the AE ride done on alternate weekends, but over the course of this block you should gradually increase the duration by adding 30 minutes or so each time you do it. Of course, your AE ride should also get increasingly longer.

Run Combined Workouts

In the Base 3 training plans below there are three combined-ability run workouts—ME + Fo, AE + Fo, and Test + AE. They are similar to the same types of workouts done on the bike in this block. Here's how to do them.

For ME + Fo, find a hill with no traffic intersections and a grade of 4 or 5 percent that takes about 5 minutes to run up. This is best if it is grass, dirt, gravel, or some other surface that is softer than pavement. If you do not have the ideal hill, find the best hill you can for our purpose here, which is to increase resistance while doing muscular endurance training. (See also the "No Hills" section under "Common Concerns of Base 3" on p. 149.) If your hill is longer, simply stop after 5 minutes of climbing and turn around for

Interval: 5-min. hills
Intensity: Zones 4 and 5a
Duration: 10–20 min.

the descent. Basically, you will warm up and then run up the hill at your heart rate in zones 4 and 5a (see Table 7.3). Your pacing device won't help on a hill; pace is only meaningful on flat terrain. (I expect GPS pacing devices to provide real-time, normalized-graded pace soon, which will correct this deficiency.)

Jog back down the hill slowly after each hard effort. The descent is best done on a soft surface to minimize pounding your legs. It's important that you go very slow and easy on the descents, as this is when the risk of injury from such a workout increases. Running downhill fast puts tremendous loads on the feet and legs. Although these hills may be run upward on pavement, it is best to run down on a much softer surface. If there are no dirt or grass hills for this workout, try to find a paved hill that has a dirt or gravel shoulder you can run on for the descents. If you have a history of running injuries, then it is best to walk down the hills after each hard effort.

Get in a total of about 10 to 20 minutes of high-effort hill climbing within a single workout. The first time you do this workout start near the low end, and add a few more minutes each week until you are doing about 20 minutes in a session.

The third combined run workout is Test + AE, found in the rest-and-test week. This workout is the same as the one you did in Base 1 and 2 (see pp. 93 and 132). Following the warm-up and completion of the test described below under "Run Field Test," recover for a few minutes by jogging slowly or walking, and then run steadily in heart rate zone 2 for the time remaining in the workout.

Bike-Run Combined Workouts

Just as in Base 2, the training plans at the end of this chapter call for a 15-minute AE run on Sundays. Do this as a "brick" by running immediately after the bike ride. The time of the "T2" transition is not critical now. It's fine to take your time to change from your biking gear to your running gear before heading back out. But do keep the transition to less than 10 minutes so you don't tighten up and lose the effects of being warmed up.

Base 1 Testing

Are you making progress toward having good base fitness? You should have been asking yourself that question frequently over the past several weeks. Every time you come to a rest-and-test week, it is time to answer that question.

Over the course of several weeks, you should be seeing improvements in each sport if training has gone well. If improvements are not evident you must give some thought to what you've been doing—or not doing—with your available training resources and make adjustments. The most common causes of fitness stagnation in the Base period are lost training time due to illness or other interruptions, too much training at inappropriately high intensities, insufficient sleep, excessive emotional stress, and inadequate diet. Often the cause is some mix of these.

If you can determine why you are not making progress, then dedicate yourself to correcting the situation. If the cause is largely out of your control and likely to continue, however—perhaps you are moving, going through a career change, or trying to meet a challenging work schedule—then now is the time to reconsider your race goals, at least for the early season.

Warm-up	10–15 min.
Main set	Swim 1,000 m at hard, racelike effort
Cooldown	As needed, easy

Divide your total time for the 1,000 by 10 to find your pace per 100 yards or meters. This is referred to as your "T-time" and is a good indicator of your fitness for endurance swimming. Over the course of the season it should gradually get faster.

SWIM FIELD TEST

Repeat the 1,000 meter or 1,000 yard T-time test that you did at the end of every previous period: Prep, Base 1, and Base 2. By now you should be getting faster, so a comparison of your new test results and your original results should show an improvement.

BIKE FIELD TEST

Your heart rate zones for the bike should be well established by now based on previous testing. But if you are unsure of your zones, repeat the 30-minute time trial that you did before (see Chapter 4). Warm up and then ride as fast as you can for 30 minutes straight. At 10 minutes into the test, click the lap button on your heart rate monitor. You will then find the average heart rate for the last 20 minutes of the test. This number is an approximation of your lactate threshold heart rate.

If you have a power meter, your average power for the entire 30 minutes (not the last 20) is your functional threshold power. Although your LTHR probably has not changed in the past several weeks, your FTPw should have. Power is likely to increase with greater fitness while heart rate remains constant. So even if you know your LTHR is correct, you should still test for FTPw.

The 30-minute test is a challenging workout, much like a race, only without other athletes to help with your motivation. You could do a race instead if there is one available during your rest-and-test week. It could be a sprint-distance triathlon or a 40 km bike time trial. Your average power for this race should be close to your FTPw.

The 30-minute test should be done *as if it were a race* for the *entire* 30 minutes, whether you are running or on your bike.

Warm-up	20–30 min.
Main set	30 min. hard, race effort
Cooldown	As needed, easy

At 10 minutes into the test, click the lap button on your heart rate monitor. Hit the lap button again at the end of the 30-minute effort. After your cooldown, see what your average heart rate was for the last 20 minutes. This number is an approximation of your LTHR.

FTPw CONFIRMATION

Do this workout on an indoor trainer.

Warm-up   10–20 min.
Test set   4-min. repeats; *1-min. recoveries between intervals*

Begin 80 watts below your FTPw (based on your most recent test). Increase
power by 10 watts with each interval. Continue until you reach your LTHR.

If there is no race available and you simply can't get motivated to do a 30-minute, solo time trial, there is another option, but you have to know your LTHR. I call it an FTPw confirmation test. It's basically a graded exercise test that consists of several 4-minute work stages separated by 1-minute recoveries. The first work stage begins at a power about 80 watts below what you believe your FTPw is based on previous testing. With each subsequent work stage, increase your power by 10 watts. This continues until your LTHR is observed. The average power for this last stage should be close to your FTPw.

RUN FIELD TEST

Your run heart rates probably will not have changed since you were last tested, as heart rate remains fairly stable even when fitness improves. What may well have changed, however, is your functional threshold pace (FTPa). If your FTPa has changed and your FTPw has not, that's a good thing. It means you've gotten faster while your heart rate has remained the same. Heart rate reflects effort, so think of it this way: You are running faster while making the same effort, and that is exactly what we want to happen.

If you are still not sure of your heart rate zones, recheck your LTHR with a 30-minute test similar to the 30-minute bike test (see Chapter 4). But if there is no doubt about your LTHR, repeat the aerobic time trial that you did earlier in the Base block (see Chapter 5). Compare your time with what it was at the end of Base 1 or Base 2. If it's been about eight weeks since your first test, you should see an improvement in your time.

LAB OR CLINIC TEST

If you did a VO$_2$max test earlier in the season, now is a good time to repeat it. It's important that you use the same testing facility as well as the same piece of testing equipment and the same technician, if possible, to eliminate some of the variables inherent with such testing. Otherwise you may not get meaningful results. Discuss the protocol in advance with the technician to make sure it is the same as that of your original test, and use the same running shoes, bike, and treadmill. In keeping with the theme of eliminating unusual variables, make sure you are rested as well. The best time to do this test is near the end of the rest-and-test week at the end of Base 3, as shown in the tables at the end of this chapter.

After the test, ask the technician to point out significant changes that have occurred since the previous test. What you want to know is whether the trend of your numbers is appropriate after several weeks of basic-ability training. There are several things I look for in such a follow-up test. The first is a lower respiratory equivalency ratio (RER) at any given intensity, which shows that aerobic endurance has improved and that fat burning is prevalent. Another is an improvement in bike power or run pace, especially at lactate threshold (your technician may refer to this as "anaerobic threshold"). A longer time to failure on a graded exercise test is another indicator that general fitness has improved. I would also like to see an increase in aerobic capacity (VO$_2$max), showing that aerobic fitness is progressing as it should.

Your Base 3 Training Plan

The tables that follow are your training plans for Base 3. As with previous chapters, they are organized by the distance of your A-priority race. Follow the plan that is appropriate to your goal event.

There are two workout categories not found in the plans for the previous blocks: aerobic endurance combined with force (AE + Fo), and muscular endurance combined with force (ME + Fo). These and all of the other workouts are described earlier in this chapter.

One of these, AE + Fo, warrants further explanation. On weekends, you should alternate the AE + Fo workouts for the bike and the run. For example, on one weekend you will do an AE + Fo run on Saturday and an AE bike ride on Sunday. The next weekend, you will reverse these by doing an AE run on Saturday and an AE + Fo bike ride on Sunday.

TRAINING PLAN — BASE 3

SPRINT-DISTANCE TRAINING **BASE 3**

T R A I N I N G   W E E K S

SPORT	SWIM	BIKE	RUN	STRENGTH	DAILY VOLUME
MON	*Rec* 0:15–0:30			SM 0:45	0:45–1:15
TUES	SS + AE 0:30–0:45	*SS* or *Rec* 0:45–1:00	ME or ME + Fo 0:45–1:00		1:15–2:45
WED		ME or ME + Fo 1:00–1:30	SS 0:30–0:45		1:00–2:15
THURS	SS + Fo + ME 0:30–0:45		SS 0:45–1:00		1:15–1:45
FRI	*Rec* 0:15–0:30	SS 1:00–1:30		SM 0:45	1:00–2:45
SAT	SS + ME + AE 0:45–1:00	*Rec* 0:30–0:45	AE or AE + Fo 1:00–1:45		1:45–3:30
SUN		AE or AE + Fo 1:30–2:30	AE 0:15		1:45–2:45
VOLUME BY SPORT	1:45–3:30	3:30–7:15	2:45–4:45	0:45–1:30	8:45–17:00
WORKOUTS	**3–5**	**3–5**	**4–5**	**1–2**	**11–17**

R E S T   &   T E S T   W E E K

SPORT	SWIM	BIKE	RUN	STRENGTH	DAILY VOLUME
MON				SM 0:45	0:45
TUES	SS 0:15–0:30		SS 0:30–0:45		0:45–1:15
WED		SS 0:45–1:00			0:45–1:00
THURS	Te 0:30–0:45		SS 0:30–0:45		1:00–1:30
FRI		Te 1:00			1:00
SAT	SS 0:15–0:30		Te 0:45–1:15		1:00–1:45
SUN		AE 1:30–2:30	AE 0:15		1:45–2:45
VOLUME BY SPORT	1:00–1:45	3:15–4:30	2:00–3:00	0:45	7:00–10:00
WORKOUTS	**3**	**3**	**4**	**1**	**11**

Notes: Rec = Recovery. Optional workouts are in italic. The AE runs on Sunday are intended to follow the bike ride. Detail on the workouts can be found in the chapter. Strength workouts appear in Appendix C.

02
OLYMPIC

OLYMPIC-DISTANCE TRAINING **BASE 3**

T R A I N I N G   W E E K S

SPORT	SWIM	BIKE	RUN	STRENGTH	DAILY VOLUME
MON	*Rec 0:15–0:30*			SM 0:45	0:45–1:15
TUES	**SS + AE** 0:45–1:00	*SS or Rec 0:45–1:00*	**ME** or **ME + Fo** 0:45–1:00		1:30–3:00
WED		**ME** or **ME + Fo** 1:00–1:30	*SS 0:30–0:45*		1:00–2:15
THURS	**SS + Fo + ME** 0:45–1:00		**SS** 0:45–1:00		1:30–2:00
FRI	*Rec 0:15–0:30*	**SS** 1:00–1:30		*SM 0:45*	1:00–2:45
SAT	**SS + ME + AE** 0:45–1:00	*Rec 0:45–1:00*	**AE** or **AE + Fo** 1:30–2:00		2:15–4:00
SUN		**AE** or **AE + Fo** 2:00–3:00	**AE** 0:15		2:15–3:15
VOLUME BY SPORT	2:15–4:00	4:00–8:00	3:15–5:00	0:45–1:30	10:15–18:30
WORKOUTS	**3–5**	**3–5**	**4–5**	**1–2**	**11–17**

R E S T   &   T E S T   W E E K

SPORT	SWIM	BIKE	RUN	STRENGTH	DAILY VOLUME
MON				SM 0:45	0:45
TUES	**SS** 0:30–0:45		**SS** 0:30–0:45		1:00–1:30
WED		**SS** 0:45–1:00			0:45–1:00
THURS	**Te** 0:30–0:45		**SS** 0:30–0:45		1:00–1:30
FRI		**Te** 1:00			1:00
SAT	**SS** 0:30–0:45		**Te** 1:15–1:30		1:45–2:15
SUN		**AE** or **AE + Fo** 2:00–3:00	**AE** 0:15		2:15–3:15
VOLUME BY SPORT	1:30–2:15	3:45–5:00	2:30–3:15	0:45	8:30–11:15
WORKOUTS	**3**	**3**	**4**	**1**	**11**

Notes: Rec = Recovery. Optional workouts are in italic. The AE runs on Sunday are intended to follow the bike ride. Detail on the workouts can be found in the chapter. Strength workouts appear in Appendix C.

TRAINING PLAN — BASE 3

HALF-IRONMAN-DISTANCE TRAINING **BASE 3**

T R A I N I N G   W E E K S

SPORT	SWIM	BIKE	RUN	STRENGTH	DAILY VOLUME
MON	*Rec* 0:30–0:40			SM 0:45	0:45–1:25
TUES	SS + AE 0:45–1:00	*SS* or *Rec* 1:00–1:30	ME or ME + Fo 1:00–1:15		1:45–3:45
WED		ME or ME + Fo 1:30–2:00	SS 0:45–1:00		1:30–3:00
THURS	SS + Fo + ME 0:45–1:00		SS 1:00–1:15		1:45–2:15
FRI	*Rec* 0:30–0:40	SS 1:00–1:30		SM 0:45	1:00–2:55
SAT	SS + ME + AE 1:00–1:15	*Rec* 1:00–1:30	AE or AE + Fo 2:00–2:30		3:00–5:15
SUN		AE or AE + Fo 3:00–4:00	AE 0:15		3:15–4:15
VOLUME BY SPORT	2:30–4:35	5:30–10:30	4:15–6:15	0:45–1:30	13:00–22:50
WORKOUTS	3–5	3–5	4–5	1–2	11–17

R E S T   &   T E S T   W E E K

SPORT	SWIM	BIKE	RUN	STRENGTH	DAILY VOLUME
MON				SM 0:45	0:45
TUES	SS 0:30–0:45		SS 0:30–0:45		1:00–1:30
WED		SS 0:45–1:00			0:45–1:00
THURS	Te 0:30–0:45		SS 0:30–0:45		1:00–1:30
FRI		Te 1:00			1:00
SAT	SS + ME 0:30–0:45		Te 1:30–2:00		2:00–2:45
SUN		AE or AE + Fo 3:00–4:00	AE 0:15		3:15–4:15
VOLUME BY SPORT	1:30–2:15	4:45–6:00	2:45–3:45	0:45	9:45–12:45
WORKOUTS	3	3	4	1	11

Notes: Rec = Recovery. Optional workouts are in italic. The AE runs on Sunday are intended to follow the bike ride. Detail on the workouts can be found in the chapter. Strength workouts appear in Appendix C.

IRONMAN-DISTANCE TRAINING BASE 3

T R A I N I N G   W E E K S

SPORT	SWIM	BIKE	RUN	STRENGTH	DAILY VOLUME
MON	*Rec 0:30–0:40*			SM 0:45	0:45–1:25
TUES	SS + AE 0:45–1:00	*SS or Rec 1:00–1:30*	ME or ME + Fo 1:00–1:15		1:45–3:45
WED		ME or ME + Fo 1:30–2:00	*SS 0:45–1:00*		1:30–3:00
THURS	SS + Fo + ME 0:45–1:00		SS 1:00–1:15		1:45–2:15
FRI	*Rec 0:30–0:40*	SS 1:00–1:30		*SM 0:45*	1:00–2:55
SAT	SS + ME + AE 1:15–1:30	*Rec 1:00–1:30*	AE 2:30–3:00 or AE + Fo 1:30–2:00		2:45–6:00
SUN		AE 5:00–6:00 or AE + Fo 3:00–4:00	AE 0:15		3:15–6:15
VOLUME BY SPORT	2:45–4:50	5:30–12:30	3:45–6:45	0:45–1:30	12:45–25:35
WORKOUTS	**3–5**	**3–5**	**4–5**	**1–2**	**11–17**

R E S T   &   T E S T   W E E K

SPORT	SWIM	BIKE	RUN	STRENGTH	DAILY VOLUME
MON				SM 0:45	0:45
TUES	SS 0:30–0:45		SS 0:30–0:45		1:00–1:30
WED		SS 0:45–1:00			0:45–1:00
THURS	Te 0:30–0:45		SS 0:30–0:45		1:00–1:30
FRI		Te 1:00			1:00
SAT	SS 0:30–0:45		Te + AE 1:30–2:00		2:00–2:45
SUN		AE 5:00–6:00	AE 0:15		5:15–6:15
VOLUME BY SPORT	1:30–2:15	6:45–8:00	2:45–3:45	0:45	11:45–14:45
WORKOUTS	**3**	**3**	**4**	**1**	**11**

Notes: Rec = Recovery. Optional workouts are in italic. The AE runs on Sunday are intended to follow the bike ride. Detail on the workouts can be found in the chapter. Strength workouts appear in Appendix C.

Part III

BUILD 1 AND BUILD 2

Research and experience tell me that the most critical time for your training begins 12 weeks prior to your A-priority race and continues until there are only 3 weeks to go. This is the Build period. How your training goes now will have more influence on your race performance than what is done at any other time in the season.

Build 1 and Build 2 are when you must do the "real" training. These will be your hardest workouts of the entire year. This is not to say that what you did in the Base period was unimportant. In fact, it was the workouts you did then that got you ready for the Build period. Without them, you would not be able to train nearly as well now as you will find you can. In the Base period you were, in effect, training to train. In the Build period you are really training, and your fitness will bloom.

This is the period that serious athletes like the most. They are finally doing what they thrive on—hard workouts. And because of this enthusiasm, it is also the most dangerous time in the season. Some time in Build you may begin to feel "bullet-proof," as if you could do anything you wanted in training and accelerate the development of fitness. Resist the temptation to leap tall buildings. When you find yourself feeling strong in workouts and going faster than you ever have in training races, you are one mistake from disaster.

At some point in the next few weeks you may well have to restrain your desire to do more—more workouts, more intensity, and more duration. Setbacks in training are more likely to occur now than at any other time. If you become injured, sick, or overtrained with just a few weeks remaining until your race, it will be devastating for your season. You'll be unable to train, fitness will be lost, and there will not be enough time remaining to get ready.

Don't ad lib. Be patient. We're almost there. Follow the plans laid out for you in the next two chapters. If you do, you will have the best triathlon you have ever experienced.

Build 1

8

AS YOU START BUILD 1 you will have 11 or 12 weeks remaining until your A-priority race. Older athletes and those who find they generally recover slowly are advised to start this block 12 weeks before race day. These athletes will do a 3-week Build 1 and a pair of 3-week Build 2s. That adds up to 9 weeks, and they will go on to spend 2 weeks in the Peak period (covered in Chapter 10) and 1 week in the Race block (covered in Chapter 11). For younger athletes and those who recover quickly, Build 1 and Build 2 will each be 4 weeks long, for a total of 8 weeks in Build, and this will also be followed by 2 in Peak and 1 for race week, so they are now 11 weeks from the race.

There is a lot to be accomplished in the next few weeks. The training will be challenging. Some of the workouts will be difficult because they are both long in duration and high in intensity. Others will be difficult because they require you to go easy when you may still be eager to work hard. But balancing hard and easy workouts is the key to success in the Build period. The harder the hard workouts are, the easier the easy ones should be. For many athletes, going easy is more difficult than going all-out. I can tell you from experience that as soon as you start making your easy workouts slightly harder than they should be, you are starting down the path to poor race performance. This issue is critical now, and I'll cover it in more detail in this chapter.

Objectives for Build 1

1. **Make workouts more like the race.** Making your workouts more racelike is the primary objective of Build 1. In Chapter 3 I explained the first rule of periodization: You must make your workouts increasingly like your A-priority race the closer you get to the race. That shift in focus should become quite apparent in Build 1. The shift actually started late in the Base period, but it will be more obvious now. You will now find a great deal of similarity between your hard workouts and what the race will be like. You will spend more time at race intensity, and the workout durations will mimic that of your race. Of course, a workout is never exactly the same as a race. The race is always harder. But now we want to begin approaching that same level of stress.

2. **Continue building muscular endurance.** The ability most closely tied to high performance in triathlon is muscular endurance. You started working on this ability in Base 2. The past several weeks of training should pay off now as your workouts become more difficult, with a greater emphasis on intervals at race effort or even slightly harder.

3. **Recover quickly between key workouts.** How fit you are on race day depends a great deal on how hard you make the hard workouts in the Build period. And, strangely enough, that depends on how easy you make the easy days. If you make the easy days too difficult at this point in your training, even by just a little bit, it will detract from your capacity for really challenging sessions when it truly counts on the hard training days. So workouts are either easy or hard in Build 1—never in between.

4. **Rehearse race strategies.** Although you may have done a race or two already, in the Build period you should definitely test yourself. Racing is the best way to do this. A race offers the opportunity to work on pacing and nutrition strategies while getting back into the mindset of competition. In the Build 1 block do at least one race. Races of the same distance as your A-priority race or slightly shorter would be ideal. One or two races in Build 1 and again in Build 2 are about right (but I'll provide more detailed guidelines later in this chapter). The exception is when training for an Ironman. I recommend doing no more than one race for the entire Build period in this case. Sprint-distance athletes can race frequently. Racing is discussed in greater detail throughout this chapter.

5. **Maintain basic abilities.** In the Base period you invested a lot of training time and energy into building your aerobic endurance, force, and speed skills. Now all you need to do is maintain them. The beauty of the human body is that it takes less energy and effort to maintain a given level of fitness than it does to build up to that level in the first place. A little bit of each type of training done regularly, but less frequently than before, will do the trick.

Coaching Tips for Build 1

In Build 1, training becomes more focused on your A-priority race than it was in the Base period. Your purpose in Base training was to create enough general fitness to be ready for the Build period. Now that we're finally there, the real fun begins. The training you will be doing in the coming weeks is more challenging than in previous blocks, with an emphasis on race fitness. You may even be doing your first races of the season. All of this raises several matters that I generally talk about with the athletes I coach.

MINDSET

The greatest shift in thinking now has to do with the time you have remaining until the goal race. With only 11 or 12 weeks left until race day, you really can't afford to be careless with your training time. Every workout must have a purpose, and that purpose must be closely related to your performance on race day. You will need to stay focused.

In addition, it may have been several months since you last raced, so now is a good time to get your head wrapped around the psychological stresses of racing again. Running one or more races can help you do this. Racing can be very disconcerting and requires a special mindset. It is nothing like going for a hard workout, even if you work out with training partners sometimes.

Realize that all of the emotional stress you experience in the last few days and final hours before the race is entirely in your head. The race itself is not emotionally demanding; only the physical aspects of racing are "real." Any mental stress you experience racing now represents a lack of self-confidence. It's better to experience it now, in minor races, than right before the most important race of your season. The way to resolve this confidence quandary is to practice becoming more confident. Practice races are a great time to do this. This topic was discussed in the "Mindset" section of Chapter 5, so go back and reread the sections about how you can relive successes, "act as if . . ." and quiet "self 1" in that chapter if you experience undue stress before races during Build 1. There is still time to train yourself in this area before the A-priority race.

Preparing for a race also involves planning and logistics. Doing this kind of planning now for less important races will help to make them fresh in your mind once again. It's better to find out at a B-priority race in Build 1 that a certain food just doesn't work for you on race morning, or that arriving at the race check-in late really adds to your stress, than to find out at your A-priority race in a few weeks. If you don't already have one, create an equipment checklist. Also make an activities timeline that you can use in future races. Refine it with each race you do between now and the A-priority race.

TRAINING SETBACKS

Illness and injury now have huge consequences for your race performance. If some niggling injury came along in the Base period, you could rest and not feel too much pressure. But now you no longer have time on your side. Setbacks, even small ones, can be expensive in terms of fitness, and lost training time will mean a lesser performance on race day.

You must avoid these setbacks by taking good care of yourself. This includes never training through a tender muscle or tendon, and it includes avoiding situations that are likely to expose you to illness. Public places such as airports bring you into contact with sick people and the things they have handled. When in such places, you can minimize the risk by keeping your left hand in your pocket and coming into contact with the world only with your right hand. Then only use your left hand when you need to touch your face or your food. Also, wash your hands frequently when you've been around lots of people in a public place such as an airport.

Now let's get back to injuries. At the first sign of something wrong with a muscle or tendon, you must back off of your training and seek medical assistance. It's not unusual for athletes to decide they can "train through" something that doesn't feel right. This is nearly always a mistake. Injuries are best dealt with sooner rather than later. The earlier you rest the tender area or begin treatment, the less training time you will lose in the long run. Take care of the problem immediately.

But what if, despite following all these guidelines, you are forced to stop training in one of the three sports while an injury heals? My advice is to simply do what you can do while you wait, maintaining safety first and foremost. For example, if the injury just affects running, it could be a great opportunity for you to become a stronger cyclist and swimmer.

Consult your doctor to make sure you understand what you can safely do at this time and what you must avoid doing. Other options for an injured runner, for example, may include stair-climbing machines, elliptical trainers, and water running. You would shift some of your former run-training time to the bike and swim, while adding in a bit of these other options just to maintain the running posture and general movement skills. Finally, to stave off injuries before they start, be very selective about the races you do in Build 1.

In this block you can race too much. The more important your A-priority race is, the less racing you should do. I'd recommend no more than one race in Build 1. If you are doing an Ironman in a few weeks, then this would be the time for your one and only practice race—preferably a half-Ironman. The exception to this limited-racing rule is that sprint-distance triathletes can race several times at the sprint distance in the Build period. In this case, the races are short enough that recovery time is less of an issue. This issue is discussed further under "Build 1 Testing" later in this chapter.

COMMON CONCERNS OF BUILD 1

At first you may be skeptical of some of the advice I'll be giving you below for the Build period. A little skepticism is healthy, but rest assured that my advice here is based on solid scientific data. I will not be discussing all of the research because I am not aiming to write a technical treatise. If you are interested in knowing more, I'd highly recommend that you do more research on your own, but make sure you search out research-driven books and online scientific discussions rather than company marketing materials or unsupported opinions.

Here we go with some challenging new ways of seeing some old topics.

Hydration

If this is your first Build 1 of the season, it's probably late winter or spring. The daily temperature is rising as the weather improves, and that usually triggers concern in athletes regarding their hydration levels—even, I'd say, too much concern. I'm not sure why, but in the past 20 years American and European runners and triathletes have come to believe that their greatest challenge in racing, especially when doing long

FURTHER READING FOR BUILD 1

Good sources of information to help with Build 1 include the Web sites Sportsci.org and Sportsscientists.com, as well as these books: *Brain Training for Runners* by Matt Fitzgerald, *Daniels' Running Formula* by Dr. Jack Daniels, *Going Long* by Joe Friel and Gordon Byrn, *Lore of Running* by Dr. Timothy Noakes, *The Paleo Diet for Athletes* by Dr. Loren Cordain and Joe Friel, *Racing Weight* by Matt Fitzgerald, and *The Runner's Body* by Drs. Ross Tucker and Jonathan Dugas.

races like the half-Ironman and Ironman, is avoiding dehydration. Perhaps it's the proliferation of sports drinks on the market and the marketing tactics used by the companies behind them. There has been heavy promotion of drinking during exercise as the way to high performance. In the 1990s the American College of Sports Medicine pretty much said the same thing as the drink manufacturers. To their credit, ACSM has softened its position on this topic in the past few years. Not so the sports drink companies.

Since the 1980s several myths associated with hydration have become commonly accepted as "wisdom." One is the claim that a 2 percent drop in body weight, ostensibly as a result of excessive dehydration, causes a significant loss of performance. Yet study after study has found that the most dehydrated athletes in any long endurance event were the top finishers. Elite marathon runners typically lose around 5 percent of their body weight when running world-class times. They certainly haven't suffered a loss of performance. Other research has shown that there is no difference in body-weight changes between those who struggle to finish and report to the medical tent in long events and those who finish strongly. Losing some weight is common in long events and does not present a problem to the body. Your bathroom scales do not tell you how much water you need. Thirst does.

Here's another myth: that by the time you become thirsty it is "too late." I have always assumed that meant too late to rehydrate—in other words, if you're in a race, you might as well stop if you suddenly realize you're thirsty. The sports drink companies tell us to drink, drink, and then drink some more because you can't trust thirst (if you see no conflict of interest in such product promotion, then I have a seafront property in Arizona you may be interested in buying!). Actually, thirst works quite well, and that fact has been supported by several studies. If it didn't work, our species would have never made it this far, since a great loss of body water results in death. You can certainly trust your thirst to tell you when it's time to drink. The only question, really, is if you are paying attention.

That's one of the purposes of training—to learn to pay attention. You need to know what to do in a race under a variety of circumstances, and circumstances include whether you are thirsty and just how thirsty and when. Drink when you are thirsty, and drink until your thirst is satisfied. If you aren't thirsty, then don't drink. That will prevent perhaps the worst thing that could happen to you in a long race—hyponatremia.

Hyponatremia is a condition marked by a low concentration of sodium in the body, and it's usually brought on by drinking too much. It doesn't matter what you drink too much of. It could be water or even a sports drink containing sodium. Sports drinks are always hypotonic. That means they have a lower sodium concentration than that of your body fluids. Drinking anything will only dilute your sodium levels, making hyponatremia all the more likely. The problem with hyponatremia is not only that it can result in a drop in performance, but that it's dangerous. In the past several years four documented deaths in marathons have been attributed to hyponatremia. One of the victims, at the 2002 Boston Marathon, drank large amounts of a sports drink at aid stations. But it doesn't matter what you drink: Hyponatremia is possible anytime you drink based on a regimented schedule instead of based on thirst. Your body is good at sorting things out and will prevent you from drinking too much or not enough—if you'll listen.

Muscle Cramping

Build 1 is the time of year when you are most likely to experience muscle cramps, as you are doing your first races of the season. No one understands why muscles cramp. Popular theories—that they're caused by dehydration, heat, or electrolyte losses, especially sodium loss—are all pure conjecture based on very old and poorly conducted research starting around 1900. Despite many studies since then, scientists have never been able to pinpoint the cause. But they've never been able to make a muscle cramp up in the lab by restricting fluids, creating a hot environment, or removing any electrolytes from the subjects' bodies. Nor have they found any significant differences in the diets or race-day nutrient intakes of athletes who have and have not cramped in marathon races and Ironman triathlons. Regardless of what you read in the marketing materials of many sports nutritional products, cramping is a great mystery.

Be wary of anyone trying to sell you a product that is guaranteed to stop cramps. That includes sport drinks loaded with sodium and other stuff. Our beliefs in this area are largely the result of excellent marketing—not science. This massive amount of misinformation about muscle cramps has been enhanced by athletic mythology that flies in the face of physiological reality.

For example, most athletes think they must replace their electrolytes after exercising to prevent muscle cramping. The truth is that when you exercise, the concentration of electrolytes in your body fluids increases—it doesn't decrease. You lose far more water through sweat than you do sodium, potassium, magnesium, and other electrolytes. Imagine a pot of water with some salt sprinkled into it. Heat the water and what happens to the concentration of salt? It increases, because far more water than sodium is lost in the form of steam. The same thing happens with your body, even if you are a "heavy salt sweater," whatever that is. The body operates on its concentration of electrolytes, not on the total amount present.

There are other theories on what causes cramps. The latest one, which appears to be gaining a following among exercise physiologists, has to do with fatigue and the nervous system. In your muscles and tendons there are safety devices called "muscle spindles" and "Golgi tendon devices." They regulate muscle tension when the muscle is stretched or loaded with an overly heavy weight, and they protect the muscle and its associated tendons from damage in certain conditions. This new theory suggests that localized muscular fatigue causes some confusion in the signals from the nervous system. The muscle spindles and Golgi tendon devices do what they think they're supposed to do when receiving a certain signal—they contract the muscle and refuse to relax. That's the cramp happening. If this is true, then to stop the cramp an athlete would need to stretch the cramping muscle. The theory is that the stretch sends the opposite signal to these protective devices and the muscle relaxes.

My experience seems to support the basic idea that fatigue is related to cramps. In the spring, when athletes are just starting to race again following a winter of base training, I get several emails asking what can be done to prevent or deal with muscle cramping during a race. I seldom get this question in the late summer, and I think the reason is that athletes are simply not as fit for the intensity and duration of races early in the year, so fatigue is more prevalent. By late summer they have raced several times and are more race-fit.

There are no studies to back up this particular theory for now. But South African exercise physiologists Ross Tucker and Jonathan Dugas suggest a few steps to prevent cramping, and in my experience they seem to work. The first is to pace the race correctly based on your known level of fitness and race readiness. Starting a race too fast will cause fatigue later in the race and could lead to cramping. (See Chapter 7 for more on pacing.) Second, they believe that a regular stretching program and weight training may help. Perhaps most important of all, they recommend that those who have problems with cramping do workouts that stress the muscles they seem to be having problems with. This may mean running high-intensity hill reps if your calf muscle tends to cramp, or hard bike intervals to fortify the hamstrings.

Stretching

We've been told that stretching may help to prevent injuries, especially in running. We've also been told that stretching will improve running performance. So for the past 25 years or so runners and triathletes have been stretching religiously.

But although stretching may prevent injury if you have tight hips or ankles, there has never been much in the way of research to support the position that it improves performance, and now there is even research supporting the opposite point of view. A few studies have shown that runners who have a great deal of flexibility in their lower legs are less economical than runners who have tight lower-leg muscles.

You'll recall from Chapter 2 that economy has to do with how much oxygen, and therefore energy, it takes to run at a given submaximal pace. Runners with tight lower-leg muscles seem to be more economical in terms of energy return. It's like the difference between a tight spring and a loose one. The tight one will recoil with greater force when compressed. If you run with a brief foot-ground contact time, as you should, the stored energy will provide some of the power necessary to drive you forward while running, just as the tight spring would do.

Could you cause an injury by not stretching the lower legs? There is no research that addresses that question, so for now I would say that the answer could be yes. If you have a tendency to get Achilles' heel, plantar fascia, or calf injuries, then I'd suggest that you do some stretching of the lower legs. This is another time when moderation is probably a wise choice. Don't overdo the stretching. A little is probably better than a lot.

Recovery

One of the more common problems I hear of from athletes in the Build period is poor recovery. This shows up as the inability to maintain the training workload in this block. Throughout the Build period you will be flirting with overtraining. In fact, your training should be stressful enough that, if you didn't allow for recovery every third or fourth week, you would be likely to experience overtraining. You would have an overwhelming sense of fatigue and find it difficult to get out of bed in the morning, let alone swim, bike, or run.

As you may notice in the plans that follow, the volume of training drops off slightly in Build 1 compared to Base 3. This is primarily due to a small decrease in workout durations, especially if you are training for a sprint- or Olympic-distance triathlon. (Ironman-distance volume stays about the same). However, as the volume drops off, the intensity of training rises. Sometimes the failure of an athlete to recover well during this block has to do with trying to maintain the same volume as in Base 3 while also increasing the intensity. That's a huge mistake. It's simply too much stress to manage if you are training at near your physiological limit. The only reason an Ironman-distance athlete can maintain volume is that the intensity of training is not all that great.

Race Distance	Duration
Sprint and Olympic	30–45 min.
Half-Ironman and Ironman	1 hr.–1 hr. 15 min.

Strides should be run on a slight downhill, preferably barefoot on a clean grassy surface.

Warm-up	10–20 min. gradually increasing effort and pace
SS set	6–8 × 30 strides, fast but not all-out
	Count 30 foot strikes on the right leg.
	90-sec. walk recoveries
Cooldown	10–45 min. easy running, zone 1

FORCE WORKOUTS

Swim Force Workouts

Interval: 25 m with drag, 50 m for strong swimmers
Intensity: Hard
Recover as needed
Duration: Frequency over volume

The swim force sets are the same in this training block as they are in the Base 3 period (see p. 153). For these force workouts, you will do short, high-effort repetitions using drag devices such as paddles or while wearing a T-shirt, with long recoveries following each repetition.

Bike and Run Force Workouts

For the bike workouts, force training may be combined with anaerobic endurance (An + Fo) for sprint- and Olympic-distance triathletes. This takes the form of hill intervals. Half-Ironman and Ironman-distance racers may do bike muscular endurance and force intervals (ME + Fo) on hilly courses. At this point we will omit force workouts for running because of the increased risk of injury as the run sessions become more challenging.

No matter what distance you are training for, you may also do your weekend muscular endurance rides and runs on hilly courses if

Interval: 3 min. hills
Intensity: Hard, RPE 9
Recover 3–5 min.
Duration: 3–5 sets

your A-priority race is hilly. These workouts are discussed in greater detail in the following sections. But be careful of doing too much hill training. The possible downsides are knee problems on the bike; calf, Achilles' tendon, and foot problems when running; and perhaps even the overdevelopment of the major mover muscles in either sport.

MUSCULAR ENDURANCE WORKOUTS

For each sport, muscular endurance training changes in Build 1. The intensity and duration of the harder efforts in these workouts begins to shift toward being more racelike.

Swim Muscular Endurance

By now your swim skills should be greatly improved compared to where you started in Prep. Working on these skills may still be an ongoing project, however. Your ME training depends on the progress you've made thus far. If you are comfortably swimming 100 meters in less than 1 minute and 50 seconds, then follow the instructions

for ME sets provided below. If you are not yet at that point, keep the focus on speed skills. Shorten the ME sets described below, replacing most of these intervals with more of the SS training explained in previous chapters. If your time for the 100 meters is between 1:20 and 1:50, you can start to do a bit more of the ME work while continuing the SS drills.

If you are ready for more muscular endurance work, it will do a lot to

Interval: 5 min.
Intensity: Hard, RPE 7 or 8
20-sec. recoveries
Duration: 3–4 sets

Pace/100 m	Distance/Interval
1:45	250–300 m
1:30	300–400 m
1:20	400–500 m

improve your race swim performance, but never allow your form to break down in order to go faster. Midrange swimmers (those doing the 100 meters anywhere from 1:20 to 1:50) are the most likely to push so hard in the water that they waste energy. They build a bubbly froth around themselves while not really going any faster than if they simply backed off of the effort and swam more smoothly. Again, never sacrifice technique for speed.

When you are working on muscular endurance for swimming, the work intervals need to be fairly long—about 5 minutes each. See the workout chart to estimate your total distance according to your pace per 100 meters. Regardless of your race distance, do three or four such intervals within an ME set. The rate of perceived exertion should be a 7 or 8 on a 10-point scale. This level of exertion should feel "hard." See Appendix B for what this means in terms of pacing. Recover for about 20 seconds after each work interval.

The Saturday An + ME + SS (for sprint and Olympic distance) and ME + AE + SS (for half-Ironman and Ironman distances) swim sets are done as shown below. The optional Tuesday ME set is described under the "Swim Anaerobic Endurance" section later in this chapter.

Duration: 45–60 min.

Warm-up	4–6 × 50 m, with descending times (faster for each subsequent 50)
An set	3 × 100–300 m at pace zone 5b (see Appendix B for zones)
	40- to 60-sec. recoveries
	[Optional: Replace the An set with 10 × 25 m and include personal limiter drills with long recoveries.]
ME set	3 × 250–500 m at zone 4–5a pace
	20-sec. recoveries
SS set	10 × 25 m, fast, with focus on technique
	Long recoveries
Cooldown	200 m, easy swim, focusing on technique

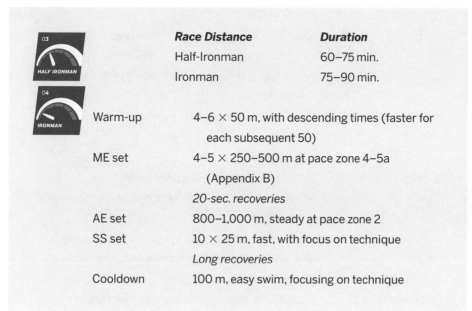

	Race Distance	Duration
	Half-Ironman	60–75 min.
	Ironman	75–90 min.
Warm-up	4–6 × 50 m, with descending times (faster for each subsequent 50)	
ME set	4–5 × 250–500 m at pace zone 4–5a (Appendix B)	
	20-sec. recoveries	
AE set	800–1,000 m, steady at pace zone 2	
SS set	10 × 25 m, fast, with focus on technique	
	Long recoveries	
Cooldown	100 m, easy swim, focusing on technique	

On Tuesdays, half-Ironman and Ironman athletes will do an SS + ME + AE swim workout as follows. The Tuesday swim for sprint- and Olympic-distance triathletes is described in the "Swim Anaerobic Endurance" section later in this chapter.

Duration: 45–60 min.

Warm-up/SS set	6 × 50 m, with descending times (faster for each subsequent 50)
ME set	3–4 × 250–500 m at pace zone 4–5a (Appendix B)
	20-sec. recoveries
AE set/ cooldown	10–20 min., steady at pace zone 2

On Thursday athletes for all distances will do the following:

Race Distance	Duration
Sprint	30–45 min.
Olympic, half-Ironman, and Ironman	45–60 min.

Warm-up/SS set	10 × 25 m, with technique focus and/or personal-limiter drills
	Long recoveries
Fo set	4 × 25 m, with paddles or drag device
	Start each 25 with a 6-stroke sprint, and finish each at ME effort.
	30-sec. recoveries
ME set	3–4 × 250–500 m at pace zone 4–5a (Appendix B)
	20-sec. recoveries
Cooldown	100–300 m, easy swim, focusing on technique

Bike Muscular Endurance

Bike training for ME is best done on the road but may be done on an indoor trainer if the weather conditions do not permit for outdoor riding. The road is better because this type of workout should help you learn how to be aerodynamic and to pace yourself properly when the terrain or wind changes.

Most triathletes (all except for Ironman-distance hopefuls) will now have two ME workouts on the bike each training week. One is on Sundays, and the other is scheduled for Wednesdays. Let's start with the Wednesday workout.

Half-Ironman and Ironman athletes are scheduled for an ME + Fo workout on Wednesdays, whereas sprint- and Olympic-distance athletes have these as optional workouts (the An + Fo workout, discussed in the following section, is the other option).To decide which workout to do, look at your average race speed on relatively flat courses. If your race times are long enough, anaerobic endurance training will have little benefit, whereas muscular endurance training will pay off handsomely. If your bike average race speed on relatively flat courses is typically slower than 21 miles per hour (34 kph) for a sprint-distance race or 18 miles per hour (29 kph) for an Olympic-distance race, then I'd recommend doing the ME + Fo workout.

The Wednesday ME + Fo bike workouts are intervals done as repeats on a low-to moderate-grade hill (a 3 to 5 percent grade). That's a rise of 150 to 250 feet over a mile. The perfect hill for this workout takes 6 to 8 minutes to climb. Yours may well be shorter. If so, start each interval on a flat section approaching the hill, using a slightly higher-than-normal gear so your cadence is less than 80 rpm, and finish each interval on the hill. If you don't have hills where you live, do these intervals on a flat stretch of road into a strong headwind, using a slightly higher-than-normal gear. If you are doing the intervals on an indoor trainer due to bad weather, it's best if you have a trainer that allows you to simulate hills.

Do each interval in the aero position while staying focused on maintaining a heart rate or power output in zone 4. Avoid zone 5. Power is preferable as a metric for this workout because it eliminates the guesswork that occurs in the early part of interval training when heart rate is climbing but hasn't yet reached the target zone. The recovery after each interval is the descent time for the hill, which should be as short as possible. If you are doing these on flat terrain or a trainer, recover for 2 to 3 minutes with easy riding. Get 30 to 40 minutes of combined work-interval time in a single session.

The following is an example of the Wednesday ME + Fo bike workouts for all race distances. For the sprint and Olympic distances, this is the optional workout to replace the scheduled An + Fo bike session.

Warm-up	10–30 min. of increasing effort and gearing
ME + Fo set	4–6 × 6- to 8-min. hill repeats, HR or power zone 4
	Ride hills at less than 80 rpm in aero position.
	Recover on the descents
Cooldown	10–30 min., spinning with decreasing effort

Now let's take a look at the Sunday ME + AE bike workouts. Note that only sprint-, Olympic-, and half-Ironman-distance athletes will do these. Ironman triathletes do AE bike workouts on Sundays in this block.

The Sunday intervals are now longer than in Base 3, but the intensity remains the same. They are now 8 to 20 minutes long, depending on your event, and done at heart rate zones 3 to 5a or power zones 3 to 5, depending on your race distance. The recovery after each is about one-quarter as long as the preceding work interval. The total combined work-interval time is 20 to 100 minutes, depending on your race distance.

The work intervals may be done on hills if the race you are training for is hilly. If possible, simulate the hills in terms of their length and grade on the racecourse. Your cadence should be the same as the cadence you will use in the race. It's a common mistake to rely on force instead of increasing cadence. In most cases your cadence should be above 80 rpm, but the exact cadence that is best will of course depend on the specifics of the race. Typically, for fast triathletes, the shorter the race is, the higher the cadence.

On Sundays, ME intervals are always combined with a finishing AE set in Build 1. Watch for decoupling in the AE portion (see Chapter 6). Following are examples of the Sunday ME + AE bike workouts for Build 1 by race distance. Note that on Sundays Ironman athletes complete a five- to six-hour AE ride as described later in this chapter.

Race Distance	Duration
Sprint and Olympic	90–120 min.
Half-Ironman	2–3 hr.

Warm-up	15 min. of gradually increasing intensity and gearing
ME set	3–5 × 8 min. in HR zone 4–5a or power zone 4–5 (Appendix B)
	2-min. easy-spin recoveries
AE set	30–45 min. in HR or power zone 2
Cooldown	Easy spinning with decreasing effort for the remainder of the ride

Warm up	15 min. of gradually increasing intensity and gearing
ME set	3–4 × 12 min. in zone 4
	3-min. easy-spin recoveries
AE set	30–60 min. in HR or power zone 2
Cooldown	Easy spinning, decreasing effort for the remainder of the ride

	Warm-up	10 min. of gradually increasing intensity and gearing
	ME set	4–5 × 15–20 min. in zone 3
		4- to 5-min. easy-spin recoveries
	AE set	30–90 min. in HR or power zone 2
	Cooldown	Easy spinning, decreasing effort for the remainder of the ride

Run Muscular Endurance

Sprint-, Olympic-, and half-Ironman-distance triathletes will do ME + AE runs on Saturdays. Ironman racers do not do muscular endurance workouts on the weekend and instead focus on aerobic endurance then. For the sprint and Olympic distances, ME bike workouts are optional on Tuesdays. Faster runners will do the An workouts, which are described later in the chapter. If your stand-alone 5K running race times (not triathlon splits) are typically slower than 22 minutes or your 10 km times are slower than 47 minutes, then I'd recommend doing the ME run workouts on Tuesdays instead of the An workouts.

Let's start with the Tuesday ME workouts. These may be done on a flat, measured section of road or on a track or treadmill. If you are using a speed-distance device such as a GPS watch or accelerometer, then the road is an excellent choice, as pacing is a key to success in such a workout. Otherwise, a track is a good choice because it allows you to check your pace every 100 meters, if you know how to read the lane markings. A treadmill may also be used for this workout, but I wouldn't recommend using one every week. Treadmills have no variation in grade or surface canting and no corners, and the repetitiveness of long runs on a treadmill may eventually contribute to overuse injuries.

Sprint- and Olympic-distance athletes who opt to do the ME workout on Tuesdays will run a zone 4 pace for a total of 15 to 20 minutes in a session. Each interval is 5 minutes long followed by 2 minutes of easy jogging or walking. Half-Ironman and Ironman racers will do three or four 8-minute intervals for a total of 24 to 32 minutes. These are done at the zone 3 pace with 2-minute walk-jogs for recovery after each.

Table 8.1 shows pace zones 3 and 4 based on a recent 5K or 10K race time. If you haven't done a running race recently, then you will need to estimate what your time might be. Find your race time in the left-hand columns. To the right are the zone 3 and zone 4 paces.

TABLE 8.1	Run Zones 3 and 4 Paces					
		ZONE 3			ZONE 4	
5K TIME	10K TIME	MILES	KILOMETERS	MILES	KILOMETERS
14:15	30:00:00	5:27–5:51	3:24–3:39	5:09–5:26	3:13–3:23
14:45	31:00:00	5:37–6:01	3:30–3:45	5:18–5:36	3:18–3:30
15:15	32:00:00	5:47–6:12	3:36–3:52	5:27–5:46	3:24–3:36
15:45	33:00:00	5:56–6:22	3:42–3:58	5:36–5:55	3:30–3:41
16:10	34:00:00	6:06–6:32	3:48–4:05	5:45–6:05	3:35–3:48
16:45	35:00:00	6:15–6:42	3:54–4:11	5:54–6:14	3:41–3:53
17:07	36:00:00	6:25–6:53	4:00–4:18	6:03–6:24	3:46–4:00
17:35	37:00:00	6:34–7:03	4:06–4:24	6:12–6:33	3:52–4:05
18:05	38:00:00	6:44–7:13	4:12–4:30	6:21–6:43	3:58–4:11
18:30	39:00:00	6:53–7:23	4:18–4:36	6:30–6:52	4:03–4:17
19:00	40:00:00	7:03–7:34	4:24–4:43	6:39–7:02	4:09–4:23
19:30	41:00:00	7:12–7:44	4:30–4:50	6:48–7:11	4:15–4:29
19:55	42:00:00	7:22–7:54	4:36–4:56	6:57–7:21	4:20–4:35
20:25	43:00:00	7:31–8:04	4:41–5:02	7:06–7:30	4:26–4:41
20:50	44:00:00	7:41–8:15	4:48–5:09	7:15–7:40	4:31–4:47
21:20	45:00:00	7:51–8:25	4:54–5:15	7:24–7:50	4:37–4:53
21:50	46:00:00	8:00–8:35	5:00–5:21	7:33–7:59	4:43–4:59
22:15	47:00:00	8:10–8:46	5:06–5:28	7:42–8:09	4:48–5:05
22:42	48:00:00	8:19–8:56	5:11–5:35	7:51–8:18	4:54–5:11
23:10	49:00:00	8:29–9:06	5:18–5:41	8:00–8:28	5:00–5:17
23:38	50:00:00	8:38–9:16	5:23–5:47	8:09–8:37	5:05–5:23
24:05:00	51:00:00	8:48–9:27	5:30–5:54	8:18–8:47	5:11–5:29
24:35:00	52:00:00	8:57–9:37	5:35–6:00	8:27–8:56	5:16–5:35
25:00:00	53:00:00	9:07–9:47	5:41–6:06	8:36–9:06	5:22–5:41
25:25:00	54:00:00	9:16–9:57	5:47–6:13	8:45–9:15	5:28–5:46
25:55:00	55:00:00	9:26–10:08	5:53–6:20	8:54–9:25	5:33–5:53
26:30:00	56:00:00	9:36–10:18	6:00–6:26	9:03–9:35	5:39–5:59
26:50:00	57:00:00	9:45–10:28	6:05–6:32	9:12–9:44	5:45–6:11
27:20:00	58:00:00	9:55–10:38	6:11–6:38	9:21–9:54	5:50–6:11
27:45:00	59:00:00	10:04–10:49	6:17–6:45	9:30–10:03	5:56–6:16
28:15:00	60:00:00	10:14–10:59	6:23–6:51	9:39–10:13	6:01–6:23

Note: Paces are based on a recent 5K or 10K race.

The ME run workouts on Tuesdays are done as follows. For sprint- and Olympic-distance triathletes, these are optional workouts that may replace the An run sessions scheduled for Tuesdays.

Race Distance	Duration
Sprint & Olympic	45 min.–1 hr.
Half-Ironman & Ironman	1 hr.–1 hr. 15 min.

	Warm-up	20–30 min. of gradually increasing effort and pace
	ME set	3–4 × 5 min. at pace zone 4 (Appendix B)
		2-min. jog-walk recoveries
	Cooldown	10 min. easy jogging
	Warm-up	15–35 min. of gradually increasing effort and pace
	ME set	3–4 × 8 min. at pace zone 3
		2-min. jog-walk recoveries
	Cooldown	10 min. easy jogging

The Saturday ME + AE runs are the most important runs of the week. For the half-Ironman and Ironman triathlete they are long enough that recovery before the long bike ride on Sunday may be difficult. For these longer distances, and perhaps even for Olympic-distance racers, it may be wise to swap the Thursday and Saturday run workouts, if possible. That will make Saturday an easier run day, allowing for a more full recovery for Sunday's long ride. The downside of doing this is that there's not much time to recover for Thursday following the Tuesday run and the Wednesday bike workout combination. This is the challenge of training for multisport. If you swap the Thursday and Saturday runs only to find out that you aren't ready to go for a long run on Thursdays, then you must cut back on either the intensity or the duration of the Tuesday or Wednesday workout. Quality in training is now far preferable to quantity, so make a decision on how to best use your resources to ensure a well-paced long run. This is often a difficult call for a self-coached athlete. But you must try to do what a good coach would do and make a decision to cut back somewhere, based on your assessment of what you need the most.

As with the Tuesday runs, the flat-road, track, or treadmill ME intervals scheduled for Saturdays (or Thursdays) will be done using either pace or heart rate to gauge intensity. Pace is preferred for sprint- and Olympic-distance athletes because the intervals are short.

These intervals are 5 to 9 minutes each, depending on your race distance. The recoveries still last about a quarter of the duration of the preceding interval. The total combined high-effort interval time for one of these sessions ranges from 15 to 72 minutes, depending on your race distance. Steadily increase the number of work intervals you do so that the combined time increases throughout Build 1. Some athletes may be able to do the maximum number right from the start. If you can do this, maintain it throughout the block each time you do this workout.

Race Distance	Duration
Sprint	1 hr.–1 hr. 30 min.
Olympic	1 hr. 15 min.–1 hr. 45 min.
Half-Ironman	1 hr. 30 min.–2 hr.

Warm-up	15 min. of gradually increasing effort
ME set	3–5 × 5 min. at HR or pace zone 4 (Appendix B)
	75-sec. easy jog recoveries
AE set	30–60 min., steady in zone 2
Cooldown	Running easily with decreasing effort

———————

Warm-up	15 min., gradually increasing effort
ME set	4–6 × 5 min. at HR or pace zone 4
	75-sec. easy jog recoveries
AE set	30–60 min. steady in zone 2
Cooldown	Running easily with decreasing effort

———————

Warm-up	10 min., gradually increasing effort
ME set	5–8 × 9 min. at HR or pace zone 3
	60-sec. walk recoveries
AE set	30–60 min. steady in zone 2
Cooldown	Running easily with decreasing effort

As with the ME bike workouts, these run sessions on Saturdays always finish with an aerobic endurance set. Whenever doing an AE set, watch for decoupling. It should be less than 5 percent by now. If it isn't, then you need to reduce the amount of muscular endurance training you are doing and just do a longer aerobic endurance set.

See some examples of the Saturday ME + AE run workout for Build 1 on p. 194 opposite.

Note that Ironman triathletes do not do an ME run on Saturdays in Build 1. Instead they do an AE run, which is described later in this chapter.

ANAEROBIC ENDURANCE WORKOUTS

Anaerobic endurance training is not for everyone. There are definite advantages to doing these workouts—for the fastest athletes. But that is where it ends. The risk of injury is greatly increased with such training. I've found this to be especially true for mid- and back-of-the-pack triathletes. For them, the downside far outweighs the upside. At the end of this chapter whenever an anaerobic endurance set or session is called for there is also an alternative muscular endurance set in italic. If you are a mid- or back-of-the-pack triathlete you should defer to the muscular endurance workouts to get the best results.

Swim Anaerobic Endurance

For the competitive triathlete one of the greatest benefits of anaerobic endurance training is found at the start of the swim. This is always the fastest part of any triathlon. If you want to be with the leaders coming out of the water, the start must be anaerobic. Depending on the duration of your race and where you are positioned on the start line, this high effort lasts for just a few minutes.

This doesn't mean the race outcome is determined by what happens in these first few minutes. It seldom is, in fact. Regardless of your race distance, there is still a long way to go to the finish line, and in nondrafting triathlons the bike and run have a lot to do with the outcome. Nevertheless, if you want to be further up in the rankings out of the water, then doing anaerobic endurance training may help you reach that goal. If that isn't one of your objectives, then you are better off developing greater muscular endurance and speed skills.

Anaerobic endurance sets for swimming are made up of short work intervals with relatively long recoveries. When you swim one of these intervals, the idea is for you to do it at a near maximal effort just as you would at the start of a race. Your breathing should be quite easy before starting an interval, however, so you should

TABLE 8.2 Swim Zone 5b Pace

TIME 1,000 m/yd	PACE/100 m (Aerobic capacity)
9:35–9:45	0:54–0:57
9:46–9:55	0:55–0:58
9:56–10:06	0:56–0:59
10:07–10:17	0:57–1:00
10:18–10:28	0:58–1:01
10:29–10:40	0:58–1:02
10:41–10:53	1:00–1:04
10:54–11:06	1:01–1:05
11:07–11:18	1:02–1:06
11:19–11:32	1:03–1:07
11:33–11:47	1:05–1:09
11:48–12:03	1:06–1:10
12:04–12:17	1:07–1:12
12:18–12:30	1:08–1:13
12:31–12:52	1:10–1:15
12:53–13:02	1:12–1:17
13:03–13:28	1:14–1:19
13:29–13:47	1:15–1:20
13:48–14:08	1:17–1:22
14:09–14:30	1:18–1:23
14:31–14:51	1:21–1:26
14:52–15:13	1:23–1:28
15:14–15:42	1:25–1:31
15:43–16:08	1:27–1:33
16:09–16:38	1:30–1:36
16:39–17:06	1:32–1:38
17:07–17:38	1:35–1:42
17:39–18:12	1:38–1:45
18:13–18:48	1:42–1:49
18:49–19:26	1:44–1:52
19:27–20:06	1:48–1:55
20:07–20:50	1:52–1:59
20:51–21:37	1:56–2:04
21:38–22:27	2:00–2:08
22:28–23:22	2:04–2:13
23:23–24:31	2:10–2:19
24:32–25:21	2:15–2:24

Note: Paces are based on a 1,000 meter or 1,000 yard time trial.

not start a new one if you are still breathing heavily from the last one; wait until you feel well recovered. The recoveries may take 40 to 60 seconds.

As with muscular endurance work, slower swimmers should cut way back on anaerobic endurance intervals or omit them entirely. Your emphasis must remain on speed skills. Better technique will produce faster times for you. Mid- to back-of-the-pack triathletes should still emphasize speed skills and muscular endurance sets over anaerobic endurance sets. Those swimming faster than 1:20 per 100 will reap the greatest rewards from anaerobic endurance training in the pool.

Pace per 100 m	Training Focus
1:50	Little to no An work
1:20–1:50	An work with SS + ME
1:20	An work

The length of the anaerobic endurance intervals depends on your swim speed. The idea is to do intervals that are between 2 and 3 minutes long. See the workout table for approximate distances based on your pace for 100 yards or meters.

Your pacing for these intervals is based on your 1,000 meter or 1,000 yard swim times from the rest-and-test week at the end of Base 3. Use Table 8.2 to find your anaerobic endurance pace per 100.

Here is an example of the SS + An + AE swim sets for sprint- and Olympic-distance triathletes scheduled for Tuesdays in the Build 1 block:

Race Distance	Duration
Sprint	30–45 min.
Olympic	45–60 min.

Warm-up/SS set	10 × 25 m, including technique focus and/or personal-limiter drills	
	Long recoveries	
An set	5 × 100–300 m at pace zone 5b (Appendix B)	
	40- to 60-sec. recoveries	
	[Optional ME set to replace An set:	
	3–4 × 250–500 m at pace zone 4–5a,	
	with 20-sec. recoveries]	
AE set/cooldown	10–20 min., steady at pace zone 2	

Pace per 100 m	Distance for An Intervals
1:35–1:55+	100–150 m
1:35–1:25	150–200 m
< 1:25	200–300 m

Bike Anaerobic Endurance

Anaerobic endurance training on the bike is done only by sprint- and Olympic-distance triathletes. These are scheduled for Wednesdays in the plans at the end of this chapter. The longer the race, the less benefit you will experience from doing anaerobic endurance work on the bike. The bike and swim portions of the race are very different from each other in terms of the need for anaerobic endurance. Whereas the swim starts extremely fast, the bike segment should be just the opposite—a steady, well-controlled effort and speed right from the start. The biggest mistake with pacing at all race distances is going out too fast at the start of the bike leg. I've seen Ironman athletes set a personal best in the first 25 miles of their 112-mile ride—and still have 87 miserable miles to go as they slowly fade.

The benefits of anaerobic endurance training for the shorter distances are an increased VO_2max and improved economy. Because of the latter, I sometimes, on rare occasions, have pro triathletes who race long courses do a bit of anaerobic endurance training in Base 3. I have never recommended this for an age-group triathlete who is racing long course. Pros typically train with greater volume than age-group athletes, which means they can fit such a workout in on top of everything else. They also have a tremendous capacity for workload that allows them to recover rapidly despite the volume. The downside of this kind of training for all triathletes, regardless of level or type of race, is the increased risk of injury and illness. There is a lot of stress placed on the knees during anaerobic training, and the immune system takes quite a beating.

Anaerobic endurance intervals on the bike are done on a hill to maintain the force ability. This type of workout increases the load on your knees, so be especially cautious. While you are climbing, sit up and hold on to the tops of your handlebars. This upright position will help to maintain your climbing force. If you are on flat terrain or using an indoor trainer, you may do the intervals in the aero position.

These high-effort intervals are about 3 minutes long and done at your aerobic capacity. Heart rate is ineffective for monitoring the intensity of these intervals because it lags so far behind the actual work you are doing. It will take 1 to 2 minutes within each 3-minute interval for a heart rate monitor to tell you how you're doing. In those first few minutes, you therefore need to use perceived exertion or a power meter to regulate the intensity. As most athletes go much too hard when gauging effort subjectively in this workout, this is when training with a power meter really pays off. By the third pedal stroke, you will know if you are at the right intensity. There is no guesswork.

When using a power meter to gauge anaerobic endurance intervals you will need to know your functional threshold power (see Chapter 3). The proper intensity for these intervals is zone 6, and it is found by multiplying your functional threshold power (FTPw) by 1.2 to set the low end of the zone and by 1.5 for the upper end. If you don't have a power meter, then you will be looking for a perceived exertion of 9 on a 1-to-10 scale. This is very hard. Stay in this range for each 3-minute interval, and recover after each interval by coasting down the hill and spinning easily for 3 minutes. Do five intervals within a workout once a week. That will give you about 15 minutes of anaerobic endurance training within a session. Doing more will give you little in the way of greater benefit but will greatly increase your risk of breaking down.

This is what the Wednesday An + Fo bike workout looks like for sprint- and Olympic-distance triathletes in Build 1:

Race Distance	Duration
Sprint	1 hr.–1 hr. 15 min.
Olympic	1 hr. –1 hr. 30 min.

Warm-up	20 min. of gradually increasing effort and gearing
An + Fo set	5 × 3 min., seated and sitting up on a hill at power zone 6 (Appendix B) or RPE 9
	3-min. recoveries
	[Optional ME + Fo set to replace An + Fo set:
	5 × 5 min. on a hill, seated and sitting up at
	HR zone 4–5a or power zone 4–5,
	quick descents for recoveries]
Cooldown	10–30 min., zone 2 power or heart rate on a flat to gently rolling course

Run Anaerobic Endurance

Anaerobic endurance runs are found on Tuesdays in the training plans at the end of this chapter. These workouts are only for the sprint- and Olympic-distance athletes. Instead of anaerobic runs, long-course triathletes do muscular endurance runs on Tuesdays. Those are described in the "Run Muscular Endurance" section above.

I've mentioned this a couple of times now, but to make sure the message is received I will say it one last time: Anaerobic endurance training is not for everyone. This is especially true for running since the effort is very high and can have negative consequences for recovery and your health. These are high-risk workouts.

If your 5K running race times are slower than 22 minutes or your 10K is slower than 47 minutes, then you are unlikely to gain much, if any, benefit from anaerobic endurance training. Muscular endurance training will be a far more effective use of your time. You'll notice, however, that in Table 8.3 I've included anaerobic endurance pace zones beyond 22 minutes for the 5K and beyond 47 minutes for the 10K. I did this because I know some back-of-the-pack runners will still want to try such training. A "can-do" attitude is common among triathletes of all abilities. I concluded that it's probably better to provide the information than to leave these athletes to their own devices in coming up with appropriate interval paces.

TABLE 8.3	Run Zone 5b Pace		
5K TIME	**10K TIME**	**MILES**	**KILOMETERS**
14:15	30:00:00	4:37–4:58	2:53–3:06
14:45	31:00:00	4:45–5:06	2:58–3:11
15:15	32:00:00	4:53–5:15	3:03–3:16
15:45	33:00:00	5:01–5:24	3:08–3:22
16:10	34:00:00	5:10–5:33	3:13–3:28
16:45	35:00:00	5:18–5:41	3:18–3:33
17:07	36:00:00	5:26–5:50	3:23–3:38
17:35	37:00:00	5:34–5:59	3:28–3:44
18:05	38:00:00	5:42–6:08	3:33–3:50
18:30	39:00:00	5:50–6:16	3:38–3:55
19:00	40:00:00	5:58–6:25	3:43–4:00
19:30	41:00:00	6:06–6:34	3:48–4:06
19:55	42:00:00	6:14–6:43	3:53–4:11
20:25	43:00:00	6:22–6:51	3:58–4:16
20:50	44:00:00	6:31–7:00	4:04–4:22
21:20	45:00:00	6:39–7:09	4:09–4:28
21:50	46:00:00	6:47–7:17	4:14–4:33
22:15	47:00:00	6:55–7:26	4:19–4:38
22:42	48:00:00	7:03–7:35	4:24–4:44
23:10	49:00:00	7:11–7:44	4:29–4:50
23:38	50:00:00	7:19–7:52	4:34–4:55
24:05	51:00:00	7:27–8:01	4:39–5:00
24:35	52:00:00	7:35–8:10	4:44–5:06
25:00	53:00:00	7:43–8:19	4:49–5:11
25:25	54:00:00	7:52–8:27	4:55–5:16
25:55	55:00:00	8:00–8:36	5:00–5:22
26:30	56:00:00	8:08–8:45	5:05–5:28
26:50	57:00:00	8:16–8:53	5:10–5:33
27:20	58:00:00	8:24–9:02	5:15–5:38
27:45	59:00:00	8:32–9:11	5:20–5:44
28:15	60:00:00	8:40–9:20	5:25–5:50

Note: Based on a recent 5K or 10K race.

Anaerobic endurance run intervals are best done on a track, but you can also use a relatively flat, measured road or a treadmill. Run four or five 3-minute intervals at pace zone 5b, with 3-minute easy jog recoveries between them. Based on your 5b pace zone found in Table 8.3, you can set a fixed distance for each interval that will last about 3 minutes. For example, if your 5b pace zone is 5:58–6:25 per mile (1,600 meters), running for 3 minutes at that pace would cover approximately half a mile (800 meters). So you could do four or five 800-meter intervals in 3 minutes to 3 minutes, 12 seconds. Or, if your 5b pace zone is 6:22–6:51, that means you are running every 100 meters in 24 to 26 seconds (this result is found by converting your mile time range to seconds and dividing by 16). At that pace, in 3 minutes you would run 692 to 750 meters (found by dividing 180 seconds by 26 and 24, respectively, and multiplying by 100). So 700-meter intervals would be just about right. That's just 100 meters short of half a mile (800 meters).

If you are running on a track, you will need to know how to read track markings to figure out the start and finish points. Of course, you can simply run for 3 minutes at the appropriate pace and not worry about the distance. Just check your pace every 200 meters (half lap) to make sure you are not going too fast, which is the most common error in the first two intervals. Your projected time for each 200 meters is found by dividing your 5b pace range by eight (there are eight 200-meter segments in 1,600 meters).

A speed-distance device such as a runner's GPS or accelerometer can be very helpful with pace setting because it allows you to have real-time pace displayed on your wrist device. This allows you to do the workout on any mostly flat stretch of road. You can also do this workout on a treadmill and use the display to gauge your pacing.

This is the anaerobic endurance run workout scheduled for Tuesdays in Build 1 for sprint- and Olympic-distance triathletes:

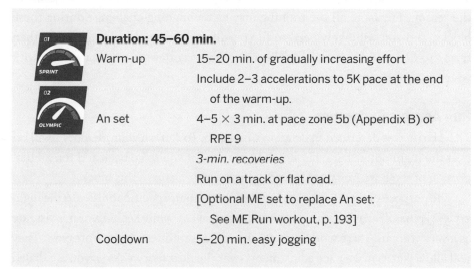

Duration: 45–60 min.

Warm-up	15–20 min. of gradually increasing effort
	Include 2–3 accelerations to 5K pace at the end of the warm-up.
An set	4–5 × 3 min. at pace zone 5b (Appendix B) or RPE 9
	3-min. recoveries
	Run on a track or flat road.
	[Optional ME set to replace An set: See ME Run workout, p. 193]
Cooldown	5–20 min. easy jogging

AEROBIC ENDURANCE WORKOUTS

For the Ironman triathlete, aerobic endurance training is the heart of race preparation. The run sessions are found on Saturdays in the Ironman training plan at the end of this chapter, and AE bike rides are on Sundays. That makes for two long workouts back to back, which may leave you tired for the Sunday ride. The reason they are planned this way is that most athletes have work schedules and lifestyles that free up only their weekends for these long workouts. If you can, swap the Thursday and Saturday runs so that your long run is on Thursday and your speed skills run is on Saturday. This will ensure that you are fairly fresh for your Sunday ride. The downside of making this switch is that you may be a bit tired for the Thursday run, since you will have had a muscular endurance run on Tuesday and a muscular endurance ride on Wednesday. You may want to try it both ways early in Build 1 to see which plan works better for you.

The long aerobic endurance workouts are the most important of the Ironman athlete's week. If you have to miss something due to other commitments in your life, try not to miss these. Rearrange the weekly workout schedule, if necessary, to somehow fit them in. Consistency is critical to having your best possible race. If you miss one of these in the last 12 weeks before the race, that means about 17 percent of your fitness-boosting bike or run preparation was lost. The workouts in the last 3 to 12 weeks are the most important of the entire season. Everything you've done up to this point was to get you ready for these 8 weeks. If you want to excel on race day, training for triathlon is demanding, especially at this point in the season. Fitting in all the training may be an ongoing challenge during these blocks, and you will likely need to fit your lifestyle around training, rather than trying to fit training around your lifestyle. You may have to negotiate deals with your family for a few weeks.

Run Aerobic Endurance

The AE run was described in detail in Chapter 6. To refresh your memory I will repeat the main points here, but it would be wise for you to go back and reread that portion of the Base 2 chapter before doing the ride again in this block.

The purpose of the AE run is to build your Ironman-specific abilities to the highest level possible. You're trying to get as fast as you can while keeping your heart rate as low as you can. These workouts may also serve as minitests of your progress. They will allow you to make pace adjustments over the next few weeks so you are dialed in by race day. I'll explain how to do that after a quick summary of this workout.

The aerobic endurance run is a very simple session. All you do is run for 2.5 to 3 hours on a mostly flat or gently rolling course. The first few minutes are a steady warm-up, leaving about 2.5 hours for the AE portion. After the warm-up, run with your heart rate in zone 2 for the rest of the session. (For your heart rate zone 2, see Appendix B.)

That's all there is to it. But what happens during the workout is the important part. This is when a runner's GPS or accelerometer, along with the right kind of software (I recommend WKO+ software, available at TrainingPeaks.com), proves invaluable. When your running aerobic endurance is optimal, the software will show that by revealing when your heart rate and speed were "coupled." This simply means that the graphed lines representing these parameters remain parallel. There may be a slight separation, but if the separation is more than 5 percent (WKO+

software provides this metric), the two are "decoupled," showing the need for improvement. Figures 6.3 and 6.4 illustrate what I am describing here.

You can measure the decoupling in the minitest that I mentioned above. As long as heart rate and speed are coupled, you continue running at that same heart rate for this session each week. If your speed and heart rate are not coupled, then you will need to lower your sights for Build 2's long aerobic endurance runs by slowing down a bit and using a lower target heart rate. If you don't, you are simply rehearsing the wrong pace for the race, and the chance of a crash and burn on race day is high.

The AE run for Ironman triathletes scheduled for Saturdays will be done as shown in the following workout.

Duration: 2 hrs. 40 min.–3 hrs. 10 min.

Warm-up	5–30 min., gradually increasing speed
AE set	2 hr. 30 min., HR zone 2 (Appendix B)
Cooldown	5–10 min., walking

Bike Aerobic Endurance with Run Brick

The bike portion of your race is the most important part of race day. It is the longest leg of the race—taking about half of your race time—and it strongly influences how well you will run. If you ride too hard, then it's likely you will have a poor marathon run. So if you want to run well, concentrate on getting as aerobically fit for the bike as you can. The greater your bike fitness, the more you can hold back on the bike and still produce a fast time, and the fresher you will be for the run.

Some Ironman athletes train by running 400 meter intervals as fast as they can so they can run well on race day. That's counterproductive. You don't need to train for a high aerobic capacity or great speed. The pace of your Ironman run is not challenging at all. You could probably go out and run a stand-alone marathon at that pace right now with little training. The challenge is running the marathon on legs that have just completed a 112-mile bike ride. If your legs are relatively fresh, you can run at goal pace without a problem. But if you aren't very bike-fit—or you rode the bike portion of the race too fast—then you have set yourself up for a slow walk-jog or even a DNF (did not finish).

The bottom line is that if you want to run well and achieve your race goal, you must put bike fitness at the top of your list of objectives. And bike fitness for an

Ironman is based primarily on aerobic endurance. You must become as fast as you can at a low heart rate. That will happen with consistent, moderate-effort training over the course of the 8 or 9 weeks of the Build period. If you've been doing long, aerobic rides throughout the Base period, you are ready to start focusing on these long race-effort rides now.

The bike aerobic endurance workout is a simple session. Ride for a total of 5 or 6 hours on a flat to rolling course. It's best to avoid very hilly courses with long climbs for this session. If your race will be on a hilly course, then you can ride such courses in Build 2 when training becomes even more racelike, but for Build 1, stick with the less hilly areas.

After warming up, ride for at least 4 hours in heart rate zone 2 (see Appendix B). This session is best done alone or with a training partner who will let you set the pace. If your partner insists on riding too hard or too easy, then avoid riding with that person again when you are scheduled for an AE ride. To achieve your goal, you must train precisely in the way that your body needs you to train—not according to somebody else's whims or demands. If you find yourself on the wrong ride because of your training partner, briefly excuse yourself and go your own way.

You will need to stay focused on your heart rate by continually checking it throughout the 4 hours. Do not start at a higher heart rate, assuming that is some-how going to result in a faster time. You will simply fatigue and fail to meet the objective for the workout of building aerobic endurance. Stay in zone 2 the entire time.

There will be some drifting in and out of zone 2 as a result of having to stop for red lights or slow down for traffic, and you will likely have lapses in your concentration and forget to stay on task. That's to be expected. Just get back into zone 2 right away when you realize you've strayed from the plan.

During the entire ride, drink when you are thirsty and eat what you will use on race day for carbohydrate calories. Use the same rate of intake you plan to use on race day. Now is the time to refine your race-day nutrition. Dehydration will not be a problem if you pay attention and keep your thirst quenched. But if you don't take in enough carbohydrate, you may find yourself slowing down. There is a narrow window for what works best here, and it is unique to every individual. Regardless of what your buddies do for energy intake or what you read some pro does, you must find what works for you.

Too few calories consumed on the bike, and you will gradually slow down later on the ride. Too many, and you may cause your gut to shut down as you start to feel bloated. You will probably need 200 to 400 kilocalories of carbohydrate per hour of riding, depending on your body size, if you stay in the proper zone right from the start. If you make a mistake in training, make it on the side of eating a little bit less than you need. And keep it simple: The more "stuff" you mix in with your calories (such as electrolytes, proteins, and fats), the greater your risk of bloating. Refine your eating plan over the course of the rides scheduled for the next few weeks.

The real key to your progress on the bike is to keep your power and heart rate coupled, just as with the run. A power meter on the bike is very helpful and does the analysis for you. Your bike aerobic endurance is solid when the graphic display of your heart rate and power are parallel for the entire ride. As explained earlier, if these are coupled, it means you are aerobically fit. If your aerobic fitness is lacking, the power graph will drift downward as heart rate remains steady. This simply means you need more of these long aerobic-endurance rides. (See Chapter 6 for more information on coupling.)

As soon as you finish the AE bike ride, transition to a 15-minute run just as you will do on race day. Start the run at a conservative effort, using this time to find a comfortable rhythm. Your heart rate should go no higher than zone 2. If it goes into zone 3, start walking. If you paced correctly you will be a bit wobbly at first, but you will soon begin to feel comfortable running. When that happens, increase your pace to lift your heart rate to zone 2. This should become easier over the course of Build 1. If you are forced to walk during this short run, there is nothing wrong with your running fitness. You simply need more aerobic endurance training on the bike.

The following workout shows how to do the Ironman aerobic endurance bike and run workout scheduled for Sundays in this block.

Duration: 5–6 hr.

Warm-up	30 min. of gradually increasing effort and gearing
Bike AE set	Ride 4 hrs. steady at HR zone 2 (Appendix B), rehearsing race-day nutrition
	30–90 min. of easy riding to recover
Run AE set	Transition as you will on race day to a 15-min. run at goal effort, watching heart rate and keeping it below heart rate zone 3
Cooldown	Walk 5–10 min. and begin the recovery process as soon as possible

"BIG DAY" WORKOUTS

As I explained in Chapter 3, training should become increasingly like the race the closer you get to race day. A problem with that rule becomes apparent, though, when you are training for an Ironman triathlon. You simply can't do workouts that are that long very often. It's too demanding for both the body and the mind. But you do need to simulate at least a healthy chunk of the race sometime before race day. This won't do as much to prepare your body as it will your mind. The issues are how long, how often, and when.

In the Build period I like to have Ironman triathletes do two workouts that I call "Big Days." For athletes training in 4-week blocks (3 weeks of quality training and 1 rest-and-test week), the first is done during Build 1 and is scheduled for a weekend 8 weeks before race day. If you are training in 3-week blocks (2 weeks on and 1 off), then do the first Big Day workout 10 weeks before race day. In both cases this will be the weekend right before the Build 1 rest-and-test week. The second Big Day workout is done 4 weekends before race day for both 4- and 3-week-block athletes. As you will see in the next chapter, that will also place this workout on the last weekend before a rest-and-test week. It's important that this workout come right before a rest break because it is so demanding.

Nevertheless, it's a simple workout. You get out of bed at the same time you plan to do get up on race day. Assuming a 7:00 a.m. race start, that should be no later than 4:30 a.m. Have breakfast just as you will on race day. Eat the same foods and eat them in the same amounts you think you will eat them then. At 7:00 a.m., start the swim portion of the workout. This is a 1-hour session in which you swim at race effort. You may either break them into 500 yard or 500 meter segments or do them nonstop. If, on race day, you will wear a wetsuit, then wear it for this swim as well. If you plan to start fast on race day to get good positioning, then do the same today. Do everything as nearly similar as possible to the way you plan to do it on race day.

After the swim, take a 90-minute break. Eat a very light meal and stay off of your legs as much as possible. Then, after the break, start a 5-hour bike ride. This should be done at the heart rate and the power or effort at which you plan to race the Ironman. Use the same bike equipment you will use on race day. This includes clothing, shoes, helmet, wheels, and anything else you will race with. Drink when you are thirsty throughout the ride. Take in calories the same way you are planning to do on race day, and pay close attention to how you feel. Your mind will wander a bit, but stay in the moment as much as possible. Focus your attention on pacing control and anything that may need to be adjusted for the actual race. You can frequently run a mental checklist: Am I thirsty? Do I need calories? How's my stomach? How's my breathing? Am I pacing properly? Are my legs strong? You might even consider taping these questions to your handlebars to help you stay focused.

After the 5-hour ride, take another 90-minute break. Get off of your legs and eat a light, mostly liquid meal. Then start a 2-hour run. Wear the same type of clothing and the same shoes that you are planning to use for the race. Don't do the run in the shirt, shorts, or socks you rode in on your bike, as they will be soiled and might give you a rash or infection. If you are planning to wear a hat and sunglasses on race day, then wear them on this Big Day. For the run, it's a good idea to wear a holster belt with fluids and/or the fuel you will use. Or you might consider planning your route so that you frequently pass locations where you can have fluids and fuel stored, even if it means returning to the same spot.

You will be a bit stiff as you start the run, so allow your body to gradually find its rhythm and tempo. Don't force the pace right away. You will also do this on race day as you exit T2. Once you have your legs working smoothly, get up to race pace, heart rate, or effort just as you will do in the race. As with the bike, stay focused on how you are feeling and how you are doing with pacing. Run the same mental checklist: Am I thirsty? Do I need calories? How's my stomach? How's my breathing? Am I pacing properly? Are my legs strong?

Here's how the Big Day workout is done.

IRONMAN BIG DAY WORKOUT

4:30 a.m.–5:00 a.m.	Wake up and eat a race-day breakfast, followed by some light stretching and mental preparation.
7:00 a.m.–8:00 a.m.	Swim 1 hour at race intensity, using race-day gear.
8:00 a.m.–9:30 a.m.	Get off of your legs and eat a light meal.
9:30 a.m.–2:30 p.m.	Ride as you will on race day, mimicking the intensity, equipment, clothing, fluids, and nutrition planned for the race.
2:30 p.m.–4:00 p.m.	Get off of your legs and eat a light, mostly liquid meal.
4:00 p.m.–6:00 p.m.	Run as you will on race day, mimicking the intensity, clothing, shoes and other gear, fluids, and nutrition planned for the race.

By the time you finish the run, you will have spent about 14 hours of your day devoted to an Ironman-specific workout. Eight of those hours will have been at race effort. You will have learned a lot about topics such as refueling, managing thirst, pacing, equipment, mental preparedness, and more. Write down what you learned and how you plan to alter your preparation and perhaps even your goals for the race.

The Big Day workout serves as a benchmark for how you are progressing physically and gives you a sense of what it will be like mentally to do an Ironman race. It's a learning and growth opportunity. The next workout like this is scheduled to occur just four weekends before race day. That will be your last opportunity to rehearse everything prior to the race.

The Big Day workouts appear in your plan on a Saturday, but if the weather is not cooperative on Saturday, you may do it on Sunday. If the weather does cooperate on Saturday, you will get a day off on Sunday and an extra day of rest. The day off is a reward. Take advantage of it and get lots of rest. You may even have time to do a few other things that are important to you, such as enjoying your family.

RECOVERY WORKOUTS

As in the plans found in previous chapters, the workouts in boldface italics in the Build 1 training plans are optional and focus on recovery or speed skills. If you have time to do these in addition to the primary workouts, you will improve your economy. The more frequently you swim, bike, or run, the more economical your body becomes at making the unique movements of that sport. And the more economical you become, the less energy you use.

The downside of doing these optional workouts is that you may become fatigued or have trouble recovering between workouts. If you find that you are often tired going into a primary workout on the training plan, then don't do the optional workouts. Doing more workouts in this case is counterproductive. If you are recovering quickly and feeling fresh most of the time, then the additional workouts may help your training progress faster. For advanced triathletes the rate of recovery may also be enhanced by doing light exercise, especially swimming and biking.

For the optional workouts listed as recovery sessions, keep the intensity very low. That means heart rate, pace, and power zone 1. No higher. Do not get sloppy with your technique when going slowly. Focus on maintaining picture-perfect form whenever you swim, bike, or run, even if the workout seems inconsequential.

The optional workouts labeled as speed skills sessions are for drills and are intended to further refine your techniques. Select the workouts you will do here based on your technique limiters and refer to the "Speed Skills" section earlier in this chapter.

STRENGTH MAINTENANCE

Strength training continues during this block to maintain the muscular strength you developed in Base 1. If you find your recovery is compromised by lifting weights, however, even if the workload is greatly reduced, as it should be in SM, then you must cut back. Your greatest gains in terms of race performance will most definitely come from swimming, biking, and running now, so strength training is of secondary importance.

The short gym workouts you will do in Build 1 should not be challenging at all. If your gym workouts leave you tired for your Tuesday workouts, then you must either omit one or more strength exercises or not do any weight lifting at all. The exercises you are most likely to feel the effects of the next day are the hip extension sets in the form of squats, leg presses, or step-ups. If your legs are weary for Tuesday's run, cut these from your routine.

Core strength training may continue in Build 1 regardless of what you do about weight lifting. In fact, for triathletes whose cores are weak it is a good idea to do one or two additional core strength sessions later in the week (see Chapter 5 for an explanation of how to assess your core strength).

Build 1 Testing

Weekend races serve as great tests of how you are coming along in your preparation for your goal event. The best time to race is at the end of a rest-and-test week, especially if the race is B-priority. If it's a C-priority race it can be done at the end of any week in your schedule. Just be aware that if you are an experienced triathlete, C races have limited value. The main reason for doing one is simply to tune up and prepare for the nuances of racing shortly before your A-priority race. I'd caution against doing any that are longer than your A race. Such races require a considerable amount of recovery time, and the return on that investment is limited. Any C races that you do should be shorter than your target race, or perhaps the same length. Iron-distance triathletes should do no more than one race in the Build 1 and 2 blocks combined, preferably a half-Ironman. Doing races of Olympic distance and shorter will only detract you from your limited training time. When it comes to the Ironman, you need all of the training time you can get. It seems there is never enough.

Of course, field testing continues to be an effective way to check your progress, too. The purpose of these tests is to determine whether you are able to hold the pace or power you want for your goal race without working too hard and for the duration needed. Our purpose of the training for the past several weeks has been to get you as fast as possible at a low heart rate or level of effort. At the end of the Build 1 block we will check to see how much you have achieved. Below I describe the field tests that I have athletes do in the rest-and-test week at the end of Build 1. Do these only if you are not racing. If you are racing, you will be checking your progress by seeing how you do in the race.

SWIM FIELD TEST

One reason that racing can be a test in itself at this point in the season is that testing is in fact very much like racing now. We want to know the answer to just one question from your Build 1 swim test, for example: Can you swim at goal race pace for a given duration without slowing down and with an appropriate effort? Because heart rate monitors are not used in swimming, this question can only be answered subjectively. Also, continually check your splits on the poolside clock to see if you are slowing down as the test set progresses.

The Build 1 swim field test is done as follows.

Warm-up	6 × 50 m, with each interval faster than the previous one, focusing on technique
	20- to 30-sec. recoveries
Test set	Swim at goal race pace for a distance based on your race distance
Cooldown	100–300 m, easy swimming focused on technique

Race Distance	Test Interval
Sprint	500 m
Olympic	750 m
Half-Ironman	1,000 m
Ironman	1,500 m

BIKE FIELD TEST

The bike field test for Build 1 sprint- and Olympic-distance triathletes may be done on an indoor trainer using your race bike. For half-Ironman and Ironman athletes the test is best done on the road because the workout is so long. On an indoor trainer you would be unlikely to do a fair test, just out of sheer boredom. If you are doing the test on the road, it's best if you have a power meter.

Sprint and Olympic triathletes must make sure that the bike and the indoor trainer are set up precisely so that the test can be repeated with the same parameters at the end of Build 2. The two critical elements for set-up are tire pressure and trainer resistance against the back wheel. If these vary from test to test, the results are of little value in measuring progress.

Gauging race-specific progress on the bike with a field test on the road is difficult to do if you don't have a power meter. You really can't measure output with only a heart rate monitor and perceived exertion. You cannot accurately judge your power by how fast you are going, because your speed on the bike is strongly affected by wind and terrain. If you have a power meter, the wind and terrain changes are inconsequential; you know how much power you applied to the pedals no matter what the other conditions might be. You simply ride at goal power and see what happens to heart rate.

Warm-up	10–20 min. of gradually increasing effort and gearing
Bike test set	Ride at goal race heart rate or power (power is preferable) based on your race distance
	5-min. recoveries
Cooldown	Ride at lower than race effort for the remainder of the workout
Run set	Quickly transition to a 15-min. run at goal race effort or pace
Cooldown	Walk for several minutes

Race Distance	Distance of Test Interval
Sprint	10 km at goal race heart rate or power
Olympic	20 km at goal race heart rate or power
Half-Ironman	5 × 20 min. at zone 3
Ironman	4 hr. at goal race power or heart rate

A watt is always a watt regardless of external variables. If you have a power meter, you can download the data from the workout and see if your heart rate remained constant or decoupled as the test set progressed. If there is any decoupling, it should be less than 5 percent. If you must use only a heart rate monitor and perceived exertion, what you want to see is speed holding steady and effort feeling manageable. If you were doing the Sunday bike workouts in the past few weeks of Build 1, you should already have a pretty good idea of how your fitness is progressing. The test will help you know for sure.

The test is also a brick workout, so run for 15 minutes once you're off the bike as you will do in the race.

Refer to p. 211 to see how the Build 1 bike field test is done.

RUN FIELD TEST

By now you should be able to run in a workout for at least half of the distance of your goal race at goal pace. If you can't do this by the end of Build 1 when you are fresh and without a bike ride preceding the run, then it means you've set your aim too high. You need to lower your goal pace. The run field test will help you determine whether your pace is right, and this test is best done on a flat course with the miles or kilometers marked. If you have a speed-distance device, then that will serve the same purpose.

The pacing question could also be stated in these terms: We want to find out whether you can maintain your goal heart rate or effort for a given distance or duration and without slowing down while using a particular pacing strategy. Or, conversely, if you are using a speed-distance device, or running on a measured and marked course, can you run the distance or duration of your test without the effort becoming too great and without your heart rate decoupling by more than 5 percent. If either of these negative outcomes occur, then you must reconsider your race goal by lowering your expectations. As with the bike, with the run you should have a pretty good idea of how race-ready you are becoming just because of how well you are handling the Saturday runs. This test only confirms what you likely already know.

The Build 1 run field test is done as shown in the following workout.

Warm-up	10–20 min. of gradually increasing effort
Test set	Run at goal race heart rate or pace (pace is preferred) based on your race distance
Cooldown	Run at slower than race effort for the remainder of the workout

Race Distance	Distance of Test Interval
Sprint	3 km at goal race heart rate or pace
Olympic	5 km at goal race heart rate or pace
Half-Ironman	10 km at goal race heart rate or pace
Ironman	2 hr. at goal race heart rate or pace

TRAINING PLAN -- BUILD 1

SPRINT-DISTANCE TRAINING **BUILD 1**

T R A I N I N G   W E E K S

SPORT	SWIM	BIKE	RUN	STRENGTH	DAILY VOLUME
MON	*Rec* 0:15–0:30			SM 0:45	0:45–1:15
TUES	**SS + An** *ME + AE* 0:30–0:45	*SS* or *Rec* 0:45–1:00	**An** or *ME* 0:45–1:00		1:15–2:45
WED		**An + Fo** *ME + Fo* 1:00–1:15	*SS* 0:30–0:45		1:00–2:00
THURS	**SS + Fo + ME** 0:30–0:45		**SS** 0:30–0:45		1:00–1:30
FRI	*Rec* 0:15–0:30	**SS** 1:00–1:15			1:00–1:45
SAT	**An** *SS* **+ ME + SS** 0:45–1:00	*Rec* 0:30–0:45	**ME + AE** 1:00–1:30		1:45–3:15
SUN		**ME + AE** 1:30–2:00	**AE** or **ME** 0:15		1:45–2:15
VOLUME BY SPORT	1:45–3:30	3:30–6:15	2:30–4:15	0:45	8:30–14:45
WORKOUTS	**3–5**	**3–5**	**4–5**	**1**	**11–16**

R E S T   &   T E S T   W E E K

SPORT	SWIM	BIKE	RUN	STRENGTH	DAILY VOLUME
MON				SM 0:45	0:45
TUES	SS 0:15–0:30		SS 0:30–0:45		0:45–1:15
WED		SS 0:45–1:00			0:45–1:00
THURS	**Te** 0:25–0:30 or *SS if race*		SS 0:30–0:45		0:55–1:15
FRI		**Rec** 1:00			1:00
SAT	SS 0:15–0:30 or *Race*	*Race*	**Test** 0:45 or *race* or *SS if race Sun*		1:00–1:15
SUN		**Te** 1:30 or *Rec or Race*	**ME** 0:15 or *no run if race Sat*		1:45
VOLUME BY SPORT	0:55–1:30	3:15–3:30	2:00–2:30	0:45	6:55–8:15
WORKOUTS	**3**	**3–4**	**4**	**1**	**11–12**

Notes: Rec = Recovery. Optional workouts are in italic. The AE or ME runs on Sunday are intended to follow the bike ride. Detail on the workouts can be found in the chapter. Strength workouts appear in Appendix C.

OLYMPIC-DISTANCE TRAINING **BUILD 1**

T R A I N I N G   W E E K S

SPORT	SWIM	BIKE	RUN	STRENGTH	DAILY VOLUME
MON	Rec 0:15–0:30			SM 0:45	0:45–1:15
TUES	SS + An *ME + AE* 0:45–1:00	*SS or Rec 0:45–1:00*	An or *ME* 0:45–1:00		1:30–3:00
WED		An + Fo *ME + Fo* 1:00–1:30	SS 0:30–0:45		1:00–2:15
THURS	SS + Fo + ME 0:45–1:00		SS 0:30–0:45		1:15–1:45
FRI	Rec 0:15–0:30	SS 1:00–1:30			1:00–2:00
SAT	An *SS* + ME + SS 0:45–1:00	*Rec 0:45–1:00*	ME + AE 1:15–1:45		2:00–3:45
SUN		ME + AE 1:30–2:00	*AE or ME 0:15*		1:45–2:15
VOLUME BY SPORT	2:15–4:00	3:30–7:00	2:45–4:30	0:45	9:15–16:15
WORKOUTS	3–5	3–5	4–5	1	11–16

R E S T   &   T E S T   W E E K

SPORT	SWIM	BIKE	RUN	STRENGTH	DAILY VOLUME
MON				SM 0:45	0:45
TUES	SS 0:30–0:45		SS 0:30–0:45		1:00–1:30
WED		SS 0:45–1:00			0:45–1:00
THURS	Te 0:30–0:40 or *Rec if race*		SS 0:30–0:45		1:00–1:25
FRI		Rec 1:00			1:00
SAT	SS 0:30–0:45 or *Race*	*Race*	Te 1:15 or *Race* or *SS if race Sun*		1:45–2:00
SUN		Te 1:30 or *Rec or Race*	ME 0:15 or *Race* or *no run if race Sat*		1:45
VOLUME BY SPORT	1:30–2:10	3:15–3:30	2:30–3:00	0:45	8:00–9:25
WORKOUTS	3	3–4	4	1	11–12

Notes: Rec = Recovery. Optional workouts are in italic. The AE or ME runs on Sunday are intended to follow the bike ride. Detail on the workouts can be found in the chapter. Strength workouts appear in Appendix C.

TRAINING PLAN — BUILD 1

HALF-IRONMAN-DISTANCE TRAINING **BUILD 1**

TRAINING WEEKS

SPORT	SWIM	BIKE	RUN	STRENGTH	DAILY VOLUME
MON	*Rec* 0:30–0:40			SM 0:45	0:45–1:25
TUES	SS + ME + AE 0:45–1:00	*SS* or *Rec* 1:00–1:30	ME 1:00–1:15		1:45–3:45
WED		ME + Fo 1:30–2:00	*SS* 0:45–1:00		1:30–3:00
THURS	SS + Fo + ME 0:45–1:00		SS 1:00–1:15 or *swap with Sat ME + AE run*		1:45–2:15
FRI	*Rec* 0:30–0:40	SS 1:00–1:30			1:00–2:10
SAT	ME + AE + SS 1:00–1:15	*Rec* 1:00–1:30	ME + AE 1:30–2:00		2:30–4:45
SUN		ME + AE 2:00–3:00	AE or ME 0:15		2:15–3:15
VOLUME BY SPORT	2:30–4:35	4:30–9:30	3:45–5:45	0:45	11:30–20:35
WORKOUTS	3–5	3–5	4–5	1	11–16

REST & TEST WEEK

SPORT	SWIM	BIKE	RUN	STRENGTH	DAILY VOLUME
MON				SM 0:45	0:45
TUES	SS 0:30–0:45		SS 0:30–0:45		1:00–1:30
WED		SS 0:45–1:00			0:45–1:00
THURS	Te 0:40–0:50 or *SS if race*		SS 0:30–0:45		1:10–1:35
FRI		Rec 1:00 or *SS if race*			1:00
SAT	SS + ME 0:30–0:45 or *Race*		Te 1:30 or *Race* or *SS if race Sun*		2:00–2:15
SUN		Te 2:30 or *Race* or *Rec if Sat race*	ME 0:15 or *no run if race Sat*		2:45
VOLUME BY SPORT	1:40–2:20	4:15–4:30	2:45–3:15	0:45	9:25–10:50
WORKOUTS	3	3	4	1	11

Notes: Rec = Recovery. Optional workouts are in italic. The AE or ME runs on Sunday are intended to follow the bike ride. Detail on the workouts can be found in the chapter. Strength workouts appear in Appendix C.

IRONMAN-DISTANCE TRAINING **BUILD 1**

T R A I N I N G   W E E K S

SPORT	SWIM	BIKE	RUN	STRENGTH	DAILY VOLUME
MON	*Rec* 0:30–0:40			SM 0:45	0:45–1:25
TUES	SS + ME + AE 0:45–1:00	*SS* or *Rec* 1:00–1:30	ME 1:00–1:15		1:45–3:45
WED		ME + Fo 1:30–2:00	*SS* 0:45–1:00		1:30–3:00
THURS	SS + Fo + ME 0:45–1:00		SS 1:00–1:15 *or swap with Sat AE run*		1:45–2:15
FRI	*Rec* 0:30–0:40	SS 1:00–1:30			1:00–2:10
SAT	ME + AE + SS 1:15–1:30 or 1:00 *Big Day* *wk 9 or 10*	*Rec* 1:00–1:30 or 5:00 *Big Day* *wk 9 or 10*	AE 2:30–3:00 or 2:00 *Big Day* *wk 9 or 10*		3:45–6:00 or 8:00 *Big Day* *wk 9 or 10*
SUN		AE 5:00–6:00 *or day off if Big Day Sat*	AE 0:15 *or day off if Big Day Sat*		5:15–6:15 or day off if Big Day Sat
VOLUME BY SPORT	2:45–4:50	7:30–12:30	4:45–6:45	0:45	15:45–24:50
WORKOUTS	3–5	3–5	4–5	1	11–16

R E S T   &   T E S T   W E E K

SPORT	SWIM	BIKE	RUN	STRENGTH	DAILY VOLUME
MON				SM 0:45	0:45
TUES	SS 0:30–0:45		SS 0:30–0:45		1:00–1:30
WED		SS 0:45–1:00			0:45–1:00
THURS	Te 0:50–1:00		SS 0:30–0:45		1:20–1:45
FRI		*Rec* 1:00			1:00
SAT	SS 0:30–0:45		Te 2:15–2:30		2:45–3:15
SUN		Te 5:00	AE 0:15		5:15
VOLUME BY SPORT	1:50–2:30	6:45–7:00	3:30–4:15	0:45	12:50–14:30
WORKOUTS	3	3	4	1	11

Notes: Rec = Recovery. Optional workouts are in italic. The AE runs on Sunday are intended to follow the bike ride. Detail on the workouts can be found in the chapter. Strength workouts appear in Appendix C.

Build 2

THE LAST 3 TO 12 WEEKS before your A race are the most critical for your success. The workouts throughout the Build period will have a greater effect on your race preparation and fitness than those done at any other time of the year. In many ways, Build 2 is the most important block of the season. If training goes well in this block, then you are practically assured of a good race.

As you start Build 2, you should have 7 or 9 weeks remaining until the race. If you recover quickly and therefore train in 4-week blocks in the Build period, there should now be 7 weeks remaining until race day. If you recover more slowly and train in 3-week blocks, then you will repeat Build 2 and have 9 more weeks to go.

Objectives for Build 2

1. **Make your hard workouts even more racelike.** As discussed in Chapter 3, the single most important aspect of any periodization plan is that the workouts become increasingly like the race as training progresses. The hard workouts in the training plans at the end of this chapter will be very racelike.

2. **Train for race intensity.** A hard workout now is one that is done at race intensity or slightly harder. It is not one in which you go as fast as possible at all times. What makes these hard workouts possible are the easy ones you

will do on other days. In Build 2, the training sessions will be either hard or easy—never in between. Recovery between hard workouts is more important in the next few weeks than in any other block.

3. **Refine race strategy.** By the end of this block you must have a very good sense of your ability to go fast and of what it will take to have a successful race performance. In Build 2 you will refine your race-day pacing and nutrition so that there are no questions about your race readiness. In the block that follows, the Peak period, you will commit your race plan to paper.

4. **Maintain basic abilities.** In this block you will maintain your aerobic endurance, speed skills, and force. These are the fundamentals that are necessary for the development of the advanced abilities—muscular endurance and anaerobic endurance—which ultimately determine your physical preparation for a fast race.

Coaching Tips for Build 2

Many athletes are dealing with the same types of issues at this point in the season. It's a time when doubts can set in about whether you can achieve the goals you have set. There are other stresses that are also unique to this period. To address these issues, when I am coaching an athlete I discuss the following in Build 2.

MINDSET

You're almost there. Build 2 will be your last hard push to build fitness before the race, so make the most of it. Race preparation is as much a mental challenge as it is a physical one. You may naturally be questioning at this point whether the goals you set are realistic, so make this a time to assess how you are doing and make adjustments in your plan, if needed.

Question Your Readiness

Can you swim, bike, and run at your goal levels? Are you close to being ready for a fast race? How do you know? These are the questions I ask the athletes I coach every time we talk in Build 2. As a self-coached athlete, you need to ask yourself the same questions. By the end of Build 2 you should be able to answer them with confidence and assurance, knowing that you can, indeed, succeed. If you cannot answer them with confidence, you can then revise your goals so that you can go into the race with the right strategy for the goals you know you can attain.

Questioning your readiness is not negative thinking. It's realistic thinking. On race day you need to know exactly what you are capable of doing. Starting the race without knowing the answers to these questions is a sure way to fail. You are not going to suddenly develop the physiology to go fast just because you're at a race. Simply hoping and wishing for a fast race isn't going to hack it. You must train for a fast race and have demonstrated in workouts that you have what it takes to go fast. If you are not ready to succeed in your race goals, then you must downgrade your race goals to something you know is possible. Do not delude yourself into believing that somehow a miracle will happen and you will go fast on race day. That may happen in the movies, but it doesn't happen in the real world. Now is your last chance to build the fitness needed for race day while constantly assessing your progress.

If you decide to set different goals, set goals that are attainable but still worth working hard to attain. They should represent the very best that you are capable of doing. A good goal has two common characteristics: It stretches you to your limits, but you believe you can do it. If the first characteristic is missing, then the goal is too easy; if the second is missing, then it's too hard.

Stay Focused on Recovery and Quality

One of the biggest mistakes I see triathletes make in Build 2 is training too hard on recovery days. In fact, after a subpar performance in a B- or C-priority race, the common solution is to work harder, especially on the easy days. Working harder on the hard days is great. That's what produces racelike fitness. But increasing the intensity of the recovery days is counterproductive. This will only leave you tired for the truly hard workouts and reduce their quality.

Being recovered is the key to quality training. The easy workouts in Build 2 must be just that—easy. You will see a lot of them on your training plan at the end of this chapter. The proper intensity for these sessions is zone 1. This is a time when heart rate is the best indicator of how hard you are biking and running. For swimming, perceived exertion is your best indicator. On a scale of 1 to 10, with 10 being max effort, your recovery swims should feel like a 2 or 3. Focus on technique in all of the swim, bike, and run recovery sessions.

On Mondays in your Build 2 plan there is an optional recovery swim and a strength maintenance session in the gym. These should only be done if you are recovering quickly after workouts, you are highly motivated to work out, and training is going great. If there is any sign at all that things are not as they should be, then any given Monday must become a complete day of rest. That means no swimming and no weights. Rest. The key to quality racing is quality workouts. Coming into your Tuesday and Wednesday sessions tired will reduce their quality and ultimately your race performance.

If you make Monday a rest day, there are certain things you can do to boost recovery. The first is to stay off of your legs whenever possible. I tell the athletes I coach to never stand without support if they can lean against something, to never lean if they can sit, and to never sit if they can lie down. Give your body a break. On a recovery day, watch your nutrition closely, too. Include healthy carbs, choosing from fruits and veggies, lean proteins, and good fats and oils from fish, nuts, avocado, olive oil, canola oil, and flaxseed oil. Avoid junk food. Keep water handy and drink whenever thirsty. Do not drink water just to be drinking. That is counterproductive. Avoid sweetened drinks. Gentle stretching will also help recovery. Other common recovery aids are massage, napping, elevating your legs, floating in water, and listening to your favorite music.

Choose Training Partners Carefully

Training partners can be beneficial to your training or they can hold you back. It's good to have a variety of training partners with different abilities—including some who are faster than you and some who are slower. Work out with faster ones when you want to push hard in a session, such as when doing anaerobic endurance intervals. Train with slower partners when you want to recover and go easy.

Be wary of training partners with a gung-ho, macho, more-is-always-better attitude. Their enthusiasm for excess can be contagious. If you follow their lead, you will make training mistakes that could lead to injury, illness, burnout, or overtraining. Also avoid training partners with great emotional peaks and valleys, those who are ecstatic one day and depressed the next. They will prove to be a burden. Stay away from triathletes who must always "win" the workout. They will cause you to lose focus.

The best training partners are those who train hard when it's time to do so but can otherwise go easy, and who have a steady, easy-going, positive approach to workouts and life in general. Such a training partner will help you succeed. If you find someone with all of these traits, you are quite fortunate. They are rare. Be very kind to such a training partner.

NUTRITION

In Build 2, everything becomes more critical to your success—not only your workouts, but also your diet, your recovery after hard sessions, and your body weight, health, and physical soundness. We do not want any setbacks with only a handful of weeks remaining until your race. Earlier in the season there was time to recover from small setbacks and still rebuild fitness. We don't have that luxury now. Lost training in Build 2 means less fitness on race day.

Refine Race Nutrition

What will you eat and drink the day before the race, the morning of the race, and during the race? You probably already know the answer to this question from prior race experience, but if you don't, Build 2 is the time to refine your race-nutrition plan. The following is what I recommend to the athletes I coach.

The day before a race, you should not make wholesale changes in your normal diet. Just slightly shift your diet toward an emphasis on carbohydrate, especially from vegetables and fruits. Your evening meal might include a baked potato, sweet potato, or yam, for example. A banana is also a good choice for a portion of this meal. These foods are rich in carbs and do not have too much fiber. Be sure to also include protein and good fats today as you normally do. Fish is a great source of both. Try out a few different versions of this meal before hard training days and see what works best for you.

You should also try out your morning pre-race meal at least once in Build 2. A good time to do this is before a B- or C-priority race, a Saturday swim, or a Sunday ride. Ironman athletes should try out their planned breakfast on the morning of their Big Day workout 4 weeks prior to the race (explained later in this chapter). Eat at least 2 hours prior to starting the race or workout, taking in 200 to 600 calories, mostly from carbs. How much you eat depends on your body size, the amount of time until the race, the length of the race, and your own experience with trying out different eating plans in training and previous races. The bigger you are, the more you should eat. The more time you have until your race start, the more you can eat. The longer the race is, the more you must eat. A longer time between breakfast and racing also means a wider variety of choices, as you will have more time to digest your meal.

Your morning, pre-race food should be something that is not too high in fiber and that has a low to moderate glycemic index, such as a potato, sweet potato, or yam; a banana or plantain; or other fruits that meet these requirements. But, most importantly, eat whatever you have found works best for you. Many athletes eat oatmeal before a race. If you prefer to eat cereal, avoid sugary products. Applesauce is popular with some due to its consistency and ready availability when traveling to a race. Look for applesauce with no sugar added. Adding protein powder to oatmeal, cereal, and applesauce will lower the glycemic index while providing additional nutrients. A sports bar with protein included works for some—just be sure to drink some water along with it. Many athletes choose liquid fuel sources for their pre-race meals due to nervous stomachs and lack of appetite first thing in the morning. Fruit or vegetable juices may serve this purpose. You could also make something in a blender or use a commercial product such as Mix 1 or Ensure. But again, be sure to try out these options on training days to see what works for you.

In the last hour before the race, take in only water. Sugar at this time is likely to cause an insulin reaction, which lowers your normal blood sugar level. With 10 minutes remaining until the start, you can take in some carb, perhaps as a gel washed down with water or a sports drink. Rehearse this in Build 2 by using the same product before working out.

During the race you will need fluids and possibly carbohydrate, depending on the race duration. For events lasting less than an hour or perhaps even up to 90 minutes, it's all right to drink a commercial sports product—though, for fit athletes, water is adequate. Solid food will likely cause an upset stomach and is unnecessary for short events. For races 90 minutes to 4 hours long, sports drinks and gels taken with water work well for most athletes.

For races longer than 4 hours, I have the athletes I coach consider fluids and fuel as two separate matters. If you try to get both from a sports drink, you're likely to get too much of one and not enough of the other, which can lead to bloating or bonk-ing. Instead, simply drink when you are thirsty (see Chapter 8). Water is the best choice, but a diluted sports drink will do. Take in carbs from a source other than a sports drink at a rate that meets your needs. For most athletes this will fall into the range of 200 to 400 calories per hour, with the precise amount depending on body size and experience with using carbs in long training sessions. The faster you go, the fewer the calories you will be able to take in without causing gastric shutdown. This is especially true when it comes to solids. Good sources of carbs might be gels, blocks, sports beans, or bars.

The bottom line here is to rehearse and refine your race nutrition in Build 2. Leave nothing to chance on race day.

Eat to Recover

In Chapter 7 I explained some principles for eating right for optimal recovery. You may recall that it involves five stages of eating throughout the day based on the tim-ing and difficulty of training. By this time in the season athletes sometimes tell me they aren't recovering well. They may be going into key workouts a bit more fatigued than they feel they should be. Some fatigue is normal. But if your fatigue level is so high that you can't achieve the prescribed power or pace of a hard workout, then it's too high. With the athletes I coach who are experiencing this, I ask questions to find out why it is happening, and I often discover that these athletes are not paying close enough attention to their diet in stages 3 and 4.

Good athletes often take things to the extreme. They think that if a little bit of something is good for you, then a lot of that thing will be great. The nutritional plan I outlined in Chapter 7 says to cut back on the starchy, high-carb foods in stage 5, which is the time of day after all training and immediate postworkout recovery is done. Doing so often results in a slight loss of excess body fat over these blocks of training along with a boost in the immune system, helping you to avoid upper respiratory infections. When athletes realize this is happening, they sometimes become overly zealous about reducing starches and sugars in their diets. As a result, they sometimes don't eat enough of these types of foods in stages 3 and 4.

Stages 3 and 4 are critical to your recovery, so make sure you are getting the carbohydrate you need at that point in the day to replenish your stores of glycogen. Stages 3 and 4 combined last as long as the duration of the preceding workout, with stage 3 taking up the first 30 minutes immediately following a hard workout. If you don't refill your muscle glycogen stores with fast-acting carbs (starch and sugar) at this time, your recovery will be incomplete, and this may well slow you down for your next hard workout. In these stages, eat as if your race success depended on it, because it does.

Allow Body Weight to Normalize

In Build 2 your body weight is likely to fluctuate a bit one way or the other. If you are eating a healthy diet—meaning lots of vegetables, fruits, and lean protein—then don't be concerned with changes of 1 or 2 pounds (1 kilogram) either up or down. Your body is simply adjusting to keep you healthy. If you have gained more than about 2 pounds since the end of Base 3, then you need to reconsider what you are eating, especially in stage 5 of recovery (see Chapter 7). A weight gain may also result from missing too many workouts. Give serious thought to both sides of the equation—calories in and calories out—as well as to the types of foods you are eating in stage 5. Eating a lot of starch and sugar in the last stage of the day is likely to add unwanted body fat. Starches and sugars rebuild glycogen stores when eaten in stages 3 and 4, but in stage 5 they are more likely to be converted to body fat.

Weight may actually come off for some in Build 2 as a result of the harder training. Again, if this is more than about 2 pounds, then you may need to closely examine your diet relative to your level of exercise. Excessive weight loss can compromise your long-term recovery, leaving you fatigued when it's time to do a hard workout. If you are overly fatigued, read the previous section, "Eat to Recover." You may not be getting enough of what you need in stages 3 and 4.

STAYING HEALTHY AND INJURY-FREE

When you train hard, your immune system is under a great deal of stress and may not be able to fend off invaders. You must help it now more than at any time in the season. If you become sick in Build 2, you will miss the most important workouts of your long buildup to the race. Go out of your way to avoid people who are sneezing, coughing, or otherwise obviously sick, whether they're at work, school, parties, or in your family. Traveling to races or for any other reasons can be particularly risky. By making it a habit to keep one hand relatively germ-free, as described in Chapter 8, and washing your hands frequently when you are around people, you increase your chances of staying healthy.

You must also avoid injury that would set you back. This means stopping a workout whenever something doesn't feel right. It could be a slight twinge in a tendon or joint or even just a sense that you aren't up to training on a given day. One missed workout is far better than missing a week or two while recuperating from an injury. Prevention is less costly than the cure.

Do not train with niggling injuries. No matter how insignificant it may seem at the time, the first step is to always rest when something isn't right. During this time, do whatever training you can that doesn't aggravate the tender spot. If, with two days of rest, the discomfort isn't gone or at least considerably better, then make an appointment to see a physical therapist, sports doctor, chiropractor, or other health-care professional immediately.

The bottom line here is that you must stay healthy and injury-free in the last few weeks before an A-priority race.

Build 2 Workouts

As with the previous blocks, your training plan at the end of this chapter is based on the distance of your A-priority race. As you read about the workouts in this block, refer to your plan to see how it all fits together. In some cases you may want to refer back to a previous chapter to read the details for training a specific ability. This is especially true if you are just starting to read this book as you enter Build 2 in your season. That's rather late in the year to start an entirely different way of training, so I'd suggest that you include only the most important workouts from the following plan while keeping much of what you previously have been doing the same. The most important workouts in the plan are those that are scheduled for the weekends.

In Build 2 the hard workouts are harder and the easy workouts are easier than in Build 1. You're either training to go faster or recovering—never in between. Although the basic abilities are included, your primary focus is on race intensity. Remember that the key to fast racing is not how many miles you do, but what you do with the miles. Logging big weekly volume numbers is not nearly as important for an athlete of your ability as going fast in training. "Fast," in this case, means race intensity. In Build 2, you will do a great deal of race-intensity training. And you must be recovered for each of these key sessions.

In Build 2 you will also maintain the basic abilities that you developed in the Base period—aerobic endurance, speed skills, and force. Aerobic endurance and force are built into your workouts in Build 2. As in previous blocks, AE training involves steady efforts at your zone 2 heart rate, power, or pace. Force training for swimming calls for the use of paddles or drag devices. On the bike, force training is combined with muscular endurance intervals on a hill. Going uphill increases the force component of the power formula explained in Chapter 2 (Power = Force × Velocity).

Good technique is critical for fast racing. All of the swim workouts in this block include speed skills sets, and speed skills are also included in your Tuesday runs in the form of strides (see Chapter 5). You will have training time dedicated to skills enhancement, but you should swim, bike, and run with good technique even when it isn't the focus of a workout. Never allow your form to break down in training in order to go faster. You must also maintain your technique in races. In fact, whether training or racing, as the pace or power increases, you must concentrate even more on maintaining good technique.

The workouts in Build 2 are quite similar to the ones you did in Build 1, but there are some slight changes. You will do more work intervals and shorter recovery intervals for anaerobic endurance and muscular endurance sessions. For sprint, Olympic, and half-Ironman athletes, the emphasis is primarily on muscular endurance, just as it was in Build 1. Ironman athletes continue to focus most of their training on aerobic endurance or slightly higher, which is race intensity. In Build 2 there is also a greater emphasis on T2 transition practice.

The courses you use for your bike and run workouts should simulate the racecourse you will encounter in your A-priority race as much as possible. If you can manage to fit it in, open-water swims in this block are also a good idea. They may replace your Saturday swim sessions. Open-water swims should always be done with a partner or in a lifeguarded area for safety. Having a swim partner also allows you to practice drafting, which is critical to a fast swim. Open-water swim workouts are *fartlek* sessions, meaning they are unstructured. I recommend that you include both fast and slow portions, depending on how you feel at the time, but spending a great deal of time at race effort.

MUSCULAR ENDURANCE WORKOUTS

Muscular endurance remains the most important aspect of your training in Build 2 regardless of your race distance. The intensity of these workouts is the same as your race intensity, unless you are training for an Iron-distance race. Iron-distance racers will still do these workouts, however, as muscular endurance training builds greater fitness, making race intensity more manageable on race day. Regardless of your race distance, these are the workouts that will do the most to improve your pace and power while preparing you for the stress of racing.

Swim Muscular Endurance

The ME intervals in Build 2 are long, about 5 minutes each, with short (15-second) recoveries. Use the following guidelines to determine the length of your ME intervals:

Avg. 100 m Time	ME Interval
1:45	250–300
1:30	300–400
<1:30	400–500

The Saturday An + ME + SS (sprint and Olympic) and ME + AE + SS (half-Ironman and Ironman) swim sets are done as described below. You may also substitute an open-water swim, done as a fartlek session with long, unstructured intervals at race intensity and faster. Again, open-water swims should be done with a partner to practice drafting.

On Tuesdays, half-Ironman and Ironman athletes will do an SS + ME + AE swim workout as follows. The Tuesday swim for sprint- and Olympic-distance triathletes is described in the "Swim Anaerobic Endurance" section later in this chapter.

Duration: 45–60 min.

Warm-up	4–6 × 50 m with descending times (faster for each subsequent 50)
An set	3 × 100–300 m at pace zone 5b (Appendix B)
	30 to 40-sec. recoveries
	[Optional: Omit the An set and replace it with SS sets, 10 × 25 m, including personal limiter drills and long recoveries]
ME set	3 × 250–500 m at pace zone 4–5a
	15-sec. recoveries
SS set	10 × 25 m, fast, with focus on technique
	Long recoveries
Cooldown	200 m, easy swim focusing on technique

Race Distance	Duration
Half-Ironman	60–75 min.
Ironman	75–90 min.

Warm-up	4–6 × 50 m with descending times (faster for each subsequent 50)
ME set	4–5 × 250–500 m at pace zone 4–5a
	15-sec. recoveries
AE set	800–1,000 m, steady at pace zone 2
SS set	10 × 25 m, fast, with focus on technique
	Long recoveries
Cooldown	100 m, easy swim focusing on technique

Duration: 45–60 min.

Warm-up/SS set	4–6 × 50 m with descending times (faster for each subsequent 50)
ME set	3–4 × 250–500 m at pace zone 4–5a (Appendix B)
	15-sec. recoveries
AE set/cooldown	10–20 min., steady at pace zone 2

The Thursday swim sets are as follows.

Race Distance	*Duration*
Sprint	30–45 min.
Olympic, half-Ironman, Ironman	45–60 min.

Warm-up/SS set	10 × 25 m, including technique focus and/or personal-limiter drills
	Long recoveries
Fo set	4 × 25 m, including 6-stroke sprint with paddles or drag device at the start of each 25, finishing each at ME effort
	30-sec. recoveries
ME set	3–4 × 250–500 m at pace zone 4–5a (Appendix B)
	15-sec. recoveries
Cooldown	100–300 easy swim focused on technique

Bike Muscular Endurance

As in Build 1, there are two ME bike workouts on the schedule in Build 2, one on Wednesdays and the other on Saturdays. For sprint- and Olympic-distance athletes, the Wednesday ME + Fo workout is an optional session that may replace An + Fo that day. If you are racing at one of these distances and you had good results doing An + Fo in Build 1, then you may continue that type of training in Build 2. If you experienced niggling injuries or soreness, especially in the knees, or slow recovery, leaving you exceptionally tired for the Thursday swim or even the Saturday run, then I'd recommend that you do the optional ME + Fo workout on Wednesdays following these workouts in Build 1.

Ironman athletes will replace the Saturday ME session with aerobic endurance training. AE is race effort, power, or heart rate for the Ironman athlete. Although it is not exactly race intensity for Ironman athletes, the Wednesday workout prepares you for the hills on the course and develops greater force so that you can improve your power on the flat sections. For all other distances, the ME workouts are done at race intensity. This is zone 3 or 4 heart rate or power, depending on your race distance.

The following is an example of the Wednesday bike ME + Fo workouts for Build 2 for all race distances. For the sprint and Olympic distances, this is an optional workout to replace the scheduled An + Fo bike session.

Warm-up	10–30 min. of gradually increasing effort and gearing
ME + Fo set	4–6 × 6- to 8-min. hill repeats at HR or power zone 4
	Ride at less than 80 rpm in aero position
	Recover on the descents
Cooldown	10–30 min., spinning with decreasing effort

On the following page are examples of the Sunday bike ME + AE workouts for Build 2 by race distance. Transition to a 15-minute run following the bike.

Run Muscular Endurance

For sprint, Olympic, and half-Ironman athletes there are three ME run workouts in Build 2. The first is on Tuesdays, which is an optional substitute for the An + Fo run workout for the two shorter distances. If your A-priority race is at one of these distances and you did the An + Fo workout in Build 1, then continue with that same session and disregard the Tuesday ME run session described here. If you didn't do the An + Fo run in Build 1, or if you did it but experienced injury, unusual soreness,

Race Distance	Duration
Sprint and Olympic	1 hr. 30 min.–2 hr.
Half-Ironman	2–3 hr.

Warm-up	15 min. of gradually increasing intensity and gearing
ME set	3–5 × 8 min. in HR zone 4–5a (Appendix B) or power zone 4–5
	2-min. easy-spin recoveries
AE set	30–45 min. in HR or power zone 2
Cooldown	Easy spinning, decreasing effort for the remainder of the ride

---

Warm-up	15 min. of gradually increasing intensity and gearing
ME set	3–4 × 12 min. in zone 4
	3-min. easy-spin recoveries
AE set	30–60 min. in HR or power zone 2
Cooldown	Easy spinning with decreasing effort for the remainder of the ride

---

Warm-up	10 min. of gradually increasing intensity and gearing
ME set	4–5 × 15–20 min. in zone 3
	4- to 5-min. easy-spin recoveries
AE set	30–90 min. in HR or power zone 2
Cooldown	Easy spinning with decreasing effort for the remainder of the ride

---

or extreme fatigue in the days following the workout, then do the SS + ME session that follows instead. This Tuesday session is the only ME workout in Build 2 for Ironman athletes who focus strictly on aerobic endurance training on the weekends.

The ME run workouts on Tuesdays in Build 2 are done as follows. For sprint- and Olympic-distance triathletes, these are optional workouts that may replace the An run sessions scheduled for Tuesdays.

Race Distance	Duration
Sprint and Olympic	45 min.–1 hr.
Half-Ironman and Ironman	1 hr.–1 hr. 15 min.

Warm-up	20–30 min. of gradually increasing effort and pace
SS set	5 × 20-sec. strides at fast pace on grass or other soft surface
	60- to 90-sec. walk recoveries
ME set	3–4 × 5 min. at pace zone 4 (Appendix B)
	2-min. jog-walk recoveries
Cooldown	10 min. easy jogging

Warm-up	15–35 min. of gradually increasing effort and pace
SS set	5 × 20-sec. strides at fast pace on grass or other soft surface
	60 to 90 sec. walk recoveries
ME set	3–4 × 8 min. at pace zone 3
	2-min. jog-walk recoveries
Cooldown	10 min. easy jogging

Note that on Sundays Ironman athletes complete a 5- to 6-hour AE ride.

The second ME run workout (ME + AE, see p. 234) is on Saturdays in Build 2. For sprint, Olympic, and half-Ironman triathletes, this is the most important run of the week. If there are scheduling conflicts that will cause you to miss training on Saturday in any given week, then rearrange the sessions so that this one is done on another day and omit one of the other runs. If your lifestyle permits, the Saturday workout is actually best done on Thursdays because then you have more time for recovery before your Sunday bike ride, which is the most important ride of the week. I've scheduled the long ME run for Saturdays simply because most athletes are unable to do long workouts on weekdays.

Race Distance	Duration
Sprint	1 hr.–1 hr. 30 min.
Olympic	1 hr. 15 min.–1 hr. 45 min.
Half-Ironman	1 hr. 30 min.–2 hr.

01 SPRINT

Warm-up	15 min. of gradually increasing effort (or 30-min. bike ride, with last 10 min. at zone 4 [Appendix B])
ME set	3–5 × 5 min. at HR or pace zone 4 *75-sec. easy jog recoveries*
AE set	30–60 min. steady in zone 2
Cooldown	Running easily with decreasing effort

02 OLYMPIC

Warm-up	15 min. of gradually increasing effort (or 30-min. bike ride, with last 10 min. at zone 4)
ME set	4–6 × 5 min. at HR or pace zone 4 *75-sec. easy jog recoveries*
AE set	30–60 min. steady in zone 2
Cooldown	Running easily with decreasing effort

03 HALF IRONMAN

Warm-up	10 min. of gradually increasing effort (or 30-min. bike ride, with last 10 minutes at zone 3)
ME set	5–8 × 9 min. at HR or pace zone 3 *60-sec. walk recoveries*
AE set	30–60 min. steady in zone 2
Cooldown	Running easily with decreasing effort

The ME + AE run combines both duration and racelike intensity, which is why it is your most important run. To make it even more racelike, ride for 30 minutes and then transition to the run. This bike set starts with about 20 minutes of gradually increasing intensity to get you warmed up and finishes with about 10 minutes of race intensity. You can then work on your T2 transition and start the run without warming up. If you decide not to do the bike portion, include a warm-up in your run before starting the SS + ME sets.

The opposite page shows examples of the Saturday Build 2 ME + AE run workout. Sprint, Olympic, and half-Ironman athletes may start with a 30-minute bike ride, with the last 10 minutes or so at race intensity, and then transition to the following run. If you do this bike workout, omit the run warm-up and start the run portion immediately with intervals. This will shorten your run by the duration of the warm-up.

Note that Ironman triathletes don't do an ME run on Saturdays in Build 2, but rather an AE run.

The third ME run of the week is on Sundays, and it is a brick run of 15 minutes. This gives you the opportunity to rehearse your second transition and become accustomed to running at race effort immediately after a hard and long bike ride. The exception here is for Ironman athletes, who will do an AE run on Sundays or a Saturday Big Day workout four weeks prior to race day (explained later in this chapter).

ANAEROBIC ENDURANCE WORKOUTS

If you did anaerobic endurance workouts in Build 1 and feel they were beneficial then, continue them in Build 2. Continue to treat these workouts cautiously, however, as the risk of injury is high, especially for running. The possibility of reward is also high. These workouts can boost aerobic capacity, improve lactate threshold, and increase economy. They are for sprint- and Olympic-distance athletes only.

The recovery intervals in the An workouts are now shortened from what they were in Build 1. The purpose of this is to make these sessions more like your upcoming race, where there will be no recoveries at all. The effort, pace, or power remain unchanged from Build 1 unless you find that you are now faster. If so, return to Chapter 8 and reread the section on "Anaerobic Endurance Workouts" (p. 195), where pace and power determinations are described.

Swim Anaerobic Endurance

Anaerobic endurance training for the swim will be part of the Tuesday SS + An + AE workout. There is also a Saturday An + ME + SS swim, but that workout is explained in the "Swim Muscular Endurance" section above. The focus of the Tuesday workout is the An set, though you will add SS and AE sets to maintain the advances you made in speed skills and aerobic endurance in previous blocks. The only change in the An set is a shortening of the recovery intervals.

If you have decided not to do anaerobic endurance training for the swim, replace the An set with the ME set in the workout description that follows. The Build 2 SS + An + AE swim sets for sprint- and Olympic-distance triathletes are as follows.

Race Distance	Duration
Sprint	30–45 min.
Olympic	45–60 min.

Warm-up/SS set	10 × 25 m, including technique focus and/or personal-limiter drills
	Long recoveries
An set	5 × 100–300 m at pace zone 5b (Appendix B)
	30- to 40-sec. recoveries
	[Optional ME set to replace An set: 3–4 × 250–500 m at pace zone 4–5a, *10-sec. recoveries*]
AE set/cooldown	10–20 min., steady at pace zone 2

Race Distance	Duration
Sprint	1 hr.–1 hr. 15 min.
Olympic	1 hr.–1 hr. 30 min.

Warm-up	20 min. of gradually increasing effort and gearing
An + Fo set	5 × 3 min. on a hill, seated and sitting up, power zone 6 or perceived exertion 9 on a 1–10 scale
	2-min. recoveries
	[Optional ME + Fo set to replace An + Fo set: 5 × 5 min. on a hill, seated and sitting up, HR zone 4–5a (Appendix B) or power zone 4–5, *quick descents for the recoveries*]
Cooldown	10–30 min. at zone 2 power or heart rate on a flat to gently rolling course

Bike Anaerobic Endurance

On Wednesdays sprint- and Olympic-distance triathletes may opt to do an An + Fo bike workout. This remains the same as in Build 1 except for a shortening of the recovery intervals from 3 minutes to 2 minutes. The performance reward for this type of training on the bike is the same as it was for the swim—improvement of VO_2max, lactate threshold, and economy. The risk is for your knees. Climbing a hill at a high power output places a lot of stress on them, so if you want to protect your knees from injury, you can skip anaerobic endurance training on the bike. Those who choose not to do the anaerobic sets can replace that portion of the workout with muscular endurance training, doing an ME + Fo set instead. See the An + Fo bike workout for sprint- and Olympic-distance triathletes scheduled for Wednesdays in Build 2, with an optional ME + Fo set.

Run Anaerobic Endurance

The Tuesday anaerobic endurance run for sprint- and Olympic-distance training in Build 2 is much the same as the parallel workout in Build 1 except for two small changes: First, a speed skills set has been added following the warm-up, and second, the recovery between An intervals has been shortened from 3 minutes to 2.5 minutes. This workout is best done on a track, but it may also be done on a soft surface such as grass or dirt. Do not run fast intervals on pavement, as the pounding the legs and feet take increases your risk of injury. As with the swim and bike ride, you may opt to replace the An set with an ME set.

Here is the SS + An run workout for sprint- and Olympic-distance triathletes scheduled for Tuesdays in Build 2:

Duration: 45–60 min.

Warm-up	15–20 min. of gradually increasing effort
SS set	5 × 20-sec. strides at fast pace on grass or other soft surface
An set	5 × 3 min. on a track or flat road at pace zone 5b (Appendix B) or RPE 9
	2.5-min. recoveries
	[Optional ME set to replace An set: 3–4 × 5 min. at pace zone 4, *2-min. jog-walk recoveries*]
Cooldown	5–20 min. of easy jogging

THE "BIG DAY" WORKOUT

If your A-priority race will be an Ironman, you will do another "Big Day" workout four weekends before your race. This will be your second (and last) Big Day training session of the season, and therefore will serve as your last chance to rehearse your race. The basic workout was described in Chapter 8. It will occur on the weekend before your Build 2 rest-and-test week regardless of whether you are training in 3- or 4-week blocks. As in Build 1, the workout is scheduled for a Saturday so that if the weather is nasty you can move it to Sunday. If you do the workout on Saturday, take Sunday off as a complete day of rest and recuperation.

You will have already learned several things from your Build 1 Big Day. By now you should be able to complete this workout much more easily than you did the first time. If you cannot, then you must give a great deal of thought to your race goals relative to your fitness. Are your goals set too high? Or were there factors beyond your control that interfered with your workout performance, such as bad weather, a head cold or other illness, or equipment failure? After the second Big Day workout, decide if your goals are appropriate and make changes to the race plan that should now be taking form in your mind. At the end of the Peak block you will commit that plan to paper.

Here's how the Ironman Big Day workout is done.

IRONMAN BIG DAY WORKOUT

4:30 a.m.–5:00 a.m.	Wake up and eat a race-day breakfast, followed by some light stretching and mental preparation.
7:00 a.m.–8:00 a.m.	Swim for 1 hour at race intensity, using race-day gear.
8:00 a.m.–9:30 a.m.	Get off of your legs and eat a light meal.
9:30 a.m.–2:30 p.m.	Ride as you will on race day, mimicking the intensity, equipment, clothing, fluids, and nutrition planned for the race.
2:30 p.m.–4:00 p.m.	Get off of your legs and eat a light, mostly liquid meal.
4:00 p.m.–6:00 p.m.	Run as you will on race day, mimicking the intensity, clothing, shoes and other gear, fluids, and nutrition planned for the race.

RECOVERY WORKOUTS

The most obvious change in the training plans for Build 2 compared to Build 1 is the increase in recovery workouts. In Build 2, if you aren't doing a hard workout, then you should be recovering. Any time you see "Rec" in your plan, the workout is very easy, with the effort, heart rate, pace, or power in zone 1. You can shorten the recovery workouts or even omit them entirely if you are feeling fatigued. Be very cautious about doing the optional recovery workouts listed (the ones with "Rec" in parentheses). Doing them when you are tired will only add to your fatigue level and reduce the quality of the workouts scheduled for the following days. These workouts are included because many advanced athletes find that an easy spin on the bike or a short swim speeds recovery. If this is not the case for you, then skip these workouts and rest.

STRENGTH MAINTENANCE

You will continue your gym workouts in Build 2 to maintain the strength you established earlier in the season. This is now the least important workout on your training plan, however. If you are not recovering well and something must be cut from the plan so you can get more rest, this is it. You may, however, be able to continue with core strength training. If you are managing the brief SM workout well and it has no negative effect on your Tuesday swim or run workouts, then continue doing it the same way as in Build 1.

Build 2 Testing

You will do the same testing in the last week of Build 2 that you did in Build 1. The purpose in testing now is to measure improvements in performance by comparing the data with earlier results. You should see quite significant changes in your performance compared to the Base period. It's possible that you won't see any improvement from the more recent test results in Build 1, however, simply because it has only been three or four weeks since the Build 1 testing. Any improvements will likely be small.

There are also many variables that are difficult to control each time you conduct a test, and these may also affect the results. The weather on the day of the test, recent work- or school-related stress, other emotional stresses such as difficulties with your finances or relationships, and poor sleep patterns just prior to testing can all change the outcome slightly. As always, you should manage as many of the controllable variables as possible, including equipment choices, the test venue, the time of day for testing, the amount of rest you get prior to the test, your diet in the 24 hours preceding the test, and the pretest warm-up. These should all be as close as possible to what they were in previous testing.

As in Build 1, you may also opt to do a race in Build 2 to see how your fitness is coming along. If it's a B-priority race, it is best done at the end of the rest-and-test week so that you are well rested and ready to go all out. C-priority races may be done at any time in Build 2. But realize that if you are tired from a hard training week leading up to a race, your results may not be a good indication of your current status. It is not a good idea to back off your training before a C-priority race in the midst of the hard training weeks of Build 2. Backing off to prepare for a minor race at this time will have negative consequences for your fitness for your A-priority race. Athletes often do this because they lose direction just before a race. They rest up for a C-priority race and miss out on having great fitness for their A-priority race. There's no avoiding the fact that skipping a workout or two before a C race will cost you fitness for your A race.

Be cautious of racing too much in Build 2. A short-course triathlete may do a couple of races in this block. In fact, a sprint-distance triathlete can race nearly every weekend and cool down afterward with an extended run or ride. Olympic-distance athletes can also add a bike or run after a short-course race, but they are better off racing no more than twice in this block. For the half-Ironman triathlete the best option is to race once in Build 2. This race should come at the end of the rest-and-test week. I'd suggest an Olympic-distance race for those who are doing a half-Ironman. An Ironman triathlete should do only one race, preferably a half-Ironman, in the entire eight or nine weeks of the Build period.

SWIM FIELD TEST

The swim field test is the same as it was in Build 1; see p. 210 in Chapter 8. The purpose here is to gauge your effort and ability to maintain a steady tempo when swimming at race pace. If you slow down as the test set progresses, then you must give a great deal of consideration to your goal.

BIKE FIELD TEST

The bike field test is also the same as it was in Build 1; see p. 211 in Chapter 8. Go back to Chapter 8 and read the details of this test because it may help you to keep the variables constant. As with the swim test, the purpose is to see if you can maintain goal race effort or heart rate without slowing down, or, if you are using a power meter, to ensure that you are not decoupling (as explained in Chapter 6). If your training has been going well and your race-pace goals are realistic, then you should have no great difficulty with this test.

RUN FIELD TEST

Do not use a treadmill for the run test unless it is calibrated, which takes special equipment. Use the same venue as you used in Build 1, if possible. It would be helpful to reread the section on the run field test in Chapter 8, p. 212 before testing again.

| Warm-up | 10–20 min. of gradually increasing effort and gearing |
| Test set | Run at goal race heart rate or pace (pace is preferred) based on your race distance |

Race Distance	Test Interval
Sprint	3 km at goal race heart rate or pace
Olympic	5 km at goal race heart rate or pace
Half-Ironman	10 km at goal race heart rate or pace
Ironman	2 hr. at goal race heart rate or pace

| Cooldown | Run at slower than race effort for the remainder of the workout |

TRAINING PLAN — BUILD 2

SPRINT-DISTANCE TRAINING **BUILD 2**

T R A I N I N G   W E E K S

SPORT	SWIM	BIKE	RUN	STRENGTH	DAILY VOLUME
MON	*Rec 0:15–0:30*			SM 0:45	0:45–1:15
TUES	SS + An *ME + AE* 0:30–0:45	*SS or Rec 0:45–1:00*	SS + An *or SS + ME* 0:45–1:00		1:15–2:45
WED		An + Fo *ME + Fo* 1:00–1:	*Rec 0:30–0:45*		1:00–2:00
THURS	SS + Fo + ME 0:30–0:45		*Rec 0:30–0:45*		1:00–1:30
FRI	*Rec 0:15–0:30*	*Rec 1:00–1:15*			1:00–1:45
SAT	An *SS + ME + SS* 0:45–1:00	*Rec 0:30–0:45 or 0:30 build to race intensity, T2 to run*	ME + AE 1:00–1:30		1:45–3:15
SUN		ME + AE 1:30–2:00	ME 0:15		1:45–2:15
VOLUME BY SPORT	1:45–3:30	3:30–6:15	2:30–4:15	0:45	8:30–14:45
WORKOUTS	**3–5**	**3–5**	**4–5**	**1**	**11–16**

R E S T   &   T E S T   W E E K

SPORT	SWIM	BIKE	RUN	STRENGTH	DAILY VOLUME
MON				SM 0:45	0:45
TUES	SS 0:15–0:30		SS 0:30–0:45		0:45–1:15
WED		SS 0:45–1:00			0:45–1:00
THURS	Te 0:25–0:30 *or SS if race*		SS 0:30–0:45		0:55–1:15
FRI		Rec 1:00 *or Race*			1:00
SAT	SS 0:15–0:30 *or Race*		Te 0:45 *or Race or SS if race Sun*		1:00–1:15
SUN		Te 1:30 *or Rec or Race*	ME 0:15 *or no run if race Sat*		1:30–1:45
VOLUME BY SPORT	0:55–1:30	3:15–3:30	2:00–2:45	0:45	6:55–8:15
WORKOUTS	**3**	**3**	**4**	**1**	**11**

Notes: Rec = Recovery. Optional workouts are in italic. The ME runs on Sunday are intended to follow the bike ride. Detail on the workouts can be found in the chapter. Strength workouts appear in Appendix C.

OLYMPIC-DISTANCE TRAINING BUILD 2

T R A I N I N G   W E E K S

SPORT	SWIM	BIKE	RUN	STRENGTH	DAILY VOLUME
MON	Rec 0:15–0:30			SM 0:45	0:45–1:15
TUES	SS + An ME + AE 0:45–1:00	Rec 0:45–1:00	SS + An or SS + ME 0:45–1:00		1:30–3:00
WED		An + Fo ME + Fo 1:00–1:30	SS 0:30–0:45		1:00–2:15
THURS	SS + Fo + ME 0:45–1:00		Rec 0:30–0:45		1:15–1:45
FRI	Rec 0:15–0:30	Rec 1:00–1:30			1:00–2:00
SAT	An SS + ME + SS 0:45–1:00	Rec 0:45–1:00 or 0:30 build to race intensity, T2 to run	ME + AE 1:15–1:45		2:00–3:45
SUN		ME + AE 1:30–2:00	ME 0:15		1:45–2:15
VOLUME BY SPORT	2:15–4:00	3:30–7:00	2:45–4:30	0:45	9:15–16:15
WORKOUTS	3–5	3–5	4–5	1	11–16

R E S T   &   T E S T   W E E K

SPORT	SWIM	BIKE	RUN	STRENGTH	DAILY VOLUME
MON				SM 0:45	0:45
TUES	SS 0:30–0:45		SS 0:30–0:45		1:00–1:30
WED		SS 0:45–1:00			0:45–1:00
THURS	Te 0:30–0:40 or Rec if race		SS 0:30–0:45		1:00–1:25
FRI		Rec 1:00 or SS if race			1:00
SAT	SS 0:30–0:45 or Race		Te 1:15 or Race or no run if Sat race		1:45–2:00
SUN		Te 1:30 or Race or Rec if race Sat	ME 0:15 or no run if race Sat		1:45
VOLUME BY SPORT	1:30–2:10	3:15–3:30	2:30–3:00	0:45	8:00–9:25
WORKOUTS	3	3	4	1	11

Notes: Rec = Recovery. Optional workouts are in italic. The ME runs on Sunday are intended to follow the bike ride. Detail on the workouts can be found in the chapter. Strength workouts appear in Appendix C.

TRAINING PLAN -- BUILD 2

HALF-IRONMAN-DISTANCE TRAINING **BUILD 2**

TRAINING WEEKS

SPORT	SWIM	BIKE	RUN	STRENGTH	DAILY VOLUME
MON	Rec 0:30–0:40			SM 0:45	0:45–1:25
TUES	SS + ME + AE 0:45–1:00	Rec 1:00–1:30	SS + ME 1:00–1:15		1:45–3:45
WED		ME + Fo 1:30–2:00	Rec 0:45–1:00		1:30–3:00
THURS	SS + Fo + ME 0:45–1:00		Rec 1:00–1:15 or swap with Sat AE + ME run		1:45–2:15
FRI	Rec 0:30–0:40	Rec 1:00–1:30			1:00–2:10
SAT	ME + AE + SS 1:00–1:15	Rec 1:00–1:30 or 0:30 build to race intensity, T2 to run	ME + AE 1:30–2:00		2:30–4:45
SUN		ME + AE 2:00–3:00	ME 0:15		2:15–3:15
VOLUME BY SPORT	2:30–4:35	4:30–9:30	3:45–5:45	0:45	11:30–20:35
WORKOUTS	3–5	3–5	4–5	1	11–16

REST & TEST WEEK

SPORT	SWIM	BIKE	RUN	STRENGTH	DAILY VOLUME
MON				SM 0:45	0:45
TUES	SS 0:30–0:45		SS 0:30–0:45		1:00–1:30
WED		SS 0:45–1:00			0:45–1:00
THURS	Te 0:40–0:50 or SS if race		SS 0:30–0:45		1:10–1:35
FRI		Rec 1:00 or SS if race			1:00
SAT	SS 0:30–0:45 or Race		Te 1:30 or Race or SS if race Sun		2:00–2:15
SUN		Te 2:30 or Race or Rec if Sat race	ME 0:15 or no run if race Sat		2:45
VOLUME BY SPORT	1:40–2:20	4:15–4:30	2:45–3:15	0:45	9:25–10:50
WORKOUTS	3	3	4	1	11

Notes: Rec = Recovery. Optional workouts are in italic. The ME runs on Sunday are intended to follow the bike ride. Detail on the workouts can be found in the chapter. Strength workouts appear in Appendix C.

IRONMAN-DISTANCE TRAINING **BUILD 2**

T R A I N I N G   W E E K S

SPORT	SWIM	BIKE	RUN	STRENGTH	DAILY VOLUME
MON	Rec 0:30–0:40			SM 0:45	0:45–1:25
TUES	SS + ME + AE 0:45–1:00	Rec 1:00–1:30	SS + ME 1:00–1:15		1:45–3:45
WED		ME + Fo 1:30–2:00	Rec 0:45–1:00		1:30–3:00
THURS	SS + Fo + ME 0:45–1:00		Rec 1:00–1:15 or swap with Sat AE run		1:45–2:15
FRI	Rec 0:30–0:40	Rec 1:00–1:30			1:00–2:10
SAT	ME + AE + SS 1:15–1:30 or 1:00 Big Day wk 9 or 10	Rec 1:00–1:30 or 5:00 Big Day wk 4	AE 2:30–3:00 or 2:00 Big Day wk 4		3:45–6:00 or 8:00 Big Day wk 4
SUN		AE 5:00–6:00 or day off if Big Day Sat	ME 0:15 or day off if Big Day Sat		5:15–6:15 or day off if Big Day Sat
VOLUME BY SPORT	2:45–4:50	7:30–12:30	4:45–6:45	0:45	15:45–24:50
WORKOUTS	3–5	3–5	4–5	1	11–16

R E S T   &   T E S T   W E E K

SPORT	SWIM	BIKE	RUN	STRENGTH	DAILY VOLUME
MON				SM 0:45	0:45
TUES	SS 0:30–0:45		SS 0:30–0:45		1:00–1:30
WED		SS 0:45–1:00			0:45–1:00
THURS	Te 0:50–1:00		SS 0:30–0:45		1:20–1:45
FRI		Rec 1:00			1:00
SAT	SS 0:30–0:45		Te 2:15–2:30		2:45–3:15
SUN		Te 5:00	AE 0:15		5:15
VOLUME BY SPORT	1:50–2:30	6:45–7:00	3:30–4:15	0:45	12:50–14:30
WORKOUTS	3	3	4	1	11

Notes: Rec = Recovery. Optional workouts are in italic. The ME and AE runs on Sunday are intended to follow the bike ride. Detail on the workouts can be found in the chapter. Strength workouts appear in Appendix C.

Part IV

PEAK AND RACE

You are now about to start the most mentally challenging period of training in the entire season. I consider it mentally challenging because serious endurance athletes do not like to hold back in training, and that's what I will ask you to do. Cutting back on training nearly always makes triathletes anxious and eventually causes doubts about race-readiness. You simply have to hang in there with me for three more weeks.

If you've made it this far in the book following the training routine I've designed for you, then you must have some level of trust in me as your coach. Keep trusting me for the next few weeks. We are beginning the final preparation for your triathlon, and I know from experience that what we're about to do works. If you modify it so as not to feel anxious, then much of what has gone before will be for naught. This training plan is a complete package. Instead of a smorgasbord where you can pick and choose what you'll do, it's a five-course meal with the menu items chosen to fit together perfectly. It's all or nothing.

One final thought before you start the last part of your training: You can't "win" the race in these three weeks, but you can certainly "lose" it. You won't become more fit in the coming weeks; instead, you'll become more race-ready. There's a difference. I'll explain that in the next chapter.

Peak

AS YOU START THE PEAK BLOCK you should have 3 weeks remaining until your A-priority race. The first two of these are the Peak block. The third week is the Race block.

Athletes often refer to the Peak training block as the "taper." Although that is descriptive of a portion of what you will do in this block, it is also misleading. "Taper" implies cutting back on training, especially volume, whether in terms of time or distance. Although it's true that you will taper your volume in the Peak block, that's not all you will do for the next two weeks. If it was, then you would be likely to have a poor race. The key to racing well for the experienced and competitive tri-athlete is training intensity, and tapering says nothing about this.

I have developed my approach to tapering over 30 years of experience in coaching athletes of all abilities, basing it on research as well as my own observations. It's actually quite simple, and yet it is very effective. All it involves is reducing the volume of training over the course of two weeks while doing a minirace-simulation workout every third day. This means that between the race simulations there are two full days of recovery. By following this method during the Peak period as well as my instructions for the Race block, you will come into excellent race form on race day.

That's it. Now all we need to do is work out the details of how you will peak for your best triathlon ever.

Objectives for the Peak Period

1. **Make your hard workouts minirace simulations.** As mentioned many times in this book, your workouts must become increasingly like the race you are preparing for as the season progresses. At no time is this more important than in the Peak block. For the next two weeks you will rehearse and refine the many elements that go into a successful race.

2. **Rest and recover completely for each minirace simulation.** Workouts are now either very hard or very easy. "Hard" is defined as "like the race." You'll do several minirace simulations in the next two weeks. The recovery days are the key to how racelike these hard workouts will be. Whenever a recovery (Rec) workout is scheduled, you must go very easy. Moderate efforts (not quite racelike but harder than easy) on these days will have no benefit for your fitness and will leave you just a bit too tired to go all-out for the next hard session. You must be completely recovered for each minirace simulation.

3. **Reduce long-term fatigue gradually.** You've been carrying a good deal of fatigue around with you over the past several weeks. You may not even be aware of it any longer because it has become so common. You've probably lost your sensitivity to fatigue. Now is the time to shed that hidden fatigue. This is what coming into race form is all about. The fatigue will melt away as you taper the volume of training and increase the number of weekly recovery workouts.

4. **Rehearse and refine your transitions.** Hard-fought, close races are sometimes won and lost in transition. Speedy transitions may make the difference in your race outcome. In the Peak block, you will practice the transitions along with your racelike workouts. This will make the sessions even more racelike. The purpose of practicing T1 (the transition from the swim to the bike) and T2 (the transition from the bike to the run) is to refine your movements. After rehearsing them, you'll be able to do them efficiently without thinking.

5. **Prepare your race plan.** By the end of the Peak block you will create a detailed, written plan for your race. This plan will help to keep your focus on what is necessary for success on race day. I like to see lots of detail in these. But any plan, even a sketchy one, is better than no plan at all. And that is what most triathletes do—they go into their most important races of the year without a plan. Your plan will give shape and focus to even the most minute details

of race day. Once you've done this activity you will never again go into an A-priority race without a plan.

Coaching Tips for the Peak Period

The closer you get to race day the more critical everything becomes. With only a couple of weeks to go, your mindset, nutrition, race plan, and other matters all need to be dialed in if you are to achieve your race goals. The following are common topics I discuss with the athletes I coach as we start peaking for the big day.

MINDSET

The Peak block is a unique time in your season. It's so different from what preceded it that some athletes don't handle these two weeks very well. Whereas in the Base and Build periods your purpose was fitness, now it is race form. I'll explain what that means shortly. For now, let's examine what you can do to make the most of the Peak block.

Mentally Prepare for Race-Simulation Workouts

If you look ahead to your two-week training plan at the end of this chapter, you will see that there are hard workouts every third day. Recovery workouts are scheduled for the two days between these hard sessions. The hard workouts are intended to simulate the intensity and other conditions of your race. These must be racelike. And they must be racelike not only in terms of intensity, but also in terms of terrain, equipment, nutrition, and anything else that defines your race. Now more than ever before in the season you will need to consider all the details of each workout so that each is a race simulation—a minirace.

Expect to Feel Guilty and Anxious

For the past several weeks you have been training long and hard, with only a few breaks from the routine. Starting with the Peak block, the volume of your training begins to decline. This is necessary for success. In order to gain race form, you must rest. In fact, that's what form is—being rested, fresh, and race-ready. You certainly do not want to stand at the starting line on race day feeling tired. There's no question about it; you simply must rest.

However, after what you've been through over the past several months, cutting back on training is likely to leave you feeling both guilty and anxious. This is normal. Nearly every athlete experiences it. But you must come to grips with these feelings and not try to relieve them by adding more hard workouts or by increasing the volume of your workouts. Stick with the plan, and you will be ready on race day. Add to it, and you will not come into form.

Research and experience tell me that in the last three weeks before the race you can have no significant impact on fitness by training hard and long. There simply isn't enough time now to get into better shape. What you can accomplish in these two weeks of the Peak block is shedding some of the fatigue that has accumulated. You've been managing it for so long that you are probably not even aware of it anymore. Losing fatigue is what race form is all about. One of our objectives in these last three weeks before the race is to have you gain form by eliminating fatigue. This is the final piece that will help to produce your best possible triathlon. Don't blow it by giving into your feelings. Stay the course!

NUTRITION

In the Peak block, the volume of training begins to decrease. By the second week of the Peak block your weekly training time will be down 20 to 30 percent compared to Build 2. This means that if you continue to eat as you did in Build 2, you are likely to add some unwanted weight. So be aware of your eating in the Peak block, especially in stage 5 (see Chapter 7). This is the portion of your day when quick recovery is no longer the focus and you are eating meals. Watch your portions so that you don't overeat out of habit.

Do not, however, cut back on stage 3 and 4 recovery nutrition following hard workouts. Gauge how much to take in based on the workload of the preceding workout. You don't need to count calories—just be aware of how hard the workout was and eat appropriately.

Your training plan at the end of this chapter includes several minirace simulation workouts. By the end of this block you should know exactly what it feels like to swim, bike, and run at the effort, heart rate, pace, or power that will lead to a personal-best triathlon. No less important is what you eat and drink on race day. Rehearse your nutrition plan in each of the racelike workouts in the Peak block. By now you should have it nailed down, but there may be just a few lingering doubts. The Peak block is the time for you to make your final decisions about fuel. By the time you write out your race plan, there should be no doubt as to what you will eat and drink during the race and when you will do so.

COMPLETE YOUR RACE PLAN

I'm sure that over the past several weeks you have been giving considerable thought to the many important aspects of your upcoming race. At the end of this training block you should be ready to finalize a detailed plan. I'd strongly suggest putting this in writing. That will force you to be more precise than if you just formed it in your head. Sometime after your combined bike-run workout on Sunday of Peak week 2, sit down and write out a plan for the race that covers everything that will be under your control. Here are some of the more important topics to address:

Race goal. Start your race plan with a clear statement of your race-day goal. You may want to reread the section of Chapter 1 related to goal setting. Does your goal still seem reasonable? Has your training gone as expected? If so, then it should be easy for you to prepare the plan. If not, consider what you are capable of doing in this race and create a plan that addresses the revised goal.

If you have been following the training plan in this book since the start of your season, then you should be well prepared. You have developed a depth of fitness that—with a little luck—will enable you to succeed. But if you came into this book at midseason, you may have missed much of the fundamental training. As a result you may not have enough fitness depth. Or you may have had setbacks in training due to illness or injury, or simply overestimated how your body would respond to training. If so, then you must be realistic and downgrade your goals for the race. On the other hand, when you originally set your goal, you may have underestimated how much progress you would make when you had the right training plan to follow. If that is the case, upgrade your goal accordingly.

Plan B. Include a plan B goal in case something out of your control goes wrong, such as a flat tire or horrible weather. Your plan B goal could be to have a personal best time for the run portion of the race, for example. Whatever you come up with should be something that would allow you to cross the finish line feeling like you still accomplished something worthwhile regardless of the circumstances.

Travel. When and how will you travel to the race? If you are flying and crossing several time zones, how will you adjust your internal clock?

Here are some suggestions. Many of my athletes like to start getting in sync with the race-venue time zone by going to bed earlier or later than usual, depending on whether they are flying east or west, starting a few days before they travel. This is especially beneficial if you are traveling east through more time zones than the number of days you will arrive before race day (for example, traveling through five zones but only arriving three days before the race). It takes about one day to adjust your biological clock for every time zone you pass through when going east.

It's about half a day per time zone when flying west. Once you are on the airplane, put your watch on the time of your destination and start thinking about meals and sleep relative to your destination, not what the time is back home.

Weather. How will you make changes in equipment and clothing if there is rain, snow, wind, cold, heat, or humidity? How will you make adjustments to pacing with unusual weather conditions?

Equipment. List the critical swim, bike, and run equipment you will use on race day. This might include which wetsuit you will use (which depends on water conditions), wheels and tires, tire pressure (lower the pressure if the pavement is wet), running shoes, and anything else that is important.

The day before the race. What will you do the day before the race? Will you do a brief workout or not? When will you do it? Where will you do it? What will you eat on that day, and when? Do you need to attend a race meeting? When will you go to bed?

Race-morning routine. What time will you get up on race day? What things will you do and in what order? Common possibilities are stretching, eating, reading, listening to music, and using the bathroom.

Pre-race nutrition. What will you eat and drink the morning of the race? When will you eat? (Chapter 7 offers suggestions for eating before a race.)

Race nutrition. What will you take in for fuel, how much will you take in, and when will you take it in? This is especially important for the bike leg of the half-Ironman and Ironman races. In Ironman, except for pacing decisions, this is the most important decision you will make. You should have rehearsed your race-day nutrition many times in the Build period. The Peak block will offer you a few more opportunities to finalize it.

I always suggest to those I coach that they keep race nutrition simple. Do you really need all of those electrolytes, protein combinations, vitamins, oils, and exotic mixtures of carbohydrate? It's doubtful. The more stuff you put in your stomach during a race, the more likely it is that your gut will shut down, resulting in bloating and a long walk or "DNF" (did not finish). (See Chapter 7 for more details on fuel and fluids during the race.)

Transitions and special needs. How will you arrange your transition stalls and flow through the transition process? If it's an Ironman, will you have special-needs bags? I tell my Ironman athletes that even if they don't intend to use them, they should at least put some of their bike and run fuel in the appropriate bags. That way, if something happens and you lose your fuel stash during the race, you know you can get more. When you get to the special-needs area and you have what you need still onboard, you can just keep on going.

Pacing. How will you pace each of the three legs of the race? Include topics such as where you will position yourself for the start of the swim and how you will start; your power, heart rate, or effort for the bike, including flat portions and hills; and your pace, heart rate, or effort for the run. This is perhaps the most important thing you will decide—and the one that most triathletes mess up, especially for the start of the bike ride. You must be willing to let other racers pass you at the start of the bike leg as you stick with your plan. Trying to "win" the first couple of miles of this portion of the race is a sure way to ruin your day. Remind yourself that those who pass you now are going much too fast and will not be able to sustain it. You must be patient, as you will pass them a bit later on when it really matters.

Course management. I suggest to the athletes I coach that they divide the bike and run courses into smaller segments and then plan how to manage each separately. One way of doing this is to simply divide each course into equal quadrants. For example, a 112 mile bike leg in an Ironman would have four segments of 28 miles (45 km) each. Or the division may be based on terrain and conditions. Perhaps one portion of the course is hilly, another flat, a third is windy, and one segment has lots of turns. Use whatever method best suits the course and the way you view it. Some athletes will give each segment a name ("Windy") and an easy-to-remember strategy for racing it ("stay very aero"). Focus on the strategy during each portion. Not only will the race go faster, but you'll do a much better job of staying in the moment.

Mindset. What will you think about during the race? This might include mantras you will repeat, mental technique checklists, songs to have in your head, or checkpoints or landmarks to look for along the course. Anything you have found beneficial for your mindset in your training or prior racing can become part of the plan for race day.

Going to Plan B. Expect the unexpected and be prepared for it. How will you handle a flat tire? What if your stomach becomes upset? What changes will you make in your eating and drinking if this happens? If it simply isn't your day and things aren't going as planned, under what conditions will you decide to go to plan B?

COMMON CONCERNS OF PEAK 1

Just because you are cutting back on training in the Peak block doesn't mean that training is unimportant. It's merely different. And it is still critically important to your race success. But there are other concerns that are also important. In this block, taking good care of yourself—psychologically, emotionally, and physically— becomes paramount.

Serious triathletes almost always burn the candle at both ends. They somehow manage to cram career, workouts, family time, sleep, and other responsibilities into each 24-hour period, day after day. If this describes you, then for the next three weeks try to reduce stress by cutting back on all the excess stuff in your life as best you can. I'm sure you know what this stuff is already. It's stuff that is unimportant in the big picture of your life but that you feel compelled to do anyway. It won't be easy, and you may need to call on family members and friends to help you out. After your race, when they have special needs, you can repay the favor.

For the three-week period of time that is left before the race, rest all you can. Get to bed earlier than usual. Sleep in when possible. Stretch gently throughout the day, especially those areas that tend to be tight and where you may have had injuries in the past. Eat quality food, including vegetables, fruits, and lean protein. Snack on nuts and dried fruit. Avoid junk food. And steer clear of sick people.

Peak Workouts

I'm going to throw a curve ball at you here and say something you may not expect: In the Peak and Race blocks, you will lose fitness. I know, that's a scary thought, and one that you strongly suspect is inaccurate. So let me explain why and how this happens—and why it's necessary to let it happen if you want your best possible race performance.

For the purpose of this discussion, let's define fitness as the capacity to manage a given level of training stress. Training stress primarily comes in the form of intensity and duration. Over the past several weeks you've been doing longer and harder workouts. We know you're more fit now than you were several weeks ago because you can handle these higher levels of stress. You gradually increased the stress of your training with longer workouts and higher efforts, and particular workouts gradually became easier for you as your fitness improved. If the workouts had not become easier for you, it would mean that your fitness had not improved. That's pretty basic.

Over the next three weeks, we're going to reduce the stress by having you recover more frequently as the workouts get shorter. As the stress is reduced, fitness is lost. If that wasn't the case, there would be no reason to train. You could just sit in front of the TV doing nothing and gain fitness—or at least not lose it. Reduced stress means reduced fitness. There's no way to get around that. Again, it's pretty basic.

So, if you are still with me, why would you want to give up even a little bit of your hard-earned fitness? The answer is that, on race day, you need freshness as well as fitness. And in order to gain freshness, you must shed the fatigue that you have gained along with the fitness. You may not think you're fatigued, but trust me, if you have been training hard for several months, you're fatigued, even if you followed my suggested training plans and had rest-and-test weeks along the way. If you aren't, then you didn't do enough. The reason you may not realize that you are fatigued is that you have lost your sensitivity to it. Every hard-training athlete is carrying fatigue by this time in the season. You need to get rid of it, and if you do, you will have a great race. If you don't, you'll race tired and have poor results.

By shedding this fatigue and gaining freshness, you will also gain "form." This is the final piece coming into place in the preparation for your race—an important part. You must not skip it because you're afraid of losing fitness. Form is necessary for a best-ever race performance.

Let's return to this idea of losing fitness. If you follow the plan I've laid out for you at the end of this chapter, you won't lose much fitness. In fact, the loss will be quite small. When I coach an athlete, I use software that quantifies fitness (and also fatigue and form). I keep the fitness loss to less than 10 percent of what it was at the start of the Peak block. If the athlete follows the plan and gains form, then I know the race will be exceptional. I've designed this part of the training plan to help you do just that. If you follow it closely, form should occur as fatigue is shed and fitness drops only slightly.

The first step you will take to decrease the stress of training is to cut back on your running. Out of the three sports in triathlon, that's the one that seems to produce the most deeply embedded fatigue, so we will start there. Cutting back on bike training will be next, and then swim training. Swim and bike volume don't change much at all in the Peak period, as the taper in these sports starts late in Peak 2 and continues into race week. The lower your volume has been, the less of a drop you will see. Why? Because if the volume starts low and is cut back severely, then there is not enough stress and too much fitness is lost.

There are only two types of workouts in the Peak block—race-intensity workouts and recovery workouts. You're either training hard or going very slow and easy— never in between. Later we will look at these two extremes in more detail, but first we will take a quick detour to discuss transitions.

TRANSITIONS

I haven't said much about transitions yet, but in the Peak block you will rehearse and refine your transition routines. In each of the combined bike-run sessions, you will practice your T2. For most triathletes this is the more critical transition. Your purpose in rehearsing it is to become so efficient that no time is wasted. The T1 transition is a bit more difficult to rehearse, but it still needs to be practiced and refined. You will get in two or three T1 rehearsal sessions before the race.

The most important lesson I have learned for efficient transitions is to make them as simple as possible. When rehearsing T2, for example, you must eliminate anything that isn't absolutely essential when moving from the bike to the run. The equipment that you need to handle must be kept to a minimum, and you must position each item so that it can be taken off or put on with as little movement as possible. Taking your feet out of your shoes in the last 2 minutes of the bike leg and leaving them clipped into the pedals when you dismount shaves precious seconds off of T2. It also makes running through the transition area safer—you're less likely to fall if you are not wearing slippery biking shoes. After you reach your assigned stall and rack your bike, the helmet comes off and your running shoes are slipped on. Lying next to your shoes is your hat, if you wear one, and it is put on as you are running out of the transition area. Follow this or whatever procedure you prefer in your combined bike-run workouts in the Peak block.

A good time to practice the T1 is after a swim workout. If you will use a wetsuit on race day, do at least one of the Peak block swim workouts in it. When you do this wetsuit swim, take your bike to the pool (or open-water venue) and rehearse your T1 at the end of the swim workout. You may also rehearse T1 at home. The most challenging part of T1 is wetsuit removal. Practice taking off your wet wetsuit many times until you can do it efficiently. If you will have your shoes clipped into the pedals before mounting, practice mounting the bike that way when training. Getting into your shoes while riding can be a bit tricky, but doing so daily in training makes it a much smoother process.

RACE-SIMULATION WORKOUTS

These workouts are the heart of your Peak block training. Simulating portions of the race will prepare you for the challenges expected on race day. It involves not only the intensity of the swim, bike, and run portions of the race, but also your transitions, the fuel you will use on race day, the terrain and other conditions of the race, the clothing and equipment you will use, and anything else that may influence how well you will perform on race day. By the end of the Peak block you should have rehearsed and refined all of the elements that will account for your success.

These race-simulation workouts get shorter with each session. That's the duration part of peaking, which produces tapering. As explained earlier, however, the most important training element now is intensity. The racelike workouts must be done at race intensity—which means they should be neither harder nor easier than race intensity. Of course, the intensity during the race may vary a bit. For example, at the start of the swim it is common to go out very fast in order to get on the feet of faster swimmers who can pull you along. But once a few minutes have passed, you will settle into a slower pace with a lower effort. Once you are into your shoes on the bike, the effort will remain steady as long as you are on a flat portion of the course. As soon as a hill appears, however, the effort will rise some. At the start of the run you are likely to begin a little slower than the pace you will reach a bit later. All of the intensities must be rehearsed now. The workouts that follow will provide you with opportunities to simulate all of these intensities.

Swim Peak Workouts

There are two swim workouts that are the same sessions you did in the Build blocks. In the plans at the end of this chapter, these are the SS + An (ME) session on Tuesday of week 1 and the SS + Fo + ME session on Friday of week 1. You can refer back to Chapter 8 for the details, but you will find the workouts later in this chapter as well. The ME + AE + SS workout on Monday of week 2 is a modified version of the session with that same name for the Saturday swim in the Build period. It has been shortened, but the emphasis on muscular endurance remains the same.

The biggest difference you will see for your swim training now is that there are two days of recovery between sessions. Starting on Thursday of the Peak week with the first race-pace workout, the swim workouts become quite short as the true peaking for swimming begins.

Notice in the plans at the end of this chapter that there is very little change in swim volume in the Peak period. Because swimming needs the shortest tapering of the three sports, the real cutback in swim volume does not occur until the Race block in the week ending with your triathlon.

An optional session that may replace any of the workouts scheduled here is an open-water swim. Swimming in open water is very different from swimming in a pool. It makes for a much more complex session, primarily because of the need for navigation. There are no lanes to guide you, of course, let alone stripes painted on the bottom. Swimming off-course in a race is a common mistake. Get in an open-water swim every chance you get in the Peak period to refine your course-navigation skills. On race day, although you will want to find someone's feet to draft on, it's still imperative that you stay on course. You can't blindly trust the swimmer ahead of you. Sighting is a skill that requires practice to refine. If you don't work on navigation you may well find yourself going fast but in the wrong direction in the race.

When doing open-water swims, you must have a swim partner for safety purposes. Having a partner also allows you to work on open-water drafting. Take turns leading and following, much as you might do on a bike ride with a partner. When following, stay close enough to be in the leader's bubbles, but not so close as to touch his or her feet. Having one's feet touched is very disconcerting and may cause the lead swimmer to kick you. Having your goggles knocked off or a bloody nose is not a good way to start the race.

Monday of Peak week 2 is your dress-rehearsal day. On that day you should get out of bed at least 2 hours before the beginning of your swim workout (you will need to go to bed early the night before) and have the same breakfast you plan to eat on race day. Then, during the swim, bike, and run portions of the workout, use the same equipment, fluids, and fuel you will use on race day. If you find something isn't right, you still have a week to correct it and try the substitute in another workout.

Race Distance	Duration	An Interval	(ME Interval)
Sprint	30–45 min.	100 m	200 m
Olympic	45–60 min.	200 m	300 m

	Warm-up / SS set	10 × 25 m, including technique focus and/or personal-limiter drills *Long recoveries*

	An set	3 × 100–200 m at pace zone 5b (Appendix B)
		30- to 40-sec. recoveries
		[Optional ME set to replace An set:
		    3 × 200–300 m at pace zone 4–5a,
		    10-sec. recoveries]

	AE set / cooldown	10–20 min., steady at pace zone 2

Duration: 45–60 min.

Warm-up	4–6 × 50 m, with descending times (faster for each subsequent 50)	
ME set	3–4 × 250–500 m at pace zone 4–5a (Appendix B)	
	15-sec. recoveries	
AE set / cooldown	10–20 min., steady at pace zone 2	

The SS + An (sprint and Olympic) swim on Tuesday of Peak week 1 and the ME + AE (half-Ironman and Ironman) swim sets follow. You may also substitute an open-water swim, done as a fartlek session with long, unstructured intervals at race intensity and faster. If you are preparing for a sprint- or Olympic-distance race and you have not been doing the An sets previously, then do the optional ME set for this workout instead.

The SS + Fo + ME swim workout for Friday of Peak week 1 is done as follows. You may also substitute an open-water fartlek swim with a partner, focusing on drafting and navigation.

Race Distance	*Duration*
Sprint	30–45 min.
Olympic, half-Ironman, Ironman	45–60 min.

Warm-up / SS set	10 × 25 m, including technique focus and/or personal-limiter drills
	Long recoveries
Fo set	4 × 25 m, including 6-stroke sprint with paddles or drag device at the start of each 25, finishing each 25 at ME effort
	30-sec. recoveries
ME set	3–4 × 250–500 m at pace zone 4–5a (Appendix B)
	15-sec. recoveries
Cooldown	100–300 m, easy swim focusing on technique

Next is the ME + AE + SS swim workout for Monday of Peak week 2. You may also substitute an open-water fartlek swim with a partner, focusing on drafting and navigation. Get out of bed early enough to rehearse your pre-race meal. This is best done at least 2 hours before start time.

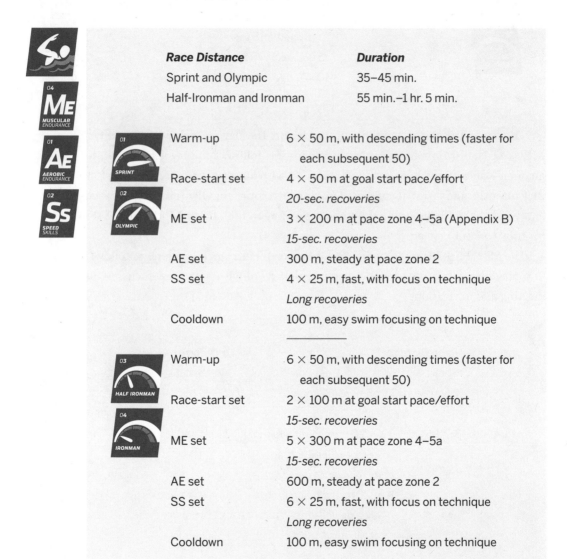

Race Distance	Duration
Sprint and Olympic	35–45 min.
Half-Ironman and Ironman	55 min.–1 hr. 5 min.

Warm-up	6 × 50 m, with descending times (faster for each subsequent 50)
Race-start set	4 × 50 m at goal start pace/effort
	20-sec. recoveries
ME set	3 × 200 m at pace zone 4–5a (Appendix B)
	15-sec. recoveries
AE set	300 m, steady at pace zone 2
SS set	4 × 25 m, fast, with focus on technique
	Long recoveries
Cooldown	100 m, easy swim focusing on technique

Warm-up	6 × 50 m, with descending times (faster for each subsequent 50)
Race-start set	2 × 100 m at goal start pace/effort
	15-sec. recoveries
ME set	5 × 300 m at pace zone 4–5a
	15-sec. recoveries
AE set	600 m, steady at pace zone 2
SS set	6 × 25 m, fast, with focus on technique
	Long recoveries
Cooldown	100 m, easy swim focusing on technique

The following is the first race-pace swim workout for Peak week 2, scheduled for Thursday.

RACE-PACE SWIM 1

Race Distance	Duration
Sprint	20–30 min.
Olympic	30–40 min.
Half-Ironman	40–50 min.
Ironman	1 hr.–1 hr. 10 min.

01 SPRINT

Warm-up	6 × 50 m, with descending times (faster for each subsequent 50)
Race-start set	4 × 50 m at race start pace—faster than goal pace
	15-sec. recoveries
Race-pace set	6 × 100 m at goal pace
	10-sec. recoveries
Cooldown	100 m, easy swim focusing on technique

———————

02 OLYMPIC

Warm-up	6 × 50 m, with descending times (faster for each subsequent 50)
Race-start set	2 × 100 m at race start pace—faster than goal pace
	10-sec. recoveries
Race-pace set	5 × 200 m at goal pace
	10-sec. recoveries
Cooldown	100 m, easy swim focusing on technique

———————

03 HALF IRONMAN

Warm-up	4 × 50 m, with descending times (faster for each subsequent 50)
Race-start set	2 × 100 m at race start pace—faster than goal pace
	10-sec. recoveries
Race-pace set	5 × 300 m at goal pace
	15-sec. recoveries
Cooldown	100 m, easy swim focusing on technique

continues

RACE-PACE SWIM 1, *continued*

Warm-up	4 × 50 m, with descending times (faster for each subsequent 50)
Race-start set	2 × 100 m at race start pace—faster than goal pace
	10-sec. recoveries
Race-pace set	7 × 400 m at goal pace
	10-sec. recoveries
Cooldown	100 m, easy swim focusing on technique

The second race-pace swim workout, is scheduled for Sunday of Peak week 2.

RACE-PACE SWIM 2

Race Distance	Duration
Sprint	15–20 min.
Olympic	20–30 min.
Half-Ironman	30–40 min.
Ironman	45–55 min.

Warm-up	4 × 50 m, with descending times (faster for each subsequent 50)
Race-start set	8 × 25 m at race start pace—faster than goal pace
	10-sec. recoveries
Race-pace set	6 × 50 m at goal pace
	5-sec. recoveries
Cooldown	100 m, easy swim focusing on technique

02 OLYMPIC	Warm-up	4 × 50 m, with descending times (faster for each subsequent 50)
	Race-start set	4 × 50 m at race start pace—faster than goal pace
		10-sec. recoveries
	Race-pace set	6 × 100 m at goal pace
		10-sec. recoveries
	Cooldown	100 m, easy swim focusing on technique

03 HALF IRONMAN	Warm-up	4 × 50 m, with descending times (faster for each subsequent 50)
	Race-start set	2 × 100 m at race start pace—faster than goal pace
		10-sec. recoveries
	Race-pace set	6 × 150 m at goal pace
		10-sec. recoveries
	Cooldown	100 m, easy swim focusing on technique

04 IRONMAN	Warm-up	4 × 50 m, with descending times (faster for each subsequent 50)
	Race-start set	2 × 100 m at race start pace—faster than goal pace
		10-sec. recoveries
	Race-pace set	9 × 200 m at goal pace
		10-sec. recoveries
	Cooldown	100 m, easy swim focusing on technique

Run Peak Workouts

There is only one stand-alone, key run workout in the Peak period, and it is scheduled for Tuesday of the first week. This is a speed skills and muscular endurance session similar to what you may have done in the Build period, depending on your race distance.

Following is this SS + ME run workout for Tuesday of Peak week 1.

Race Distance	Duration
Sprint and Olympic	45–60 min.
Half-Ironman and Ironman	1 hr.–1 hr. 15 min.

Warm-up	10–20 min. of gradually increasing effort and pace
SS set	5 × 20-sec. strides at fast pace on grass or other soft surface
	60- to 90-sec. walk recoveries
ME set	3–4 × 5 min. at pace zone 4
	2-min. jog-walk recoveries
Cooldown	10 min. easy jogging

Warm-up	15–30 min. of gradually increasing effort and pace
SS set	5 × 20-sec. strides at fast pace on grass or other soft surface
	60- to 90-sec. walk recoveries
ME set	3–4 × 8 min. at pace zone 3
	2-min. jog-walk recoveries
Cooldown	10 min. easy jogging

Bike Peak Workouts

As with running, on the bike there is only one stand-alone workout in the Peak block, but it is a key session. It will be on Wednesday of the first week and focuses on muscular endurance and force. It is the same for all race distances. All other key bike rides in Peak are combined with runs and are explained later in this chapter.

Here is the ME + Fo bike workout scheduled for Wednesday of Peak week 1.

Duration: 1 hr.–1 hr. 30 min.

Warm-up	15–20 min. of gradually increasing effort and gearing
ME + Fo set	4–6 × 5 min. hill repeats (20–30 min. of total climbing intervals) at HR or power zone 4 and at racelike cadence, in aero position
	Recover on the descents
Cooldown	10–20 min., spinning with decreasing effort

Combined Bike-Run Peak Workouts

There are four combined bike-run workouts in the Peak block. Two of them emphasize the bike and two emphasize the run. These sessions gradually get shorter as the Peak block progresses. You may be tempted to make them longer. Don't do it. In the Peak block, the intensity of training must be kept racelike while the duration of the workouts gets shorter. This approach allows your body to come into peak form.

This late in the season, you're simply not going to improve your endurance anyway. Endurance takes many weeks to develop, and there isn't enough time remaining to have any meaningful impact on it. If you don't have excellent endurance by now, it's too late. If you've been faithfully following the plan in this book, then your endurance should be at a very high level now. Our purpose is to maintain it while emphasizing intensity.

In these combined bike-run workouts, you should rehearse your T2 transition so that by race day you can do it without thinking.

Note that the half-Ironman and Ironman combined workouts are rather long sessions. You may need to make adjustments to your daily work schedule and other normal responsibilities to fit them in.

The first bike-run combined workout, with an emphasis on the run, is scheduled for Friday of Peak week 1 (see pp. 268–269).

The second bike-run combined workout, with a bike emphasis, will be on Monday of Peak week 2 (see pp. 270–271). For this workout use the equipment and clothing you will use in your race. Also use the fluids and fuels you will use in the race at the same rate you will use them on race day.

BIKE-RUN COMBINED WORKOUT 1

For the bike and run race-pace sets, choose a course that is similar to the racecourse.

Race Distance	Duration
Sprint	1 hr. 5 min.
Olympic	1 hr. 15 min.
Half-Ironman	1 hr. 45 min.
Ironman	2 hr. 15 min.

01 SPRINT

Warm-up on bike	20 min. of gradually increasing effort and gearing
Bike race-pace set	10 min. at goal race intensity (effort, heart rate, or power)
Transition 2	Quickly change into running gear as you will in the race
Run race-pace set	Immediately after T2, start 5 × 3 min. at race intensity
	3-min. jog recoveries
Cooldown	5 min. of easy running and walking

02 OLYMPIC

Warm-up on bike	20 min. of gradually increasing effort and gearing
Bike race-pace set	10 min. at goal race intensity (effort, heart rate, or power)
Transition 2	Quickly change into running gear as you will in the race
Run race-pace set	Immediately after T2, start 5 × 5 min. at race intensity
	3-min. jog recoveries
Cooldown	5 min. of easy running and walking

03 HALF IRONMAN	Warm-up on bike	20 min. of gradually increasing effort and gearing
	Bike race-pace set	15 min. at goal race intensity (effort, heart rate, or power)
	Transition 2	Quickly change into running gear as you will in the race
	Run race-pace set	Immediately after T2, start 6 × 9 min. at race intensity
		1-min. walk recoveries
	Cooldown	5 min. of easy running and walking

04 IRONMAN	Warm-up on bike	20 min. of gradually increasing effort and gearing
	Bike race-pace set	20 min. at goal race intensity (effort, heart rate, or power)
	Transition 2	Quickly change into running gear as you will in the race
	Run race-pace set	Immediately after T2, run 90 min. at race intensity
	Cooldown	5 min. of walking

BIKE-RUN COMBINED WORKOUT 2

For the bike and run race-pace sets, choose a course that is similar to the racecourse.

Race Distance	Duration
Sprint	1 hr. 5 min.
Olympic	1 hr. 25 min.
Half-Ironman	2 hr. 5 min.
Ironman	2 hr. 45 min.

01 SPRINT

Warm-up on bike	20 min. of gradually increasing effort and gearing
Bike race-pace set	4 × 4 min. at goal race intensity (effort, heart rate, or power) *3-min. recoveries*
Transition 2	Quickly change into running gear as you will in the race
Run race-pace set	Immediately after T2, run 10 min. at race pace
Cooldown	5 min. of easy running and walking

02 OLYMPIC

Warm-up on bike	20 min. of gradually increasing effort and gearing
Bike race-pace set	5 × 6 min. at goal race intensity (effort, heart rate, or power) *2-min. recoveries*
Transition 2	Quickly change into running gear as you will in the race
Run race-pace set	Immediately after T2, run 20 min. at goal race pace
Cooldown	5 min. of easy running and walking

03 HALF IRONMAN	Warm-up on bike	10 min. of gradually increasing effort and gearing
	Bike race-pace set	6 × 10 min. at goal race intensity (effort, heart rate, or power)
		3-min. recoveries
	Transition 2	Quickly change into running gear as you will in the race
	Run race-pace set	Immediately after T2, run 30 min. at goal race pace
	Cooldown	5 min. of easy running and walking

04 IRONMAN	Warm-up on bike	10 min. of gradually increasing effort and gearing
	Bike race-pace set	2 hr. at goal race intensity (effort, heart rate, or power)
	Transition 2	Quickly change into running gear as you will in the race
	Run race-pace set	Immediately after T2, run 30 min. at goal race pace
	Cooldown	5 min. of walking

The third bike-run combined workout, with an emphasis on the run, will be on Thursday during Peak week 2.

BIKE-RUN COMBINED WORKOUT 3

For the bike and run race-pace sets, choose a course that is similar to the racecourse.

Race Distance	Duration
Sprint	55 min.
Olympic	1 hr.
Half-Ironman	1 hr. 20 min.
Ironman	1 hr. 45 min.

Warm-up on bike	20 min. of gradually increasing effort and gearing
Bike race-pace set	10 min. at goal race intensity (effort, heart rate, or power)
Transition 2	Quickly change into running gear as you will in the race
Run race-pace set	Immediately after T2, start 5 × 2 min. at race intensity
	2-min. jog recoveries
Cooldown	5 min. of easy running and walking

Warm-up on bike	20 min. of gradually increasing effort and gearing
Bike race-pace set	10 min. at goal race intensity (effort, heart rate, or power)
Transition 2	Quickly change into running gear as you will in the race
Run race-pace set	Immediately after T2, start 5 × 3 min. at race intensity
	2-min. jog recoveries
Cooldown	5 min. of easy running and walking

03 HALF IRONMAN		
	Warm-up on bike	20 min. of gradually increasing effort and gearing
	Bike race-pace set	15 min. at goal race intensity (effort, heart rate, or power)
	Transition 2	Quickly change into running gear as you will in the race
	Run race-pace set	Immediately after T2, start 4 × 9 min. at race intensity
		1-min. walk recoveries
	Cooldown	5 min. of easy running and walking

04 IRONMAN		
	Warm-up on bike	20 min. of gradually increasing effort and gearing
	Bike race-pace set	20 min. at goal race intensity (effort, heart rate, or power)
	Transition 2	Quickly change into running gear as you will in the race
	Run race-pace set	Immediately after T2, run 1 hr. at race intensity
	Cooldown	5 min. of walking

The fourth bike-run combined workout, scheduled for Sunday of Peak week 2, will have an emphasis on the bike leg.

BIKE-RUN COMBINED WORKOUT 4

For the bike and run race-pace sets, choose a course that is similar to the racecourse.

Race Distance	*Duration*
Sprint	55 min.
Olympic	1 hr. 10 min.
Half-Ironman	1 hr. 40 min.
Ironman	2 hr.

Warm-up on bike	20 min. of gradually increasing effort and gearing
Bike race-pace set	4 × 3 min. at goal race intensity (effort, heart rate, or power)
	2-min. recoveries
Transition 2	Quickly change into running gear as you will in the race
Run race-pace set	Immediately after T2, run 10 min. at goal race pace
Cooldown	5 min. of easy running and walking

Warm-up on bike	20 min. of gradually increasing effort and gearing
Bike race-pace set	5 × 4 min. at goal race intensity (effort, heart rate, or power)
	2-min. recoveries
Transition 2	Quickly change into running gear as you will in the race
Run race-pace set	Immediately after T2, run 15 min. at goal race pace
Cooldown	5 min. of easy running and walking

03 HALF IRONMAN	Warm-up on bike	20 min. of gradually increasing effort and gearing
	Bike race-pace set	5 × 8 min. at goal race intensity (effort, heart rate, or power)
		3-min. recoveries
	Transition 2	Quickly change into running gear as you will in the race
	Run race-pace set	Immediately after T2, run 20 min. at goal race pace
	Cooldown	5 min. of easy running and walking

04 IRONMAN	Warm-up on bike	10 min. of gradually increasing effort and gearing
	Bike race-pace set	1 hr. 15 min. at goal race intensity (effort, heart rate, or power)
	Transition 2	Quickly change into running gear as you will in the race
	Run race-pace set	Immediately after T2, run 30 min. at goal race pace
	Cooldown	5 min. of walking

RECOVERY WORKOUTS

To come into good form for the race, you must reduce the duration of your workouts, do a race-like workout every third day, and recover quickly between the race-like sessions. The recovery workouts should not be taken lightly. If you make a recovery workout too hard, the quality of your next racelike workout will be compromised. This is the most common mistake I see in the athletes I coach. These sessions should be primarily zone 1 in effort, heart rate, power, or pace. There may be a few cumulative minutes of zone 2, but these should be brief incursions lasting no longer than a couple of minutes at a time. Strictly avoid zones 3 and higher. Your purpose is only to recover; you are not trying to boost race fitness on these days.

Swim Recovery Workouts

Swim recovery time should be devoted to the ongoing refinement of your swimming skills. This is a good time to use swim aids such as a snorkel, a pull buoy, and fins. Pull buoys may prove to be especially beneficial if your legs are tired.

Bike Recovery Workouts

It's best to avoid other riders when doing recovery bike workouts in the Peak period. You're much more likely to keep the intensity at the zone 1 level when riding alone than when riding with others. Also avoid hills, if possible. Using an indoor trainer for these rides is a great way to keep them easy. If you have a road bike in addition to your triathlon bike, this is a good time to use it. The road bike allows for a more relaxed posture, which promotes recovery.

Run Recovery Workouts

Running is the sport that is most likely to compromise recovery between hard workouts. You'll be walking a thin edge here between maintaining run fitness, primarily economy (as described in Chapter 2), and recovering for your next racelike session.

But you have options if you are not recovering well. The first is to select the shorter end of the run workout's prescribed range in your plan. The second is to take walking breaks frequently during recovery runs. This is perfectly acceptable, and nothing is lost. I have those I coach do it a lot when they're feeling tired. The third option to promote recovery when a "Rec" run session is called for in your plan is to reduce the duration by half or more, or even to omit the workout, perhaps replacing it with an easy swim or ride. Do not jeopardize your recovery if you are fatigued. Do whatever it takes to get rested up.

STRENGTH MAINTENANCE

I have mentioned a couple of times in previous chapters that strength training in the gym becomes a lower priority the closer you come to race day. This is especially the case in the Peak period. Strength training should now be a mere shell of what it was in the Prep and early Base periods.

I commonly have athletes stop doing leg work by this block. They may even cut out shoulder and arm training as well. That leaves just core strength training, which doesn't require going to a gym and is less taxing than other kinds of strength work. Again, one of the primary concerns of the Peak block is being recovered and ready to push the limits in your racelike workouts. Nothing should stand in the way of doing that, including gym training.

SPRINT-DISTANCE TRAINING **PEAK**

P E A K   W E E K   1

SPORT	SWIM	BIKE	RUN	STRENGTH	DAILY VOLUME
MON				SM 0:45	0:45
TUES	SS + An *ME* 0:30–0:45		SS + ME 0:45–1:00		1:15–1:45
WED	*Rec* 0:15–0:30	ME + Fo 1:00–1:30			1:00–2:00
THURS	Rec 0:20–0:30	Rec 0:45–1:00	Rec 0:30–0:45		1:35–2:15
FRI	SS + Fo + ME 0:30–0:45	#1 B + R 0:30	#1 B + R 0:35		1:35–1:50
SAT	Rec 0:20–0:30	Rec 1:00–1:15	*Rec* 0:30–0:45		1:20–2:30
SUN		*Rec* 0:45–1:00	Rec 0:30–0:45		0:30–1:45
VOLUME BY SPORT	1:40–3:00	3:15–5:15	2:20–3:50	0:45	8:00–12:50
WORKOUTS	4–5	4–5	4–5	1	13–16

P E A K   W E E K   2

SPORT	SWIM	BIKE	RUN	STRENGTH	DAILY VOLUME
MON	ME + AE + SS 0:35–0:45	#2 B + R 0:50	#2 B + R 0:15	*SM* 0:45	1:40–2:35
TUES		*Rec* 0:45–1:00			0–1:00
WED	Rec 0:15–0:30		Rec 0:30–0:45		0:45–1:15
THURS	#1 Race pace 0:20–0:30	#3 B + R 0:30	#3 B + R 0:25		1:15–1:25
FRI		Rec 0:45			0:45
SAT	*Rec* 0:15–0:30		*Rec* 0:30–0:45		0–1:15
SUN	#2 Race pace 0:15–0:20	#4 B + R 0:40	#4 B + R 0:15		1:10–1:15
VOLUME BY SPORT	1:25–2:35	2:45–3:45	1:25–2:25	0–0:45	5:35–9:30
WORKOUTS	4–5	4–5	4–5	0–1	12–16

Notes: Rec = Recovery. Optional workouts are in italic. Detail on the workouts can be found in the chapter. Strength workouts appear in Appendix C.

TRAINING PLAN — PEAK

OLYMPIC-DISTANCE TRAINING PEAK

PEAK WEEK 1

SPORT	SWIM	BIKE	RUN	STRENGTH	DAILY VOLUME
MON				SM 0:45	0:45
TUES	SS + An *ME* 0:45–1:00		SS + ME 0:45–1:00		1:30–2:00
WED	*Rec 0:15–0:30*	ME + Fo 1:00–1:30			1:00–2:00
THURS	*Rec 0:20–0:30*	*Rec 0:45–1:00*	*Rec 0:30–0:45*		1:35–2:15
FRI	SS + Fo + ME 0:45–1:00	#1 B + R 0:30	#1 B + R 0:45		2:00–2:15
SAT	Rec 0:20–0:30	Rec 1:15–1:30	*Rec 0:20–0:30*		1:35–2:30
SUN		*Rec 0:45–1:00*	*Rec 0:30–0:45*		0:30–1:45
VOLUME BY SPORT	2:10–3:30	3:30–5:30	2:30–3:45	0:45	8:55–13:30
WORKOUTS	4–5	4–5	4–5	1	13–16

PEAK WEEK 2

SPORT	SWIM	BIKE	RUN	STRENGTH	DAILY VOLUME
MON	ME + AE + SS 0:35–0:45	#2 B + R 1:00	#2 B + R 0:25	*SM 0:45*	2:00–2:55
TUES		*Rec 0:45–1:00*			0–1:00
WED	Rec 0:15–0:30		Rec 0:30–0:45		0:45–1:15
THURS	#1 Race pace 0:30–0:40	#3 B + R 0:30	#3 B + R 0:30		1:30–1:40
FRI		Rec 1:15–1:30			1:15–1:30
SAT	*Rec 0:15–0:30*		*Rec 0:45–1:00*		0–1:30
SUN	#2 Race pace 0:20–0:30	#4 B + R 0:50	#4 B + R 0:20		1:30–1:40
VOLUME BY SPORT	1:40–2:55	3:35–4:50	1:45–3:00	0–0:45	7:00–11:30
WORKOUTS	4–5	4–5	4–5	0–1	12–16

Notes: Rec = Recovery. Optional workouts are in italic. Detail on the workouts can be found in the chapter. Strength workouts appear in Appendix C.

HALF-IRONMAN-DISTANCE TRAINING **PEAK**

P E A K W E E K 1

SPORT	SWIM	BIKE	RUN	STRENGTH	DAILY VOLUME
MON				SM 0:45	0:45
TUES	ME + AE 0:45–1:00		SS + ME 1:00–1:15		1:45–2:15
WED	*Rec* 0:15–0:30	ME + Fo 1:00–1:30			1:00–2:00
THURS	Rec 0:20–0:30	Rec 1:00–1:30	Rec 0:45–1:00		2:05–3:00
FRI	SS + Fo + ME 0:45–1:00	#1 B + R 0:35	#1 B + R 1:05		2:25–2:40
SAT	Rec 0:20–0:30	Rec 1:30–2:00	*Rec* 0:30–0:45		1:50–3:15
SUN		*Rec* 1:00–1:30	Rec 0:45–1:00		0:45–2:30
VOLUME BY SPORT	2:10–3:30	4:05–7:05	3:35–5:05	0:45	10:35–16:25
WORKOUTS	4–5	4–5	4–5	1	13–16

P E A K W E E K 2

SPORT	SWIM	BIKE	RUN	STRENGTH	DAILY VOLUME
MON	ME + AE + SS 0:55–1:05	#2 B + R 1:30	#2 B + R 0:35	*SM* 0:45	3:00–3:55
TUES		*Rec* 1:00–1:30			0–1:30
WED	Rec 0:15–0:30		Rec 0:45–1:00		1:00–1:30
THURS	#1 Race pace 0:40–0:50	#3 B + R 0:35	#3 B + R 0:45		2:00–2:10
FRI		Rec 1:30–2:00			1:30–2:00
SAT	*Rec* 0:15–0:30		*Rec* 1:00–1:15		0–1:45
SUN	#2 Race pace 0:30–0:40	#4 B + R 1:15	#4 B + R 0:25		2:10–2:20
VOLUME BY SPORT	2:20–3:35	4:50–6:50	2:30–4:00	0–0:45	9:40–15:10
WORKOUTS	4–5	4–5	4–5	0–1	12–16

Notes: Rec = Recovery. Optional workouts are in italic. Detail on the workouts can be found in the chapter. Strength workouts appear in Appendix C.

IRONMAN-DISTANCE TRAINING **PEAK**

P E A K   W E E K   1

SPORT	SWIM	BIKE	RUN	STRENGTH	DAILY VOLUME
MON				SM 0:45	0:45
TUES	ME + AE 0:45–1:00		SS + ME 1:00–1:15		1:45–2:15
WED	*Rec 0:15–0:30*	ME + Fo 1:00–1:30			1:00–2:00
THURS	Rec 0:30–0:40	Rec 1:00–1:30	Rec 0:45–1:00		2:15–3:10
FRI	SS + Fo + ME 0:45–1:00	#1 B + R 0:40	#1 B + R 1:35		3:00–3:15
SAT	Rec 0:30–0:40	Rec 1:30–2:00	*Rec 0:30–0:45*		2:00–3:25
SUN		*Rec 1:00–1:30*	Rec 0:45–1:00		0:45–2:30
VOLUME BY SPORT	2:30–3:50	4:10–7:10	4:05–5:35	0:45	11:30–17:20
WORKOUTS	4–5	4–5	4–5	1	13–16

P E A K   W E E K   2

SPORT	SWIM	BIKE	RUN	STRENGTH	DAILY VOLUME
MON	ME + AE + SS 0:55–1:05	#2 B + R 2:10	#2 B + R 0:35	*SM 0:45*	3:40–4:35
TUES		*Rec 0:45–1:00*			0–1:00
WED	Rec 0:15–0:30		Rec 0:45–1:00		1:00–1:30
THURS	#1 Race pace 1:00–1:10	#3 B + R 0:40	#3 B + R 1:05		2:45–2:55
FRI		Rec 1:00–1:30			1:00–1:30
SAT	*Rec 0:15–0:30*		*Rec 1:00–1:15*		0–1:45
SUN	#2 Race pace 0:45–0:55	#4 B + R 1:25	#4 B + R 0:35		2:45–2:55
VOLUME BY SPORT	2:55–4:10	5:15–6:45	3:00–4:30	0–0:45	11:10–16:10
WORKOUTS	4–5	4–5	4–5	0–1	12–16

Notes: Rec = Recovery. Optional workouts are in italic. Detail on the workouts can be found in the chapter. Strength workouts appear in Appendix C.

Race Week

THIS IS IT. FINALLY! The week you've been preparing for over the past several months. You're now down to only a few days until the race. This is a unique week. It's nothing like what you've done previously this season. It will probably seem too easy to you. That's a common reaction from the athletes I coach. They want to train hard right up until the day before the race. That's not a good idea. You can't "win" the race this week, but you can certainly "lose" it.

Your training plan at the end of this chapter has you doing exactly what I have the triathletes I coach do in the week of the race. This plan has been refined over two decades and has proven to work for hundreds of athletes. If you've followed the training plans in this book closely and continue on as planned this week, you should have your best triathlon ever in a few days.

Objectives for Race Week

1. **Maintain training intensity.** The key to fast racing for the experienced triathlete is intensity, not workout duration or weekly volume. That truth is never more apparent than in the Race block. This week you will do a considerable amount of race-intensity work in the form of very short intervals. But the workouts will also be short, and they will get even shorter as the week

progresses. Volume will decline at a far greater rate than at any other time in your preparation.

2. **Taper workout durations.** Your workouts are shortened this week compared to the Peak period of the past two weeks. And that means that your training hours, meters or yards, and miles or kilometers for the week will taper significantly right up until the day before the race. There are also two days of no training at all. The reason for this is that rest is essential now if you want to be fresh for the race.

3. **Rest.** There are a considerable number of research studies showing that a combination of rest and intensity in the last few days before an important race produces the best results. So this is exactly what your training plan calls for. I've done this hundreds of times with the athletes I've coached and can attest to how well it works. If you follow the plan at the end of this chapter, by race day you'll come into excellent race form and will be amazed at how well you race.

4. **Commit the race plan to memory.** Success on race day also comes down to following the race plan you created in the Peak block (see Chapter 10). If your plan is solid and you follow it throughout the race, your chances of achieving your goal are very high. Having a race plan but not following it is a sure way to fail. You must commit the race plan to memory this week. Below I will discuss this aspect of race preparation in more depth (see "Committing to Your Race Plan").

Coaching Tips for Race Week

Race week can be a stressful time given that you've been training for months for the race and that now it's all coming down to the last few days and hours. There may be a lot of self-doubt and worry. The best way to cope with this added pressure is to confirm that you are mentally and physically ready. If you have been following the training plans in this book, you should be in great physical shape. It's mental fitness that challenges athletes the most during race week. The following are topics I often discuss with the athletes I coach to help them make final preparations for race-day success.

MINDSET

Are great race performances due to physiology or psychology? In other words, to have your best possible race, which is more important to the outcome—your mental abilities or your physical abilities? You might guess that race success is 90 percent mental, 90 percent physical, about 50–50, or some other mix. Here's how I see it: If you are set on having your best triathlon, then it has to be 100 percent of both. What I mean by that is that you can't rely on only one of these. You need to fully develop your abilities in both areas. Although the purpose of this book is first and foremost to help you with your physical training, there are some mental qualities that I have found to either help or hinder an athlete's progress. I will summarize these here.

Committing to Your Race Plan

In the week leading up to the race, review your race plan daily. Commit it to memory. Most important, commit to sticking with your plan on race day. All too often I hear of athletes creating a plan and then abandoning it in the heat of competition. It's usually the pacing plan that is scrapped, especially in the first few minutes on the bike when emotions are running high. You must not do this. Commitment to the plan is necessary.

I review the plan with the athletes I coach and make sure they understand that I will hold them accountable to it. As a self-coached athlete, you must do the same for yourself. After the race, you will review how you did with the plan. Did you follow it? If not, why not? You've spent months preparing for this day, and you've invested a great deal of time, money, and energy getting ready for it. You've created a plan based on the best information available—so if you deviate from it, you better have a very good reason for it.

Also, beware of goal inflation this week and on race day. Yes, you are feeling great with all of the rest, but that doesn't mean you have become a superhero capable of performing miraculous deeds. That may seem funny now, but people do it. Somehow, right before or during the race some triathletes get the notion that they can race much faster than they had planned. When this thought crosses your mind, it's time to mentally review your plan once again. Tell yourself that if you are still feeling exceptionally strong late in the race, you can go faster then—but you must not go any faster than planned early on in the race. Stick with the plan!

During the race you must execute the plan, stay in the present moment, and simply do your best at all times. Take the race in little chunks. Quietly celebrate the completion of each chunk and then focus on the next—as planned. There will be good and bad "patches." Stay positive in the bad patches while always moving forward. Keep the plan in your thoughts throughout race week. Read it over at least once a day. Make all your decisions this week, and especially on race day, based on what the plan tells you. Do not trust your emotions. If you have done the training and you stick with the race plan, you will be ready and race well.

Avoid the Desire to "Prove" You Are Ready

Athletes can have a tendency to do too much training the closer they get to the race. Be sure to avoid this mistake: There is nothing to be gained from extra training, but a lot to lose. Following the training plan provided at the end of this chapter will have you rested and sharp come race day.

If you know there are things you have done in the past in your training that helped prepare you for a race, then do them. Your experience is very important. But avoid the all-too-common urge to do one last mega-workout this week. I see this frequently. I've been going to the Hawaii Ironman for years, and I'm always amazed at how many athletes are doing exceptionally long workouts the week of the race. They seem to be trying to prove to themselves that they are ready. It's too late to do that now. If you make any training mistakes this week, make them on the side of doing too little.

Rest is the most important aspect of training now. Make the workouts short, with just enough intensity to maintain fitness. On race day, you will be glad you did.

Relax the Day Before the Race

The day before a big race is psychologically challenging for almost all athletes. You'll probably feel nervous and have the race uppermost in your mind throughout the day. The more experience you have had with racing, the less stressful this usually is, but for most athletes, a bit of stress is inevitable. That doesn't mean there is nothing you can do to relieve your stress, however.

The workouts in your training plan for this week may temporarily relieve some of the anxiety, especially the swims. But the anxiety will return, usually in the form of self-doubt, and you cannot work out every time you are experiencing it, because you must rest to be fresh. At the heart of this anxiety is a lack of self-confidence. To counter it, every time you notice you're thinking about the race and getting butterflies in your stomach, recall a previous race or racelike workout in which you did well. Relive the high points of that event as a way of reminding yourself that you have what it takes. Then do a mental review of the race plan once again. Never allow your mind to wander into the area of negative thoughts. Whenever such a thought creeps into your head, relive a positive race or racelike-workout experience.

I like to see those I coach do something the day before the race to take their minds off of the race. It needs to be something that is both mentally and physically relaxing. Possibilities include going to a movie, taking a guided bus tour of the city you're racing in, watching TV, listening to music, reading, or spending time with friends. Avoid anything that requires walking, spending time in the hot sun, or be-ing around other nervous triathletes.

Always think positive thoughts.

Let Go of the Uncontrollables

Right before the race you may find something that isn't to your liking, such as the weather, surf conditions, wind, or other competitors. You have no control over these things. The only things you can control are your thoughts and actions. Determine how you will deal with the unexpected obstacles and then move on. Do not dwell on it. Fretting wastes mental energy, raises self-doubt, and diverts you from your goal.

From this point forward the only things that are controllable are your course knowledge, understanding of the rules, race strategy, equipment, positioning at the start and during the race, pacing, technique, nutrition, and hydration. Stay focused on these.

Cope with Starting-Line Anxiety

The morning of the race your anxiety will undoubtedly be at a peak. You may not have slept very well. That's to be expected and isn't a problem, since you've been resting up throughout the week. Start your race morning with as normal a routine as you can given where you are staying. Anything you normally do when you are at home is perfect: having a cup of coffee, stretching, reading the paper, checking email, eating breakfast, and so on. If you have a common race-morning routine that has helped before, follow it. And in all the excitement, don't forget the toilet break.

Thoughts about the race will continually creep into your head. Take this as a good thing; it means your mind is preparing for the race. All race thoughts this morning should be positive. Do not allow your mind to wander into the negatives. What I mean by "positive" is partly this: Always think about what you are going to do in the race, not what you are not going to do. If you focus on what you are not going to do, you may end up doing it.

This is a good time to review your goal and your race plan one last time. Both should be fully committed to memory by now, so this should go quickly. It may also be a good time to remind yourself why you race. I expect the answer is personal satisfaction. You're not doing this for anyone but yourself. You're accountable only to yourself. Reminding yourself of this may decrease the pressure you may be feeling.

The day before the race I like to remind the athletes I coach that they don't have to do anything superhuman on race day. If you've trained well, you are ready to go.

You've done all of this before. When the race starts, all you have to do is "flip the autopilot switch" and do exactly what you've rehearsed many times.

Focus on Performance

Racing is not about effort; it's about performance. Would you want your surgeon to make a good effort or have a good performance? It's no different for an athlete. Good performance demands that you do things correctly—in other words, "as planned."

Race performance is not about numbers. It's not how high your average power or heart rate is during the race. Those numbers have to do with effort. Performance, in contrast, is about time. You're not racing to see how big your numbers can be. If you are, it can lead you to make poor decisions during a race. When you are faced with a long, steep descent on the bike, for example, should you pedal hard to keep your heart rate and power high, or should you coast? I hope you answered "coast." Post-race numbers mean nothing if you wasted energy and posted a poor race result. All the little decisions you must make throughout the race should be based on performance only. Let the numbers fall where they may.

Stay in the Moment During the Race

While racing, avoid the urge to think about the outcome. All too often, athletes think about what their finish times or age-group placement will be if they continue at a certain speed. Or they dwell on mistakes they made earlier in the race. Don't fall into these traps. In fact, don't think about the future or the past—think only about the current moment. What are you doing now? How do you feel? Are you thirsty? Is your technique good? Are you following the plan? Now is the only thing that matters.

Follow the Race Plan

This is the last time I will say this, I promise: Follow the race plan!

NUTRITION

The day before your race you may need to change your normal eating habits a little. The biggest change is that you may want to eat more carbs than you normally eat, especially if you are doing a half-Ironman- or Iron-distance race. This week, since you've been tapering your workouts, your body has been storing carbohydrate in the form of glycogen, especially in the swim, bike, and run muscles, so you'll have a lot of fuel onboard come race day. But to be on the safe side, it doesn't hurt to take in a bit more the day before. Good sources are fruit (either fresh or dried), and potatoes, sweet potatoes, and yams. It's okay to relax a bit today and have a dessert after dinner (unless having dessert typically hinders you from doing well in workouts the following day).

Past experience has a lot to do with eating the day before the race. Many athletes know they need to reduce their intake of fiber because of a nervous stomach and slow digestive processing. Some find that an all-liquid evening meal works best the night before a race. Others know from experience that they need to finish their evening meal by a certain time to ensure a proper bowel movement the next morning. Taking in small amounts of food frequently throughout the day, rather than in three big meals, seems to work well for many. Do whatever you have found works best for you.

Do not fluid load. There is no need to chug down gallons of water or sports drink the day before a race. I see athletes doing this at every race I go to, but fluid loading will only dilute your body chemistry and cause you to have to go to the bathroom frequently. You cannot store water like a camel. Simply continue to drink when you are thirsty, just as you normally would.

Even though you reduced calories starting in the Peak block and are continuing to be aware of your food intake, you may gain some weight this week due to carbohydrate storage. For every gram of carbohydrate stored, the body also stores 2.7 grams of water. When training is reduced, as it is this week, your body begins stashing away extra fuel. So you can expect your body weight to go up by perhaps 1 or 2 pounds (0.5 to 1 kilograms). It's really not a big deal. Having a little extra water in your system at the start line can actually be beneficial, so don't sweat it. Just be aware of your eating so you will not overeat out of habit. You won't need as many calories now as you did in earlier blocks of the season.

COMMON CONCERNS OF RACE WEEK

The closer you get to race day, the more critical every aspect of your preparation becomes. Below I go over some of the advice I typically give to athletes as we begin the Race block.

Traveling to a Hot Climate, a High Altitude, or a Race Far Away

Traveling two days before race day generally works well and is recommended for most races. But the sooner you can arrive, the better off you will be, especially when the heat or humidity of the race location is greater than it is where you train, or when the altitude will be 2,000 feet (600 m) or more higher than where you live. Also, if you are traveling east through two or more time zones, or west through more than four, you may need to arrive sooner than two days before the race just to adjust to the clock change. It takes 10 to 14 days of exposure to a much hotter environment than you are used to for complete adaptation to occur.

A difference of 10 degrees Fahrenheit (4°C), especially when the race temperature is above 80°F (25°C), is probably enough to cause a significant reduction in performance. For example, in Kona, Hawaii, both the temperature and humidity are typically very high for the Hawaiian Ironman World Championship Triathlon. The sooner you can arrive, the better adapted you will be on race day. Even if you can arrive only a week early, that is much better than one or two days early. You can do all of your workouts scheduled for this week in the heat of the day to speed your adaptation. However, you can keep the air conditioning turned on in your hotel room. Being hot all week if you are not one of those rare people who enjoy the heat will do nothing to improve your readiness; it will only make you miserable during your rest and relaxation time. Cool off as soon as the workout is over each day.

Adaptation to altitude begins as soon as you arrive at the race venue, but it is not significant unless you arrive several days early. Recent research has suggested that the earlier you can get to the race altitude, the better your performance is likely to be on race day. If you are coming from a lower altitude, you can expect your race performance to be compromised to some extent. It takes two to four weeks for a significant adaptation to occur.

For every 1,000 feet (300 m) of altitude gain, expect about a 2 percent slowing of your race time if you are not adapted. It will be less than that if you arrive more than two days early and have begun to adapt. For example, if you live at sea level and your race is in Boulder, Colorado, at roughly 5,000 feet (1,500 m), and you arrive two days before the race, you can expect to race roughly 10 percent slower than you would back home. After a few weeks in Boulder, however, the drop in performance from sea level would be about 5 percent.

Traveling through several time zones is physically stressful, as the body does not like quick changes in sleeping and eating routines. Such patterns are regulated to a great extent by sunrises and sunsets, and it takes a few days to adjust to the change. While you are adjusting, you may feel lethargic and sleepy. Traveling east is more stressful than traveling west. Remember to arrive one day early for every time zone you are crossing when traveling east, or half a day early for every time zone when traveling west (see Chapter 10 for more information). The adjustment to a new time zone may begin even before you leave home if you can begin going to bed and getting up earlier or later, depending on the time zone you will be traveling to. By starting the process at home, you can reduce some of the time you will need to adjust to the new schedule on-site. Even a 1-hour shift before the trip can save you the stress of one or two time zones on arrival.

Protecting Your Health

I once went to a World Championship in Mexico. Many of the athletes woke up on race day with diarrhea. What a shame. After all those weeks of preparing for their biggest race of the season, they spent much of their race time in portable bathrooms. Feeling under the weather on race day is a horrible experience, so do all you can to protect your health this week.

This may mean drinking only bottled water or other bottled beverages, choosing your restaurants carefully, avoiding people as best you can, not touching objects such as doorknobs, and washing your hands frequently. You've been thinking a lot about how to get to the finish line, but your first and most basic goal is to arrive at the start line healthy.

Race Week Workouts

This is the final training plan of the buildup to your race. You've been training hard for several weeks now, so your fitness is at a high level. The primary purpose of this week's plan is rest and recovery. Notice that the volume of training drops off much more than it did in the Peak block. The daily training volume tapers down purposefully. You may be inclined to do more this week than you see on the training plan tables at the end of the chapter. Don't do it. There is nothing to be gained now by training longer. What you need is R&R. As you shed fatigue, you will gain freshness and begin to come into race form. By the end of this week you will be race-ready.

There are two weekly plans suggested for each race distance. The first of each pair is designed around a Saturday race, and the second is for a Sunday race. Be sure to select the right one based on your race day.

The race-week workouts fall into three categories. The first category makes up most of the week's training. These are the short, race-intensity interval workouts. The second category is for the workouts you will do the day before the race. And the last consists of optional recovery bike rides.

RACE-INTENSITY INTERVAL WORKOUTS

Pacing is critical to goal success in triathlon. The interval workouts scheduled for the first part of this week focus strictly on race intensity. Each has only three parts:

warm-up, race-intensity intervals, and cooldown. By the end of this week you will have rehearsed your optimum race intensity for a particular section of each leg of the race several times. Because your pacing in each sport is unlikely to be perfectly steady, the intervals will focus on the intensity that is the most critical for each sport. In the swim, that is likely to be the start; for the bike it is hills, even if they are small ones; and for the run it is the start.

Swim Race Intervals

Regardless of your race distance, the swim intervals in the Race block are 100 yards or meters with 45-second recoveries. The intensity for each interval is what you expect your start pace to be. If your swim goal is to position yourself with the leaders, then that will be a very fast, anaerobic effort for each 100. If you will swim at your own pace for the start, it will still probably be the fastest portion of your swim.

Here are the details for this workout.

100 M RACE INTERVALS

Warm-up	200 m, swimming continuously, with descending times (faster for each subsequent 50)
SS set	100 m, including technique focus and/or personal-limiter drills
Intervals	4, 3, or 2 × 100 m, depending on your race distance, with each done at race-start effort
	45-sec. recoveries at wall
Cooldown	100 m, easy swim focusing on your technique limiter

Bike and Run Race Intervals

The bike and run workouts this week are best done as combination workouts ("bricks") so you can continue to rehearse the T2 transition. The intervals are 90 seconds, with 3-minute easy recoveries after each. The intensity of the bike intervals is what you expect to be the highest in the race, which is more than likely on hills. By now you should know the racecourse very well, especially the hills, which are usually the most challenging part of the bike portion. Even if the course is relatively flat, there will still probably be small hills where you will ride at a slightly higher effort than when on the flats and downhills (see the "Power and Pacing" section of Chapter 2). Try to find a training course that has similar terrain to the most challenging portion of the race bike leg and do your 90-second intervals there.

When you finish the bike part of this workout, practice going quickly and efficiently from the bike to the run. You should have a T2 transition area set up to make it as realistic as possible.

Immediately out of the bike-to-run transition, start a 90-second run interval at the same pace, heart rate, or effort you have planned for the race. The training plan below tells you how many intervals to do each day this week. Recover between intervals with a 3-minute, very slow jog.

The workout for the bike and run intervals is as follows.

90-SECOND RACE INTERVALS

Bike warm-up	15–30 min. of gradually increasing power, heart rate, effort, and cadence
Bike intervals	4, 3, or 2 × 90-sec., done at race intensity (see plan for total sets)
	3-min. recoveries
Transition 2	Quickly change into running gear as you will do in the race
Run intervals	3, 2, or 1 × 90-sec., done at race intensity (see plan for total sets)
	3-min. recoveries
Cooldown	15–20 min. of easy running, focusing on technique

PRE-RACE WORKOUTS

In this section I'll describe the workouts you will do the day before your race. The purpose of these workouts is primarily to make sure you and your equipment are ready to go. But there is also another reason for them. In the early days of my coaching, I had athletes rest completely the day before the race. What I often found was that they felt "flat" on race day. They were lethargic and felt like they had to try hard just to generate power. I started to change my approach and had them work out with some intensity the day before the race, but without much volume. Once I made that change, I heard of them feeling flat far less often. With this approach, there is a complete day of rest two days before the race.

I find that a few athletes, however, race better if they take off on the day before the race rather than two days before. You may know what works best for you based on experience. If a day of rest right before the race is what has worked for you in the past, then swap the scheduled day off so you get a day off before the race. You can do the final workout two days before the race instead. If you don't know which is the better option for you, then follow the plan below and do your short, racelike workout the day before the race.

Pre-Race Swim

The pre-race swim is best done at the race swim venue and at the same time as your race start. You will be able to see where the sun will be while you're in the water, determine how to navigate around buoys, and locate landmarks on shore that you can use to stay on course. Rehearse portions of the course that are challenging for navigation. If you will use a wetsuit in the race, then use it for your pre-race swim as well.

The pre-race swim session is only about 15 minutes long. Warm-up for a few minutes with a focus on technique, and then do a few short accelerations to race effort. These should be 10 to 20 seconds long, with 2- to 3-minute easy-swim recoveries. This session is best done with a training partner so you can rehearse drafting just as you will do in the race. If the race swim venue is not available for this workout, then the next best option is to swim at another open-water location. If an open-water swim is not possible, then do a pool swim. Practice getting your head out of the water to navigate while still including a few accelerations as described earlier.

PRE-RACE WORKOUT

Duration	15–20 min.
Warm-up	3–5 min. of gradually increasing effort, focusing on technique
Main set	4–5 × 10- to 20-sec. accelerations to race pace
	2- to 3-min. easy swim recoveries
Cooldown	2–3 min., easy swim focusing on technique

Pre-Race Bike and Run

Like the pre-race swim, this workout is best done on the racecourse. Although you may have done your intervals earlier in the week on a course with very challenging hills, today is not a good day to push your limits on the bike or the run, however. In fact, a relatively flat section of the course or any other road is best. I like to have the athletes I coach ride a portion of the racecourse near the start of the bike leg, if possible, as this is when they will be most likely to deviate from the plan. Rehearsing this section of the ride may help you stick to the plan on race day.

On the bike, warm up and then do a few 10- to 20-second accelerations to race intensity, especially the intensity you will use early in the race. Ride slowly and easily for 2 to 3 minutes after each one. This ride should last about 30 minutes.

After the ride, quickly transition to a 15-minute run in which you also include a few 10- to 20-second accelerations to race pace or effort. These are too brief to judge your effort by heart rate. Jog or walk easily for 2 to 3 minutes after each acceleration, and walk for a few minutes to cool down at the end.

Wear clothing similar to what you will use on race day. All of your other equipment should be exactly what you will use on race day—bike, wheels, tires, bike shoes, helmet, sunglasses, running shoes, and hat. This is your last chance to make sure everything is ready. Immediately following the workout check that all the bolts on your bike are appropriately tight before taking your bike to the transition area, if that is required.

PRE-RACE WORKOUT

Bike warm-up	10–15 min. of gradually increasing effort or power and cadence
Bike main set	30 min., with a few 10- to 20-sec. accelerations to race intensity in the aero position
	2- to 3-min. recoveries
Transition 2	Rehearse T2 just as you will do it on race day
Run main set	15 min., with a few 10- to 20-sec. accelerations to race pace or effort
	2- to 3-min. jog-walk recoveries
Cooldown	2–3 min. of walking

BIKE RECOVERY WORKOUTS

There are one or two optional recovery bike rides on the training plan depending on if your race is Saturday or Sunday. The first of these is scheduled for two days before your race. This may be a travel day for you so training may not even be possible. Most athletes are best advised to take a full day of rest two days before their race, but if you are very nervous, a short, easy ride may have a calming effect.

If your race is on Saturday you may want to go for an easy ride on Sunday to recover (and celebrate), but it is not necessary. In the Transition block next week you will be cutting back considerably on exercise time to give your mind and body a break. Sunday may also be a travel day for you as you head back home.

STRENGTH

This is the first week since you started this training plan when there is no strength work scheduled. With just a few days remaining until your race, there is nothing to be gained by lifting weights. If you have been doing gym-based workouts and feel guilty about doing nothing on Monday of race week, it's all right to do some core strength training. But remember that your primary purpose this week is rest.

SPRINT-DISTANCE TRAINING **RACE**

S A T U R D A Y   R A C E

SPORT	SWIM	BIKE	RUN	STRENGTH	DAILY VOLUME
MON					0:00
TUES	3 x 100 0:25	3 x 90 sec 0:45	2 x 90 sec 0:25		1:35
WED	2 x 100 0:20	2 x 90 sec 0:40	1 x 90 sec 0:20		1:20
THURS		*Rec 0:30*			0–0:30
FRI	Pre-race 0:15	Pre-race B + R 0:30	Pre-race B + R 0:15		1:00
SAT	Race split	Race split	Race split		Race time
SUN		*Rec 1:00*			0–1:00
VOLUME BY SPORT	1:00 + Race split	1:55–3:25 + Race split	1:00 + Race split	0:00	3:55–5:25 + Race time
WORKOUTS	4	4–6	4	0	12–14

S U N D A Y   R A C E

SPORT	SWIM	BIKE	RUN	STRENGTH	DAILY VOLUME
MON					0:00
TUES	4 x 100 0:30	4 x 90 sec 0:50	3 x 90 sec 0:30		1:50
WED	3 x 100 0:25	3 x 90 sec 0:45	2 x 90 sec 0:25		1:35
THURS	2 x 100 0:20	2 x 90 sec 0:40	1 x 90 sec 0:20		1:20
FRI		*Rec 0:30*			0–0:30
SAT	Pre-race 0:15	Pre-race B + R 0:30	Pre-race B + R 0:15		1:00
SUN	Race split	Race split	Race split		Race time
VOLUME BY SPORT	1:30 + Race split	2:45–3:15 + Race split	1:30 + Race split	0:00	5:45–6:15 + Race time
WORKOUTS	5	5–6	5	0	15–16

Notes: Rec = Recovery. Optional workouts are in italic. Detail on the workouts can be found in the chapter.

TRAINING PLAN — RACE

LYMPIC

TRAINING PLAN -- RACE

OLYMPIC-DISTANCE TRAINING **RACE**

S A T U R D A Y   R A C E

SPORT	SWIM	BIKE	RUN	STRENGTH	DAILY VOLUME
MON					0:00
TUES	3 x 100 0:25	3 x 90 sec 0:45	2 x 90 sec 0:25		1:35
WED	2 x 100 0:20	2 x 90 sec 0:40	1 x 90 sec 0:20		1:20
THURS		*Rec 0:30*			0–0:30
FRI	Pre-race 0:15	Pre-race B + R 0:30	Pre-race B + R 0:15		1:00
SAT	Race split	Race split	Race split		Race time
SUN		*Rec 1:00*			0–1:00
VOLUME BY SPORT	1:00 + Race split	1:55–3:25 + Race split	1:00 + Race split	0:00	3:55–5:25 + Race time
WORKOUTS	4	4–6	4	0	12–14

S U N D A Y   R A C E

SPORT	SWIM	BIKE	RUN	STRENGTH	DAILY VOLUME
MON					0:00
TUES	4 x 100 0:30	4 x 90 sec 0:50	3 x 90 sec 0:30		1:50
WED	3 x 100 0:25	3 x 90 sec 0:45	2 x 90 sec 0:25		1:35
THURS	2 x 100 0:20	2 x 90 sec 0:40	1 x 90 sec 0:20		1:20
FRI		*Rec 0:30*			0–0:30
SAT	Pre-race 0:15	Pre-race B + R 0:30	Pre-race B + R 0:15		1:00
SUN	Race split	Race split	Race split		Race time
VOLUME BY SPORT	1:30 + Race split	2:45–3:15 + Race split	1:30 + Race split	0:00	5:45–6:15 + Race time
WORKOUTS	5	5–6	5	0	15–16

Notes: Rec = Recovery. Optional workouts are in italic. Detail on the workouts can be found in the chapter.

HALF-IRONMAN–DISTANCE TRAINING **RACE**

SATURDAY RACE

SPORT	SWIM	BIKE	RUN	STRENGTH	DAILY VOLUME
MON					0:00
TUES	3 x 100 0:25	3 x 90 sec 0:45	2 x 90 sec 0:25		1:35
WED	2 x 100 0:20	2 x 90 sec 0:40	1 x 90 sec 0:20		1:20
THURS		Rec 0:30			0–0:30
FRI	Pre-race 0:15	Pre-race B + R 0:30	Pre-race B + R 0:15		1:00
SAT	Race split	Race split	Race split		Race time
SUN		Rec 1:00			0–1:00
VOLUME BY SPORT	1:00 + Race split	1:55–3:25 + Race split	1:00 + Race split	0:00	3:55–5:25 + Race time
WORKOUTS	4	4–6	4	0	12–14

SUNDAY RACE

SPORT	SWIM	BIKE	RUN	STRENGTH	DAILY VOLUME
MON					0:00
TUES	4 x 100 0:30	4 x 90 sec 0:50	3 x 90 sec 0:30		1:50
WED	3 x 100 0:25	3 x 90 sec 0:45	2 x 90 sec 0:25		1:35
THURS	2 x 100 0:20	2 x 90 sec 0:40	1 x 90 sec 0:20		1:20
FRI		Rec 0:30			0–0:30
SAT	Pre-race 0:15	Pre-race B + R 0:30	Pre-race B + R 0:15		1:00
SUN	Race split	Race split	Race split		Race time
VOLUME BY SPORT	1:30 + Race split	2:45–3:15 + Race split	1:30 + Race split	0:00	5:45–6:15 + Race time
WORKOUTS	5	5–6	5	0	15–16

Notes: Rec = Recovery. Optional workouts are in italic. Detail on the workouts can be found in the chapter.

TRAINING PLAN — RACE

IRONMAN-DISTANCE TRAINING

S A T U R D A Y   R A C E

SPORT	SWIM	BIKE	RUN	STRENGTH	DAILY VOLUME
MON					0:00
TUES	3 x 100 0:25	3 x 90 sec 0:45	2 x 90 sec 0:25		1:35
WED	2 x 100 0:20	2 x 90 sec 0:40	1 x 90 sec 0:20		1:20
THURS		*Rec 0:30*			0–0:30
FRI	Pre-race 0:15	Pre-race B + R 0:30	Pre-race B + R 0:15		1:00
SAT	Race split	Race split	Race split		Race time
SUN		*Rec 1:00*			0–1:00
VOLUME BY SPORT	1:00 + Race split	1:55–3:25 + Race split	1:00 + Race split	0:00	3:55–5:25 + Race time
WORKOUTS	4	4–6	4	0	12–14

S U N D A Y   R A C E

SPORT	SWIM	BIKE	RUN	STRENGTH	DAILY VOLUME
MON					0:00
TUES	4 x 100 0:30	4 x 90 sec 0:50	3 x 90 sec 0:30		1:50
WED	3 x 100 0:25	3 x 90 sec 0:45	2 x 90 sec 0:25		1:35
THURS	2 x 100 0:20	2 x 90 sec 0:40	1 x 90 sec 0:20		1:20
FRI		*Rec 0:30*			0–0:30
SAT	Pre-race 0:15	Pre-race B + R 0:30	Pre-race B + R 0:15		1:00
SUN	Race split	Race split	Race split		Race time
VOLUME BY SPORT	1:30 + Race split	2:45–3:15 + Race split	1:30 + Race split	0:00	5:45–6:15 + Race time
WORKOUTS	5	5–6	5	0	15–16

Notes: Rec = Recovery. Optional workouts are in italic. Detail on the workouts can be found in the chapter.

Part V

YOUR NEXT TRIATHLON

I hope your race went just as you had hoped it would. If you followed the training plan and guidelines I laid out for you in the previous chapters, then chances are your race went well. I certainly hope you've been celebrating your success. Celebrations are magical times in our lives that mark our passage and remain with us forever. Let loose, enjoy the moment, and share your happiness with those around you. You've certainly earned it.

But since it's not always possible to control all of the variables that affect your life, your training, or the races themselves, there is a slight possibility that you did not achieve your goal. That's one of the risks you take when setting challenging goals. High achievers are not always successful in their first attempts. History is marked with those who failed time and again only to become the best the world had ever known in their respective fields. Excellence in sport, as in anything else in life, often is nourished by and grows from failure. If you did not achieve your goal, hang in there, learn from your experience, and rededicate yourself to reaching your potential.

In Part V I will continue giving you the same advice I give to those I coach. Chapter 12 describes the Transition period, the interim between one season and the next or one portion of a season and the next. I've known athletes to skip the Transition period when they are highly motivated. Some fear losing fitness. It's generally not a good idea to avoid taking this much-needed break. The break in serious, focused training makes for a long and successful triathlon career. The athletes I coach are always better off because of it.

Chapter 13 describes what you need to know to make your next A-priority triathlon even better than the one you just completed.

Transition

YOU DID IT! The race is now history. No matter how you performed, log the details into your training diary. You will want all the facts for future reference. And no matter what happened, it's time to take a much-deserved break from training.

This is the start of the Transition block. If your race was at midseason, this block may last a few days or a week. If it was your last race of the season then the block should be somewhat longer. In fact, if it is the end of your season, I recommend making this block at least 2 weeks long, and perhaps as long as 6 weeks, depending on how you feel. When your last race of the season is an Ironman, it's probably a good idea to extend the Transition block to at least 4 weeks.

The name of this block implies that a change is taking place, and that is exactly what's happening. You're transitioning from the last season to the next season. The transition is primarily physical, but it has to do with mindset as well. This chapter will guide you through the changes that are taking place in both areas. Then, in Chapter 13, we'll start to look ahead to the next triathlon. Looking behind at what you have done and looking ahead to what's coming up really go hand in hand. So after you evaluate every aspect of your race, while you are still in the Transition block, read the next chapter and begin to think about the future.

Objectives for the Transition Block

1. **Rest and recuperate.** Recovery is the most important objective for you over the next several days. Your primary purpose during this week is to recharge your batteries. This period is often referred to as "R&R"—rest and recuperation. That means it's quite acceptable—in fact, it's even healthy—to take one or more days off from exercise at this point in your annual training cycle.
2. **Assess your season.** In the Transition block you need to give a lot of thought to what you did as you prepared for your A-priority race and what you would like to do differently next time. Your purpose here is not to find fault with yourself, but to grow as an athlete so that your next big race is even more successful.
3. **Stay physically active.** It's all right to "exercise" during the Transition period, but there should be no purpose to your workouts other than to satisfy your daily addiction to sweat. By "no purpose," I mean no expected performance outcomes in mind. You're not training to improve fitness now. It's more play than training. Simply have fun.

Coaching Tips for the Transition Block

This is a time unlike any other in your season. Most athletes find it is difficult to let go of hard training and watch their hard-earned fitness slowly erode. But you must do this. And there are many other things happening now that are unique to this portion of the training year. Here is what I talk with my athletes about as they start into the Transition block.

MINDSET
In the Transition block, what you think about is more important than what you do. You will be cutting way back on physical training, but mental training continues. Some of the most important mental tasks you will do as an athlete take place during this period, because you now have the time to reflect and plan. You will determine how your season and your race went, and you will start making decisions in preparation for your next A-priority race.

Assess Your Race Performance

How did your race go? What did you learn? Did you stick with the race plan? What did you do well? What would you do differently if you could do the race again, knowing what you know now? Now is the perfect time to determine what you learned in this race. Reflecting on your performance while the race is still fresh in your mind will help you do a better job of preparing for the next one. If the race didn't go as planned, it's all the more important to ask these questions and to seek answers.

I tell the athletes I coach that the main difference between a "good" race and a "bad" one is that after a bad one you learn something. Or at least you better learn something. If you don't, you'll undoubtedly make the same mistake again in the future.

There are lots of things that can go wrong in a race and some probably did go wrong for yours, at least to some degree. I've yet to see the perfect race. A poor race plan or no plan at all, too little training or too much training, inadequate pre-race and race-day nutrition, improper pacing, not enough tapering or too much tapering, bad equipment choices, and poor preparation for race-day variables such as heat, humidity, hills, rough water, rain, and wind are all common pitfalls.

Poor pacing is probably the most common mistake of all. In the heat of the moment, especially at the start of the bike, the tendency is to go much too hard. Did you train for pacing in this part of the race? Did you meticulously rehearse your pacing, in fact, for each leg of the race, as the training plans in this book called for in the final three weeks? How did you monitor intensity at this time? Did you rely on your emotions or your intellect?

Prepare a checklist of possible things you could do to improve next time. Make some notes below the checklist as you think about what you would do differently. If you have a coach, ask him or her to help evaluate your race, or sit down with a training partner and review your notes. Having someone who can view your performance dispassionately is very helpful. Whatever you do, don't make the same mistakes again the next time. Use your recent experience to grow as an athlete.

Evaluating your performance takes honesty and a great deal of thought. Each person has a unique physical and mental makeup. We are very complex—and in training and racing there are lots of variables. The challenge when assessing your performance is to figure out what you can change in order to do better next time and what was truly outside of your control.

Race outcomes aren't always going to be what we plan for and hope will happen, and sometimes we just have to let go of some of it. If the competition was simply tougher than what you expected despite your efforts to choose the right race, or an unforeseen equipment failure set you back, that's just life. If the setbacks were things that you could prevent from happening next time, consider them carefully and write them down. If you don't write them down, there's a good chance you will forget about them and repeat the same errors.

Consider each item carefully before deciding whether it's something to include on the list or not. Equipment failures are not always outside of your control, for example. Do you have a decent bike that fits properly? How about your wheels, shoes, wetsuit, goggles, and clothing? Did the battery go dead on your heart rate monitor, power meter, GPS device, or accelerometer during the race, leaving you with only your poorly developed sense of perceived exertion to gauge intensity? At first glance this may seem beyond your control, but if you had put in a fresh battery during race week, you could have prevented it from happening.

One issue that truly is outside of your control is your genetic makeup. However, you might be able to do a better job of matching yourself to the right race. With this racing season completed, you have a lot more information to go on to determine what your genetically based capabilities are. How much slow-twitch or fast-twitch muscle do you have? How difficult is it for you to get down to racing weight? Do you seem to be better at short races than long ones—or the other way around? Using all the new information at your disposal to plan your next season means taking these basic facts into consideration. If what you have found out means that you should become a sprint-distance triathlete instead of an Ironman athlete, or vice versa, so be it.

Your mindset may also have contributed to your performance in some way. Perhaps you threw in the towel as soon as the competition heated up, or you just couldn't seem to stay focused during the race. Maybe you were so nervous before the race that you made lots of rookie errors, such as starting much too fast. Evaluate these factors as well as the physical ones.

If you did not do as well as expected, keep in mind that you may not be able to figure out a cause. That's all right. Do your best to evaluate your performance, and be open to hearing what your coach or perceptive training partners have to say. Then keep your head up and press ahead.

Avoid the Urge to Do a "Redemption" Race

The bottom line after your last race of the season is that you have enough information now to figure out what to change next year. And this means that, if you didn't do as well as expected, you should not simply look for the next race you can do, hopefully very soon, so you can prove to yourself that you're okay after all. You may feel that your luck turned against you and that you need another race to prove you can do better. The truth is, you're seeking salvation for your shortcomings in the new race, with the hope of making your world right again. "Redemption races" are seldom the best course of action.

At redemption races, the athlete is usually too tired, too sore, or too tapered to race well. This often results in a second "bad" race, one that brings not salvation, but eternal damnation. Athletes who do these unplanned races can sink into a morass of mental self-abuse so deep that it causes them to quit the sport. They all too often come to the conclusion that they are indeed worthless when it comes to racing. I've even seen athletes who come to believe they are no longer good people because of a poor race performance. Sometimes we tie too much of our self-worth to race performances. You are not your last race.

My advice is to avoid doing redemption races altogether. The only exception would be if you did not finish the race you planned for because of some obvious and easily fixed problem, such as a mechanical issue with your bike. If that happened, you are not completely fatigued, and you may legitimately decide to do another race. The replacement race will give you a chance to get some better information about how you can perform after following these training plans, although the timing may not be perfect.

Let Go of Peak Fitness

You've been focused on purposeful training for several months, and you reached a peak of fitness and form before your race. Now you must let go of it, and that is hard to do. In fact, most serious athletes simply can't do it. They try to maintain this high level and eventually implode as a result. You simply cannot be in top physical condition all the time. Trying to maintain peak form will, without doubt, lead to burnout, staleness, overtraining, or whatever you like to call it. Do not "train" now. You need that R&R!

Once you get a few days of rest, your goal should be to simply stay active. You can still swim, bike, and run, but do some other things you enjoy as well. This may be in-line skating, canoeing, snowshoeing, skiing, rock climbing, basketball, hockey, tennis, volleyball, mountain biking, or any other physical activity. They can entirely replace the triathlon sports, or they can augment them. Don't get serious about preparing for a triathlon at this time.

Do not follow a training plan or even consider what you will do tomorrow or the next day. Decide when you wake up what you will do that day—or if you will do anything at all. It's okay to rest.

Spend time with your family and friends. Do things that "normal" people do, such as watching TV, going to movies, eating out, hanging out with friends, surfing the Web, or whatever turns you on besides triathlon. *Do not train!*

NUTRITION

When it comes to your nutrition, the Transition block is like no other. In the first few days after your race, eat anything that sounds appealing to you. This could be pastries, soft drinks, processed foods, and all the other stuff you used to eat before you became a triathlete. You more than likely avoided some or all of these foods as you prepared for your race. Take a break from the monastic lifestyle for a few days. When you start feeling guilty about eating so much junk food, it's time to move back toward a healthier diet focused on vegetables, fruits, and lean protein.

Eat as much as you want, at least until you begin to feel like a glutton. That may only take a day or so. You will probably gain a couple of pounds this week. That's all right. Your body is going to store a lot of carbohydrate in the first day or so after the race. And with every gram of carbohydrate stored away as glycogen, the body also stores away nearly three grams of water. This will all come off when you get back into training later on. So don't worry about it. In fact, it's probably best to not even weigh yourself this week.

COMMON CONCERNS OF THE TRANSITION PERIOD

Getting lots of rest now is critical to your health. I can't tell you how many times I've seen athletes come down with a cold, sore throat, viral infection, or other symptoms of illness in the week following a hard-fought race. Your immune system is in a weakened state for several hours and perhaps even for several days following a race that pushed you to your limits.

Besides keeping your distance from other people who may be carrying a bug, the best thing you can do is rest. Sleep is especially beneficial now. Take a nap after the race, if possible. The night after the race, allow yourself to sleep a long time and wake up slowly—no alarm clocks today. This may mean scheduling your return trip home later in the day or taking a day of vacation from work. Do whatever is necessary to rest as much as possible in the days after the race.

Enjoy Life

For many months you've been focused on training for your race. You've made lots of sacrifices that have also affected your family and friends. Now is the time to pay them back for putting up with your drive to succeed. Dedicate the first few days away from serious training to them. Live like a "normal" person for a change. Spend time with your family and do what they like, or visit with friends. Eat out to celebrate. Heck, you might even throw a party. Do all of the things you give up when you are training hard. Enjoy life to its fullest now, as you will soon return to the monastic lifestyle of the serious athlete to prepare for the next race.

Take Care of Your Body

I'd suggest getting a massage or two in the week after the race. The first one may be a day or two after the race and should be a light flushing massage. This should prove to be very relaxing and therapeutic. Later in the week after the race, when the stiffness and soreness have subsided, you may be ready for a deeper sports massage.

It's a good idea to gently stretch your muscles once or twice daily post-race. In doing so you may discover some soreness that you weren't aware of, and you can gently self-massage these tender areas.

Also, be aware of any sore spots to make sure they are healing. Don't stress them with exercise. The muscles most likely to be sore are the primary movers for running and their associated tendons in the calf muscles and feet. Your knees or other joints may also be tender. I'd suggest not running for a few days after the race to allow all of these areas to heal.

If you have very sore tendons or joints in the first three days after the race that don't go away with rest, then make an appointment with a medical practitioner to assess the damage and provide therapy. It's common for muscles to be sore and stiff, and they do not normally require medical attention. But unusual joint and tendon soreness that do not heal with rest should not be accepted as normal. It's best to get this taken care of right away rather than waiting until you are ready to go back into hard training again.

Your Transition Training Plan

There is no training plan for the Transition block, but you may still exercise as described above under "Let Go of Peak Fitness." That means no goals, no objectives, and no purpose other than having fun.

Rather than tell the athletes I coach what to do during this block, I simply set limits on what they may and may not do and leave the rest up to them. For example, I advise exercising no more than once a day. In addition, it's best now to do something other than (or in addition to) swimming, biking, and running, as discussed above.

Any triathlon-type sessions you do in Transition should be no longer than the shortest you did during your buildup to the race. For example, if your shortest swim in the Base or Build periods was 30 minutes, then that will be your longest swim now. If your shortest ride was an hour, then ride no longer than an hour a day now. Follow the same guideline for your running.

The intensity of any exercise session should be zone 1, primarily, with an occasional foray into zone 2. That means very easy. It should feel ridiculously, even embarrassingly, slow. It's best to avoid swim, bike, and run groups you normally train with, as the tendency will be to keep up or even "win" the workouts. Instead, swim for the fun of it, ride flat courses with good scenery, and stop and smell the flowers while running.

Actually, there are special guidelines for running. As mentioned earlier, I suggest no running for the first three to five days after your race, as this is the sport most likely to give you orthopedic problems such as sore knees, tight tendons, or deeply fatigued muscles. It's best to err on the side of doing too little running now. When you do start back into running, keep these sessions under 45 minutes and strictly in zone 1. Runs are best done on grass or dirt for the first several run sessions.

There is no strength training, per se, in the Transition block. If you enjoy going to the gym and lifting weights, it's all right to continue doing so now. But, just as with the other activities mentioned above, keep it brief, easy, and without purpose other than having fun.

Depending on when your race occurred, the Transition block will last a few days (early season) to a few weeks (late season). In either case, once you have recovered both mentally and physically it's time to start preparing for your next triathlon.

Your Next Triathlon ⟍13⟍

YOU HAVE LOTS of decisions to make as you look ahead to your next triathlon. If you have several months until your next A-priority race, then what you do after the current Transition is no great mystery: You return to the Prep period and reread Chapter 4. Chapter 13 will help you address some important postseason questions and concerns as you start planning for the season ahead. If your race was midseason and you have another important race coming up soon, you are probably somewhat pressed for time and need to make some quick decisions about what to do in training. This chapter will help you make those decisions.

Either way, the purpose of this chapter is to help you focus your attention in order to make your next A-priority triathlon even better than the one you just completed.

GROWING AS A TRIATHLETE

In your recent A-priority race you should have learned something that will make you a better athlete. The longer you've been in the sport, the fewer lessons there are to learn. Regardless, you should come away from every race with at least one new insight or tool. In the previous chapter, you analyzed what you could have done differently, either in the race or in your preparation for it, knowing what you know now. That leads to the next question: How should you prepare for your next race?

If you evaluated your race according to the guidelines supplied in Chapter 12, you can now start thinking about how you can tweak your training for your next race. The changes may involve seasonal periodization, weekly routines, types of workouts, nutrition, equipment, mental preparation, training partners, training courses, and many other aspects of training. It's not necessary to commit to these changes yet—that can come later. Now is the time for brainstorming. It's a good idea to start taking notes on the changes you may want to make for next time. There may only be a couple of small ones if your race went well. On the other hand, you may have a long laundry list of things that must be done next time. That's fine: It means you learned a lot of things that you can soon put into practice.

A couple of days or a couple of weeks after the race, depending on how much time you have for your Transition block, start organizing your thoughts about the next race. If your race came at midseason, this organizing must happen quickly, as you may only have a few weeks until you stand on a starting line again. If your race was at the end of the season, you have more time to contemplate how things went and can prepare your next race plan gradually. Your focus will turn to the future as you let go of the recent past.

COMMON POSTSEASON QUESTIONS

Let's take a step back and do some deep thinking. Now is the best time in the season to contemplate some truly big-picture issues along with some others that aren't quite so big. Let's start with the toughest questions and work our way down.

Is Triathlon the Right Sport for Me?

This question may be easy for you. Perhaps you enjoyed the triathlon so much that you know for sure that you want to continue. You love the sport and couldn't imagine doing anything else. Or perhaps you feel that you couldn't face another triathlon if someone paid you for it. In that case, your answer is also clear. But this is a tough question for some. If you fall in between the two extremes, it's worth taking a day or two to consider how triathlon fits into your life and whether a change in sport could be a good idea.

For example, I've known athletes who simply could not fit training for three sports into their already jam-packed lives. Going to a single sport made their lives much more manageable. Another option for some is to race duathlons so there is one less activity to fit in. It could also be that you are experiencing nagging injuries from one of the sports that simply won't go away no matter what you do, or at least in time to start training for the next season's set of races. Running is the most likely culprit. If this is the case, you could take up bike racing or swim in masters competitions. Or maybe you really like one of the sports far more than the others and would enjoy competing only in that one area. If you decide you want to change sports, now is the time. If you have no interest in changing sports, and feel enthusiastic about continuing, then it's full speed ahead.

Am I Racing the Right Distance?

The Iron-distance triathlon is very popular right now. If you are racing that distance, is it right for you, or are you doing it because it's "cool"? Not everyone is cut out to do ultradistance training and racing. Some people just don't have enough time in their week to do the long workouts that are necessary to achieve an Ironman goal. Some people doing Ironman races may be much better at shorter ones. Some I've known have even tried short-course triathlons and enjoy them more than the Ironman-distance races, but were continuing to struggle with long-course racing because their friends were all doing it. Or perhaps you are racing Olympic distances even though your speed is not great and your endurance is. If this description fits you, maybe you should move up to the half-Ironman distance.

Give these questions a great deal of thought before you start planning for your next season. You should do what is right for you. Now is the time to make a major shift of this type if one is needed.

Do I Need a Coach?

If you really want to succeed at a high level in triathlon, you need a coach. Many athletes think coaches are only for the pros. Indeed, most pros do have coaches in their corners, because they understand the benefits of having one. A good coach will design a training plan unique to your strengths and weaknesses, help you fit workouts around your career and lifestyle, suggest a nutritional strategy for training and racing, help you mentally prepare for hard races, motivate you to do your best, and answer your questions. He or she will also educate you so that you eventually become better at self-coaching.

If you would like to have a coach but can't afford one, there are less expensive options. You can purchase a generic training plan designed for your race distance, age group, experience in the sport, available training time, and equipment (such as a power meter, heart rate monitor, or GPS/accelerometer). You can find such training plans at TrainingPeaks.com. There you will also find an online "VirtualCoach" that inexpensively designs a personalized weekly training plan specific to your needs after you answer a few key questions.

Should I Upgrade My Equipment?

Sometimes what's standing between an athlete and success is poor equipment. The bike is the most likely culprit here. When I go to races, I often see athletes riding bikes that don't fit them properly. Other athletes have bikes that fit well enough but are set up poorly. Sometimes just a small adjustment, such as saddle height or handlebar reach, makes a big difference. It's a shame to do all of that training only to be held back by a poor bike fit.

As you begin training for a new season, remember to get a new bike fit to make sure yours does fit you. If it does, the next biggest return on investment comes from aerobars and wheels. The models are always changing, so I won't go into detail here. I will say, however, that well-designed aerobars and wheels can make you significantly faster than basic ones.

The return you will receive from investments in other types of equipment changes are less significant if considered one at a time, but in combination they can still add up to a lot. This includes helmets, clothing, bike shoes, and drinking systems. Running shoes are also critical to performance, especially when it comes to injury avoidance. If your gear is all top-of-the-line, then you're set for the next race, at least in this category.

Should I Retest?

In Chapter 5 I suggested that you go for testing in a lab or clinic to get a better handle on your lactate threshold for each sport as well as other metrics such as aerobic capacity, metabolic rate, and economy. You'll recall that these are called VO_2max or gas-analysis tests. Such testing is available at many medical clinics, university exercise physiology departments, health clubs, triathlon stores, bike shops, and running stores. They are commonly done for biking and running, but rarely for swimming.

If you had such a test done back in Base 1, you may want to consider having it done again now, or at least soon after you have recovered from your race. This will give you a good idea how much change has taken place over the course of the season. It will also serve as a baseline as you begin training for your next A race. If your next A-priority race isn't for several months, and you haven't had the test done before, then I recommend having the test done when you're in Base 1 again.

PREPARING FOR YOUR NEXT A-PRIORITY RACE

Once you've fully evaluated your race, asked the big questions listed above, and know what your new set of goals and objectives are, you can begin planning your upcoming race calendar.

The most difficult scenario is when the next A-priority race on the calendar is less than 6 weeks after the last one. That's especially true for half-Ironman and Ironman races. For the shorter distances, the challenge isn't as great, since the time needed to recover is far shorter than with the long-course races. However, the athlete must still determine the best way to rebuild fitness and come into form in a short period of time.

The key question is how to periodize training when you don't have time to begin again back in Prep. Usually, depending on how much time you have, you should go back to Base 3, Build 1, or Build 2, but there is no formula to help you decide. Answering the questions below may help, but the best answer will depend on your unique circumstances.

How Much Recovery Time Do You Need?

The longer your A-priority race was and the harder you pushed yourself, the more time you'll need to shed fatigue, heal sore soft tissues, and recover mentally from focused training. If your race was a long one, it's best not to have another A-priority race for at least 4 weeks. Six weeks is better, and 8 weeks is nearly perfect. Following a sprint- or Olympic-distance triathlon, you can be ready to go back into serious training within a few days—a week at the most.

How Long Is Your Next A-Priority Race?

Longer races, especially the half-Ironman and Ironman distances, require a lot of low-intensity, long-duration training. The shorter races are more dependent on high-intensity, low-duration training. So the key question here is when you will be ready to race either long or fast again. If your last race was long and your next race is also long, then you can rebuild fitness rather quickly once you have recovered. But if your last race was short and the next one is long, it will take more time to prepare. It's a bit easier to build fitness for a short race if the last one was long, as speed seems to come more quickly than endurance.

How Sound Is Your Base Fitness?

Should you return immediately to the Build period, or should you go back to Base training for a while? The answer to this question depends on how sound your Base fitness is.

Chapter 3 described three fitness abilities that must be developed in the Base period before you can move on to the Build period—aerobic endurance, muscular force, and speed skills. The first, aerobic endurance, is the most critical at this juncture because it is the most basic of all the triathlon abilities. If it is weak, then any advanced-ability training you do for muscular endurance and anaerobic endurance will likely have little benefit for faster racing.

If you went through a 3-week taper as prescribed in the training plans in Chapters 10 and 11, and you are now taking a week or more to recover from your A-priority race, then your aerobic endurance is certain to have faded. This can be checked by doing aerobic threshold workouts for each sport and looking for decoupling as described in Chapter 5. It will probably take 2 or more weeks of focused training to adequately rebuild it in each sport. For a sprint- or Olympic-distance race you can bring this back to a high level quickly. But if your next race is a half- or full-Ironman, it will take several weeks of aerobic endurance training to be ready to race well again.

So the answer to the question of which training period you should go to next for a second A-priority race within the same season is, "It depends." Without knowing your answers to the above questions, I cannot make that call for you. I can tell you, however, that I return nearly all of those I coach to Base training, usually Base 3, for at least 2 weeks if we have at least 6 weeks separating their races. If you make a mistake in periodization, make it on the side of overdeveloping your Base fitness, especially aerobic endurance.

THE KEYS TO FUTURE SUCCESS

Triathletes are amazing people. I've coached athletes in many endurance sports, including track and field, road cycling, mountain biking, road and trail running, rowing, and even endurance horse racing. On the whole, triathletes are the most driven to succeed. That is good, but it can also be bad. Triathletes often train too much, too long, and too intensely. That inevitably leads to overtraining, burnout, illness, and injury. Over the past 30 years, I've helped many triathletes get out of the rut they've dug for themselves by teaching them to train moderately and consistently. These are the keys to success in sport.

If your last A-priority race didn't go as you hoped it would, and it's because you were unable to perform to your potential on race day, then excessive and inconsistent training may be the cause. You can't let this happen again. You must learn to harness and direct your desire to succeed. How can you do that? It starts with training moderation.

Moderation in training means that you seldom explore your physical limits. Too many triathletes try to do the hardest workouts they are capable of more frequently than they should. Their long workouts are much too long, and their intensity is often too high. Most seem to believe that peak fitness comes from finding their limits on a near-daily basis. That is a sure way to derail your training. Moderation when it comes to workout duration and absolute intensity is the key.

That said, moderation is a moving target. As your fitness improves, what would have been a hard workout a few weeks ago becomes moderate. So within the same season the level of moderation rises. The same sort of thing is going on from season to season. If you are training properly, your capacity to handle a given training load increases over the long term. What was a hard workout last year is moderate this year.

Consistency results from moderation. Consistent training means you don't miss workouts—ever. Missed workouts are the result of immoderate training. You try to do too much: too much intensity, too much duration, too much working out, and too much stuff in your life. If you train and live with moderation, you will be consistent. If you are consistent, you will race faster. It's not about how hard the workouts are, in the final analysis. It's how consistently you do them.

A couple of weeks after I start coaching a triathlete, I ask if the training is harder or easier than it was when the athlete was self-coached. The answer nearly always is that it's easier. I have the athletes do less than they did before, and they get faster and fitter than they did on their self-coached plan. I simply focus our attention on weaknesses that must be improved for success in the next A-priority race. You'll recall from Chapter 3 that these weaknesses are called limiters. If you want to improve as an athlete, you must know your limiters and then train moderately and consistently with your primary focus on them.

YOUR NEXT TRIATHLON

Determine the limiters, train moderately, and train consistently. That describes 90 percent of what I focus on with the athletes I coach. The rest is just the details. If you follow this training philosophy, I know you will steadily improve as a triathlete and that your race goals—and achievements—will continue to rise.

I've often found that middle-of-the-pack finishers can become top competitors in their age groups at local races within a season once they adopt my approach. Within a couple of seasons, they can be contenders in national competitions. Some go on to race competitively on the world stage. When they first come to me, these athletes exhibit a lot of natural ability but are training in ways that constrain their development, usually by training excessively and inconsistently. Once I correct their training programs, they become more fit and their talent is revealed. As their fitness improves, they become more confident.

You can experience the same sort of growth by following the guidelines in this book. You may not have achieved a high race goal the first time you followed the plan. That's the nature of training—your body adapts slowly over a long period of time. It's also the nature of competition. If it was easy, it wouldn't be any fun. You certainly should have learned a lot, however, including how to modify the plan to better fit your unique limiters and lifestyle. I'm certain that if you continue to implement the training plan presented in these chapters and stick to the basic guidelines found here, what seemed like a stretch for you this season will be easily managed soon.

If you achieved your season's race goal, then it's time to do some thoughtful self-assessment and decide where you will go next in the sport. If you continue to train consistently and follow the guidelines in this book, your next triathlon should be even better.

Appendix A
Annual Training Plan Template

The training plans at the end of each training-period chapter should cover your entire season, but the Annual Training Plan that follows can help you see the season at a glance.

Athlete:
Annual hours:
Seasonal goals:
1.
2.
3.
Training objectives:
1.
2.
3.
4.
5.

Wk#	Mon	Race	PRI	Period	Hours	Weights	SWIM							BIKE							RUN						
							Endurance	Force	Speed Skills	Muscular Endurance	Anaerobic Endurance	Power	Testing	Endurance	Force	Speed Skills	Muscular Endurance	Anaerobic Endurance	Power	Testing	Endurance	Force	Speed Skills	Muscular Endurance	Anaerobic Endurance	Power	Testing
01																											
02																											
03																											
04																											
05																											
06																											
07																											
08																											
09																											
10																											
11																											
12																											
13																											
14																											
15																											
16																											
17																											
18																											
19																											
20																											
21																											
22																											
23																											
24																											
25																											
26																											
27																											
28																											
29																											
30																											
31																											
32																											
33																											
34																											
35																											
36																											
37																											
38																											
39																											
40																											
41																											
42																											
43																											
44																											
45																											
46																											
47																											
48																											
49																											
50																											
51																											
52																											

Appendix B
Pace and Heart Rate Zones

These tables are simply consolidated from the various training blocks to make it easier to define your training zones.

TABLE B.1	Swimming Pace, Zones 1–5c					
Time	**Active Recovery**	**Aerobic Endurance**	**Tempo**	**Lactate Threshold**	**Aerobic Capacity**	**Anaerobic Capacity**
1,000 m/yd	**ZONE 1**	**ZONE 2**	**ZONE 3**	**ZONE 4–5a**	**ZONE 5b**	**ZONE 5c**
9:35–9:45	1:13+	1:09–1:12	1:04–1:08	0:58–1:03	0:54–0:57	0:53–max
9:46–9:55	1:15+	1:11–1:14	1:06–1:10	0:59–1:01	0:55–0:58	0:54–max
9:56–10:06	1:16+	1:12–1:15	1:07–1:11	1:00–1:06	0:56–0:59	0:55–max
10:07–10:17	1:17+	1:13–1:16	1:08–1:12	1:01–1:07	0:57–1:00	0:56–max
10:18–10:28	1:18+	1:14–1:17	1:09–1:13	1:02–1:08	0:58–1:01	0:57–max
10:29–10:40	1:20+	1:15–1:19	1:10–1:14	1:03–1:09	0:58–1:02	0:57–max
10:41–10:53	1:22+	1:17–1:21	1:12–1:16	1:05–1:11	1:00–1:04	0:59–max
10:54–11:06	1:23+	1:19–1:22	1:13–1:18	1:06–1:12	1:01–1:05	1:00–max
11:07–11:18	1:24+	1:20–1:23	1:14–1:19	1:07–1:13	1:02–1:06	1:01–max
11:19–11:32	1:26+	1:21–1:25	1:15–1:20	1:08–1:14	1:03–1:07	1:02–max
11:33–11:47	1:28+	1:23–1:27	1:17–1:22	1:10–1:16	1:05–1:09	1:04–max
11:48–12:03	1:29+	1:24–1:28	1:18–1:23	1:11–1:17	1:06–1:10	1:05–max
12:04–12:17	1:32+	1:26–1:31	1:20–1:25	1:13–1:19	1:07–1:12	1:06–max
12:18–12:30	1:33+	1:28–1:32	1:22–1:27	1:14–1:21	1:08–1:13	1:07–max
12:31–12:52	1:35+	1:30–1:34	1:24–1:29	1:16–1:23	1:10–1:15	1:09–max
12:53–13:02	1:38+	1:32–1:37	1:26–1:31	1:18–1:25	1:12–1:17	1:11–max
13:03–13:28	1:40+	1:34–1:39	1:28–1:33	1:20–1:27	1:14–1:19	1:13–max
13:29–13:47	1:41+	1:36–1:40	1:29–1:35	1:21–1:28	1:15–1:20	1:14–max
13:48–14:08	1:45+	1:39–1:44	1:32–1:38	1:23–1:31	1:17–1:22	1:16–max
14:09–14:30	1:46+	1:40–1:45	1:33–1:39	1:24–1:32	1:18–1:23	1:17–max
14:31–14:51	1:50+	1:44–1:49	1:36–1:43	1:27–1:35	1:21–1:26	1:20–max
14:52–15:13	1:52+	1:46–1:51	1:39–1:45	1:29–1:38	1:23–1:28	1:22–max
15:14–15:42	1:56+	1:49–1:55	1:42–1:48	1:32–1:41	1:25–1:31	1:24–max
15:43–16:08	1:58+	1:52–1:57	1:44–1:51	1:34–1:43	1:27–1:33	1:26–max
16:09–16:38	2:02+	1:55–2:01	1:47–1:54	1:37–1:46	1:30–1:36	1:29–max
16:39–17:06	2:04+	1:57–2:03	1:49–1:56	1:39–1:48	1:32–1:38	1:31–max
17:07–17:38	2:09+	2:02–2:08	1:53–2:01	1:43–1:52	1:35–1:42	1:34–max
17:39–18:12	2:13+	2:05–2:12	1:57–2:04	1:46–1:56	1:38–1:45	1:37–max
18:13–18:48	2:18+	2:10–2:17	2:01–2:09	1:50–2:00	1:42–1:49	1:41–max
18:49–19:26	2:21+	2:13–2:20	2:04–2:12	1:53–2:03	1:44–1:52	1:43–max
19:27–20:06	2:26+	2:18–2:25	2:08–2:17	1:56–2:07	1:48–1:55	1:47–max
20:07–20:50	2:31+	2:22–2:30	2:12–2:21	2:00–2:11	1:52–1:59	1:51–max
20:51–21:37	2:37+	2:28–2:36	2:18–2:27	2:05–2:17	1:56–2:04	1:55–max
21:38–22:27	2:42+	2:33–2:41	2:22–2:32	2:09–2:21	2:00–2:08	1:59–max
22:28–23:22	2:48+	2:38–2:47	2:27–2:37	2:14–2:26	2:04–2:13	2:03–max
23:23–24:31	2:55+	2:45–2:54	2:34–2:44	2:20–2:33	2:10–2:19	2:09–max
24:32–25:21	3:02+	2:52–3:01	2:40–2:51	2:25–2:39	2:15–2:24	2:14–max

Note: Paces are based on a 1,000 m/yd time trial. Paces for each zone represent the minutes and seconds for 100 m/yd.

TABLE B.2	Cycling Heart Rate, Zones 1–5c					
LTHR	**Active Recovery**	**Aerobic Endurance**	**Tempo**	**Lactate Threshold**	**Aerobic Capacity**	**Anaerobic Capacity**
	ZONE 1	**ZONE 2**	**ZONE 3**	**ZONE 4–5a**	**ZONE 5b**	**ZONE 5c**
137	<109	109–122	123–128	129–140	141–145	146+
138	<110	110–123	124–129	130–141	142–146	147+
139	<110	110–124	125–130	131–142	143–147	148+
140	<111	111–125	126–130	131–143	144–147	148+
141	<112	112–125	126–131	132–144	145–148	149+
142	<113	113–126	127–132	133–145	146–149	150+
143	<113	113–127	128–133	134–145	146–150	151+
144	<114	114–128	129–134	135–147	148–151	152+
145	<115	115–129	130–135	136–148	149–152	153+
146	<116	116–130	131–136	137–149	150–154	155+
147	<117	117–131	132–137	138–150	151–155	156+
148	<118	118–132	133–138	139–151	152–156	157+
149	<119	119–133	134–139	140–152	153–157	158+
150	<120	120–134	135–140	141–153	154–158	159+
151	<121	121–134	135–141	142–154	155–159	160+
152	<122	122–135	136–142	143–155	156–160	161+
153	<123	123–136	137–142	143–156	157–161	162+
154	<124	124–137	138–143	144–157	158–162	163+
155	<125	125–138	139–144	145–158	159–163	164+
156	<126	126–138	139–145	146–159	160–164	165+
157	<127	127–140	141–146	147–160	161–165	166+
158	<128	128–141	142–147	148–161	162–167	168+
159	<129	129–142	143–148	149–162	163–168	169+
160	<130	130–143	144–148	149–163	164–169	170+
161	<130	130–143	144–150	151–164	165–170	171+
162	<131	131–144	145–151	152–165	166–171	172+
163	<132	132–145	146–152	153–166	167–172	173+
164	<133	133–146	147–153	154–167	168–173	174+
165	<134	134–147	148–154	155–168	169–174	175+
166	<135	135–148	149–154	155–169	170–175	176+
167	<136	136–149	150–155	156–170	171–176	177+
168	<137	137–150	151–156	157–171	172–177	178+
169	<138	138–151	152–157	158–172	173–178	179+
170	<139	139–151	152–158	159–173	174–179	180+
171	<140	140–152	153–160	161–174	175–180	181+
172	<141	141–153	154–160	161–175	176–181	182+

continues

TABLE B.2	Cycling Heart Rate, Zones 1–5c *(continued)*					
LTHR	**Active Recovery**	**Aerobic Endurance**	**Tempo**	**Lactate Threshold**	**Aerobic Capacity**	**Anaerobic Capacity**
	ZONE 1	**ZONE 2**	**ZONE 3**	**ZONE 4–5a**	**ZONE 5b**	**ZONE 5c**
173	<142	142–154	155–161	162–176	177–182	183+
174	<143	143–155	156–162	163–177	178–183	184+
175	<144	144–156	157–163	164–178	179–184	185+
176	<145	145–157	158–164	165–179	180–185	186+
177	<146	146–158	159–165	166–180	181–186	187+
178	<147	147–159	160–166	167–181	182–187	188+
179	<148	148–160	161–166	167–182	183–188	189+
180	<149	149–160	161–167	168–183	184–190	191+
181	<150	150–161	162–168	169–184	185–191	192+
182	<151	151–162	163–170	171–185	186–192	193+
183	<152	152–163	164–171	172–186	187–193	194+
184	<153	153–164	165–172	173–187	188–194	195+
185	<154	154–165	166–172	173–188	189–195	196+
186	<155	155–166	167–173	174–189	190–196	197+
187	<156	156–167	168–174	175–190	191–197	198+
188	<157	157–168	169–175	176–191	192–198	199+
189	<158	158–169	170–176	177–192	193–199	200+
190	<159	159–170	171–177	178–193	194–200	201+
191	<160	160–170	171–178	179–194	195–201	202+
192	<161	161–171	172–178	179–195	196–202	203+
193	<162	162–172	173–179	180–196	197–203	204+
194	<163	163–173	174–180	181–197	198–204	205+
195	<164	164–174	175–181	182–198	199–205	206+
195	<164	164–174	175–181	182–198	199–205	206+

Note: Based on lactate threshold heart rate (LTHR).

TABLE B.3   Running Pace, Zone 1–5c

Time		Active Recovery	Aerobic Endurance	Tempo	Lactate Threshold	Aerobic Capacity	Anaerobic Capacity
5K	10K	ZONE 1	ZONE 2	ZONE 3	ZONE 4–5a	ZONE 5b	ZONE 5c
14:15	30:00:00	6:38+	5:52–6:37	5:27–5:51	5:09–5:26	4:37–4:58	4:36–max
14:45	31:00:00	6:50+	6:02–6:49	5:37–6:01	5:18–5:36	4:45–5:06	4:44–max
15:15	32:00:00	7:02+	6:13–7:01	5:47–6:12	5:27–5:46	4:53–5:15	4:52–max
15:45	33:00:00	7:13+	6:23–7:12	5:56–6:22	5:36–5:55	5:01–5:24	5:00–max
16:10	34:00:00	7:25+	6:33–7:24	6:06–6:32	5:45–6:05	5:10–5:33	5:09–max
16:45	35:00:00	7:36+	6:43–7:35	6:15–6:42	5:54–6:14	5:18–5:41	5:17–max
17:07	36:00:00	7:48+	6:54–7:47	6:25–6:53	6:03–6:24	5:26–5:50	5:25–max
17:35	37:00:00	8:00+	7:04–7:59	6:34–7:03	6:12–6:33	5:34–5:59	5:33–max
18:05	38:00:00	8:11+	7:14–8:10	6:44–7:13	6:21–6:43	5:42–6:08	5:41–max
18:30	39:00:00	8:23+	7:24–8:22	6:53–7:23	6:30–6:52	5:50–6:16	5:49–max
19:00	40:00:00	8:34+	7:35–8:33	7:03–7:34	6:39–7:02	5:58–6:25	5:57–max
19:30	41:00:00	8:46+	7:45–8:45	7:12–7:44	6:48–7:11	6:06–6:34	6:05–max
19:55	42:00:00	8:58ı	7:55 8:57	7:22 7:54	6:57–7:21	6:14–6:43	6:13–max
20:25	43:00:00	9:09+	8:05–9:08	7:31–8:04	7:06–7:30	6:22–6:51	6:21–max
20:50	44:00:00	9:21+	8:16–9:20	7:41–8:15	7:15–7:40	6:31–7:00	6:30–max
21:20	45:00:00	9:32+	8:26–9:31	7:51–8:25	7:24–7:50	6:39–7:09	6:38–max
21:50	46:00:00	9:44+	8:36–9:43	8:00–8:35	7:33–7:59	6:47–7:17	6:46–max
22:15	47:00:00	9:56+	8:47–9:55	8:10–8:46	7:42–8:09	6:55–7:26	6:54–max
22:42	48:00:00	10:07+	8:57–10:06	8:19–8:56	7:51–8:18	7:03–7:35	7:02–max
23:10	49:00:00	10:19+	9:07–10:18	8:29–9:06	8:00–8:28	7:11–7:44	7:10–max
23:38	50:00:00	10:31+	9:17–10:30	8:38–9:16	8:09–8:37	7:19–7:52	7:18–max
24:05	51:00:00	10:42+	9:28–10:41	8:48–9:27	8:18–8:47	7:27–8:01	7:26–max
24:35	52:00:00	10:54+	9:38–10:53	8:57–9:37	8:27–8:56	7:35–8:10	7:34–max
25:00	53:00:00	11:05+	9:48–11:04	9:07–9:47	8:36–9:06	7:43–8:19	7:42–max
25:25	54:00:00	11:17+	9:58–11:16	9:16–9:57	8:45–9:15	7:52–8:27	7:51–max
25:55	55:00:00	11:29+	10:09–11:28	9:26–10:08	8:54–9:25	8:00–8:36	7:59–max
26:30	56:00:00	11:40+	10:19–11:39	9:36–10:18	9:03–9:35	8:08–8:45	8:07–max
26:50	57:00:00	11:52+	10:29–11:51	9:45–10:28	9:12–9:44	8:16–8:53	8:15–max
27:20	58:00:00	12:03+	10:39–12:02	9:55–10:38	9:21–9:54	8:24–9:02	8:23–max
27:45	59:00:00	12:15+	10:50–12:14	10:04–10:49	9:30–10:03	8:32–9:11	8:31–max
28:15	60:00:00	12:27+	11:00–12:26	10:14–10:59	9:39–10:13	8:40–9:20	8:39–max

Note: Paces are based on a recent 5K or 10K running race.

TABLE B.4   Running Heart Rate, Zones 1–5c

LTHR	Active Recovery	Aerobic Endurance	Tempo	Lactate Threshold	Aerobic Capacity	Anaerobic Capacity
	ZONE 1	ZONE 2	ZONE 3	ZONE 4–5a	ZONE 5b	ZONE 5c
140	<120	120–126	127–133	134–143	144–149	150+
141	<120	120–127	128–134	135–144	145–150	151+
142	<121	121–129	130–135	136–145	146–151	152+
143	<122	122–130	131–136	137–146	147–152	153+
144	<123	123–131	132–137	138–147	148–153	154+
145	<124	124–132	133–138	139–148	149–154	155+
146	<125	125–133	134–139	140–149	150–155	156+
147	<125	125–134	135–140	141–150	151–156	157+
148	<126	126–135	136–141	142–151	152–157	158+
149	<127	127–135	136–142	143–152	153–158	159+
150	<128	128–136	137–143	144–153	154–158	159+
151	<129	129–137	138–144	145–154	155–159	160+
152	<130	130–138	139–145	146–155	156–160	161+
153	<131	131–139	140–146	147–156	157–161	162+
154	<132	132–140	141–147	148–157	158–162	163+
155	<132	132–141	142–148	149–158	159–164	165+
156	<133	133–142	143–149	150–159	160–165	166+
157	<134	134–143	144–150	151–160	161–166	167+
158	<135	135–143	144–151	152–161	162–167	168+
159	<136	136–144	145–152	153–162	163–168	169+
160	<137	137–145	146–153	154–163	164–169	170+
161	<137	137–146	147–154	155–164	165–170	171+
162	<138	138–147	148–155	156–165	166–171	172+
163	<139	139–148	149–155	156–166	167–172	173+
164	<140	140–149	150–156	157–167	168–174	175+
165	<141	141–150	151–157	158–168	169–175	176+
166	<142	142–151	152–158	159–169	170–176	177+
167	<142	142–152	153–159	160–170	171–177	178+
168	<143	143–153	154–160	161–171	172–178	179+
169	<144	144–154	155–161	162–172	173–179	180+
170	<145	145–155	156–162	163–173	174–179	180+
171	<146	146–156	157–163	164–174	175–180	181+
172	<146	146–156	157–164	165–175	176–182	183+
173	<147	147–157	158–165	166–176	177–183	184+

continues

TABLE B.4	Running Heart Rate, Zones 1–5c (continued)					
LTHR	Active Recovery	Aerobic Endurance	Tempo	Lactate Threshold	Aerobic Capacity	Anaerobic Capacity
	ZONE 1	ZONE 2	ZONE 3	ZONE 4–5a	ZONE 5b	ZONE 5c
174	<148	148–157	158–166	167–177	178–184	185+
175	<149	149–158	159–167	168–178	179–185	186+
176	<150	150–159	160–168	169–179	180–186	187+
177	<151	151–160	161–169	170–180	181–187	188+
178	<152	152–161	162–170	171–181	182–188	189+
179	<153	153–162	163–171	172–182	183–189	190+
180	<154	154–163	164–172	173–183	184–190	191+
181	<155	155–164	165–173	174–184	185–192	193+
182	<155	155–165	166–174	175–185	186–193	194+
183	<156	156–166	167–175	176–186	187–194	195+
184	<157	157–167	168–176	177–187	188–195	196+
185	<158	158–168	169–177	178–188	189–196	197+
186	<159	159–169	170–178	179–189	190–197	198+
187	<160	160–170	171–179	180–190	191–198	199+
188	<160	160–170	171–179	180–191	192–199	200+
189	<161	161–171	172–180	181–192	193–200	201+
190	<162	162–172	173–181	182–193	194–201	202+
191	<163	163–173	174–182	183–194	195–201	202+
192	<164	164–174	175–183	184–195	196–202	203+
193	<165	165–175	176–184	185–196	197–203	204+
194	<166	166–176	177–185	186–197	198–204	205+
195	<166	166–177	178–186	187–198	199–205	206+
196	<167	167–178	179–187	188–199	200–206	207+
197	<168	168–178	179–188	189–200	199–207	208+
198	<169	169–179	180–189	190–201	202–208	209+
199	<170	170–180	181–190	191–202	203–209	210+
200	<171	171–181	182–191	192–203	204–210	211+

Note: Based on lactate threshold heart rate (LTHR).

Appendix C
Strength Training

ANATOMICAL ADAPTATION (AA)

AA is the initial phase of strength training and usually occurs in the late fall or early winter during the Prep period. Its purpose is to prepare the muscles and tendons for the greater loads of the Maximum Strength phase. More strength training exercises are done at this time of year than at any other, since improved general body strength is a goal and other forms of training are minimal. Machines can be used in this period, but some free-weight training is beneficial. If desired, do some circuit training, as this can add an aerobic component to this phase.

In the AA phase, as in most others, the athlete should increase the loads gradually; many multisport athletes find that increasing the loads by about 5 percent every four or five workouts is about right.

MAXIMUM TRANSITION (MT)

MT is a brief phase at the end of the Prep period that occurs between the AA and MS phases. Its purpose is to prepare the body for the greater loads to follow. You should be ready to begin MS after only a few MT workouts. You will increase the loads during this phase, but in order to avoid injury, be cautious and don't increase them too rapidly.

MAXIMUM STRENGTH (MS)

The purpose of the MS phase is to improve force generation. As resistance gradually increases and repetitions decrease, more force is generated. This phase, usually included during the Base 1 period, is necessary to teach the central nervous system to recruit high numbers of muscle fibers. With practice, your nervous system will be able to do this easily. Care must be taken not to cause injury in this phase, especially with free-weight exercises such as the squat. Select loads conservatively at the start of the phase and in the first set of each workout. However, you may gradually increase the loads throughout this phase up to the goal levels based on body weight (BW). Generally, women and those new to weight training will aim for the lower ends of the ranges, whereas men and those used to weight training will go for the upper ends.

Only the exercises with specified load goals are done following the low-rep, high-load routine in the MS phase (see Table C.2). All other exercises, such as abdominal and personal weakness areas, continue with the AA-phase routine of light weights and 20 to 30 repetitions per set.

Once you've achieved the aforementioned goals, you may increase your repetitions, but the loads should remain constant. For example, a 150-pound male triathlete doing the leg press has a goal of 435 pounds (150 × 2.9). Once he can lift this weight six times, he will increase the repetitions beyond six while keeping the load at 435 pounds. There is no reason to go beyond eight MS workouts once the goal weights are achieved. But if you have not reached the goal loads after twelve MS workouts have been completed, end the phase and go on to the next.

Some athletes will be tempted to do more than one hip-extension exercise, or to increase the loads beyond the goals listed above. Others will want to extend this phase beyond the recommended number of workouts. Doing so is likely to result in muscle imbalances, especially in the upper leg, which may contribute to hip or knee injuries. During the MS phase, your endurance performance may suffer and your legs and arms may feel "heavy." As a result, your pace for any given effort will be slow.

STRENGTH MAINTENANCE (SM)

This phase maintains the basic strength you have established in the previous phases, while the hills, intervals, open-water swims, and steady-state efforts you are doing will maintain your power and muscular endurance. Stopping all resistance training at this point may cause a gradual loss of strength throughout the season. It is particularly important for women and masters athletes to maintain their strength during race season. Some athletes, particularly males in their twenties, seem capable of maintaining adequate levels of strength without continuing a weight training program throughout the late Base, Build, and Peak periods.

In the SM phase, only the last set is meant to stress the muscles. This set is done at about 80 percent of your one-repetition maximum (that is, the maximum load that a muscle group can lift in a single repetition). The one or two sets that provide the warm-up for this last set are done at about 60 percent of one-repetition maximum.

Hip-extension training (squats, step-ups, and leg presses) is optional during the maintenance phase. If you find that hip-extension exercises help your racing, continue doing them. If, however, working the legs only deepens your fatigue level, eliminate them. You can continue to work on your core muscles and personal weakness areas to maintain your strength needs. Starting seven days before A-priority races, eliminate all strength training to allow for peaking.

Table C.1 instructs you on how to vary the sets, repetitions, and load for the exercises in each phase of training. In the MT and MS Phases, you will base your load on body weight (BW) for selected exercises, as explained in the overview. You will find these load goals in Table C.2. The exercise progression for your strength workouts follows. You'll notice that there are some additional exercises in the AA strength workout. The exercise progression for the MT, MS, and SM strength workouts is the same with one exception: In the Strength Maintenance Phase, the hip extension exercise is optional.

TABLE C.1   Guidelines for Strength Training Phases

PHASE	AA ANATOMICAL ADAPTATION	MT MAXIMUM TRANSITION	MS MAXIMUM STRENGTH	SM STRENGTH MAINTENANCE
Load (% 1RM)	40–60	BW goal*	BW goal*	60, 80
Sets/session	3–5	3–4	3–6	2–3
Reps/set	20–30	10–15*	3–6*	6–12*
Speed of lift	slow	slow to moderate	slow to moderate	slow to moderate
Recovery (min.)	1–1.5	1.5–3*	2–4*	1–2*

Note: Only exercises specified in Table C.2 follow this guideline. All others continue AA guidelines.

TABLE C.2   Defining Load Goals Based on Body Weight (BW)*

EXERCISE	LOAD GOAL
Squat	1.3–1.7 x BW
Leg press (sled)	2.5–2.9 x BW
Step-up	0.7–0.9 x BW
Seated row	0.5–0.8 x BW
Standing, bent-arm lat pull-down	0.3–0.5 x BW

Note: This table helps you calculate your load goals for the MT and MS phases. All other exercises continue with the setsand reps specified for the AA phase.

AA Strength Workout

		Exercise	Muscle Group
1	*Pick one:*	**Hip Extension** (*see exercises opposite*)	quadriceps, gluteus, hamstrings
2		Standing, Bent-Arm Lat Pull-Down	latissimus dorsi, rotators
3	*Pick one:*	**Hip Extension** (*see exercises opposite, different from exercise 1*)	
4	*Pick one:*	Chest Press	pectorals, triceps
		Push-up	pectorals, triceps
5		Seated Row	upper & lower back, lower lats, biceps
6	*Pick one:*	**Personal Weakness** (*see exercises, p. 331*)	
7		Abdominal with Twist	rectus abdominus, external obliques

	Exercise	Muscle Group
Hip Extension Exercises		
	Squat (with bar or machine)	quadriceps, gluteus, hamstrings
	Step-up (with bar or dumbbells)	quadriceps, gluteus, hamstrings
	Leg Press	quadriceps, gluteus, hamstrings
Personal Weakness Exercises		
	Heel Raise	gastrocnemius
	Knee Extension	meidal quadriceps
	Leg Curl	hamstrings

Note: For instruction on sets, repetitions, and load see Table C.1 and C2. More detailed instruction on the exercises can be found in *The Triathlete's Training Bible*.

MT, MS, and SM Strength Workouts

		Exercise	Muscle Group
1	*Pick one:*	**Hip Extension** (*see exercises below*)	quadriceps, gluteus, hamstrings
2		Seated Row	upper & lower back, lower lats, biceps
3		Abdominal with Twist (follow AA guidelines in Table C.1)	rectus abdominus, external obliques
4	*Pick one:*	**Personal Weakness** (*see exercises opposite,* follow AA guidelines in Table C.1)	
5		Standing, Bent-Arm Lat Pull-Down	latissimus dorsi, rotators

Hip Extension Exercises   (These exercises are optional in the SM Phase.)

 Squat (with bar or machine)   quadriceps, gluteus, hamstrings

 Step-up (with bar or dumbbells)   quadriceps, gluteus, hamstrings

 Leg Press   quadriceps, gluteus, hamstrings

Exercise	Muscle Group

Personal Weakness Exercises (All exercises follow AA guidelines in Table C.1.)

Heel Raise   gastrocnemius

Knee Extension   meidal quadriceps

Leg Curl   hamstrings

Note: For instruction on sets, repetitions, and load see Table C.1 and C2. More detailed instruction on the exercises can be found in *The Triathlete's Training Bible.*

References

Allen, Hunter, and Andrew Coggan. 2010. *Training and Racing with a Power Meter*, 2nd ed. Boulder, CO: VeloPress.

Bjelakovic, G., D. Nikolova, L. L. Gluud, R. G. Simonetti, and C. Gluud. 2007. "Mortality in Randomized Trials of Antioxidant Supplements for Primary and Secondary Prevention: Systematic Review and Meta-Analysis," *Journal of the American Medical Association* 297 (8):842–857.

Cordain, Loren, and Joe Friel. 2005. *The Paleo Diet for Athletes: A Nutritional Formula for Peak Athletic Performance.* Emmaus, PA: Rodale books.

Daniels, Jack. 2005. *Daniels' Running Formula*, 2nd ed. Champaign, IL: Human Kinetics.

Fitzgerald, Matt. 2007. *Brain Training for Runners: A Revolutionary New Training System to Improve Endurance, Speed, Health, and Results.* New York: NAL Trade.

———. 2009. *Racing Weight: How to Get Lean for Peak Performance.* Boulder, CO: VeloPress.

Gallwey, T. 1974. *The Inner Game of Tennis.* New York: Random House.

Gleim, G. W., and M. P. McHugh. 1997. "Flexibility and Its Effects on Sports Injury and Performance." *Sports Medicine* 24 (5):289–299.

McGinley, C., A. Shafat, and A. E. Donnelly. 2009. "Does Antioxidant Vitamin Supplementation Protect Against Muscle Damage?" *Sports Medicine* 39 (12):1011–1032.

Noakes, Timothy. 2002. *The Lore of Running*, 4th ed. Champaign, IL: Human Kinetics.

Tucker, Ross, and Jonathan Dugas with Matt Fitzgerald. 2009. *The Runner's Body: How the Latest Exercise Science Can Help You Run Stronger, Longer, and Faster.* Emmaus, PA: Rodale Books.

Verstegen, Mark. 2006. *Core Performance Endurance: A New Fitness and Nutrition Program That Revolutionizes the Way You Train for Endurance Sports.* Emmaus, PA: Rodale Books.

Index

About the Author

J OE FRIEL is the founder and president of Training Bible Coaching, a company with endurance coaches around the world who learn and apply the coaching philosophy and methods described in this book. Training Bible Coaching's athletes include recreational and elite triathletes, duathletes, cyclists, mountain bikers, runners, and swimmers.

Joe has an extensive background in coaching, having trained endurance athletes since 1980. His clients have included novices, elite amateurs, and professionals. The list includes an Ironman Triathlon winner, USA and foreign national champions, world championship competitors, and an Olympian.

As well as *The Triathlete's Training Bible*, Joe is the author of *The Cyclist's Training Bible*, *Cycling Past 50*, *Precision Heart Rate Training* (co-author), *The Mountain Biker's Training Bible* , *Going Long: Training for Ironman-Distance Triathlons* (co-author), *The Paleo Diet for Athletes* (co-author), *Your First Triathlon*, and *Total Heart Rate Training*. He is the editor of the VeloPress series Ultrafit Multisport Training. He holds a master's degree in exercise science and is a USA Triathlon– and USA Cycling–certified elite coach. He helped to found the USA Triathlon National Coaching Commission and served two terms as chair.

Joe is also a columnist for *Inside Triathlon* and *VeloNews* magazines and writes feature stories for other international magazines and Web sites. His opinions on matters related to training for endurance sports are widely sought and have been featured in such publications as *Runner's World*, *Outside*, *Triathlete*, *220*, *Women's Sports & Fitness*, *Men's Fitness*, *American Health*, *Masters Sports*, *Walking*, *Bicycling*, the *New York Times*, and even *Vogue*.

He conducts yearly seminars and camps on training and racing for endurance athletes and provides consulting services to corporations in the fitness industry and to national governing bodies.

As an age-group competitor, he is a former Colorado State Masters Triathlon Champion and a Rocky Mountain region and Southwest region duathlon age-group champion, has been named to several All-American teams, and has represented the United States at the world championships. He also competes in USA Cycling bike races.

Joe Friel may be contacted through his Web site at trainingbible.com.